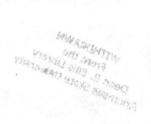

Studies in medieval literature and languages

W. Rothwell
W. R. J. Barron
David Blamires
Lewis Thorpe *editors*

Studies in medieval literature and languages

in memory of Frederick Whitehead

Manchester University Press
Barnes & Noble Books · New York

© 1973 Manchester University Press

Published by the University of Manchester
at the University Press
316–24 Oxford Road, Manchester M13 9NR

UK ISBN 0 7190 0550 7

USA

Harper & Row Publishers Inc
Barnes & Noble Import Division

US ISBN 06 495998 8

Printed in Great Britain by
Butler & Tanner Ltd. , Frome and London

Contents

Contents

T. B. W. Reid
Frederick Whitehead, 1909–71

FrederickWhitehead was from an early age clearly destined for a career of the highest academic distinction. Educated atWednesbury Grammar School and Jesus College, Oxford, he graduated in 1930 with first-class honours in Modern Languages, and spent the next few years mainly in research at Oxford and Paris. His Oxford D.Phil. was awarded for a thesis, presented in 1933, on the development of Latin *u* and Germanic *w* in the Romance languages, for which his supervisor was Alfred Ewert. At the same time he was already working, under the influence of Eugène Vinaver, in the domain of Arthurian romance (his first article on an Arthurian topic was published, also in 1933, in the recently founded journal *Medium Aevum*); he prepared a thesis for the Doctorat d'Université of the Sorbonne on the early forms of the Tristan romances, but although this was in page proof in 1939 the outbreak of war resulted in its never being presented or published. These two broad fields of study, the history of the Romance languages and medieval literature (chiefly French and Provençal, but also when the occasion arose Latin, German or English), were to remain his principal preoccupations throughout his teaching career, though he also developed an informed if somewhat sceptical interest in modern descriptive linguistics. After a temporary appointment at Oxford he became Assistant Lecturer in French at the then University College of Hull; in 1939 he was appointed Lecturer at the University of Manchester on the retirement of Mildred K. Pope from the Chair of French Language and Romance Philology, and in 1952 he was promoted to a readership in Old French Language and Literature. Though he had long suffered from recurrent periods of ill-health—through which he was devotedly supported by his wife Evelyn—his sudden death on 2 October 1971 came as a quite unexpected shock to his family, friends and colleagues.

Whitehead was a gifted and selfless teacher.Whether the subject was French historical phonology or morphology, Old Provençal poetry, or aspects of medieval French literature ranging from the detailed study of individual texts to the evolution of genres, his lectures and especially his seminars and research classes inspired a lively interest in most students and a lasting enthusiasm in many. To students, both graduate and undergraduate, he gave up much of his time and energy, as he did also to numerous organisations for the advancement of scholarship, from Manchester University groups such as the Philological Club, the Medieval Society (of which he was for many years secretary) and the Linguistic Seminar (which he helped to found), to the city's Literary and Philosophical Society and the International Arthurian Society.

Whitehead will long be remembered with affection and respect by all those who came into personal contact with him; but he leaves an even more durable legacy in his published work. Most of this is concerned with medieval French literature, and more particularly with courtly romance. In a series of articles in journals and contributions to collective volumes he dealt authoritatively with a number of important topics in Arthurian literature, from Beroul and Chrétien through the French prose romances to its latest flowering in Malory. His edition of the courtly though non-Arthurian *Chastelaine de Vergi* (1944) is in many respects characteristic of the manner and merits of his approach: the text of the base manuscript is treated with the utmost respect 'on this side idolatry', but all variant readings are carefully considered; the narration and its conventions are placed with well informed scholarship in their historical context; the art and method of the author are laid bare with delicate judgement. Characteristic, too, is the fact that in his second edition (1951) he completely rewrote his introduction, partly in order to discuss more fully certain difficulties of interpretation but also because he was no longer satisfied with some of the views he had expressed in the first edition.

Whitehead's most widely known work is no doubt his edition of the *Chanson de Roland* (1942), which has remained a standard textbook in the universities of the English-speaking world. Together with several articles (notably that in the Ewert volume of 1961), it bears witness not only to his abiding interest in the *chansons de geste* as a genre but also to what was perhaps his greatest single quality as a scholar, his mastery of the principles and practice of textual criticism in every sense of the expression. While always arguing rigorously from the transmitted data, he shows a sympathetic and imaginative understanding of the intentions and resources of the author, combined with an equally profound insight into the working situation of the scribe. His great gifts for the appreciation and elucidation of both the linguistic values and the aesthetic qualities of medieval literary works thus, as Vinaver has said, 'abolished any distinction between philological and literary approaches, and so reaffirmed the integrity of the discipline in all its various applications'. The same spirit can be recognised in the numerous reviews he wrote for *French Studies*, *Medium Aevum* and other journals: often themselves original contributions to knowledge, they are always based on a searching though charitable examination of the work in question in a context of wide reading and balanced judgement. It is a matter for the deepest regret that so many of the fruits of his research and reflexion remain unpublished—not only his two theses, and a projected edition of the *Tristan* of Thomas, but a much more elaborate edition of the *Chanson de Roland* with a complete English translation. Something of what these missing volumes might have contained may be suggested by the studies here presented; for they cannot fail to reveal the extent of Whitehead's illuminating influence on his pupils, among whom many of his colleagues would wish to be numbered.

Frederick Whitehead's bibliography

exclusive of articles in Cassell's *Encyclopaedia of Literature* and in the *Encyclopaedia Britannica*

Books

La Chanson de Roland, critical edition, Oxford (Blackwell), 1942. Now in its fifth reprint.

La Chastelaine de Vergi, critical edition, Manchester University Press. First edition 1944. Second, revised, edition 1951.

Articles

'On certain episodes in the fourth book of Malory's *Morte Darthur*,' *Medium Aevum*, II (1933), pp. 199–216.

'Tristan and Isolt in the Forest of Morrois', *Studies presented to M. K. Pope*, Manchester, 1939, pp. 393–400.

'The two-branch stemma' (in collaboration with C. E. Pickford), *Bibl. Bull. of the International Arthurian Society*, III (1951), pp. 83–90.

'L'Origine de la légende du Graal—Quelques points de méthode', *Bibl. Bull. of the International Arthurian Society*, III (1951), p. 97.

'Dialect words', *Journal of the Lancashire Dialect Society*, III (1953), pp. 2–9.

'La Crise morale dans le roman de Tristan'. *Bibl. Bull. of the International Arthurian Society*, VI (1954), pp. 99–100.

'Shannon's so-called communication theory' (in collaboration with W. Mays), *Proceedings of the Seventh International Congress of Linguists, 1952*, London, 1956, pp. 209–11.

'The early Tristan poems', in *Arthurian Literature in the Middle Ages*, Oxford, 1959, pp. 134–44.

'The *Livre d'Artus*' (in collaboration with R. S. Loomis), *Arthurian Literature in the Middle Ages*, Oxford, 1959, pp. 336–8.

'Ofermod et desmesure', *Cahiers de civilisation médiévale*, III (1960), pp. 115–117.

'The textual criticism of the *Chanson de Roland*: an historical review.' *Studies presented to A. Ewert*, Oxford, 1961, pp. 76–89.

'Menéndez Pidal and the *Chanson de Roland*', *Bulletin of Hispanic Studies*, XXXIX (1962), pp. 31–3.

'Lancelot's penance', in *Essays on Malory*, ed. J. A. W. Bennett, Oxford, 1963, pp. 104–13.

'Lancelot's redemption', in *Mélanges de linguistique romane et de philologie médiévale offerts à M. Maurice Delbouille*, II, Gembloux, 1964, pp. 729–39.

'La collision homonymique et la sémantique évolutive', in *Actes du Xe Congrès international de linguistique et philologie romanes, 1962, Strasbourg*, 1965, pp. 225–230.

'Yvain's wooing', *Medieval Miscellany presented to Eugène Vinaver*, Manchester University Press, 1965, pp. 321–36.

'L'Ambiguité de Roland', in *Studi in onore di Italo Siciliano*, Florence, 1966, pp. 1203–12.

'Norman French: the linguistic consequences of the Conquest,' *Memoirs and Proceedings of the Manchester Literary and Philosophical Society*, CIX (1966–67), pp. 78–83.

'Bleston: or, Manchester transformed', *Journal of the Lancashire Dialect Society*, XVIII (1969), pp. 2–4.

'La poésie épique et la contrainte métrique', *Société Rencesvals IVe Congrès internationale, Actes et Mémoires*, Heidelberg, 1969, pp. 117–19.

'Observations on the Perlesvaus', in *Mélanges de langue et de littérature du moyen âge et de la renaissance offerts à Jean Frappier*, Geneve, 1970, pp. 1119–27.

'Les Rêves symboliques de Charlemagne à la veille de la bataille de Roncesvaux', *Actes du Ve Congrès international de la Société Rencesvals* (Oxford, 1970).

'Comment on three passages from the text of the Oxford *Roland*', in *History and Structure of French*, Oxford, 1972, pp. 257–62.

'The introduction to the *Lai de l'Ombre*: sixty years later' (in collaboration with C. E. Pickford), XCIV (1973), pp. 145–56.

Dr Whitehead also contributed the section on 'French Medieval Literature' in *The Year's Work in Modern Languages Studies*, IX (1939), and X (1940).

A large number of reviews appeared also in *Medium Aevum, French Studies*, etc.

W. R. J. Barron

French romance and the structure of *Sir Gawain and the Green Knight*

When, some twenty years ago, as a postgraduate student, I had the pleasure of working under the late Ernest Hoepffner, then *doyen* of the Faculté des lettres at Strasbourg, he would occasionally refer to the discovery of medieval manuscripts in the great houses of Britain, where, he seemed to feel, there was yet more material, French as well as English, to be brought to light. If, he would suggest, I gave my vacations to searching 'ces vieux châteaux d'Ecosse' what might I not discover!—perhaps the French source of 'cet admirable *Gauvain et le Chevalier Vert*'. He was not, I think, wholly serious; but he was certainly not alone, at that time, in believing that *Sir Gawain and the Green Knight* derived directly from a French romance.

The earliest commentators, over a hundred years before, when the dependence of Middle English courtly literature upon French models was unquestioningly assumed, had taken the poet's reference to 'þe bok' at its face value.[1] The first editor, Madden, found what he regarded as the 'immediate original' in the *Livre de Caradoc*, part of the First Continuation of Chrétien's *Perceval*, an identification supported by a later investigation of detailed correspondences.[2] Gaston Paris, however, found equally convincing parallels with the thirteenth century *Hunbaut* and rejected both as possible originals, suggesting instead a common source for French and English versions alike.[3] That source he assumed to have been French, though he pointed out that elements of the common plot also existed in Celtic literature. Jessie Weston found details of the 'champion's bargain' episode in the Irish epic *Fled Bricrend* more clearly reproduced in *Gawain* than in the French analogues, and Kittredge, in the first detailed source study, worked

---

1 See l. 690. All references are to the edition by J. R. R. Tolkien and E. V. Gordon, revised by N. Davis, Oxford, 1967.

2 Sir F. Madden, ed. *Syr Gawayne*, Bannatyne Club, London, 1839; Miss M. C. Thomas, *Sir Gawayne and the Green Knight: a Comparison with the French Perceval*, Zürich, 1883.

3 See *Histoire littéraire de la France*, XXX, Paris, 1888.

out an elaborate hypothesis involving at least three lost French intermediaries between the Celtic legend and the English romance.[4] His
theory connected with one or other of the intermediaries not only the
Livre de Caradoc but also the prose *Perlesvaus*, derived in part from
Chrétien's *Perceval* and its continuations, and the early thirteenth century verse romance *La Mule sans Frein*. These supplied analogues for
only one of the narrative threads in *Gawain*—the beheading game; for
another—the temptation—Kittredge found somewhat vague parallels
in various thirteenth century poems, *Yder*, *Le Chevalier à l'Epée* and
Hunbaut, in the last of which it is associated but not interconnected
with a limited form of the beheading game. Hulbert, however, suggested that the connection between the two motifs was archetypal,
implicit in a variant version of the 'champion's bargain', itself a reflection of an earlier Celtic story in which a *fée* used a shape-shifter to
test the valour of her chosen lover in the beheading game.[5] R. S.
Loomis initially accepted this conception of the unity of the narrative
in its folk-lore form,[6] but he and other folklorists soon produced a
bewildering plethora of parallels to and 'sources' for the plot outline
and many incidental details not only in Irish and Welsh legend but
even in Indian mythology.[7]

Contemporary editors, preoccupied by textual problems and points
of interpretation, gave general consent to the idea of a French original
derived ultimately from Celtic legends.[8] But the source studies gave
only vague and conflicting conceptions of the nature of that original,

4 J. L. Weston, *The Legend of Sir Gawain*, London, 1897; G. L. Kittredge,
   A Study of Gawain and the Green Knight, Cambridge, Mass., 1916.
5 J. R. Hulbert, 'Syr Gawayn and the Grene Knyȝt', *Modern Philology*, XIII
   (1916), pp. 433-62, 689-730.
6 R. S. Loomis, *Celtic Myth and Arthurian Romance*, New York, 1927.
7 A. Buchanan, 'The Irish framework of *Gawain and the Green Knight*', P.M.L.A.,
   XLVII (1932), pp. 315-38; W. A. Nitze, 'Is the Green Knight story a veget-
   ation myth?', *Modern Philology*, XXXIII (1936), pp. 351-66; R. S. Loomis,
   'More Celtic elements in *Gawain and the Green Knight*', *Journal of English
   and Germanic Philology*, XLII (1943), pp. 149-84; R. M. Smith, 'Guinganbresil
   and the Green Knight', *Journal of English and Germanic Philology*, XLV (1946),
   pp 1-25; A. K. Coomaraswamy, '*Sir Gawain and the Green Knight*: Indra
   and Namuci', *Speculum*, XIX (1944), pp. 104-25.
8 Tolkien and Gordon (*Sir Gawain and the Green Knight*, Oxford, 1925, p. xiv)
   accepted Kittredge's assumption of an original in which beheading game and
   temptation were already united; Miss Day (*Sir Gawain and the Green Knight*,
   ed. Sir. I. Gollancz, with introductory essays by Mabel Day and Mary S.
   Serjeantson, London, 1940, pp. xxxii-vii) thought the combination was the
   work of the English poet.

and the over-enthusiasm of the Celticists tended to confuse the issue.[9]
Students, while strongly attracted by the verbal subtlety of the poem,
were often frustrated in attempting to understand how a particular
detail related to the overall meaning, on which scholarship had so far
thrown very little light. But in the 1950s many scholars turned from
source investigations to analytical and interpretative studies, and the
past decade in particular has produced a veritable avalanche of publications in which the source question has, for the most part, been
tacitly ignored. There can be no doubt that the change of emphasis has
been beneficial: despite some interpretative excesses and a tendency to
see symbolism behind every detail, there is gradually evolving some
consensus of opinion on the theme of the poem and general appreciation of its working methods—a process complicated by growing
realisation of its extreme complexity and subtlety.

But the French source of *Gawain*—figment or reality—is a restless
ghost which refuses to be laid. In the past decade it has risen three
times in different manifestations. L. D. Benson has returned to the
earliest of all theories and contends that 'Madden and Thomas were
right: the principal and direct source of the beheading episode in *Sir
Gawain* is *Le Livre de Caradoc*'.[10] Professor Smithers, interpreting the
host's name, Bertilak *de Hautdesert*, as meaning 'of the high hermitage'
and assuming that it refers to the Green Chapel, attributes much in the
conception of the chapel to the direct influence of an episode in the
prose *Queste del Saint Graal*, which, he believes, suggested the con-
fessional element in the poem, while the general influence of the
Vulgate romances resulted in marked emphasis on the spiritual rather
than the secular aspects of Gawain's chivalry.[11] And, more recently,
D. D. R. Owen has argued that the *Gawain* poet 'used as his chief and
immediate sources two French romances which hitherto have been
thought to provide only more or less distant analogues to his poem',
Le Chevalier à l'Epée and *La Mule sans Frein*.[12] It is, perhaps, significant

---

9 Later, Loomis ('Objections to the Celtic origin of the "Matière de Bretagne" ',
   Romania, LXXIX (1958), pp. 47–77) modified many of his more extreme
   identifications while still accepting the 'champion's bargain' as the ultimate
   source of the beheading game in Arthurian romance.
10 L. D. Benson, 'The source of the beheading episode in *Sir Gawain and the
   Green Knight*', *Modern Philology*, LIX (1961–62), pp. 1–12, at p. 2.
11 G. V. Smithers, 'What *Sir Gawain and the Green Knight* is about', *Medium
   Aevum*, XXXII (1963), pp. 171–89.
12 D. D. R. Owen, 'Burlesque tradition and *Sir Gawain and the Green Knight*',

that each has made his source identification the basis of a thematic interpretation: source study is no longer felt to be an end in itself. Unfortunately, presuppositions as to the material on which a poet worked can be a dangerous basis on which to judge his thematic intentions, especially if the poem in question is a masterpiece of a highly unconventional kind.

This is not the place to take issue with any of the source studies on points of detail. Obviously the existence of three mutually con-tradictory theories must weaken faith in all three, and personally I remain unconvinced that the immediate source of *Sir Gawain*, in whole or in part, has been identified. I ought, however, to indicate why I feel that preconceptions as to the nature of the source may be mis-leading critically. In Benson's conception the *Gawain* poet took the *Caradoc* episode as part of his matter because it offered him a theme 'that concerns the ideal of knighthood itself and the relation of that ideal to the churlishness represented by the Green Knight'.[13] In inter-preting the beheading episode as a testing of courtliness by churlish-ness he seems to me to confuse aim and agent, ignoring the fact that the real challenge comes not from the Green Knight but from the courtly code, with its demanding absolutes, and that the real conflict is within Gawain, aspiring knight and fallible human being.[14] Smithers' study, based on a tenuous and, I think, mistaken identification, involves a similar imbalance of emphasis.[15] His insistence that 'the poet's con-cern (which is at least partly reflected in Gawain's concern) is with spiritual and Christian and ecclesiastical values, and therefore with the spiritual rather than the secular aspect of the knightly ethos as em-

---

Forum for Modern Language Studies, IV (1968), pp. 125–45, at p. 125. Professor Owen is preparing, in co-operation with Professor R. C. Johnston, an edition of both poems incorporating a full account of the parallels with *Sir Gawain*.

13 Benson's source study formed the basis of his book *Art and Tradition in Sir Gawain and the Green Knight*, New Brunswick, N.J., 1965; see here p. 37.

14 For a similar objection see the review by Arthur Heiserman ('Gawain's clean courtesy, or, The task of telling of true love', *Modern Language Quarterly*, XXVII (1966), pp. 449–57; 'I think that a categorical presumption . . . warps his study of *Sir Gawain*. Romance, he says, "exists to demonstrate the superiority of chivalry" (p. 21). This unfortunate presumption forces him to see in Gawain an embodiment of chivalry, and in Bercilak the *vilain* who "must always suffer defeat". It also seems to coerce the *Gawain* poet's use of his inheritance' (p. 504).

15 In Bertilak's name *de Hautdesert* must surely refer to his castle rather than to the Green Chapel, which lies in a valley bottom and is not a hermitage. Cf. Tolkien and Gordon (revised Davis), pp. 128–9.

bodied in Gawain'[16] surely conflicts with the ideal expressed in the central symbol of the poem, Gawain's pentangle, with its emphatic insistence on the unity of Christian and chivalric virtues, each equally vital and all subordinated to the whole, the hero's *trawþe*.[17] *Gawain* is certainly concerned with spiritual knighthood, but as an indissoluble component of true chivalry, not as the rival of secular knighthood. Equally, though there is a persistent undercurrent of humour in the poem, I cannot be convinced that it derives, as Owen suggests, from the vein of burlesque running through *Le Chevalier à l'Epée* and *La Mule sans Frein*. This is not to deny the persistence in French romance of a tendency to ridicule Gawain, particularly as a philanderer, or that the *Gawain* poet was aware of it.[18] But can anything in these particular texts have taught him to exploit the tradition with such skill?—introducing it so obliquely in a passing reference to the *vrysoun* about the hero's helmet, embroidered with turtle doves and true-love flowers 'As mony burde þeraboute had ben seuen wynter / in toune' (ll. 613–14), yet in puzzling juxtaposition with armour and heraldic charge, symbols of knighthood general and particular; hinting at it in Gawain's reception by Bertilak's courtiers, who, in praising his skill in 'talkyng noble', ambiguously associate it with 'luf-talkyng' (ll. 910–27); letting the lady taunt him with it again and again (ll. 1226–40, 1249–58, 1291–1301, 1480–91, 1508–34) as she sits on the edge of his bed urging:

> '. . . ȝe, þat ar so cortays and coynt of your hetes,
> Oghe to a ȝonke þynk ȝern to schewe
> And teche sum tokenez of trweluf craftes.'   [ll. 1525–27]

until what first appeared a laughing reminder of a younger Gawain— 'I be not now he þat ȝe of speken' (l. 1242)—becomes a trap from which there seems no honourable escape:

> For þat prynces of pris depresed hym so þikke,
> Nurned hym so neȝe þe þred, þat nede hym bihoued
> Oþer lach þer hir luf, oþer lodly refuse.   [ll. 1770–2]

But quite apart from the danger of pre-judging the redactor's thematic intention, source studies inevitably concentrate undue atten-

---

16 *Loc. cit.*, p. 183.
17 Cf. J. A. Burrow, *A Reading of Sir Gawain and the Green Knight*, London 1965, p. 50.
18 Cf. L. D. Benson, *op. cit.*, pp. 104–9.

tion upon the mechanics of plot-making. Dr Owen's procedure 'as a
first step in my demonstration of the dependence of *Sir Gawain* on
the French romances . . . is to treat the French texts like a jigsaw
puzzle, break them up, and see what new pattern we can make with
a selection of the pieces'.[19] This somewhat mechanistic procedure is
scarcely likely to illuminate the creative process, and it has the inevitable effect of diminishing the poem as a work of art with its own
rationale, very different perhaps from that of its components.[20] It is
not, of course, my intention to suggest that *Sir Gawain* is a masterpiece
too sacrosanct to be exposed to the normal procedures of academic
investigation, only to be approached by a rare breed of intuitive
critics, textual analysts to a man and guided solely by the light of
reason and good taste. I do, however, feel that the present dichotomy
between source study and critical analysis is harmful and unnecessary.
The source-hunters cannot see the poem for the plot motifs and the
analysts are haunted by the possibility that their masterpiece of the
creative imagination may be only a redaction from the French after
all. Yet both are trying to understand the process by which the poem
was produced. And both would no doubt accept that *Sir Gawain* is
thoroughly rooted in romance tradition and that its plot components,
like so much Arthurian material, may well derive from the Celtic
matter rationalised and reinterpreted in chivalric terms by French
writers of the twelfth and thirteenth centuries. They differ in that one
group looks for the immediate source of the English poem amongst
a number of texts which the other regards as no more than analogues,
indicative of the type of traditional material available to the poet but
all too remote to throw any light on the creative process.

Yet some dialogue between the two would surely benefit the work
of both. The source-hunters might well be guided in their search by
a more critical awareness of what they are looking for: not a collection

19 *Loc. cit.*, p. 127.
20 As an example of the source-hunter's tendency to think that he has exploded
   the creative mystery when he has demonstrated how the pieces of the jigsaw
   were reshuffled, I quote Professor Owen again, I hope not unfairly: 'It is possible, then, to envisage the genesis of *Sir Gawain* in terms of the poet's use of his
   two basic sources, the borrowing of a few details from other romances that
   he knew, one or two relatively minor additions, and his own work of inspired amplification. At the same time he has modified some of the original
   features in a way that gives us an insight into both his literary skills and his
   intellectual approach to his subject-matter, if this is not too grand a term.'
   (*Loc. cit.*, p. 143.)

of plot motifs but the creative starting point of a masterpiece, thematically complex, structurally elaborate, highly distinctive in many respects. Those who value the poem for its inherent qualities should not
fear that source study will diminish its stature—remembering that the
medieval concept of literary originality was latitudinarian, and redaction ranged from hack translation to fundamental re-creation. If
the manifest source of *Sir Gawain* were to come to light, it would
probably stimulate even greater critical interest in the poem itself and
sharpen awareness of its unique qualities. Until it does, those who
believe in its existence might reasonably examine each new 'immediate
original' in terms of its artistry as well as its narrative content, while
those who remain sceptical might consider where amongst the
analogues and the tradition to which they belong the *Gawain* poet
could have acquired his sense of form, his mastery of ambiguity and
thematic obliquity, his verbal and metrical subtlety.

There is space here for only a limited exercise along these lines in
relation to structure, the most concrete aspect of the poem. Superficially, the structure of *Sir Gawain and the Green Knight* is conventional: of the four sections into which the poem is divided by narrative movement and the presence of large capitals in the manuscript, the
first and fourth are concerned with the beheading game, the others
with adventures which arise on the hero's mission to receive the
return blow. It sounds like a fragment of the Vulgate cycle, where
the technique of *entrelacement* repeatedly inserts one narrative into the
course of another. But there the interruptions multiply in seemingly
endless series, the interlacing winding ever onwards towards an in-
finitely postponed conclusion. *Sir Gawain*, however, is no fragment,
but a tightly organised whole, strictly self-contained, whose components—structural, narrative and thematic alike—are not interwoven
in linear development but fitted neatly inside one another like a nest of
Chinese boxes. Romance convention is observed in the adventures
which arise on the journey from Camelot to the Green Chapel, but the
traditional trials of the knight errant are dismissed in a half-humorous
catalogue which mocks the excesses of conventional romance:

> Sumwhyle wyth wormez he werrez, and with wolues als,
> Sumwhyle wyth wodwos, þat woned in þe knarrez,
> Boþe wyth bullez and berez, and borez oþerquyle,
> And etaynez, þat hym anelede of þe heȝe felle;   [ll. 720–3]

Instead, the interval between challenge and return blow is largely

devoid of action, divided between passive resistance to the forces of
Nature and relaxation in a courtly world of hunting, feasting and
refined conversation. Yet in this interlude of inactivity is the heart of
the matter: Gawain having won his struggle against the fear of death,
presents himself for the return blow at the climax of the action only
to find that the crisis is already past, that he has been tested and found
wanting.

The interlude itself is elaborately structured upon a triple pattern:
on each of three days, while his host hunts in the forest, Gawain is
besieged in bed by his hostess, whose pressing attentions he avoids
without discourtesy to her or disloyalty to her husband, to whom each
evening he passes on her kisses, fulfilling the exchange-of-winnings
compact made with the lord. The functioning of this triple structure
in relation to theme and narrative is extremely complex. Superficially,
its very elaboration seems part of the whole atmosphere of courtly
festivity in Bertilak's castle, ordered and formal, a Christmas game
played out according to well understood rules, no more significant,
apparently, than the exchange of winnings itself, a social compact
between gentlemen for their mutual amusement. The threefold pattern, so familiar from folk-tales, is reassuring: Gawain having once
successfully resisted temptation and kept the compact, the implication
is that he will succeed on the second and third days also—as, indeed,
superficially he does, paying over the last three kisses as faithfully as
the first. But it is also disturbing: in folk-tales the events of the third
day so often break the established pattern—as, indeed, in this case also.
The compact itself has something of the same ambivalent duality:
seemingly casual, threatening at worst a social lapse, yet serving as
cover for a serious attack upon Gawain's honour by the lady, leaving
him apparently no alternative but to fail in *cortaysye* towards her by
rejecting her advances or in *felaȝschyp* to her husband by accepting
them, offending at the same time against his own *clannes*, physical and
spiritual. The ambiguity of form and meaning is reflected in the whole
atmosphere of the sequence, superficially comic—at the hero's expense,
in itself unusual and disconcerting—yet with ominous undertones:

> Gret perile bitwene hem stod,
> Nif Maré of hir knyȝt mynne.   [ll. 1768-9]

As the lady's motives in pursuing Gawain remain obscure—'For to
haf wonnen hym to woȝe, what-so scho þoȝt ellez' (l. 1550)—much
of the temptation's ominous atmosphere depends upon its structural

treatment. Each interview between them is inset within the narrative of that day's hunt, the timing so indicated that both episodes seem to take place simultaneously. Thematically there is an obvious connection: the lady is hunting Gawain as her husband hunts deer, boar and fox. But it is the underlying contrast which most contributes to the ambivalent effect of the temptation. Bertilak, in culling Nature's excess to provide food, is fulfilling his proper social function, and the hunting is presented as a natural activity, exhilarating and uncomplicated. The lady, however, is profoundly unnatural in hunting the male, and the bedroom scenes, with their uneasy ambiguities, are made to seem all the more unhealthy by contrast.

For some commentators the contrast is heightened by a more detailed correspondence between the lord's quarry on each day and Gawain's reaction to the lady's advances, at first startled and timorous like the deer, then brusque and forceful like the boar, finally cunning and deceitful like the fox.[21] Others, with whom I would agree, see the third day as a deliberate breach of the pattern established on the first two, so that the contrast which had been in the lady's disfavour becomes a similarity wholly to Gawain's discredit.[22] Having, perhaps, taken the initial parallelism of wooing and hunting as no more shocking than that paradox of courtly love poetry which makes Venus a huntress[23]—akin to the lady's perverse use of the courtly code in claiming Gawain as her 'prisoner' and at the same time declaring herself his 'servant', to his embarrassment and our amusement—we are slow to realise the ominous significance of the parallels between the hero's behaviour and that of the fox. Our modern familiarity with fox-hunting may prevent us from noticing that the lord's quarry on the third day is unusual: the fox, considered as vermin unfit for food, comes unexpectedly after the noble game hunted on previous days. His popular reputation in beast-fable as thievish, cunning and cowardly is demonstrated by his behaviour, meticulously observed, in the course

21 See, for example, H. L. Savage, *The Gawain-Poet: Studies in his Personality and Background*, Chapel Hill, N.C., 1956, pp. 31–48.

22 See J. A. Burrow, *op. cit.*, p. 98: 'I myself cannot see that the second temptation scene differs from the first as the boar-hunt differs from the deer-hunt; but where the fox-hunt and the third temptation are concerned, I see that each differs from both its predecessors in the same sort of way. Each involves a departure from the noble and exemplary conduct of the previous days. In each we recognise death as a terrifying thing which men and animals alike try to escape by every device in their power regardless of dignity or duty.'

23 See J. A. Burrow, *op. cit.*, p. 86.

of the chase until, at the end of the day, with the hunt hard on his heels, he finds the lord full in his path with drawn sword, starts back in fear and is torn to pieces by the hounds. Meanwhile, in the secure and sheltered world of the castle, Gawain, hard pressed by the lady and reminded by her proffered gift of the green girdle which can protect its wearer from any blow of the fate which awaits him next day, accepts and cunningly conceals what properly belongs to his host, Sir Bertilak. Shrinking from the fear of death, he has fallen into sin, the death of the soul.

This is the heart of the poem, structurally and thematically, the innermost of the Chinese boxes. Yet, here as elsewhere, structural parallelism is combined with structural variation, superficially diverting attention from the theme, underscoring it in retrospect. The pattern of the first two days having established the association of hunting and wooing, we may not notice that the lady has risen to leave, apparently abandoning her seduction, before Gawain makes his fatal error, and though she begs a glove as a love token and offers first a rich ring and then the girdle—later referred to as a *drurye*—the former is refused, and the latter accepted not out of love but fear of death. It is Death the hunter who has pursued Gawain throughout the passing year, haunting his dreams and troubling his thoughts in the midst of the lady's wooing:

> And ay þe lady let lyk as hym loued mych;
> Þe freke ferde with defence, and feted ful fayre.
> Þaȝ ho were burde bryȝtest þe burne in mynde hade,
> Þe lasse luf in his lode for lur þat he soȝt
>   boute hone,
>   Þe dunte pat schulde hym deue,
>   And nedez hit most be done.[24]   [ll. 1281–7]

And he sees the girdle not as a *drurye* but as a talisman against death:

> Þen kest þe knyȝt, and hit come to his hert
> Hit were a juel for þe jopardé þat hym iugged were:
> When he acheued to þe chapel his chek for to fech,
> Myȝt he haf slypped to be vnslayn, þe sleȝt were noble.   [ll. 1855–8]

The shadow of the beheading game falls across the temptation, whose

24 As I differ from Tolkien and Gordon on the text and its interpretation at this point, I quote from my forthcoming edition and translation of *Sir Gawain*, to be published by Manchester University Press. I would translate here: 'Though she was the fairest woman the knight had ever known, the less warmth there was in his manner because of the fate that he was going to without respite, the blow that was to strike him down, and must inevitably be struck.'

narrative pattern, artificially neat, half hides the fact that the temptation is not love of the lady but love of life.

Two further examples of this use of structural anticipation to conceal—and, in reflection, reveal—thematic intention immediately follow. The established pattern of the day leads us to expect that, when his temptress has withdrawn, Gawain will rise, dress, go to the chapel, then to breakfast and pass the time until evening in pleasant relaxation amongst the ladies of the castle. So he does on this third day also—but with one significant difference. In the chapel he seeks out a priest in privacy:

> Þere he schrof hym schyrly and schewed his mysdedez,
> Of þe more and þe mynne, and merci besechez,
> And of absolucioun he on þe segge calles;
> And he asoyled hym surely and sette hym so clene
> As domezday schulde haf ben diȝt on þe morn.   [ll. 1880–4]

The substitution of confession for Gawain's daily attendance at mass may seem an unimportant variation, readily explainable as a natural preparation for his encounter with the Green Knight next morning. But can his confession be valid while he retains the green girdle, breaking the terms of his compact with Sir Bertilak? The compact may be no more than a 'game', but Gawain has given his word, and for the knight of the pentangle, pledged to a code of absolutes which admits no breach of perfection, however venial, his *trawþe* ('honour, integrity') is as deeply involved as in that other ill-omened compact whose impending settlement has driven him to take the girdle. And there is every indication that he means to keep it; before going to chapel, he

> Lays vp þe luf-lace þe lady hym raȝt,
> Hid hit ful holdely, þer he hit eft fonde.   [ll. 1874–5]

If this concealment indicates an intention already formed, then the confession was invalid and Gawain will go to face death in a state of sin, his *pure pentaungel* flawed, his trust no longer in Christian chivalry but in a dubious talisman dishonestly obtained. If, however, it is no more than a considerate precaution to protect the lady's reputation from malicious observers until her gift can be surrendered to her husband, then the confession was valid, since Gawain genuinely means to make restitution.

The perceptive reader will await the completion of the daily pattern with tense anticipation. Here too there are variations, but of a trifling kind which merely underline the normality of the evening's events. Gawain passes the day with such apparent pleasure that others comment:

> 'Þus myry he watȝ neuer are,
> Syn he com hider, er þis.'   [ll. 1891–2]

Signs of an easy conscience? Or of an attempt to conceal an uneasy one? When Bertilak returns from the hunt he has no need, as on the earlier days, to summon Gawain, who is already waiting in the hall and proposes that he should be first to present his day's winnings, not the host, as on the previous occasions. He does so—but the three kisses only, nothing else; and receives in return the fox skin, worthless to him but a disturbing symbol for readers who have recognised the congruity of his behaviour with that of the animal in the course of the day. For such readers the poet's personal interjection at the close of the third section, as the temptation gives way again to the beheading game, must seem ominous:

> Ȝif he ne slepe soundyly say ne dar I,
> For he hade muche on þe morn to mynne, ȝif he wolde,
>   in poȝt.
>   Let hym lyȝe þere stille,
>   He hatȝ nere þat he soȝt;   [ll. 1991–5]

Others who accept the narrative patterning at a superficial level and ignore its minor variations will find their conventional expectations fulfilled by its formulaic repetitions. Their suspicions unaroused, they will see no unnatural association between the green girdle and the Green Knight and detect no irony in the juxtaposition of chivalric symbol and magic talisman as Gawain, arming himself next morning, binds the girdle over his surcoat charged with the pentangle. Regarding the temptation as the conventional interval of adventures between the posing of a chivalric dilemma and its solution, they should see no particular threat in the terrifying description of the Knight of the Green Chapel given by Gawain's guide as they make their way there, or in his offer to conceal his flight if the hero cannot face the ordeal before him. But anyone who has noted the structural variations and interpreted their significance will tremble for Gawain, whom fear of death has once already tempted into breach of his chivalric code. The suspense grows more and more acute as the threefold motif of the temptation begins to intrude upon the dual pattern of the beheading

game, where much in the final section recalls the sequence of the first:
the noise which heralds the Green Knight's appearance, his bizarre
dress, hair and colouring, his great axe, his legalistic re-statement of
the terms of the compact, and the mingling of courtesy and mockery
in his manner to Gawain. He claims only a single blow, but he aims
three; and as the axe descends for the third time suspicion grows into
certainty that the blows relate to the exchange-of-winnings compact
and that Gawain's dishonesty upon the third day will be punished at
the third stroke. A flash of insight brings recognition that the Green
Knight and Sir Bertilak are somehow one and the same, that the
Christmas 'games' of Camelot and Hautdesert are equally serious, that
Gawain to fulfil the terms of the one has broken the terms of the
other, that his confession was invalid and he stands in spiritual as well
as mortal peril.

For the hero, as for readers less conscious of the interrelations of
structure and theme, the shock of realisation is still to come as the
Green Knight, his personality fused with that of Bertilak, links the
two compacts without explanation, and accuses Gawain of lack of
lewté in retaining the girdle, while at the same time praising him highly:

'As perle bi þe quite pese is of prys more,
  So is Gawayn, in god fayth, bi oþer gay knyȝtez.'   [ll. 2364-5]

Appreciation of the hero's violent reaction, the bitterness of his self-
reproach and his determination to wear the green girdle as a badge of
shame is partly conditioned by structure: by the placing of the pentangle description, implying absolute standards of chivalric integrity, at
the beginning of the temptation sequence, and its ironic association
with the girdle at the beginning of the fourth section as the beheading
game is renewed. Understanding of the full extent of Gawain's failure
will depend upon recognition of a much more subtle parallelism which
contains its own ironic variation. The form in which he admits his
shortcomings to the Green Knight leaves no doubt that he is aware his
confession to the priest at Hautdesert was invalid:

'I biknowe yow, knyȝt, here stylle,
  Al fawty is my fare;
  Leteȝ me ouertake your wylle
  And efte I schal be ware.'   [ll. 2385-8]

The Green Knight, in reply, accepts the role of confessor:

'Þou art confessed so clene, beknowen of þy mysses,
  And hatȝ þe penaunce apert of þe poynt of myn egge,

I halde þe polysed of þat plyȝt, and pured as clene
As þou hadeȝ neuer forfeted syþen þou watȝ fyrst borne;'   [ll. 2391-4]

The frank and full confession made to an invalid person, a layman,
underscores the invalidity of the incomplete confession made to
a priest. And structural patterning alone, without comment on the
poet's part, conveys one of the most profound and delicate aspects
of the theme.

Though awareness of its operation may dawn upon individual
readers at different points in the narrative, in retrospect the same
principle can be seen at work throughout the poem: structural repeti-
tion and innovation are so combined as to suggest a superficial con-
formity to the conventions and values of romance while drawing
attention—at times obliquely, at others emphatically—to departures
from the accepted norms of procedure, behaviour and judgement.
The feast which begins the action of the poem is matched by that
which reopens it at the beginning of the second section. The formal,
corporate life of the Round Table continues, but the *rechles merþes* of
the first occasion have become an uneasy façade concealing anxiety
for Gawain, the court's agreement 'To ryd þe kyng wyth croun, /
And gif Gawan þe game' (ll. 364-5) is forgotten in general criticism of
Arthur for exposing the knight to danger, and their silent acquiescence
in his acceptance of the challenge has become a conviction that it will
end in disaster, expressed with an excess of emotion:

Wel much watȝ þe warme water þat waltered of yȝen,
When þat semly syre soȝt fro þo wonez
        þad daye.   [ll. 684-6]

Their tears on this occasion must be set against the laughter with which
they greet Gawain's admission of his failure at yet another assembly of
the Round Table which ends the poem. The poet makes no comment
on their reaction nor on their instant adoption of the green girdle,
Gawain's badge of shame, as a badge of honour; but the structural
parallelism surely implies instability of opinion and superficiality of
judgement on the court's part? And on the part of readers who associate
themselves with the court's reactions?

There is a similar trap for unwary readers in the obvious parallelism
of the two descriptions of Gawain arming, one before he sets out
from Camelot, the other before he leaves Hautdesert; the former
minutely detailed, the latter brief but superficially conveying the same
effect. Both suggest the social standing of the knight in the richness of

his arms and his moral stature through their conventional symbolism, but the former gives pride of place to the heraldic badge, the pentangle, which proclaims his personal code of perfection, on which, in the latter, the green girdle, symbol of his imperfection, is superimposed. The similarities and contrasts raise obvious questions. Of what material use can armour be in a contest where the hero cannot defend himself? Can the virtue of the pentangle coexist with the girdle? Can the latter protect where the former has failed? But there are other, less obvious, structural ironies: the girdle in the second arming scene is the converse of the pentangle in the first, but it also has its obverse there in the *vrysoun* about Gawain's helmet, badge of his amorous reputation, of which Bertilak's court and the lady so persistently remind him; yet for him the green girdle is no *drurye* and he is ultimately trapped not by love but by his passionate desire to preserve the integrity of his pentangle. Meaning lies in the dissimilarities which disappoint our conventional expectations; life, as the poet reminds us, is rarely so neatly patterned as romance:

> A ȝere ȝernes ful ȝerne, and ȝeldeȝ neuer lyke,
> Þe forme to þe fynisment foldeȝ ful selden.   [ll. 498–9]

Time itself provides the most fundamental structural element in the poem, and here too there are patterns of congruity and disparity. The narrative is related in natural sequence, and almost every event is precisely dated as to the season of the year, particular day, and even time of day at which it occurs. The general effect is realistic, increasing the readers' consciousness of the relation of the incidents to their own time-ordered world; significantly, where these are most conventional in nature, if not in detail, as on Gawain's journey through the trackless forests of romance and his return to Camelot, the passage of time is left conventionally vague. And the careful recording of milestones in time heightens awareness of the remorseless passing of the year which is to end in Gawain's submission to the Green Knight's blow. Everything in this time scheme serves as a reminder that, like the narrative itself, the life of man is linear and ends in death. But there is another, very different, time scale in the poem, the cyclic time of nature in which, as the famous passage on the passing of the year reminds us:

> . . . al rypeȝ and roteȝ þat ros vpon fyrst,
> And þus ȝirneȝ þe ȝere in ȝisterdayeȝ mony,   [ll. 528–9]

Man is subject to cyclic time also, but for him the year seldom ends as it began; for Gawain it begins in feasting, merry-making and a Christmas 'game', but its outcome may be very different:

> Gawan watʒ glad to begynne þose gomneʒ in halle,
> Bot þaʒ þe ende be heuy haf ʒe no wonder;   [ll. 495–6]

Nature renews herself perennially, but the life of the individual may be cut short. The interaction of these two time schemes has obvious thematic implications which extend the poem's relevance beyond the fate of its particular hero.

The poem itself, though linear in narrative sequence, is cyclic in structure, beginning with references to the fall of Troy, the founding of Britain by the eponymous Brutus, and the *Brutus bokez* of Arthurian literature, and ending with the same references in reverse order. The effect is to place the events of the romance within the context of 'world history'—Troy being for medieval Europe the imagined source of the secular values of chivalry—of the legendary history of Britain, inheritor of those values, and of the *Arthurez wonderez* in which they were most fully expressed. This particular adventure, it is implied, like all Arthurian romance, is of a kind with the storied past of Britain:

> Where werre and wrake and wonder
> Bi syþeʒ hatʒ wont þerinne,
> And oft boþe blysse and blunder
> Ful skete hatʒ skyfted synne.   [ll. 16–19]

The implications for Britain's reputation are ambiguous, but so also is the reputation of that Trojan exile, the archetypal founding father, who

> Watʒ tried for his tricherie, þe trewest on erthe.   [l. 4]

The contribution of this structural element, the outermost of the Chinese boxes, is to generalise the content of the inner structures, suggesting that Gawain's experiences are relevant for all the heirs of Trojan chivalry. What Gawain himself has learnt from the adventure is not didactically expressed; he is silent after the court's decision to adopt his green girdle as a badge of honour. And the Round Table's own response is dubious and superficial. But the poem's return to its starting point, now perhaps viewed in a very different light, may remind us that though the life of the individual is linear the life of the race is cyclic and mankind may learn from experience. Here, as elsewhere in *Sir Gawain*, structure and meaning are one.

There is much more to the matter than this, but enough has perhaps been said to demonstrate the complex interrelation of theme and structure for which an 'immediate original' might be expected to account—in part at least. The hypothetical sources and analogues so far cited scarcely suggest such a high degree of narrative organisation. Some of them have been little studied, but in general their structure is simply that of the narrative of events in natural sequence. They fall, broadly speaking, into two categories. There are those such as *Yder*, *Hunbaut*, *Le Chevalier à l'Epée* and *La Mule sans Frein*, comparatively brief, where elements of the *Gawain* plot occur amongst a plethora of other adventures and on too limited a scale to have significant internal structure. Others, such as the *Perceval* continuation and *Perlesvaus*, are large-scale works in which *entrelacement* provides the basic structural pattern; but here again the *Gawain* analogue is only a fragment of the whole, without distinctive structural unity. Until an 'immediate original' is discovered in which beheading game and temptation are linked by the exchange of winnings in such a way as to make them mutually interdependent, the *Gawain* poet must be credited with the structure of the romance. And to credit him with structure is also to credit him with theme.[25]

This is not, however, to suggest that he had nothing to learn from French romance. On the internal evidence of the four poems generally attributed to him, he was well read in Latin and French and, to some extent at least, in Italian also. It is unlikely, since he is unusually reticent about his learning, that we know the full extent of his French reading, but he evidently knew much courtly literature, including the *Roman de la Rose*.[26] It would certainly be surprising if he had not experienced the influence, direct or indirect, of the greatest of courtly poets, Chrétien de Troyes, and his famous dictum on the art of romance composition:

Por ce dist Crestïens de Troies
que reisons est que totevoies

25 Cf. J. Gardner, *The Complete Works of the Gawain-Poet*, Chicago, 1965, p. 26: 'And to the extent that all elements in the poem are interrelated to form a coherent and balanced whole—both literal and symbolic—from which no part can be removed without serious damage to the poem on both levels, we can be absolutely certain that the interrelationship, together with the resulting aesthetic effect, is to be credited to the *Gawain*-poet himself. Once the structure of the poem has been understood, once it has been recognised that we are dealing here not with borrowing but with total transformation of old material, the search outside the poem for the poem's meaning becomes pure pedantry.'
26 See A. C. Spearing, *The Gawain-Poet*, Cambridge, 1970, pp. 12–18.

doit chascuns panser et antandre
a bien dire et a bien aprandre;
et tret d'un conte d'avanture
une molt bele conjointure
par qu'an puet prover et savoir
que cil ne fet mie savoir
qui s'escïence n'abandone
tant con Dex la grasce l'an done:[27]

Much ink has been spilt over this passage, and in particular on what Chrétien meant by *conjointure*, most recently and helpfully discussed by Professor Vinaver.[28] At a meeting of the Manchester Medieval Seminar, when he and Dr Whitehead were present, I once attempted a definition of the term in relation to two others, *matière* and *sen*, used by Chrétien in discussing his art:

> the organisation of elements in a narrative (*matière*) into a significant pattern according to an apparent principle or in relation to a particular theme (*sen*), often, where Chrétien is concerned, leaving other elements uninvolved, possibly as a means of creating narrative tension through the reader's expectation as to what their relevance to the *conjointure* will eventually prove to be, or merely as features of the inherited story-matter (*conte d'aventure*) felt to be irrelevant to the *conjointure*.

This is not an exact description of the constructional principle in *Sir Gawain* but, as Professor Vinaver points out, those who followed Chrétien in the evolution of the romance were to have a more rigid concept of *conjointure*:

> The varied and incoherent poetic legacy of the twelfth century will fall into carefully thought out narrative sequences, missing links will be found, and a vast architectural design will emerge. The Perceval story will beome the story of Galahad, the hero of a rigidly coherent *Queste del Saint Graal* in which every detail of the action will have its explicitly stated motive and no episode will be allowed to remain outside a carefully thought out scheme.[29]

27 *Erec et Enide* (ed. Mario Roques, Paris, 1968) ll. 9–18.
28 E. Vinaver, *The Rise of Romance*, Oxford, 1971, pp. 33–52. Professor Vinaver translates the *Erec* passage as follows: 'Since in his opinion it is reasonable that everyone should always endeavour to speak well and teach the right things, Chrétien de Troyes draws from a tale of adventure a very fine *conjointure*, whereby it may be proved and made known that he is not wise who does not use his learning so long as God gives him grace' (p. 34).
29 *Ibid.*, p. 51.

Writing towards the end of the fourteenth century, the *Gawain* poet may well have made his own amalgam of both concepts, combining complexity and regularity of structure with innovations and irregularities which imply thematic significance in what is superficially a *conte d'aventure*.

Internal analysis is making us increasingly aware of how the *sen* of *Sir Gawain and the Green Knight* depends upon the *conjointure*, not least upon those elements which at first sight do not seem to be involved in it. But many problems remain—such, for example, as the full significance of Morgan's role in the romance—and no doubt hidden ironies which knowledge of the source or sources might make explicit for us.[30] In ignorance of them we cannot know whether the process of re-creation was as fundamental as that of Chrétien,[31] though the text alone may convince us that the poet was of comparable stature. Certainly, if his subtle use of structure to draw meaning from his story matter is evidence of his artistic principles, he would have shared Chrétien's contempt for those who:

> depecier et corronpre suelent
> cil qui de conter vivre vuelent.[32]

The jigsaw principle would scarcely have appealed to either of them.

---

30 Cf. J. Gardner (*op. cit.*, p. 26): 'But internal analysis does have a limitation, nevertheless. What it cannot show, and what must therefore be left to the scholarship of the future, is the straight or ironic play of text against source. Reading the *Gawain* may be roughly equivalent to reading *The Waste Land* without knowledge of Eliot's sources.'

31 See J. Frappier, *Chrétien de Troyes*, Paris, 1968, p. 228: 'Il est d'ailleurs probable, à en juger par la comparaison avec les contes gallois de *Gereint*, d'*Owein et Lunet*, de *Peredur*, que Chrétien a trouvé dans ses sources la première charpente de ses romans. Son invention réelle aura été d'organiser avec autant de finesse que de clarté un assemblage raide encore et rudimentaire, d'en tirer une *conjointure* qui demeurait latente, simplement virtuelle.'

32 *Erec et Enide* (ed. Roques), ll. 21–2.

David Blamires
The sources and literary structure of *Wigamur*

The German Arthurian romances of the classical period have always been highly valued in modern times for their artistic skill and genuine poetic power. Wolfram's *Parzival*, Gottfried's *Tristan* and, to a somewhat lesser degree, Hartmann's *Erec* and *Iwein* have elicited a lasting tribute from succeeding generations of scholars—and not only scholars, as the translations into modern German and English make amply clear. Besides these works of genius, however, there exists a fairly extensive corpus of other Arthurian romances. Some of it is contemporary with the classical works or even antedates them, as, for example, Eilhart von Oberg's *Tristrant* and Ulrich von Zatzikhoven's *Lanzelet*. These two poems in particular have had their devotees, especially among those critics concerned with Arthurian source studies. But there is also a mass of later Arthurian material, much of it of ponderous length, which has been consigned by most scholars to a literary dustbin. It has been dismissed as derivative, the work of untalented imitators, and discredited by the historians of medieval literature. Among these later Arthurian romances we find the anonymous and much neglected *Wigamur*.

No one in his right mind would claim that *Wigamur* is a work of commanding literary significance, but after three readings of it I cannot feel it is as worthless as most writers on the subject have thought. *Wigamur* has had a pretty bad press. Gervinus mentions the 'schon vorbrechende Verwilderungen in der Technik', though he goes on to say that the poem has 'eine dichterische Gewandtheit der Sprache . . . , die gegen das Ende des Jahrhunderts schon selten wird', but concludes with the dismissal 'sonst eine Erzählung des ganz gewöhnlichen Schlages dieser Gattung und sichtlich eine platte Erfindung'.[1] Sarrazin, who published the first monograph on the poem, considered it 'ein

---

1 G. G. Gervinus, *Geschichte der deutschen Dichtung*, II, fifth edition, Leipzig, 1871, p. 44.

sehr unbedeutendes poetisches Product', although its 'naive, treuher-
zige, wenn auch unbeholfene Darstellung' is better than that of the
Pleier's works.[2] Of more recent scholars de Boor says, 'Die ganze
hölzerne und armselige Erzählweise, der ungepflegte Stil, die Hilf-
losigkeit in Vers- und Reimkunst würden eher auf einen jener späten
Dichter des 14. Jahrhunderts weisen, die zu der höfischen Dichtung
nur noch über den Stoff Zugang haben.'[3] Walshe merely declares that
it 'consists of practically nothing but plagiarisms'.[4] With these four
judgements one would imagine that *Wigamur* could scarcely have any
attractions, though, to be fair, both Sarrazin and de Boor have some
quite positive things to say too. Their negative remarks do, however,
point to some of the problems that one has to deal with in trying to
assess and place *Wigamur*. There is the literary crudity of the work,
which is related to its manuscript tradition. There is the date. There
is the matter of sources and what the poet made of them. Each of these
matters poses awkward problems, but I hope to show that the way in
which these questions have been tackled or avoided in the past has
contributed to the low esteem in which the poem is at present held.

Let us begin with the manuscript tradition. The main manuscript
is a fifteenth century paper one at Wolfenbüttel (W), but it has various
serious gaps to disturb our understanding of the poem, one of these
being a rather long one at the very end. The dialect shows some
Swabian features, but the poem itself seems to be of Bavarian origin.
The manuscript is swarming with errors, misunderstandings, omissions
and some totally incomprehensible lines, most of which must be
accounted to the scribe's lack of intelligence and carelessness. The
corrupt state of manuscript W has a lot to do with the adverse comments of scholars, since this is the printed text that one has to work
with. It was published by J. G. Büsching in vol. I, part 4, of von der
Hagen and Büsching's *Deutsche Gedichte des Mittelalters* (Berlin, 1808)[5]
before any other manuscript was known. The text amounts to just
over 6,000 lines. Büsching reproduced the manuscript very closely,
while inserting modern punctuation and capitals, expanding abbrevia-

---

2 Gregor Sarrazin, *Wigamur. Eine litterarhistorische Untersuchung*, Strasbourg,
   1879, p. 33.
3 Helmut de Boor, *Geschichte der deutschen Literatur*, III, part 1: *Die deutsche Literatur im späten Mittelalter. Zerfall und Neubeginn, 1250–1350*, Munich, 1962, p. 80.
4 M. O'C. Walshe, *Medieval German Literature*, London, 1962, p. 196.
5 Line references are to Büsching's edition, amplified by Carl von Kraus,
   Mittelhochdeutsches Übungsbuch, 2nd ed., Heidelberg, 1926, for manuscripts
   M and S.

tions and sparingly correcting rhymes. He did not attempt to recast it in the classical Middle High German norm. Although Ferdinand Khull promised a new edition[6] and Jenisch produced a volume of *Vorarbeiten zu einer kritischen Ausgabe des Wigamur*,[7] there has in fact been no further edition of the poem, despite the discovery of two sets of fragments in the late nineteenth century.

In 1879 R. M. Werner published the Salzburg fragments (S), now in the Österreichische Nationalbibliothek, Vienna, which correspond to lines 4744–5658 of Büsching's edition, though with the omission of 5160–409.[8] The manuscript is mid-fourteenth century in date. The second set of fragments was published by F. Keinz and is in the Bayerische Staatsbibliothek, Munich (M).[9] The fragments come from the Swabian-Bavarian dialect border and are dated about the turn of the thirteenth and fourteenth centuries. They provide about 1,400 lines of text, some of which helps to fill in the gaps in W. This means that while for most of the poem W is our only source, there is also a brief section for which M is the only witness. For comparative textual criticism there are three passages, from 4883 to 4904 and again from 4953 to 5159 and from 5409 to 5658, where all three manuscripts provide a text. Unfortunately, however, these texts pose quite as many problems as they solve in regard to establishing a critical edition. There are very many places at which it is impossible to decide precisely what the author wrote, although the narrative outline is reasonably clear.

There is nothing like working with a corrupt text or manuscript for colouring one's judgement of literary values, and I am inclined to think that this has largely influenced the received opinions of literary scholars. But the fact that we in the twentieth century know of three manuscripts of *Wigamur*, while, for example, there is only one of Hartmann's *Erec* and one of *Kudrun*, the 'heroic' epic that ranks second only to the *Nibelungenlied*, may give us some guide to the popularity of the poem. There are in addition references to Wigamur in other medieval works, which show that he was a well known hero. Albrecht

6 See Ferdinand Khull, 'Zu Wigamur', *Zeitschrift für deutsches Altertum*, XXIV (1880), p. 97.

7 Diss., Königsberg, 1918.

8 R. M. Werner, 'Fragmente einer pergamenths. des Wigamur', *Zeitschrift für deutsches Altertum*, XXIII (1879), pp. 100–11.

9 F. Keinz, 'Wigamur. Münchener Bruchstücke', *Germania*, XXVII (1882), pp. 289–330.

von Scharfenberg uses him as a walk-on character in the *Jüngerer Titurel*,[10] which was written about 1270. He is also listed in a catalogue of literary heroes in the early fourteenth century poem *Friedrich von Schwaben* (ed. Jellinek, line 4818), along with Lanzelet, Tristan, Iwein and many others. The earliest reference occurs in a *Leich* by Tannhäuser (active between 1227/8 and 1266)[11] where, in a farrago of deliberate confusions about literary matters, the poet says:

> Her Wigamur vor Camvoleis,
> wol tet erz, als wirz han vernomen.   [*Leich* 4, l. 61–2]

It was of course Gahmuret, the father of Parzival, who was the chief hero of the tournament at Kanvoleis (see *Parzival*, book 2), but Tannhäuser's attribution of this to Wigamur makes it obvious that the latter was a famous hero in the mid-thirteenth century. Because of his assessment of the aesthetic standards of the poem de Boor in his literary history would like to date *Wigamur* to the fourteenth century and suggests that the name might have been invented in another connection and simply taken over by the author of our poem for his hero. This does not seem plausible. There is no evidence of any poem about Wigamur other than the one we have here, and the independent use of the name and character by two thirteenth century poets clearly indicates a mid-thirteenth century origin. Furthermore, the formation of the name Wigamur on the pattern provided by Wigalois points to a time at which Wirnt's romance was reasonably new. Although *Wigalois* is extant in nearly forty manuscripts and fragments over the whole period of the later Middle Ages, it is likely that any imitation would occur near the time at which it first impinged on the literary scene, i.e. between 1210 and 1215.[12] It may be awkward to have to admit that works of art do not always fit into organised patterns of development (or decay) in matters of taste. With *Wigamur* it is more economical to accept that the poem which we have is the one whose hero achieved popularity sufficient for him to be alluded to by two other thirteenth century poets rather than to assume that Tannhäuser might have been referring to a now lost poem. We are left, therefore,

10 See Büsching's edition, p. vi; for the date of *Der jüngere Titurel* see the edition by Werner Wolf (Berlin, 1955, 1964, 1968; *Deutsche Texte des Mittelalters*, XLV, LV, LXI), XLV, p. ix.
11 See Johannes Siebert, *Der Dichter Tannhäuser. Leben—Gedichte—Sage*, Halle, 1934, pp. 1–27.
12 See Friedrich Neumann, 'Wann verfasste Wirnt den Wigalois?', *Zeitschrift für deutsches Altertum*, XCIII (1964), pp. 31–62.

with a mid-century date not earlier than *c.* 1215 and probably not later than *c.* 1266. It would be wise not to push these dates too far either way.

Before going on to discuss further features of *Wigamur*, it will be as well to give a fairly detailed summary of the plot, since the text is not easily accessible. Matters of source and treatment can then be dealt with in a more informed way.

In structure the poem is a biographical romance and starts with Wigamur's childhood. He is the son of Paldriot, king of Lendrie. In early childhood, when Paldriot is away at a festival at Caridol, to which he has been invited by Artus, Wigamur is abducted by a wild woman called Lespia, who carries him off to her cave at the bottom of the sea, where she keeps him with her two daughters. Lespia later captures a centaur-like monster, who is fettered in a corner away from the children, who are commanded to keep their distance from him lest he should kill them. Meanwhile Paldriot manages to take Lespia prisoner, and on threat of death she directs him to her cave. The cave, however, is found deserted of life; Lespia's two daughters are lying there dead; the monster together with Wigamur has escaped. The monster then educates Wigamur in a variety of courtly accomplishments, disabuses him of thinking Lespia to be his mother, and finally releases him from the sea, armed only with a bow and arrows, ready to proceed to the land of Doloyr. (1–418)

Running through the forest, Wigamur arrives at a castle which is being besieged by a party of knights, who are astonished at his strange appearance. They wreak havoc at the castle, burn it and carry off its lord. Wigamur then investigates the scene, finds a horse and equips himself with armour from a dead knight. The horse goes, without being given any direction, to the land of Doloyr, where Wigamur encounters the knight Glakotelesfloyr. Although he is completely inexperienced, Wigamur defeats Glakotelesfloyr in battle, at which the latter offers to become Wigamur's *man*. Since Wigamur has no idea of feudal practices, he interprets *man* as meaning 'husband' and cannot understand what Glakotelesfloyr is getting at. On receiving the explanation, he asks further questions about the burnt castle and learns that it belongs to the king of Pontrafort, who has done the king of Doloyr great harm, hence the destruction. He is to be hanged for it the following morning. Wigamur eventually lets Glakotelesfloyr go without imposing any conditions on him, though not without some anxiety on this score. This is the last we hear of Glakotelesfloyr, unless he is identical with the knight Gletechleflors, who crops up for a brief episode at a tournament organised later by Artus. (419–793)

Wigamur's horse now finds its way back to the deserted castle, where our hero discovers a beautiful maiden sitting alone in great fear. Her name is Pioles. She is the daughter of the king of Troyswarlanz and is betrothed to Harzier, king of Nordin, who was taking her home with him when he heard of a tournament at Pelrapier, to which he decided to go. He had left Pioles in the care of the king of Pontrafort. Following the destruction of the castle she is in great distress. Wigamur tries to comfort her, and she helps him to remove his armour, which he cannot get off. They rest for the night, in a completely blameless way, as the poet, anxious to safeguard Wigamur's moral reputation, explicitly informs us. The next morning Wigamur is about to depart with no further thought, but realises when Pioles begs him to kill her rather than abandon her in the forest that he must do something for her. He searches all day for help, but finds nothing. On returning he shoots a pheasant, which they eat with bread and water. They spend a second night together as before. The following morning Wigamur again rides off for help, through the forest and up a high mountain, where he reaches a castle guarded by a dwarf. The dwarf gives him food and warns him of his master, Lespurant, who has killed Johiot, the true lord of the castle, and holds his two daughters, Ligronite and Flogrisite, captive. Wigamur indignantly tells the dwarf that his master should not delay in returning their property and possessions to the maidens, but he has to go back to Pioles. He spends another night with her. (794–1099, plus M 1099, 1–93.) At this point there is a serious gap in W, which is not remedied by M or S. It is apparent, however, from later in the story that Wigamur must have returned to the castle, defeated Lespurant and left Pioles, together with Johiot's two daughters, in the care of the dwarf.

We next find Wigamur in a castle (named much later as Dalm-flamur, 4122) with a mysterious bath made of the stone *aptor*. It takes on a different appearance according to whether the onlooker is chaste or not. The bath has silver pipes flowing with both hot and cold water, and is surrounded by all kinds of trees, both northern and Mediterranean in habitat. Whoever bathes here and is false becomes bodily weakened; whoever is pure becomes joyful and full of wisdom. Wigamur bathes here and is well looked after. The lord of the castle (again not named until much later as Yttra, 4124) asks where he comes from, and Wigamur recounts the story of Lespia and his subsequent life, but says he won his horse and armour from a man who would not leave fighting him. The lord gives him a horse and a palfrey. Wigamur becomes famous throughout the land of Doloyr. (1100–355)

Wigamur now declares he wishes to go to Caridol. The lord, who turns out to be Artus's uncle, says that he himself had educated Artus as a boy and gives Wigamur a fine sword for his expedition. Wigamur first goes to the land of Stolleputria, where he rescues an eagle from a vulture. The eagle accompanies him ever after in gratitude, Wigamur thus becoming known as 'the knight with the eagle'. He spends the night in a friendly castle and then sets off for the forest of Mygaret. (1356–525)

One day Wigamur encounters a young lady riding a white mule. She is called Eudis of the Round Mountain and is in dispute with her aunt, Affrosydones, about the possession of a magic fountain sheltered by an evergreen lime tree. Whoever drinks three times from the fountain remains as young and strong as if he were thirty. The water also tastes like whatever a person wishes to drink. Eudis has had the fountain for ten years, but her aunt now threatens to take it from her by force. A duel has been arranged for their respective knights at Caridol. Wigamur modestly offers his help, and the two go to Eudis's castle for the night, after which they go to Caridol for the duel. Affrosydones has Diatorforgrant as her dueller. Artus sits in judgement on the duel, which is twice broken off, since neither knight seems to be getting the better of the other in what is a distressing experience for all concerned. In the third bout, however, Wigamur deals Diatorforgrant a death-blow, and Artus judges that Eudis has won the right to the fountain. Eudie offers lime tree, fountain and her land to Wigamur in gratitude, but he declares himself unsuited to this honour and says he wants no other reward than Eudis's goodwill. (1526–973)

Artus then hears that the land of Deleprosat needs a ruler, and organises a tournament to find the best knight for it. All the contestants declare Wigamur to be the winner, but he once more says he is too poor, unknown and lacking in kinsmen. Artus gives him a fine horse. Eudis, seeing that Wigamur persists in declining the crown of her land, presents Artus with a magnificent tent and departs. (1974–2429)

Artus entrusts Wigamur to Walwan's care and proposes a festival near the forest. During this another beautiful maiden on a white mule rides up and asks Artus and his queen to wait on her mistress, the queen of Holdrafluz, the following day at the fountain of Sinfroylas. When they get there Ysope, the queen of Holdrafluz, tells them she is being oppressed by the king of Sarzin, who is a heathen and wishes to make her his wife. Artus promises assistance, as does Wigamur, and the queen rides off home. Artus collects his knights, and Unarc, Walwan and Wigamur proceed to the coastal town of Podogar, which the heathens are besieging. Wigamur fights with Grymuras, Walwan with Drasbarun, and Unarc with Turbar(t). The three heathens are defeated and forced to promise their fealty to the queen of Holdrafluz. When Artus arrives he sends a letter to Marroch, the king of Sarzin, accusing him of wickedness in wishing forcibly to marry a Christian queen. This spurs Marroch on to attempt to destroy Queen Ysope and all her possessions. In the ensuing battle Wigamur takes Marroch prisoner. He forces him to recompense the queen for the damage done, to leave her alone for ever, to receive his land as a fief from Artus and to pay tribute for it. Ysope considers what reward she can give Artus and Wigamur. Her people would like Wigamur as their king, but she knows he has already declined this in Eudis's case and at the Arthurian tournament following it. She therefore merely presents magnificent gifts. Artus prepares to return to Caridol, and Wigamur requests permission to leave him. This is reluctantly given, and Wigamur rides off to the town of Lydasar, the scene of strife between Atroglas and Paldriot. (2430–3474)

Wigamur's host in Lydasar informs him of the struggle for the inheritance of Amilot's land between Atroglas, the deceased's maternal uncle, and Paldriot, the deceased's paternal uncle. Wigamur joins the duke of Troyswarlanz (i.e. Pioles's father) in offering his services to Atroglas, king of Rerat. They determine to invade Paldriot's country, Lendrie. Meanwhile Paldriot assembles his followers, and a well-matched battle ensues. Eventually it is agreed to determine the result by a duel in single combat. Wigamur is chosen for Atroglas's side and is promised his fourteen year old (cf. 5907) daughter Dulceflur in marriage if he wins. Paldriot decides to join the duel himself and tries to force Atroglas to be his opponent, wishing to have an equal to fight. Wigamur therefore retells his life story, beginning with Lespia, in order to establish his credentials. At this Paldriot realises he is about to fight his own son. The battle is broken off, and the natural solution is that Wigamur should be accepted as Dulceflur's rightful husband and the dispute be concluded. Paldriot abdicates his own land of Lendrie in Wigamur's favour and provides him with instruction in courtly and chivalric conduct. Back at Nogragroys, the capital of Rerat, the reception and Dulceflur's appearance are described at copious length, and the marriage is entered upon through the exchange of rings. (3475–4644)

During the festivities a messenger appears with an invitation to a tournament at Musygralt, for which the prize is the crown of the land of Queen Dinifogar. Since Wigamur has exchanged rings with Dulceflur, he is allowed to go to the tournament, at which many famous knights are gathered, among them Lehelin, Gamuret, Yther and Artus. Eventually three knights stand out for their prowess at the tournament—Gamuret, Lipondrigun and Wigamur. Dinifogar points out that she has not called the tournament through any moral laxity (*vnkeuscheit*, 5051) but because she is being threatened by a heathen king, Gramgrinot. Wigamur does not want to join in a final joust to decide the outcome, being married; Gamuret is Dinifogar's nephew and thus excluded by proximity of kinship; and Lipondrigun, we are told by Dinifogar, has in fact killed her father. Atroglas explains that after Dinifogar's father had invaded Lipondrigun's land, the latter had killed him with a spear on a hunting expedition (this is described as *gross mord*, 5170). Wigamur thereupon challenges Lipondrigun to a duel, in the course of which he breaks his sword. Lipondrigun then thinks he is about to win, but Wigamur seizes him with his arms, forces him to his knees and is ready to strangle him with his bare hands when Lipondrigun gives in and agrees to give his fealty to Atroglas. (4645–5262)

Whilst Wigamur is being cared for after the battle, Lipondrigun surreptitiously takes his leave and encounters Dulceflur with her maid, Myglares, on their way to Musygralt. In return for the disgrace inflicted on him the day before he abducts Dulceflur, but lets her maid go. As soon as the knights hear the news from Myglares they go off in hot pursuit and receive information about what has happened from the king of Sabalet. They have to travel a vast distance through difficult country, and *en route* they meet the duke of Nordin lamenting the loss of his bride Pioles. Wigamur realises that they are not far from where he had entrusted Pioles to the dwarf eight years previously, and goes off to fetch her. He finds her alive and well, together with the princesses Ligronite and Flogrisite. Pioles is overjoyed to think she will be united with Harzier again. This done, the knights continue their pursuit of Lipondrigun, whom Wigamur finally defeats. At this point a further leaf is missing in W, and one can only guess at what happens here. We have no further information about what happens with regard to Lipondrigun or Dinifogar. (5263–6040)

Atroglas, Wigamur and Harzier take Dulceflur and Pioles back to Nogragroys, and one must assume that great festivities take place, with probably a double marriage between Wigamur and Dulceflur, formalising the previous exchange of rings, and Harzier and Pioles. This is conjectural, however, as another lacuna of four leaves occurs after line 6094. The poem concludes with a brief note of the birth of the hero's son, Dulciwigar. (6041–106)

Such is the plot of *Wigamur*, and apart from the oddity of Dinifogar's tournament, which manifestly produces no victor worthy of her hand and thus renders the object of the exercise otiose, it presents a coherent and not unattractive whole. The various episodes are reasonably balanced in proportion to each other, and there is a noticeable progression in their order. This, however, is something to consider later, for the most serious charge that scholars level against the author of *Wigamur* is that he simply plundered other works for his motifs and was not much better than a plagiarist. This merits further investigation.

Our author begins his work by a reference to reading in books many strange tales about how King Paldriot ruled the country of Lendrie. On several later occasions he alludes to what he read in the *abenteur* or what it told him (see 2534, 2696, 3312, 3473). No source has in fact been found for *Wigamur*, and G. D. West's *Index of Proper Names in French Arthurian Verse Romances, 1150–1300*[13] gives no clue to the derivation of any of the multifarious strange names to be found uniquely in the German poem. The reference to a source is thus to be interpreted as a literary device to give a guarantee of the romance's value. The poet's sources are in actuality to be found in the German Arthurian and other romances that he was acquainted with. They are Ulrich's *Lanzelet*, Wolfram's *Parzival*, Hartmann's *Iwein*, Gottfried's *Tristan*, Wirnt's *Wigalois* and the anonymous *Herzog Ernst* (presumably the B version). Both Sarrazin and Khull give the impression that *Wigamur* is basically a patchwork of motifs ignorantly put together from these various poems, but if one examines these scholars' parallels carefully one soon realises, especially with Khull, that most of them fall into the category of verbal commonplaces or general similarities of expression. It would be tedious to refute this aspect of the two nineteenth century scholars' work, but Khull's contention that the poet

13 Toronto, 1969.

used Hartmann's *Erec* as well as his *Iwein* is based solely on a lengthy list of commonplaces of courtly action and attitudes.[14] Such common turns of phrase provide no evidence whatever of borrowing. There are, however, several motifs which clearly are drawn from the works just mentioned (with the exclusion of *Erec*) and which thus show how influential they were in the literary scene.

However, both scholars assemble the common motifs and expressions in a completely mechanical way, sometimes not even correctly, and frequently with wrong line references; there is no attempt to assess what the *Wigamur* poet made of them. The following table, listing motifs in chronological order, may perhaps give a better idea of the extent of the borrowing.

Wigamur	*Other poems*
Name of hero	Calqued on *Wigalois*
Abduction of hero by a mermaid	*Lanzelet*, 180 ff.
Further abduction by another sea monster	
Education in the knightly arts by sea monster	*Lanz.*, 278 ff.
Desire to leave his alien environment (no immediate aim in view)	Lanzelet wishes to go to tournaments, *Lanz.*, 302 ff.; Parzival wishes to leave Soltane in search of Artus and knighthood, *Parz.*, 126, 9 ff.
Ignorance as to his true origin	Lanzelet cannot learn his name until he kills Iweret, *Lanz.*, 307 ff.; Parzival learns his name from Sigune, *Parz.*, 140, 3 ff.
First adventures as a fool (*Dümmling*)	*Lanz.*, 389 ff.; *Parz.*, 129, 5 ff.
Ignorance about riding	*Lanz.*, 404 ff., 442 f.
Storming of the castle of Pontrafort	Slight similarities with the general situation and geographical position in siege of Pelrapeire, *Parz.* 180, 15 ff.
Acquisition of armour from a dead knight; Wigamur finds him dead, but in retelling the story he says he won it from a knight in battle, 1299 ff.	Parzival kills Ither and robs him of his armour, *Parz.*, 155, 19 ff.
Encounter with Glakotelesfloyr	

14 *Op. cit.*, pp. 106–8.

Wigamur	*Other poems*
Discovery of Pioles, separated from her lover, Harzier	
Pioles entrusted to the dwarf	
Adventure in the castle with the stone of virtue (a bath)	*Wigalois*, 1477 ff. (a stone, not a bath)
Description of the bath	*Herzog Ernst B*, 2655 ff.
Open-air surroundings of the bath, 1164–5, 1168–73, 1184–8, 1192–201	*Tristan*, 16733–60 (almost word-for-word correspondence)
Departure for Artus's court	*Parz.*, 128, 13 ff.
Rescue of the eagle from the vulture	Iwein's rescue of the lion from the dragon, *Iwein*, 3828 ff.
Wigamur fights a duel on behalf of Eudis's claims against her aunt, Affrosydones; duel ends with the death of Diatorforgrant	Iwein and Gawein fight to determine the rights of inheritance of the two daughters of the Count of the Black Thorn; duel broken off, *Iw.*, 6877 ff
Eudis's fountain tastes like whatever one wishes to drink	Grail provides whatever food one wishes to eat, *Parz.*, 238, 8 ff.
Arthurian tournament	
Ysope, queen of Holdrafluz, attacked by Marroch, the heathen king of Sarzin	Larie attacked by Roaz, the heathen king of Glois, *Wigalois*, 3607 ff.
Dispute between Atroglas of Rerat and Paldriot of Lendrie about the inheritance of Amilot	
Accidental encounter of father and son, no search involved	Wigalois sets out deliberately in search of his father, Gawein, whom he does not discover until the end of the poem, *Wigalois*, 1273 ff., 11370 ff.
	? *Jüngeres Hildebrandslied*
Duel between father and son; discovery of identity	
Father instructs son, 4281–323	*Wigalois*, 11521 ff.
Arrangement of marriage between Wigamur and Dulceflur	
Tournament at Musygralt for the hand of Dinifogar	Tournament at Kanvoleis for the hand of Herzeloyde, *Parz.*, 58, 27 ff.
Wigamur's duel with Lipondrigun	
Lipondrigun's escape and abduction of Dulceflur	
Pursuit of Lipondrigun	

Wigamur	*Other poems*
Reunion of Harzier and Pioles	
Defeat of Lipondrigun	
Marriages of Wigamur and Dulce- flur and Harzier and Pioles	
Birth of Dulciwigar	Birth of Lifort Gawanides, *Wigalois*, 11626 ff., glance at future history of Loherangrin, *Parz.*, 823, 27 ff.

The borrowings made by the author of *Wigamur* are plain to see. They are extensive, but they are not mindless. The only totally unchanged motifs are those relating to the description of the bath, with its piped hot and cold water and its exotic surroundings. Most of the other episodes contain some modification of the source. Thus the mermaid episode is duplicated in *Wigamur* with the introduction of the second abduction at the hands of the sea centaur. Then, when Wigamur departs from the sea he has no immediate goal, whereas Lanzelet is out to find possibilities of tourneying and Parzival already wishes to find Artus's court. Wigamur sets out for Caridol only after his sojourn in the castle with the mysterious bath of virtue. Furthermore, Wigamur's ignorance about his origin and identity is not dispelled until he is about to duel with his father. Lanzelet learns his name after killing Iweret, a task given to him as necessary before he can achieve this self-knowledge. Parzival discovers his identity at his first encounter with Sigune, after experiencing something of the nature of compassion. The test with the stone of virtue from *Wigalois* is expanded into a much longer episode, the stone is changed into a bath, and the whole section abounds in elaborate description.

The motif of the animal released from suffering and henceforth serving its rescuer in lifelong devotion is altered from the lion and dragon of *Iwein* to an eagle and vulture in *Wigamur*. Unfortunately, however, the *Wigamur* poet makes no further use of the help that his hero has now acquired; the only difference is that Wigamur is now frequently referred to as 'the knight with the eagle'. The legal dispute to be solved by the outcome of a duel portrays a different relationship between the two ladies and ends with the death of Wigamur's opponent, whereas in *Iwein* the duel has to be broken off because of the even matching of the duellists, and judgement is passed over to Artus. The nature of the dispute is also different in that in *Iwein* it concerns the rights of inheritance on the death of the contestants' father, whereas in *Wigamur* it concerns the rightful possession of the magic fountain that Eudis has already held for ten years. When we come to the encounter of father and son in a duel—a motif which is well known in medieval German and also in world literature[15]—the difference from *Wigalois*, if this can actually be counted as the immediate source, is apparent. Wigalois is deliberately seeking his father; Wigamur meets his father by accident and without any specific intention. In the matter of fatherly instruction which follows the encounter we still feel a basis of courtliness behind everything that Gawein says to Wigalois, but with Paldriot the mood seems to have shifted from courtly idealism to a somewhat more down-to-earth moral code. This is in keeping, of course, with *Wigamur*'s later date. Finally, the tournament arranged by Dinifogar to find herself a husband and protector turns out much less satisfactorily for her than does Herzeloyde's tournament at Kanvoleis. The *Ausblick* with the birth of Dulciwigar fits into the context of the cyclical idea of romance that finds expression in medieval German literature with Wolfram's *Titurel* and Albrecht's *Jüngerer Titurel*, Wisse and Colin's *Neuer Parzival* and the anonymous *Loherangrin*, all being ultimately dependent on *Parzival*. The so-called 'heroic' epics of the thirteenth century and later, especially those in which Dietrich von Bern is the central character, are also linked in a similar way. It is part of the literary mode of the period.

But even with the differences that *Wigamur* exhibits in relation to its obvious sources, one could scarcely claim any outstanding literary merit in the poem. It does not possess the weird fascination of *Wigalois*, with its intricately detailed descriptions of fantastic beings and mechanised landscapes, though the curious bath of virtue and Eudis's magic fountain and evergreen lime tree may be thought to reach out in this direction. Nor is there an attempt at character portrayal in any depth. During the initial episodes of the poem we hear plenty about Wigamur's youthful foolishness, but it is not displayed to us with the varied deft touches that Wolfram uses with Parzival. The only occasion on which a streak of humour appears is when Wigamur fails to understand the feudal meaning of *man* as 'vassal' and thus imagines that Glakotelesfloyr wants to become his *man* in the sense of 'husband'.

Once Wigamur has reached a degree of maturity he becomes a conventional hero of blameless morality. The author of the poem certainly seems affected by clerical ideas about sexuality in that the

15 See Wolfgang Harms, *Der Kampf mit dem Freund oder Verwandten in der deutschen Literatur bis um 1300*, Munich, 1963.

element of chastity is continually emphasised in Wigamur's development. Here is a clear difference from the literary model, Lanzelet, with
his careless succession of mistresses, and Wolfram's Gahmuret, with his
two wives and mistress Ampflise. Wigamur's relationship with Pioles,
though she does not engage his affections, has a strong affinity with
that of the young Parzival and Condwiramurs. Wolfram's young
couple spent their first three nights of marriage chastely (see *Parz.*,
201, 19 ff.), an action which is capable of a detailed psychological
interpretation in the light of Parzival's development and the necessity
for the future Grail king to have a pure wife.[16] The poet of *Wigamur*
is much blunter. He wishes to make it quite clear that there is nothing
of dubious morality happening between his hero and Pioles: 'an aller
schlacht schanden mayl / Belayben sye die nacht nu' (987 f.). That is
the first occasion, and the second is similar: 'Mit lieb sy die nacht
vertrybenn, / Vnuermailiget sy da belibenn' (1076 f.). On the third
occasion the poet tells us that each cared more for the other than for
him- or herself and then goes on: 'Die aventvre sus berihtet much. / Sie
waren aber die nacht da' (M 1099, 88 f.). No further information is
given. Wigamur and Pioles are not lovers, but the poet seems to go
out of his way to emphasise Wigamur's sexual purity. He is also
curiously *unconcerned* about the fate of Eudis after Wigamur has rejected her in marriage, of Ysope in a similar situation, and finally of
Dinifogar. It is extremely unusual in romances for courtly ladies to be
abandoned to eternal virginity when they have the key to territorial
power in their persons and actually desire a husband. Most poets seem
to feel that a narrative is only properly concluded when all those who
are marriageable are well and truly wed. Such a view helps to explain
the otherwise slightly incongruous set of marriages with which *Kudrun*,
for example, concludes. The discontented ladies of *Wigamur* are a
literary oddity, but it is quite possible that they are a logical consequence in the biography of a hero conceived as an opposite to Ulrich's
Lanzelet. None the less, the episode with Pioles is probably the most
successful section of the whole poem, for the situation is described with
a quite appealing, simple pathos.

If we turn from the borrowed motifs to the narrative structure
of the poem as a whole, we can see a fairly clear progression in
Wigamur's adventures. Although these episodes are apparently only
loosely linked, they do not follow each other in haphazard sequence.

16 See Marlis Schumacher, *Die Auffassung der Ehe in den Dichtungen Wolframs
von Eschenbach*, Heidelberg, 1967, pp. 37–47.

Since there is no psychological interest in the poem, we need to look for meaning in the structure and content of the plot itself, as Wehrli has done so fruitfully with regard to *Wigalois*.[17] There are similarities with the fairy tale, as is often the case with Arthurian romance, and the symbolism may be interpreted in a like manner.

Wigamur's childhood experiences establish him as a hero of an unusual kind. He is not himself of supernatural birth, but his upbring-ing, first of all with the wild woman Lespia for either twelve (1290) or ten (4064) years, then by the sea centaur for eight years (4091), firmly places him among the ranks of the heroes. Not only is he like Lanzelet in this respect but he has affinities with the Hagene of *Kudrun*, who is abducted by a griffin, from which, however, he quickly escapes. Wigamur then has to make his way into the courtly world, possessing many skills but lacking in ordinary knowledge. He is favoured by his physical strength and skill in battle—capacities which loom large in almost all medieval narrative poems—but it is only bit by bit that these are added to by other accomplishments. His encounter with Glakotelesfloyr provides him with an opportunity to prove himself superior to the average knight. It is perhaps for this reason that we hear no more of Glakotelesfloyr in the course of the poem, for Wigamur quickly passes this stage of his career. His later tasks and struggles express more than a simple test of strength.

We thus come to the tripartite episode with Pioles, where Wigamur gradually realises the nature of a knight's duty towards a lady in distress. This is a problem he cannot solve by mere strength. In it he learns how to respond to the needs of another human being and that he cannot simply ride away and leave Pioles unprotected and unpro-vided for. It is a situation for which he can find only a temporary solution. He entrusts Pioles to the care of a dwarf, having disposed of the latter's master, Lespurant, whom the dwarf describes as 'tivuels valant' (M 1099, 23), and thus overcomes the forces of darkness. It is only some eight years later (5646) that Wigamur is able to reunite Pioles with her husband-to-be, Harzier, almost at the conclusion of his career. The episode with Pioles links directly with the next stage in Wigamur's progress, for it is as a result of the purity of his conduct *vis-à-vis* Pioles that our hero successfully passes the test of his virtue contained in the adventure with the marvellous bath and proves him-

17 Max Wehrli, 'Wigalois', *Der Deutschunterricht*, VI (1965), Heft 2, pp. 18–35, reprinted in Max Wehrli, *Formen mittelalterlicher Erzählung*, Zürich, 1969, pp. 223–41.

self no ordinary knight. This corresponds to an initiation ritual of the most rigorous kind, since failure brings with it a deprivation of strength, while success brings renewed vitality and power. The immersion in a bath has links with the Christian idea of baptism, though these are not explicit here. The incident is perhaps also related to Lanzelet's adventure in Schatel le mort, where all who enter immediately become cowards and from which Lanzelet is released only by being carried out from the castle in order to fight against Iweret, who is besieging it. Wigamur provides a further contrast to Lanzelet in that he passes the test of virtue by his own unaided strength and purity, whereas Lanzelet requires the assistance of others and actually succumbs to the spell of the wicked Mabuz.

Having achieved the moral qualities needed for the test of virtue, Wigamur proceeds to his next adventure, in which he acquires his sobriquet of the 'knight with the eagle'. Through his intervention in the fight between the eagle and the vulture he gains alliance with the animal world. The symbolism of Iwein's lion has been discussed in considerable detail for both its Christian and its archetypal significance.[18] The alliance of story heroes with birds is more widespread in medieval German narratives. There is, for example, the swan in Konrad von Würzburg's *Schwanritter*, the unnamed bird-messenger in *Kudrun*, and—perhaps the best known—the raven messenger in *Oswald*. The eagle is of course popularly known as the 'king of the birds', and it is in this capacity that it is to be thought of in *Wigamur*.[19] Unfortunately, however, for the literary impact of the motif, the poet makes no further use of the eagle except as a more or less standing companion to Wigamur, without any meaningful participation in the story. It remains a purely external device. The poet fails to make use of the symbol he has stumbled on.

From here Wigamur goes on to the duel with Diatorforgrant about the magic fountain and the evergreen lime tree. This is a familiar theme from both *Lanzelet* and *Iwein*, though there may be, at least on the surface, some differences in *Wigamur*'s treatment of it. The fountain here is clearly related to the fairy-tale idea of the water of life, for it keeps both man and woman young as long as they live and it

18 See, for example, Hugh Sacker, 'An interpretation of Hartmann's *Iwein*', *Germanic Review*, XXXVI (1961), pp. 15–16; A. T. Hatto, ' "Der aventiure meine" in Hartmann's *Iwein*', *Festschrift* F. Norman London, 1965, pp. 97–8.

19 See Wolfgang Stammler, *Spätlese des Mittelalters*. II. *Religiöses Schrifttum*, Berlin, 1965, p. 46 (*Melker Physiologus*), pp. 131–2 (notes).

possesses 'Alle selde vnd auch gůte' by nature (1614 f.). Its further marvellous property is to taste of whatever the drinker wishes. Three draughts of it preserve one in perfect health. There is also, however, the evergreen lime tree with the birds singing. In the case of *Iwein* it is not out of the question to associate the lime tree and fountain with archetypal male and female symbols,[20] but in *Wigamur* the matter is complicated by the fact that Eudis, the owner of the fountain, is being challenged for possession of it by her aunt, Affrosydones, and that the challenge is then fought out by Wigamur and Diatorforgrant. More-over, when the duel is over Wigamur does not, as would be logical, marry Eudis. In view of this, it seems safer to interpret the adventure simply with respect to the 'water of life' theme and consider the setting, the conventional *locus amoenus*, as representing the idyllic surroundings proper to the central symbol.

There then follows the Arthurian tournament, at which Wigamur distinguishes himself against a large number of knights, though none of them belongs to the category of famous Arthurian heroes. This, however, procures recognition of Wigamur's prowess in the Arthurian circle and thus befits him for his next encounter. This is with Marroch, king of Sarzin, the representative of the pagan world. At this point, and to a lesser extent in the tournament of Musygralt, we get an extension of the exploits of the Arthurian circle of knights into the orbit of the epics which focus on the Near East and the Islamic world, of which the so-called *Spielmannsepen* are the best-known representa-tives. This is only one of a number of places at which *Wigamur* provides points of contact with these popular poems, originating in the late twelfth century but maintaining their popularity until the end of the Middle Ages in different literary forms. (The *Spielmannsepen* also tend to have an ascetic approach towards sex in that the chaste mar-riage often appears as an ideal at the end of the story.) The encounter with the Saracen king in *Wigamur* is not given any very subtle treat-ment, and the opposition of Christianity to paganism remains largely a conventional matter. But it does tie in with the depiction of Wigamur as the kind of ascetic knight whose conduct might have been modelled on the ideal of chivalry aimed at by the Knights Templar, the Knights of St John of Jerusalem or the Teutonic Knights. Once more our hero resists any blandishments offered by the lady on whose behalf he has fought. Ysope, like Eudis before her, remains without a husband.

In a sense the culmination of the story occurs when Wigamur meets

20 See Sacker, *op. cit.*, pp. 9–10.

his father as an opponent in battle. It is unfortunate that this is not more skilfully dealt with by the poet, since the theme has great potentialities for an interesting build-up, tension and resolution. But as in many other cases the poet does not seem to realise what sort of material he has to shape. The encounter of father and son takes place in a spirit that de Boor sees as related to that between Hildebrant and Alebrant in the *Jüngeres Hildebrandslied*,[21] this being the version of the duel between father and son that the *Wigamur* poet is most likely to have been familiar with. There are, however, many other important aspects to the encounter, which are the result of a careful attention to the plot. It is quite in keeping that Paldriot, finding that Atroglas is not going to be his opponent, should demand to know the identity of the knight chosen to fight him. The motivation for Wigamur's recapitulation of his history, and thus for the recognition, is well founded. But when Wigamur finds that his opponent is his father, all he can do is to say lamely that Atroglas must choose another knight in his place. This curious scene of recognition is attributed to divine agency (4158 ff.), and an attractive solution is found to the problem of the inheritance over which the two kings were fighting. Atroglas's daughter is pledged in marriage to Paldriot's son, and Paldriot forthwith abdicates all his lands to Wigamur. The son has discovered his identity and inheritance, he has gained the most beautiful of all maidens, Dulceflur, for his wife, and he has replaced his father as king of Lendrie.[22]

It would appear that a satisfactory conclusion has been reached, but the festivities are interrupted by a last-minute call from Queen Dinifogar, whose lands are being attacked by the heathen Gramrimort. This episode has several flaws in it, since we never hear of any of the knights involved in Dinifogar's tournament being called to fight the heathen oppressor, and Dinifogar is left at the end without a champion. Wigamur none the less shows himself to be the equal of Gamuret, who stands here as the flower of Arthurian knighthood, and Lipondrigun, who, though obviously adroit in battle, turns out to be a murderer and a thorough cad. When he escapes and manages to abduct Dulceflur in the process we have all the elements for an exciting eleventh-hour chase, with everything going wrong just as the hero is about to achieve his final goal. But as in all such chases, whether they belong

21 De Boor, *op. cit.*, p. 81. De Boor also draws in *Biterolf* here, which uses the same motif.
22 See also Harms, *op. cit.*, pp. 140–2.

to the concluding pages of an Arthurian romance or the last minutes of a television western, the hero does kill the villain and rescues his wife-to-be. In addition Wigamur returns to Pioles, with whom his career of virtue began, and reunites her with her lover Harzier. In this way all the important strands of the story are finally tied together.

The story of *Wigamur* is an attractive one, composite though it is in point of origin. It is not told with the degree of sophistication that we should expect from a Hartmann, a Gottfried or a Wolfram. The poet's talents are more on a level with those of Ulrich von Zatzikhoven. But for all that *Wigamur* is not a work that should be dismissed as unworthy of study. The story is related at a length well suited to the content, and the episodes are carefully matched and balanced. There are many felicitous passages and visually interesting scenes, and the descriptions of the various characters and the courtly festivities would have delighted the medieval audience. It is worth asking, finally, whether it doesn't merit a new edition to make it more accessible.[23]

23 This paper was read in substantially the same form at a conference of the British branch of the International Arthurian Society held at the University of Leeds on 15–18 September 1971. Dr Whitehead died only a few days after attending this conference.

Fanni Bogdanow

The transformation of the role of Perceval in some thirteenth century prose romances

While in all the medieval French prose romances where Perceval appears he is either the principal Grail hero, as in Chrétien's *Conte del Graal*, the several continuations of the *Conte del Graal*,[1] the *Didot–Perceval* and the *Perlesvaus*, or one of three chosen knights as in the Vulgate and Post-Vulgate cycles, the prose *Tristan*, the *Livre d'Artu* and the *Prophécies de Merlin*, yet the character and even parentage of Perceval vary from romance to romance. Jessie Weston, who in her book on the *Legend of Sir Perceval* dealt with certain features of Perceval's biography in a number of the earlier romances, concluded that the varying versions 'all go back ultimately to the same original source' and that there must have existed prior to Chrétien's *Conte del Graal* 'a well-known, . . . minutely detailed story, familiar more or less to all writers, and exactly reproduced by none'.[2] The attitude underlying her approach was typical of that of so many scholars of her time: a tacit assumption that the extant texts must be a corruption of more complete and more authentic versions and that 'our extant literature stands at the end, and not the beginning, of the evolutionary process'.[3] A study of the available material suggests, however, that this

1 The First and Second Continuations do not bring the *Conte del Graal* to a conclusion, and it was left to Manessier to terminate the romance. Gerbert expanded the work yet further by adding a long series of adventures in between the end of the Second Continuation and the beginning of Manessier. Gerbert's and Manessier's continuations postdate the Vulgate Cycle. Editions: *Le Roman de Perceval ou le Conte du Grael*, ed. W. Roach (T.L.F.), Geneva and Paris, 1956; 2nd edn., 1959. *Perceval le Gallois ou le Conte du Grael*, ed. C. Potvin, Mons, 1865–71 (edn. of all the continuations except Gerbert's, of which Potvin gives extracts); *The Continuations of the Old French Perceval*, ed. W. Roach (Am. Philos. Soc.), Philadelphia: *First Continuation*, I–III (I, 1949; repr. 1965; II, 1950; repr. 1965; III: 1, 1952; III: 2, 1955); *Second Continuation*, IV, 1971; Gerbert de Montreuil, *La Continuation de Perceval*, ed.. Mary Williams (C.F.M.A.), I, 1922, II, 1925.

2 Jessie Weston, *The Legend of Sir Perceval* (Grimm Library, Nos. 17 and 19), 1906–09; I, p. 85. 3 *Op. cit.*, II, p. 243, n. 1.

is certainly not the case and that, as regards Perceval, the variations in treatment can best be explained as an attempt by the successive writers to shape and interpret Perceval's role in accordance with their particular conception of certain themes and the overall structure of the various romances.

Nothing is known about Perceval before his first appearance in Chrétien. Before assuming the title role in the *Conte del Graal* he is singled out in *Cligés* as *uns vasax de grant renon* (4773). In the *Conte del Graal*, in contrast, Perceval begins his career as the *nice et bestiax* (1299), the uncouth youth brought up by his widowed mother in isolation, who is destined to improve and to obtain *de chevalerie . . . tot le pris* (1061–2), but who on account of his *niceté*, which takes the form of thoughtlessness, of disregard for the feelings of others and of an inability to apply sensibly the advice he receives, causes his mother's death, a sin which, together with his *niceté*, was to prevent Perceval from asking the unspelling question on his first visit to the Grail castle. At the time Perceval was unaware of his failure, and when, at the height of his triumph and after winning renown throughout Arthur's land, he is rebuked by the Ugly Damsel, he sets off again in search of the Grail castle, but is so filled with grief and despair that he forgets God for five years until on a Good Friday he meets some penitents. Filled with remorse, Perceval visits his hermit uncle, who finally makes him aware of his sin against his mother and enjoins penance so that he might recover *totes ses graces* (6472).

While the underlying theme is serious, the treatment of Perceval is most of the time light-hearted and humorous, and is closely linked with Chrétien's conception of his characters and the structure of his romances. Chrétien delights in making gentle fun of his heroes, nearly all of whom have a comic flaw which explains their initial failure in whatever they undertake. Perceval's flaw is his *niceté*, and the structure demands that while Perceval should undergo a gradual apprenticeship in chivalry before he is finally hailed

> chevaliers esprovez
> De haute proesce et de bele   [4594–5]

he must until well after the Grail scene remain a *nice* on the intellectual and religious planes. Hence with considerable humour Chrétien develops in Perceval the idea that

> Molt grief chose est de fol aprendre.   [1173]

Throughout Chrétien smiles at Perceval, and by the time Perceval
meets the penitents he is still in one respect as much a *nice* as he was
earlier on, for he is so ignorant of all religious matters that with great
naiveté he asks the penitents what they had been doing in the hermitage.
Only after Perceval's repentance of his sins will he finally cast off his
niceté.

Chrétien did not complete his *Conte del Graal*, but he implies that
once Perceval has expiated his sins, and only then, he will succeed in
the greatest of all the adventures, that of the Grail. It is in this sense
that the author of the Second Continuation interpreted Perceval's role.
For him Perceval is already *li senez*,[4] and after various adventures,
including a return to his parents' home, where Perceval meets his
sister, and a second visit to the hermit uncle to do penance,[5] Perceval
at last reaches the Grail castle for a second time. He succeeds in joining
the pieces of the Broken Sword, but a small crack still remains indicating that, while he is the best knight of those living at present,[6]
he is not yet sufficiently perfect for his predestined task:

> mes si preuz ne si bon n'estoit.   [IV, 32548]

Whatever qualities Perceval requires to be perfect in the Second Continuation, chastity is not one of them. Perceval enjoys the love not
only of Blanchefleur but also of the Damsel of the Chessboard,[7] and
while the author stresses that

> Molt par est fox qui Dieu oblie
> Por conquerre pris terrien,   [IV, 32486-7]

he does not suggest that Perceval's amorous pursuits are the cause of
his comparative failure. Nowhere is Perceval reproached for his *luxure*.
Perfection here implies valour coupled with certain moral and religious
values which do not, however, necessarily include virginity:

> Se ç'avenoit [qu'] aucun prodom,
> Qui plains fust de chevalerie,
> Loiaux de foi et sans boisdie,
> Qui Dieu cremit et Dieu amast,

4 *The Second Continuation*, ed. Roach, IV, l. 23864. Perceval plays no significant
  part in the First Continuation.
5 *Op. cit.*, IV, 23533-4221. The character of Perceval's sister was invented by
  the author of the Second Continuation.
6 *Op. cit.*, IV, 32564-75.
7 *Op. cit.*, IV, 22834-40, 28132-41.

Et qui sainte eglyse anorast
Que Diex apelle s'espousee,
S'il tenoit an sa main l'espee,
Ne cuit que gaires demorast,
Por que les aciers asamblast,
Qu'elle ne fust manois sodee.[8]   [IV, 32520–9]

The *Didot–Perceval*, which in the two manuscripts in which it has
been preserved is preceded by the prose renderings of Robert de
Borron's *Joseph* and *Merlin*, was composed, probably early in the
thirteenth century, by an anonymous writer whose aim was to supply
the third part of the Grail trilogy announced but not written by Robert
de Borron. While the author of the *Didot–Perceval* derived much of
his material from Chrétien and the Second Continuation, he modified
Chrétien's conception of Perceval's role and that of his family so
as to adapt it to the scheme of the trilogy as a whole. Perceval's function now is not only to heal the Maimed King by asking the unspelling

8 The attitude of Manessier and Gerbert, who were probably both influenced by
  the Vulgate *Queste*, differs from that of the Second Continuation. In Manessier, where a hermit advises Perceval to give up his former chivalric life (ed.
  Potvin, V, 40363–6), Perceval is represented as chaste on his third visit to
  Blanchefleur's castle (VI, 41645–70) and spends his last years as a priest in a
  hermitage (VI, 45295–350). But it is Gerbert in particular who stresses that the
  Grail hero must be chaste (ed. Williams, 2559–62). Perceval and Blanchefleur do not consummate their love here (6561) and Perceval resists the
  advances of other damsels,

      Que trop feroie grant pechié
      Se je avoie despechié
      Vo pucelage ne le mien.   [650–3]

  While, however, as in the Vulgate *Queste*, virginity is considered the highest
  virtue (6830–5), in contrast to the Vulgate, marriage is in Gerbert permissible
  for the Grail hero, and indeed Gornemant tells Perceval that only if he keeps
  his promise to marry Blanchefleur will he learn the secrets 'et de la lance et du
  Graal' (5170–7). Perceval and Blanchefleur decide on their wedding night to
  remain virgins,

      Car abstinence les atise
      Et biens et loiautés et fois,
      Qui lor enseigne et fait defois
      Qu'il n'enfraignent virginité,   [6860–4]

  but the following morning a divine voice, after informing Perceval in which
  circumstances the *delit carnel* is permissible, predicts that among Perceval's
  descendants will be the Swan Knight and the three conquerors of Jerusalem
  (6882–932). Cf. below, nn. 55 and 56.

question; his destiny is to become the third and last Grail Guardian. In order to link the *Didot-Perceval* with the *Joseph* and *Merlin*, Perceval's father, not named in Chrétien, is here identified as Alain, one of Bron's sons, who, it is predicted in the *Joseph*, is to beget the third Grail Guardian. As for the Maimed King, he is no longer Perceval's uncle on the maternal side, but his grandfather Bron. Though Perceval is referred to as *sot*,[9] the theme of his *niceté* is neither developed[10] nor linked with the death of his mother. In Chrétien, Perceval's sin was to have left home and not to have turned back when he saw his mother collapse. In the *Didot-Perceval*, where Perceval is from the beginning predestined for his great role, Perceval's father, shortly before expiring, urged his son, in compliance with instructions from the Holy Ghost, to go to Arthur's court, as Bron could not be healed until the coming of his grandson.[11] When his mother discovers that Perceval has secretly set off for court she dies out of fear at the thought that her son may have been devoured by wild beasts.[12] But while the *Didot-Perceval* is not interested in the comic treatment of the theme of Perceval's gradual progress from a *nice* to a perfect knight, yet the theme of Perceval's initial imperfection is central for the plan of the work. When Perceval attempts to sit in the Perilous Seat, the stone beneath it splits open, as he is not yet sufficiently perfect, and a voice announces that only when a knight of Arthur's court has done such deeds of arms that he has *le pris de la chevalerie del siecle* (215–16) and has asked the question about the Grail will the adventures of Logres come to an end, the Maimed King be healed and the stone be joined together again.[13] Perceval is taken by his sister to their hermit uncle to do penance for his sin concerning his mother *before* he reaches the Grail castle for the first time,[14] but as Perceval is not yet *le meillor del monde*[15] he fails to ask the unspelling question and on account of his

9 *The Didot-Perceval according to the Manuscripts of Modena and Paris*, ed. W. Roach, Philadelphia, 1941, p. 238, l. 1813.

10 The author states briefly that at Arthur's court Perceval learnt 'molt de sens et de cortesie, car saciés que quant il issi de ciés sa mere que il ne savoit riens' (p. 140, ll. 26–8).

11 *Didot-Perceval*, p. 139, ms. D, ll. 4–15; cf. p. 177, ms. E, ll. 652–4, ms. D, ll. 628–36.   12 *Op. cit.*, p. 140, ms. E, ll. 19–21.

13 *Op. cit.*, pp. 150–1, ms. E, ll 198–221.

14 In the *Didot-Perceval* Perceval, on account of his sin concerning his mother, has difficulty in finding the Grail castle, and it is only after he has done penance that he reaches the castle (p. 180, ll. 692–702; pp. 183–3, ll. 737–54).

15 *Didot-Perceval*, p. 209, ms. E, ll. 120–1.

failure falls, as in Chrétien, into despair which leads him to forget God for seven years. After Perceval has visited his hermit uncle for a second time and has done penance[16] he finally reaches the Grail castle and this time is successful. Under the influence of Robert de Borron's *Joseph*, where the sin of *luxure* is condemned, Perceval's improvement here is linked with his eventual renunciation of earthly love. He had begun by doing his deeds of valour for the love of Gauvain's sister, Elainne,[17] but later rejects the love of the Damsel of the Chessboard, having no desire 'de faire pecié et Nostre Sire ne li voloit soufrir a faire',[18] and he ends his days in God's service as the Grail guardian.

In the Vulgate *Lancelot–Grail* Cycle, Perceval, despite his chastity and his ascent to a higher spiritual level, is no longer the best knight in the world, the one destined to sit in the Perilous Seat and heal the Maimed King.[19] He is now only one of three elect who achieve the Quest, the prose *Lancelot* having, in order to link the Lancelot and the Grail themes more closely, replaced Perceval as the principal Grail hero by Lancelot's son, Galaad, the pure knight who succeeds where Lancelot on account of his *luxure* fails. The object of the Quest is now to see the Grail openly, 'li encerchemenz des repostailles Nostre Seigneur', and not to ask an unspelling question, and while Perceval, unlike Galaad, does not merit the highest degree of mystical revelation, he has a vision of the Grail mysteries at the final reunion at Corbenic, and subsequently, together with Galaad and the third elect, Boors, accompanies the Grail to Sarras. He renounces earthly chivalry, and spends the rest of his days in a hermitage.

The *Lancelot*, which combines Perceval's youthful adventures preceding the *Queste* with the main theme of the latter part of the *Agravain*, the search for Lancelot, prepares for Perceval's new role from his first

16 *Op. cit.*, pp. 219–20, ms. E, ll. 1449–70.

17 *Op. cit.*, pp. 144–8.

18 *Op. cit.*, p. 219, ms. E, ll. 147–8.

19 Perceval's adventures are related in two branches of the Vulgate Cycle: the *Agravain* section of the *Lancelot* proper, which deals with his youth (*The Vulgate Version of the Arthurian Romances*, ed. H. O. Sommer, Washington, D.C., 1912; V, 383–93, 404–7), and the *Queste del Saint Graal* (ed. A. Pauphilet, C.F.M.A., 1949). The manuscripts of the prose *Lancelot* fall into two broad groups, the 'version de Londres' as represented by Sommer's edition and the 'version de Paris' as represented by ms. B.N. fr. 120, etc. (see A. Micha, 'La tradition manuscrite du *Lancelot* en prose', *Romania*, LXXXV (1964), pp. 293–318, 478–517; LXXXVI (1965), pp. 330–59; LXXXVII (1966), pp. 194–233). The account of Perceval's youth is somewhat shorter in the Sommer version (cf. *La Folie Lancelot*, ed. Bogdanow, Tübingen, 1965, p. 249).

arrival at Arthur's court in circumstances different from those in Chrétien and the *Didot–Perceval*. Perceval's father is no longer Alain, and in addition to the two brothers killed in battle Perceval now has another brother, Agloval, who, having searched in vain for two years for Lancelot, visits his widowed mother and despite the latter's objections offers to take Perceval to Arthur's court. Pretending that he only wishes to accompany Agloval for a short distance, Perceval obtains his mother's permission to leave home, and when later on Perceval's squire returns and the mother learns the truth she dies of grief. While the newly knighted Perceval is sitting at the table for the *chevaliers de moindre renommee* a miracle happens similar to the one in Chrétien, but here a damsel who has never before spoken, after looking at Perceval for a long time, begins to weep, addresses him as 'Sergens Jhesu Crist, vierge chevaliers et nets' and bids him sit at the Round Table to the right of the Perilous Seat where the Good Knight will sit whom he resembles by his virginity.[20]

Although in the *Agravain* Perceval is no less responsible for his mother's death than in Chrétien—perhaps even more, for here he deliberately deceives her—yet in the *Queste*, in contrast to the earlier romances, Perceval's sin has no thematic significance. When Perceval's aunt, the recluse, informs him of his mother's death, she in no way reproaches Perceval or enjoins penance. On the contrary, she explains Perceval's reluctance to return to his mother as a consequence of fraternal love which binds the companions of the Round Table.[21] Indeed, it would have been inconceivable for one of the three elect to be a repentant sinner who has, as in Chrétien and the *Didot–Perceval*, to recover 'totes ses graces'. The role of repentant sinner is transferred to Lancelot, who is excluded from the final Grail ceremony. The nature of the Grail theme as conceived by the Vulgate *Queste* demands that Perceval be endowed from the beginning with all the virtues needed for his predestined role. He is 'un des chevaliers dou monde qui plus parfetement creoit en Nostre Seigneur',[22] but in contrast to Galaad, who is so perfect that he is never in danger of sinning, Perceval has one weakness, his *niceté*, on account of which he is at times brought to the brink of sinning.

This *niceté* is not the comic uncouthness of Chrétien's Perceval. Neither the *Agravain* nor the *Queste* has any use for Chrétien's

20 *Vulgate Version*, v, 385. 25–36.
21 *La Queste del Saint Graal*, ed. Pauphilet, p. 77.3–8.
22 *Op. cit.*, p. 95.13–14.

humorous treatment of the *Dümmling* theme. As the knight who
in the *Agravain* finds Lancelot on the Isle de Joie Perceval has to have
a certain dignity,[23] and as one of the elect he cannot be ignorant of
religious practices. Already in the *Agravain* Perceval, while distinguishing himself at arms, never omits to hear 'messe et matines et toutes les
heures du jour' if he has the opportunity, keeps himself 'caastes et
nets' and confesses weekly.[24] And when he and Hector, both badly
wounded, are healed by the passing of the Grail, Perceval does not
fail to ask Hector the significance of the Grail: 'Graal, fait Perceval,
sire, que puet chou estre?'[25] Perceval's *niceté* as conceived by the
Queste is his inability to recognise the devil even when warned in
advance, and it is on one such occasion that a *preudome* says to Perceval,
'Ha! Perceval, toz jors seras tu nice.'[26] Unlike his counterpart in
Chrétien and the *Didot–Perceval*, however, Perceval does not go
through a period during which he forgets God, and the conception
of a Perceval who has gradually to perfect himself is replaced by that
of a Perceval who has to guard against losing the virtues he has, above
all his virginity. He is faced with a series of temptations intended to
test him, 'por savoir et conoistre se vos estes ses feels serjans et ses
loiaux chevaliers',[27] and Chrétien's theme of Perceval's despair is
skilfully adapted for this purpose. In despair at having lost sight of
Galaad, Perceval, unsuspecting, 'come cil qui ne se prent garde de
l'agait a l'anemi',[28] accepts a diabolical horse which leads him to a
deserted island where, though forewarned, Perceval almost surrenders
to the charms of the devil in the form of a woman. But at the last
moment Perceval is saved from *pechié mortel* when providentially he
crosses himself: 'car j'eusse esté vaincuz se ce ne fust la grace du Saint
Esperit qui ne me lessa perir'.[29] Perceval immediately repents of his
sinful intention and in penance strikes himself through the thigh. He
has won through: after hearing a voice proclaim, 'Perceval, tu as

23 In contrast to Chrétien, Perceval is in the prose *Lancelot* not ignorant of arms
     or of correct social behaviour: on leaving home Perceval not only arms him-
     self, but prepares Agloval's arms and horse for him, and at Arthur's court it is
     not Perceval's clumsiness, as in Chrétien, but his distinction while serving at
     table before being knighted which brings Perceval to Arthur's notice
     (*Vulgate Version*, v, 384.3–4, 385.8–12).

24 *Vulgate Version* v, 389.20–2.   25 *Op. cit.*, v, 392.42.

26 *Queste*, ed. Pauphilet, p. 112.25–6.

27 *Op. cit.*, p. 99.32–3.

28 *Op. cit.*, p. 92.9.

29 *Op. cit.*, p. 114.28–9.

vaincu et es gariz',[30] he is allowed to join the company of the elect and is present at the *haute aventure* when Galaad is invested with the 'espee as estranges renges', an honour denied to Lancelot.

The Post-Vulgate *Roman du Graal*, a *remaniement* of the Vulgate cycle,[31] while continuing to present Perceval as one of the three elect, not only changes considerably the presentation of Perceval in the *Queste* but introduces certain variants into the account of Perceval's youthful adventures and links up the death of his father and brothers with the theme of the feud between Gauvain and Perceval's family. This latter theme was not invented by the Post-Vulgate but taken over from the First Version of the prose *Tristan*, where an account of Perceval's youth, adapted from the *Agravain* and combined with details from Chrétien, precedes Perceval's journey to Cornwall to free Tristan from Marc's prison.[32] The author of the *Agravain*, who, like Chrétien, was not interested in Perceval's father and dead brothers except in so far as references to them were essential to explain why Perceval's mother brought Perceval up in isolation, neither names Perceval's dead father and brothers nor explains the circumstances in which they

30 *Op. cit.*, p. 115.16.

31 On the Post-Vulgate, see my *Romance of the Grail*, Manchester and New York, 1966.

32 Perceval's youth and his journey to Cornwall are related in the First Version of the prose *Tristan* (ms. B.N. fr. 757) immediately after Lamorat and Drian's death (E. Loeseth, *Le Roman en prose de Tristan, analyse critique*, Paris, 1891, §§308–18; the substance of Loeseth, §§308–13 has been publ. from ms. B.N. fr. 757 by A. Hilka, *Zeitschrift für romanische Philologie*, LII (1932), pp. 513–36). Five mss. of the Second Version of the prose ⌐Tristan (B.N. fr. 772, 101, 340, 349; Chantilly, Musée Condé 648) have the same account of Perceval's youth as B.N. fr. 757, but mss. B.N. fr. 335–6, B.M. Add. 5474, Royal 20 D II, Aberystwyth 5667, Vienna 2537, 2539–40, 2542 pass from Loeseth §282 to §338a and so omit Perceval's youth and the delivery of Tristan. Instead these latter mss., as well as certain others (B.N. fr. 94, 99, 103, 334, 776; Chantilly, Musée Condé 646; New York, Pierpont Morgan Library 41) give a brief account of Perceval's arrival at Arthur's court earlier in the narrative (Loeseth, §254). At the point where Arthur announces that he will hold a court at Whitsuntide (Loeseth, §388) mss. B.N. fr. 97, 101, 349, 758, Chantilly, Musée Condé 648, Vienna 2542, B.M. Add. 5474 insert from the prose *Lancelot* an account of Galaad's birth, Lancelot's madness and Perceval's youth up to the point where Perceval finds Lancelot on the *Isle de Joie* (publ. from BM. Add. 5474 by H. O. Sommer, *Modern Philology*, V (1907–8), pp. 55–84, 181–200, 322–41). Three other mss. (B.N. fr. 99, Chantilly 646, Pierpont Morgan 41) pass from Lamorat and Drian's death on to the account of Perceval's youth and Lancelot's madness as found in B.M. Add. 5474, etc. (cf. Loeseth, p. 239, n. 3).

died.[33] In the Vulgate *Queste*, where Perceval's father is named Pellehen,[34] Perceval's brothers are said to have died 'por lor outrage',[35] but Perceval's aunt refers to their death only as a warning for Perceval. Now in the prose *Tristan* Perceval's father is the valiant King Pellinor de Listenois,[36] who in addition to Perceval and Agloval has three other sons, two of whom in particular—Lamorat and Drian—are famed for their valour. As it would not redound to their credit to have died 'por lor outrage', the prose *Tristan* links up their death and that of their father with the theme of Gauvain's treachery. Gauvain, who throughout the prose *Tristan* is represented as a villain, slew Pellinor in order to avenge his father, King Lot, killed by Pellinor. But this vengeance did not suffice Gauvain, for he hated all Pellinor's elder sons, in particular Lamorat and Drian, because they were better knights than he was, and after seeking them for many years he killed them too in treason.[37] It was after hearing of Lamorat's and Drian's deaths that Perceval's mother went to live in a deserted plain, and when eventually Perceval went to Arthur's court Gauvain began to hate him too, all the more as Gaheriet, unaware of his brother's

33 Chrétien, however, gives us the following details about Perceval's father and brothers: after being maimed in one leg Perceval's father became impoverished and when, on Utherpendragon's death, the poor people were exiled, Perceval's family went to live in the Gaste Forest. Perceval's two elder brothers went to serve the king of Escavalon and King Ban of Gomorret, and when the news came that both had been killed in battle the same day the father died of grief (408–81).

34 *Queste*, ed. Pauphilet, p. 201.24. Variant forms are *Pellehem, Pellean*.

35 *Op. cit.*, p. 73.1.

36 It is the author of the Vulgate *Merlin* continuation who first named Perceval's father Pellinor de Listenois (or Pellinor de la Salvage Forest Souvraine), but the details he gives about Pellinor differ from those in the prose *Tristan* and the Post-Vulgate (see below, p. 62).

37 Loeseth, *Analyse*, §§306–7. For the author of the prose *Tristan* Lamorat was a very much better knight than Perceval: '. . . Il ne fu si bon chevalier ne si preu d'armes con fu Lamorat, et se si grant honeur li avint comme a celui jor qu'il vit partie des merveilles del Saint Graal et fu .i. des .xii. compaignons qui la queste menerent a fin, ce ne li avint mie tant par la bonté de sa chevalerie con li avint par la bonté de sa char, qui loiaument garda a Nostre Seigneur virginité, tant comme Parceval demoura en vie. Car il fu verité que tot ainsi comme Perceval vint virges en terre, tot ainsi s'en departi il virges et presenta a Nostre Seignour sa char nete et pure de toute chaleur et de toute ardeur de luxure. Ce fu la bonté de Perceval. Et si ne di je mie mie qu'il ne fust bon chevalier a merveilles de la terriane chevalerie, mes sanz faille il ne fu mie si bon chevalier comme Lamorat ses freres, ne non fu nus de celui lignage ne devant ce n'avoit esté' (ms. B.N. fr. 772, f. 35a; cf. Loeseth, *Analyse*, §306).

treachery, expressed the hope that Perceval would one day avenge the death of his kin.[38]

The author of the Post-Vulgate *Roman du Graal*, who throughout is careful to integrate with the texture of his romance as a whole the various themes derived from his sources, relates the death of Lamorat and Drian very much as does the prose *Tristan*,[39] but assigns a larger role to Perceval's father, Pellinor, and traces the causes of the feud back to the time of Mordred's birth: having heard that a child born on May Day would cause the destruction of Logres, Arthur has all the children born that day exposed on the sea in a rudderless boat; King Lot, thinking that his son Mordred too has perished, makes war on Arthur and is slain by Pellinor, who has come to Arthur's aid. At his father's funeral Gauvain, then aged eleven, swears to avenge his father,[40] and when years later he has carried out his vengeance Perceval's mother retires, as in the prose *Tristan*, to a tower in a solitary plain. Apart from minor details the Post-Vulgate version of Perceval's youth, up to his departure from Arthur's court, is the same as that of the *Tristan*.[41] Having been brought up among women Perceval is 'assez plus nice chose que mestier ne luy fust',[42] but as in the *Didot–Perceval* the theme of Perceval's *niceté* is not developed and is not linked with the death of Perceval's mother. Determined to become a knight, Perceval sets off for court secretly early one morning and his mother, distraught with grief, sends Agloval after Perceval to bring him back. As soon as she sees Perceval again her heart fails for joy, but it is not Perceval alone who thinks that the mother has only fainted; Agloval is of the same opinion, and both brothers leave for court without another glance at their mother.

As in the *Agravain*, so in the Post-Vulgate, the events at Arthur's court mark Perceval out as predestined to be 'uns des plus souverains chevaliers de la Queste del Saint Graal', and, as befits Perceval's role, he is chaste in thought and deed. Although in the prose *Tristan* too Perceval is one of the three elect, the author, anxious to humiliate Gauvain, included a version of Perceval's *reverie* adapted from

38 *Zeitschr. f. rom. Phil.*, LII (1932), p. 527.
39 For the Post-Vulgate account of Lamorat and Drian's death, see my *Folie Lancelot*, pp. 72–81.
40 *Merlin*, ed. G. Paris, Paris (S.A.T.F., 1886), I, 158–9, 203–12, 247–9, 254–63; II, 75–6.
41 For the Post-Vulgate account of Perceval's youth, see *La Folie Lancelot*, pp. 82–100.
42 *La Folie Lancelot*, p. 83.35.

Chrétien's incident of the three blood drops in the snow. Perceval, who here dreams of the Helaine Sans Per of the *Didot–Perceval* and not of Blanchefleur, has already unhorsed Keu and Mordred and does not wish to joust a third time, but Gauvain, who here lacks the courtesy so characteristic of Chrétien's Gauvain, insists on a combat and is so badly wounded that he has to take to his bed for a month.[43] The Post-Vulgate omits this episode, substituting for it, among other adventures linking up with the feud theme, the Blanchefleur episode, remodelled in such a way as to present Perceval as both chaste and *senez*.[44] The necessity for Blanchefleur's compromising nocturnal interview with Perceval is avoided, for Perceval does not, as in Chrétien, refrain from questioning his hostess at the right time, but begs her at table to tell him why she is *corroucee*. Nor does Perceval make his help conditional on her granting him her *druerie*. He offers his services because it would be 'grant aumosne et grant cortoisie',[45] and whereas in Chrétien Perceval, after defeating Aguigeron, spends his time 'Dalez s'amie tot a aise' until he has the opportunity of doing battle with Clamadam, in the Post-Vulgate Perceval, commending himself to God 'com cil qui estoit uns des chevaliers du monde de meilleur creance',[46] defeats Clamadam and Aguigeron together. Then, having forced Clamadam to make amends to the damsel, Perceval departs, 'qu'il n'y volt plus demorer pour priere que la damoiselle luy sceust faire ne homme de leans'.[47]

While the First Version of the prose *Tristan* refers only briefly to the events of the *Queste*, barely mentioning Perceval at all,[48] the Post-Vulgate *Roman du Graal* includes a complete redaction of the *Queste*, based on the Vulgate but considerably remodelled.[49] For the author of the Post-Vulgate the *Queste* is not a means of doctrinal exposition but a chapter in the history of Logres. Hence the author does not hesitate to cut out most of the theological disquisitions of the Vulgate and to modify the roles of the characters as conceived by the Vulgate. In the second and final version of the Post-Vulgate *Queste* as represented by

43 *Zeitschr. f. rom. Phil.*, LII (1932), pp. 530–5.
44 *La Folie Lancelot*, pp. 141–7.
45 *Op. cit.*, p. 143.106.
46 *Op. cit.*, p. 145.71.
47 *La Folie Lancelot*, p. 147.278–9.
48 There is only one reference to Perceval (see Loeseth, *Analyse*, §420).
49 The First Version of the Post-Vulgate *Queste* was incorporated in a partially modified form in the Second Version of the prose *Tristan* (see my *Romance of the Grail*, pp. 88–120).

the Portuguese *Demanda*[50] and certain French manuscripts (B.N. fr. 112 and 343) the theme so important in the Vulgate—that Perceval, on account of his *niceté*, almost sins—is practically eliminated. Perceval is never referred to as *nice*, and most of the time he appears no less saintly than Galaad himself. More than once he is addressed by a *preudome* as 'saincte creature et saint corps, saincte char, necte et verge, . . . saint homme et . . . loyal sergent de Nostre Seigneur'.[51] Like Galaad, he brings through his goodness and holy life healing and relief to those he meets. An old hermit, brought to despair by the devil and on the point of hanging himself, hails Perceval as his deliverer, for at his approach the devil fled:

> 'Persival, you are the friend of God and you are welcome, for you delivered me from an evil and painful death[52] . . . As soon as you approached here and made the sign of the cross, the devil left me instantly . . . and I immediately recovered my reason . . . Certainly, if you were not a holy man and of godly life and filled with the grace of Our Lord, such a beautiful adventure would not have occurred through you.'[53]

Similarly, when in a warning vision Lancelot is struck on the thigh by Yseut's burning hand and he cries out to Perceval for help, the fire burning in Lancelot's thigh is extinguished as soon as Perceval places his hand on it 'pour la bonté de Parceval et pour l'amour que Nostre

50 *Demanda do Santo Graal*, ed. A. Magne (1st edn. Rio de Janeiro, 1945; 2nd edn., I, 1955; II, 1970).
51 Ms. B.N. fr. 112, *Livre* IV, f. 99c.
52 'Ay, Persival! vos sodes amigo de Deus e vos sejades bem vindo, que me livrastes de morte maa e de nojossa.' (*Demanda*, §183.)
53 'Tam toste como quisestes aqui entrar e vos sinastes, logo se partio de mim o demo . . . e logo torney em meu sem . . . Certas, se vos nom fosedes santo homem e da santa vida, e comprido de graça de Nosso Senhor, ja per vos nom aver[i]a tam fremossa aventura' (*Demanda*, §189). In the *Prophécies de Merlin* (ed. from ms. 593 in the Bibl. Municipale of Rennes by Lucy Allen Paton, Modern Language Association of America, New York and London, 1926), where Perceval continues to be presented as Pellinor's son, his role in the *Queste* is predicted, but none of his adventures during the *Queste* is related, as the *Queste* is outside the time span of the extant *Prophécies*. Nor does the *Prophécies* deal with Perceval's *enfances*. Perceval is essentially a utility enabling the author to bring some variety into Merlin's endless prophecies: a hermit, Helias de Norhomberlande, who is destined not to die until the coming of Perceval, hands over to Perceval a book written by Merlin. Particularly interesting, however, is that, as in the Post-Vulgate *Queste*, Perceval is able, through his goodness, to save others from the power of the devil. Thus it is thanks to Perceval's prayers that the Sage Clerc is able to speak safely to

Seigneur avoit a luy'.[54] And there is no need for a hermit to explain the significance of this miracle: Perceval himself interprets it for Lancelot and exhorts him to confess his mortal sin: 'Et certes je cuit se vous fussiés bien confés puis que vous entrastes en ceste queste, qui est queste et encerchement des grans merveilles de Nostre Seigneur, ja ceste aventure ne vous fust survenue si soudainement.'[55]

The temptation scene of the Vulgate was, however, too integral a part of the Perceval story for the Post-Vulgate author to pass it over completely, but he so shortened and revised the incident that the purpose which it had in the Vulgate, to test Perceval and to bring out his *niceté*, is no longer apparent.[56] Perceval's despair, his acceptance of a diabolical horse and his various mystical adventures on the deserted island leading up to the supreme temptation have been omitted. As in the Vulgate, the devil takes on the guise of a beautiful damsel claiming to have been disinherited and in need of help, but she does not arrive in a black boat which should have been a warning to Perceval. Instead Perceval finds her asleep in a tent by the sea-shore, and while as in the Vulgate he offers his help in return for her love, in the Post-Vulgate alone Perceval adds that he would marry her and make her queen of

---

Merlin's father, a devil whom Merlin had shut up in a stone: 'Je sai apertement que vous estes mout dignes au Sauveeur du monde, que seulement por vostre proiere sui je eschapés' (ed. Paton, I, p. 236, ch. cxci; cf. I, p. 228, ch. clxxx).

54 Ms. B.N. fr. 112, *Livre* IV, f. 100a.

55 *Loc. cit.* It is interesting to note that Gerbert's Perceval, like the Perceval of the Post-Vulgate *Queste*, not only receives but also gives holy advice. For instance, in contrast to the *Perlesvaus*, where the author represents the Chevalier au Dragon as being consumed by flames after his unsuccessful combat with Perlesvaus (ed. Nitze, p. 253), in Gerbert Perceval exhorts the vanquished Chevalier au Dragon to confess his sins and repent so that he may gain everlasting joy:

> Si te confesse, si t'esmonde
> De che qu'as mesfait en cest monde,
> Et si en soies repentans;
> Car navree est cent mil tans
> T'ame que tes cors n'est assez.

> Et prie merchi et pardon
> A Dieu, et si fai veu et don
> Que ja mais pechié ne feras;
> Et ses tu que tu en aras?
> Joie et sancté en paradis
> Et leece mais a toudis.   [9899–921]

56 *Demanda*, §§246–9. Cf. *Queste*, ed. Pauphilet, pp. 87–115.

a rich and fine land. Nor is Perceval in immediate danger of committing *pechié mortel*. While he is talking to the damsel a voice from heaven warns him that 'he is ill advised and giving up all joy for all sorrow'.[57] He falls to the ground in a swoon, and when he comes round and sees the damsel laughing he realises at once that she is a devil.

In order to strengthen the links between the various branches, the author of the Post-Vulgate *Roman du Graal* continues the themes began in the early part of his romance right through into the *Queste* section. The feud theme is developed in such a way as to contrast Perceval's loyalty with Gauvain's treachery. Perceval would gladly have avenged his father and brothers, but when his aunt, the recluse, advises him against his undertaking, as it would be disloyal to kill a knight of the Round Table, Perceval agrees to leave it to God, the great avenger, to inflict retribution.[58] Later, when Perceval encounters Gauvain, he offers to forgive him if he will tell him the truth, but Gauvain, full of cowardice, refuses to admit his guilt[59] and at the first opportunity leaves Perceval's company, 'for he was very much afraid that he would kill him for the death of his father and brothers'.[60] The theme reappears once more at the point where Gauvain leaves Corbenic. As he departs in shame, Yvain de Cenel's sister reproaches him with having slain Perceval's father, compares his *malvestié* with Perceval's *bonté* and pre-

---

57 'Ay, Persivall, como aqui ha tam maao conselho! Deyxas toda lidice por toda tristeza' (*Demanda*, §248). In Manessier, in a temptation scene closely modelled on that of the Vulgate *Queste*, the devil takes on the shape of Blanchefleur, and as in the Vulgate Perceval would have committed a mortal sin if he had not, *si com Diex volt par sa miracle* (Potvin, VI, 40708), caught sight of the cross on the pommel of his sword and made the holy *singnacle* (VI, 40476–768). In Gerbert, in contrast, Perceval is above temptation: when here the devil appears to him in the form of the Fisher King's daughter, he immediately without the least hesitation rejects her advances (ed. Williams, 2518–86). Indeed, Gerbert has almost completely transferred to Perceval Galaad's role of the Redeemer, and for Gerbert Perceval's function is to undo the work of the devil:

> feras
> Tel chose dont tu desferas
> Ce qu'anemis avoit ovré:
> Par toi esteront recovré
> Li bien avec les Dieus amis
> Que destruisoit li anemis. [5705–10]

58 *Demanda*, §221.   59 *Demanda*, §237.
60 'Ca avia muy gram pavor de ho matar polla morte de seu padre e de seus irmãos' (*Demanda*, §245).

dicts that Perceval will leave Corbenic in greater honour than Gauvain does: 'Et sachiez que Perceval, li loiaux chevaliers, qui pere vos occeistes en felenie et en traïson, istra de leienz a mult greignor honor que vos ne faites.'[61] While Gauvain degenerates, Perceval ascends, and the two knights who in Chrétien walked hand-in-hand, the best of friends, end up by becoming enemies. The transformation of the one, as of the other, was determined largely by the differences in the nature of the various romances in which they appear.

It was perhaps inevitable that in an age when writers attempted to elucidate and motivate the themes inherited from their sources someone should endeavour to explain why in some romances Perceval is second to Galaad. The *Livre d'Artu*, which was written to replace one of the branches of the Vulgate Cycle, the Vulgate *Merlin* continuation, attempts to do just this. The explanation is significantly linked with yet another account of the fate of Perceval's father and is in part a development of some hints in the Vulgate *Merlin* continuation. According to the latter, Perceval's father, King Pellinor, who had thirteen sons and two brothers, Kings Pelles and Alain, is not dead by the time Perceval sets out for court but maimed, as also is Alain.[62] But the Vulgate *Merlin* continuation does not say in what circumstances Pellinor received his wound, and it is left to the author of the *Livre d'Artu* to elucidate this in such a way as to provide at the same time an explanation for Perceval's role. Pellinor, here the father of sixteen sons and the cousin of King Pelles and King Alain,[63] had in his care the Grail and one day as he lay in his bed he began to think so

61 Ms. B.N. fr. 343, f. 93a–b.

62 The following are some of the references to Pellinor's family in the Vulgate *Merlin* continuation (*Vulgate Version*, II): (a) 'parole del roy Pelles de Listenois et del frere al roy Pellinor et le roy Alain qui frere estoient germain de peire et de meire' (II, 346.18–19); (b) 'du roy Peiles de Listenois n'atendons nul secors, car il garde le roy Pelinor son frere qui gist malades . . .' (II, 125.9–11); (c) 'roy Pellinor de la Salvage Forest Souvraine qui avoit .xi. fils qui estoient en l'eage de .xvii. ans des plus nes et en avoit .i. novelement venu a la court le roy Artu por aprendre d'armes, et ce estoit li douzimes, et du trezime estoit la meire enchainte' (II, 359.29–32).

63 Cf. the following passages: (a) 'Alain, le frere au roi Pellinor et le frere au roi Pelles du Chastel de Corbenic qui cosin germain estoient au roi Pellinor, le roi mahaignié de la cuisse de la Lance Vencheresse' (ms. B.N. fr. 337, f. 193b; cf. *Vulgate Version*, VII, 146.7–9); (b) 'Laienz furent li frere Agloval tuit .xiiii., et lor peres qui encores gisoit en langor des plaies que la Lance Vencheresse li fist parmi les cuisses ambedeus, et Percevals li petiz qui encores aprenoit a aler, tant estoit de petit aage' (VII, 236.18–20).

deeply about the marvels of the Grail that he came to doubt them. Immediately a fiery lance descending from heaven struck him through both thighs and a voice announced that this was divine vengeance for his disbelief. Not only was his name henceforth to be changed from King of the Gaste Forest Soutaine to li Rois Pecherres, but his son Perceval, on account of his father's sin, was not to become Grail Guardian until after the death of Galaad:

> C'est li vengemenz de ce que tu as mes oevres mescreues et moi deshonoré par ta pensee fole et mauvaise. Et por ce que tu es cil que j'avoie tant es-saucié de lignage sor toz autres lignages et que ge t'avoie baillié en garde mon sanc et ma char, et tu t'en desesperoies, por ce le te ferai ge si comparer que toz les jorz que tu vivras t'en menberra. Et le jor que tu garras rendras l'arme du cors. Tu soloies avoir non li Rois de la Gaste Forest Soutaine. Or avras non li Rois Peschierres, car petit avras de santé se lors non que tu seras en riviere. Et le jor que Pellinor, tes cosins, garra, tu garras et morras. *Et par ce que tu as mescreu mes miracles que je demostroie par cest païs, por ce sera tes fils Perceval reusez d'avoir le Graal en sa garde jusque aprés la mort au fill de la fille le roi Pelles, car se tes pechiez ne fust de ce que mescreu as tes filz l'eust avant en sa garde.*[64] [*Vulgate Version*, VII, 243.30–9]

And as if to reconcile still further the conflicting traditions, Perceval and Galaad are represented as sharing the task of healing the various maimed kings. According to the Vulgate *Merlin* continuation, Pellinor, who is being looked after by Pelles in Corbenic, cannot expect 'garison tant que cil vendra laiens qui les aventures du Saint Graal metera a fin',[65] and Alain will not be healed 'devant ce que li mieudres chevaliers del monde viegne a lui et li demant dont cele maladie li vint et quel chose li Graaus est que l'en sert',[66] but it is by no means clear whether it is the same knight or not at whose coming the two kings are to be healed. In the *Livre d'Artu*, however (where Pellinor goes to live in the *Chastel de la Merveille* after the death of fourteen of his sons killed in battle defending their mother's home against the pagan King Agripes and li Giromelanz),[67] it is stated clearly that Alain, Pellinor

---

64 As in all the romances except the *Perlesvaus* Perceval's mother is represented as a widow, the *Livre d'Artu*, in order to avoid any contradiction with the earlier tradition, explains that Perceval's mother was called *la Vueve de la Forest* because her husband was so badly maimed that he could not walk: 'Et por ce que il fu einsi mahaigniez que aidier ne se pot fu clamee sa femme de tout li pueple la Vueve de la Forest' (*Vulgate Version*, VII, 243.40–2).
65 *Vulgate Version*, II, 125.11–12.   66 *Ibid.*, II, 125.12–15.
67 'Mes si tost come li rois Pelinor sot que tuit si .xiiii. fil estoient mort, si ne vost onques puis estre en son recet, einz s'en ala sejorner u Chastel de la Merveille

and Pellinor's cousin, Pellinor du Chastel de Corbenic,[68] are to recover
at the coming of Perceval when he has asked the question about the
Grail, even though he is not worthy of seeing the Grail 'fors par
dehors':

> Ne li rois Alains ne li rois Pelletor[69] ne li rois Pellinor ne garront de lor
> plaies tant que li chevaliers gise en lor ostel et ait demandé cui l'en sert do
> Saint Graal. Et ja si tost ne l'avra demandé que cil ne soit gariz chiés cui il
> le demandera, encore ne soit il mie dignes du veoir fors par dehors.
>
> [*Vulgate Version*, VII, 146.23–6]

Mordrain, on the other hand, the king who is served by the Grail,
will be restored to health at the coming of the glorious knight Galaad,
in whose arms he will expire:

> Por ce ne garra mie li rois qui en est serviz, ainz le covendra avant a vivre
> .iiii.c. anz que l'avanture soit menee a fin, et morra entre les braz au glorielx
> chevalier qui l'aventure traira a fin.   [*Vulgate Version*, VII, 147.26–8]

And although Perceval's achievement is not as great as Galaad's, yet
'tant com il esploita valut, car moins ot a faire en l'aventure a chief
mener, qui trop estoit granz'.[70]

All this suggests that it is the successive authors' conception of their
themes, the necessities of the plot and the desire to rationalise and
render more coherent the material derived from their predecessors
which account for the ever-changing presentation of the characters as
they are transferred from one romance to another. The change of
Perceval from a *nice* to almost a saint was a gradual one and is significantly reflected by the successive authors' description of his appearance. For Chrétien Perceval is the youth with the bright and laughing
eyes.[71] For the author of the prose *Tristan* the most striking feature
about Perceval is his resemblance to his illustrious brother Lamorat,

---

avec la mere au roi Artus que Merlins i avoit portee, mes nu savoient nules
genz fors cil qui le Saintisme Graal avoient en garde' (*Vulgate Version*, VII,
244.9–12; cf. *ibid.*, VII, 236–43).

68 Pellinor's cousin, Pellinor du Chastel de Corbenic, is the brother of Perceval's
mother (see *Vulgate Version*, VII, 237.4–5, where Agloval says to his mother,
'Et vostre freres, roi Pelinor, du Chastel de Corbanie, coment le fait
il?').

69 Pelletor is no doubt a scribal error for Pellinor.

70 *Vulgate Version*, VII, 245.33–4.

71 'Cler et riant furent li oeil / En la teste au vallet salvage' (974–5).

slain by Gauvain.[72] But for the author of the final version of the Post-Vulgate *Queste*

> God showed Perceval such great mercy that he was so handsome and joyful in appearance that it seems there was not a knight in the world who enjoyed more the joys, delights and pleasures which the knights errant had at this time. And no body seemed to be more enamoured than he or indulge more in the pleasures of the world, but what he felt in his heart was different from what he showed outwardly.[73]

The evolution of Perceval's role, as of the medieval romances in general, is the result of a creative process, constantly renewed.

72 'Or le face Diex preudome, fet li rois, car certes il est biax enfés et bien resemble au haut lignage dont il est estrez et plus a Lamorat que a nul autre' (*Zeitschr. f. rom. Phil.*, LII (1932), p. 526). In the *Prophécies de Merlin* Perceval is described as resembling his father Pellinor: 'il resenbloit a la façon du vis le roi Pelinor' (ed. Paton, I, p. 287, ch. ccxlviii).

73 'E Deus lhe fazia tanta mercee, que era tam fremosso e tam ledo per semelhança, que no mundo nom avia mais ledo cavaleyro de ledices e de prazeres e d[e] sab[o]res que os cavaleiros andantes aviam em aquel tempo; nom semelhava que n[ẽ]huũ nom avia mais namorado ca elle, nem que mais se deitasse ao sabor do mundo, mas al avia dentro e al avia de ffora' (*Demanda*, §182). In the *Perlesvaus*, which was written after the *Lancelot* proper, though not necessarily before the *Queste*, the author has transferred to Perceval, here called Perlesvaus, the description of Galaad in the prose *Lancelot*: 'Il a le chief d'or e regart de lion e no[m]blil de virge pucele e cuer de valeur e teches sanz vilenie' (*Perlesvaus*, ed. W. A. Nitze *et al.*, Chicago, 1932–37, I, ll. 911–12). Cf. *Vulgate Version*, IV, 27.7–8).

M. Currie

Some notes on hypothetical sentences in fifteenth and sixteenth century French

Our knowledge of hypothetical sentences in medieval and sixteenth century French has remained largely unchanged since the publication of Robert-Léon Wagner's thesis *Les Phrases hypothétiques*.[1] The notes that follow take M. Wagner's work as a starting point, and have two aims: to throw some additional light on the use of the imperfect subjunctive, and to make a few brief additions and corrections to M. Wagner's historical list of hypothetical sentences.[2]

The use of the imperfect subjunctive

In medieval French the imperfect subjunctive is used in hypothetical sentences of two main types: those referring to the past (type A, *Sempres caïst, se Deus ne li aidast*), in which the pluperfect subjunctive is also used; and those referring to the present or future (type BC, *S'altre le desist, ja semblast grant mençunge*), in which the imperfect indicative – conditional are also used. The imperfect subjunctive can be used in both clauses of a hypothetical system or in only one of them, or in an independent principal. Most of the time these various cases can be considered together, and the only general distinction which has to be made is that between types A and BC. The secondary

1 *Les Phrases hypothétiques commençant par 'si' dans la langue française, des origines à la fin du XVIe siècle*, Paris, 1939. Reviewed by E. Lerch, *Zeitschr. f. rom. Phil.*, LXI (1941), pp. 375–87.
2 The texts referred to several times in this article have been read in the following editions: *Alixandre l'Orphelin*, ed. C. E. Pickford; Brantôme, *Dames galantes*, ed. M. Rat; *Cent Nouvelles Nouvelles*, ed. (ms) P. Champion, (Vérard) Le Roux de Lincy; Charles d'Orléans, ed. P. Champion; *Heptaméron*, ed. M. François; Montaigne, *Essais*, ed. A. Thibaudet; *Ovide moralisé en prose*, ed. C. de Boer; Rabelais, ed. J. Boulenger and L. Scheler; *Recueil Trepperel*, ed. E. Droz and H. Lewicka; *Quinze Joyes*, ed. (Rouen ms.) J. Rychner, (Péronne ms.) J. Crow, (*editio princeps*) F. Heuckenkamp; *Saintré*, ed. P. Champion and F. Desonay.

distinction between (B) a present and (C) a future hypothesis is unnecessary for our purpose, and is often impossible anyway (p. 343).

The question of archaic usage arises more than once in *Les Phrases
hypothétiques*. If, of two equivalent constructions, one is relatively
uncommon and seems to be associated chiefly with 'refractory' verbs
(*être*, the modal auxiliaries and a few others which are slow to adapt
completely to the prevalent construction), M. Wagner is inclined to
see it as obsolete and archaic. Thus the imperfect subjunctive in hypothetical sentences which refer to the past is considered archaic after the
middle of the fourteenth century. Later than this, the imperfect subjunctive is certainly uncommon in most cases. For prose usage of the
fifteenth century M. Wagner notes few examples of few verbs
(pp. 151-2): *devoir* (seven examples), *pouvoir* (one), *savoir* (one), *cuider*
(one), *être* (nine), *avoir* (four), *valoir* (two) and *faire* (one), and of these
faire alone is an 'indifferent', i.e. non-refractory, verb. To this list can
be added a few more examples,[3] the most interesting occurring in the
Cent Nouvelles, of which we possess one version in manuscript and
another in the later printed edition of Antoine Vérard (1486).

> *Cent Nouvelles*, p. 34, (le guet) qui l'eust en Chastellet logié, si a ceste
> heure le *trouvast*. (Vérard *l'eust trouvé*.)
>
> p. 64, luy, qui pour rien ne *courroucast* pere et mere. (V.)
>
> p. 98, bien en fussent mortes de deuil s'elles en *sceussent* la vérité. (V.
> *eussent sceu*.)
>
> p. 146, si je ne *cuidasse* qu'on feïst aultre chose en mariage, je ne m'y fusse ja
> boutée. (V. *eusse cuidé*.)
>
> p. 161, Elle *amast* trop mieulx se trouver avecques son amy, qu'elle cuidoit
> bien avoir espousé ce jour. (V.)
>
> p. 25, ce qu'elle eust voluntiers refusé si ce ne *fust* pour mieulx faire.
> (V. *ce n'eust esté*.)
>
> p. 79, si ne *fust* . . . , elle se *fust* offerte. (V.)
>
> But Vérard I, 159, Ceste mauldicte manière dura plus de dix jours et
> encores *durast*, se la bonne mère à l'espousée n'y eust pourveu du remède.
> (Ms. *et encores eust*.)

Examples such as these represent a very small proportion of the
hypothetical sentences referring to the past in the *Cent Nouvelles*.

---

3 *Ovide moralisé*, pp. 82 *peüst* (any single verb unaccompanied by *si* or *qui* always
represents a hypothetical principal), 164 *voulsist*, 78 *cuidasse*, 185 *si feïst*, 210
se je ne feusse 'but for me', 327 *feïsse*, 322 *eüst*, 235 *feïst*, 381 *feïsse*, 148 *osassent*,
291 'finalbement cheüt icelle nef entre les undes plus pesantement que ne
feïssent Athos et Pindus, se ilz *feüssent* tresbuchez du hault en bas.' *Comte
d'Artois*, p. 60, *se fust*.

However, they suggest three things, as do the examples in other texts: that the subjunctive is certainly not restricted to the refractory verbs; and that it is no longer used regularly in both clauses of a hypothetical system, although there are examples of this use (n. 3 and below, *Quinze Joyes*, p. 76). Thirdly, it appears from the variation between the two versions that the printed edition shows an erratic preference for the modern construction. If we consider that the printed text of the *Cent Nouvelles* shows a close general similarity with that of the ms., although it is not necessarily based upon it, and that the date of composition of the *Cent Nouvelles* has never been put earlier than 1450, the variation between the two versions may reflect a change which is still in progress in the second half of the fifteenth century, and which, since the variation is erratic, is not completed yet.

In the light of this, the variation between the *editio princeps* of the *Quinze Joyes de Mariage* (1480–90) and two earlier manuscript versions is also interesting, despite the fact that the printed text is not based on any of the extant mss., and that the date of composition may be as early as 1400.

> *Quinze Joyes* (Rouen ms., 1464), p. 39, mon pere et ma mere me cuiderent marier a lui, mes jamés ne le *feisse*. (Péronne ms., 1468–70, *editio princeps*, *l'eusse fait*.)
>
> p. 63,—Sainte Marie, fait il k'est il bien traistre! Quar jamés ne me *doubtasse* de lui. (P., *e.p.*)
>
> p. 76, Ainxin est gouverné le bon homme, qui a vescu honnourablement, et se *gouvernast* bien, et son mesnage, qui le *voullist* croire. (P.)
>
> p. 110, je ne *cuidasse* jamés qu'il venist a celle heure!
>
> p. 33, (ses parens) ne l'eussent pas baillee au bon homme, si ce ne *fust* ung petit eschapeillon que elle avoit fait en sa jeunesse. (P., *e.p.*)
>
> p. 47, Et si ne *fust* de paour de deshonneur, elle eust bien crié aultrement. (P., but *e.p. se n'eust esté*.)

Here the two mss., which are not related closely, concur in four examples out of five; and of the four examples where a parallel exists, the printed text has the modern construction in two cases for R and in one case for P.

The slight tendency of a printed edition to prefer the modern construction seems significant when it occurs in two texts. It seems more significant still when no trace of such a tendency is evident in the use of the imperfect subjunctive in hypotheses referring to the present or future—a use which is also relatively uncommon and, according to M. Wagner, also archaic. There is, then, some evidence that the imperfect subjunctive A is not obsolete quite as early as has been stated, and that the process of obsolescence still drags on towards the end of the fifteenth century. Two further considerations suggest that the process is not finished even then.

Firstly, it is hard to accept that the fixed expression (*se*) *ne fust*, while replaceable in the fifteenth century by the later form (*se*) *n'eust esté*, is archaic by this time (pp. 194–5). If it is, the tendency to archaise seems to be widespread, for (*se*) *ne fust*, which has no regular alternative before the end of the fourteenth century, may still be somewhat more common than *n'eust esté* in the fifteenth.[4] It continues quite late into the sixteenth century, and is not used only by Rabelais to add an old-fashioned touch to a tale (p. 180).

> Dufour, *Femmes célèbres*, p. 98, Eureux eust esté, *si ne fust* que sa meschante
> femme Messaline du lieu publicque ne bougeoit.[5]

4 Cf., besides the four examples of *se ne fust* already quoted from the *Quinze Joyes* and the *Cent Nouvelles* (which also has *si n'eust esté*, p. 166): *Saintré*, pp. 303, 386; *Ovide moralisé*, pp. 120, 170, 196, 228, 259, 288, 394; Mathieu d'Escouchy, III, 264, against two examples of *n'eust esté*, I, 314, 421; and (*ne fust*) *Comte d'Artois*, pp. 36, 40, 58, 94, 107, 115, 123, 129, 136, 148, against two examples of *n'eust esté*, pp. 81, 101 and four of *se n'eust esté*, pp. 12, 36, 77, 95; Villon, *Epître à Marie d'Orléans*, v. 73.

M. Wagner considers that (*se*) *ne fust* is relatively less common in the fifteenth century. But by adding his examples of (*se*) *ne fust* and (*se*) *n'eust esté* to those noted here we have thirty-five of the former and thirty of the latter.

M. Wagner's opinions on archaic usage are sometimes arrived at rather too easily. 'Or, confrontons à Christine de Pisan un poète qui lui est de peu postérieur et dont la langue, au dire de son érudit éditeur Pierre Champion, représente le français parlé dans l'Ile-de-France, Charles d'Orléans; nous ne relevons pas chez lui un *seul* imparfait du subjonctif (A), signe qu'il y avait chez notre poétesse volonté consciente d'archaïsme' (p. 228).

Even if this statement was factually correct (which it is not: 'Je pry a Dieu qu'il te maudie, Faulse Mort, plaine de rudesse! Se prise l'eusses en vieillesse, Ce ne fust pas si grant rigueur', *Ballades*, LVII, v. 14), the conclusion would not follow necessarily.

Sometimes his opinions on archaic usage are hard to reconcile. Cf. 'L'auteur du premier [*sc.* les *Quinze Joyes*], qui, on aura d'autres occasions de le voir, affecte de prêter à ses personnages des tours d'un archaïsme très consciemment voulu . . .' (p. 195), and 'Si l'on interroge après cela un texte du XVe siècle qui nous est très utile, les *XV Joyes de Mariage*, rédigé dans une langue savoureuse assez proche, selon toute vraisemblance, de celle que parlaient les bourgeois d'une société fortunée . . .' (p. 403).

5 Cf. Sala, *Tristan*, p. 206; *Franc-Archier de Cherré*, v. 133; *Pionnier de Seurdre*, v. 564.

Brantôme, *Dames galantes*, p. 263, Et estoit [la ville] prise, *ne fut* que les dames de la ville se presenterent à la muraille avec armes, eau et huille bouillante et pierres.

Secondly, the last few examples of the imperfect subjunctive, apart from (*se*) *ne fust*, which we find in the first half of the sixteenth century appear to reflect the final stage in its obsolescence. In the fifteenth century it is uncommon in both clauses of a hypothetical system but can still occur in either of them. Now it is restricted to the principal clause.

Rabelais, *Pantagruel*, p. 332, et n'eust esté qu'ilz estoient très bien antidotéz, le cueur . . . , ilz *feussent* suffocquéz.

Gargantua, p. 37, possible n'estoit longuement les réserver [les tripes], car elles feussent pourries.'

Maître Pierre Faifeu, p. 32, v. 22, *qui eust deu—peust*; p. 35, v. 8, *mieulx vaulsist*.

A continuous usage such as this, gradually changing and shrinking, does not look like an archaism artificially preserved by a few writers for their own reasons. Significantly, the obsolescence of the other alleged archaism, the imperfect subjunctive in present/future hypotheses, ends in the same way, but roughly half a century later. If they are both archaisms and both cultivated by 'conservative' authors, as M. Wagner thinks, how is it that one is far more frequent and outlives the other?

M. Wagner's opinions concerning the use of the imperfect subjunctive in present/future hypothetical sentences are closely connected with his account of earlier usage. According to this account, the syntactical functions of the two types, *si* + imperfect indicative – conditional and *si* + imperfect subjunctive – imperfect subjunctive, are the same by the end of the twelfth century (p. 304). Semantically, also, the two types are generally indistinguishable. In theory, the former might seem more suitable to express a hypothesis with some chance of fulfilment, and the latter more suitable to express a hypothesis which cannot be fulfilled. In fact, both types express either hypothesis indifferently, and the few works or authors, e.g. *La Mort Artu* (p. 390) or Rutebeuf (pp. 395–6), which observe a systematic distinction between them do not reflect the general usage of Old French. On the other hand, their relative frequency and their stylistic value are different. In the twelfth century *si* + imperfect subjunctive – imperfect subjunctive is already so clearly in the minority that it cannot be taken as a serious rival to its alternative (pp. 267, 363 ff.), and may have disappeared from everyday language earlier still (p. 300).[6] It is an archaism belonging to literary usage, above all poetic usage (pp. 374 ff.), which preserves it for its archaic flavour and its capacity to supply both rhymes of a couplet. It survives in thirteenth century prose, thanks to the influence of poetry and Latin, as an artificial, learned construction belonging to 'la syntaxe figée'.[7] It does not occur with any regularity except in the case of certain refractory verbs which resist the general predominance of *si* + imperfect indicative – conditional, and even this resistance is relatively infrequent. When used by certain authors it can convey a variety of affective overtones: anxiety, regret, impatience, anger and, above all, discretion in a principal clause expressing desire (pp. 385 ff.). But such overtones are not inherent in the mood itself (p. 438), and the imperfect subjunctive is at all times 'un élément de style extérieur à la syntaxe des phrases hypothétiques françaises' (p. 539). By the

6 'Que concluerons-nous de cette exception, si ce n'est que, peut-être, bien avant le début du XIIe siècle, la tournure: *Se* + *imparfait du subjonctif B . . . imparfait du subjonctif B* était, dans la langue courante, délaissée au profit de: *Se* + *imparfait de l'indicatif . . . forme en-*rais' (p. 300). This point is insisted on: 'la fréquence du type centré autour de deux subjonctifs n'est pas [*sc.* in the twelfth century] telle qu'on puisse prétendre que ce système était un élément vivant et productif de la langue parlée' (p. 364); 'un tour syntaxique que nous avons tout lieu, par ailleurs, de croire étranger au langage courant des français du XIIe siècle (p. 387); also pp. 395, 398, 415.

This view seems to be the one most favoured, but we also find the opposite: 'A dire le vrai, si nous n'avions pas, dans un ou deux textes, la preuve à peu près sûre que le tour: *Se* + *imparfait du subjoncitif . . . imparfait du subjonctif* était encore en usage en Normandie vers la fin du XIVe siècle, nous n'oserions pas affirmer, sur la seule foi des chroniqueurs ou de l'auteur de la chantefable, que les français, entre 1200 et 1300, l'utilisaient dans leurs relations familiales' (p. 392). The evidence which shows that the subjunctive is still used in Normandy seems to be three examples (of which one is a concessive clause and invalid) taken from the *Actes de la chancellerie d'Henri VI concernant la Normandie* (p. 349).

This contradiction between two different views of the imperfect subjunctive may arise because both seem to be equally speculative.

7 Here again there is some contradiction in M. Wagner's opinons. While the archaic, artificial character of the imperfect subjunctive is mentioned several times (e.g. pp. 12, 13 n. 1, 53, 56, 293, 385, 386 n. 1), we read on p. 361, 'Nous concluerons dès lors que, si l'imparfait du subjonctif est, chez les prosateurs du XIIIe siècle, un élément de syntaxe vivant dans les propositions hypothétiques relatives au présent ou à l'avenir, ou intemporelles ainsi que dans les propositions assimilées, il est surtout un *élément de style* dont on tentera plus loin de discuter la valeur et la portée.'

fourteenth century the subjunctive is less frequent still. Prose usage, with a few exceptions, admits only the refractory verbs, but verse is less restricted. The subjunctive is not a living construction in the spoken language, although it occurs at the end of the century in certain conditions: in popular speech, which often archaises, and in refined speech, where it survives in certain fixed expressions and adds a touch of elegance, 'une note élégante, polie, une pointe de préciosité comparable à celle que, de nos jours, constitue, à Paris, l'emploi d'un passé défini au cours d'un récit oral' (p. 403).[8]

If the imperfect subjunctive is archaic by the twelfth century, we can expect it to be well and truly archaic by the fifteenth. In M. Wagner's view, if the French language had developed freely the subjunctive would have been discarded long before (p. 374). The last 200 years of the history of the subjunctive are summed up as follows.

> Si, partant du règne de Charles VI (1380–1442) à cheval sur les XIVe et XVe siècles, et descendant le cours du temps jusqu'à Montaigne, nous étudions la destinée du type centré autour de deux subjonctifs,[9] nous remarquerons que *seuls* figurent dans cet emploi les verbes auxiliaires: *être, pouvoir, devoir, vouloir*, les verbes *valoir, convenir, falloir, voir, cuider* et enfin les verbes *aimer, oser, demander, dire*; pas un autre qu'eux n'est relevé par nous dans nos fiches, ainsi qu'en font foi les exemples qui suivent. [p. 345; the date of the first examples shows that this restriction of use applies from 1380].

Subsequently this list is extended to cover *chaloir* and any verb accompanied by *volontiers* (pp. 407–8). But any other instance occasionally found in verse constitutes a *hapax*, induced by the needs of rhyme or alliteration, etc. (p. 406 n. 3).

There are twenty-two exceptions among the examples quoted by M. Wagner. Eighteen of them are in verse, which leaves only two examples from the *Quinze Joyes*, one from the *Débat des Hérauts* and one from Commines, which are at variance with his statement. However, this small proportion is not representative of prose usage. The

---

8 This view seems to be consistent only with the view expressed on p. 392 (above, n. 6).

9 A footnote makes it clear that this statement covers not only hypothetical sentences with both clauses in the subjunctive but also odd subordinates and independent principals in the subjunctive. M. Wagner also includes among his examples hypothetical sentences with the subordinate in the imperfect indicative and the principal in the subjunctive. Accordingly, any occurrence of the imperfect subjunctive is valid for consideration.

Quinze Joyes has more examples of the subjunctive. I quote them all, and indicate when the two other versions of this text (mentioned above) have a comparable construction.

> *Quinze Joyes* (Rouen ms., 1464), p. 9, A Dieu plaise que je ne vive gueres! Au moins fussés vous quite de moy, et n'*eussés* plus de desplaisir de moy. (*Editio princeps*, 1480–90, au moins ne *fissies* vous compte de moy et *neussies* plus de desplaisir pour moy.)
>
> p. 14, mais, ce m'aist Dieux, si ce ne fust vostre honneur et le mien, je n'en *parlasse* ja. (Péronne ms., 1468–70, *e.p.*)
>
> p. 25, je amasse mieulx qu'elles fussent a leurs mesons, et si *feissent* elles si elles savoient bien le plesir que elles me font. (P.)
>
> p. 37, Pleust a Dieu, mon amy, que vous ne le feissés jamés si je ne vous en *parlasse*. (P., *parloie*.)
>
> p. 55, Si je fusse femme qui me gouvernasse mauvesement je ne me *mervoillasse* pas. (P. ne *m'esmerveilleroie gaires*; *e.p. ne men esbahisse tant*.)
>
> p. 112, Ha a, mes chieres amies, fait elle, si ma fille eust fait faulte, il ne m'en challist, quar moy mesmes la *estranglasse*. (P.)

Variation in usage is noticeable only between the two mss., which are roughly contemporary. The printed text shows no tendency to replace the subjunctive, and in fact uses it once where the mss. use the indicative.

> *Editio princeps*, p. 26, (le) poisson qui est en la nasse qui auroit bon temps son le *lessast* viure en languissant. (Rouen ms., P., *lessoit*.)

In contrast, the *Quinze Joyes* has numerous instances of the imperfect indicative and conditional. However, there is no doubt that the imperfect subjunctive is the minority construction. The only problem is the importance to be attached to it as a minority construction. The examples quoted of indifferent verbs are interesting not so much because they suggest that the restriction of the use of the subjunctive may have been exaggerated, but because all, except the last, appear in dialogue. Similarly, some of the examples where only refractory verbs are used appear in dialogue.

> *Quinze Joyes*, p. 46, si je *peusse* tant fere que elle prenist ce que vous li donnez, vostre besoigne *fust* faicte.[10] (*E.p. je scai bien que selle voulist—fust*.)

Whether the passages of dialogue in the *Quinze Joyes* may be taken

---

10 Refractory verbs occur with indifferent verbs in most of the examples already quoted. Cf., dialogue, pp. 31 *fussent – si fussent*, 23 *fusse*, 75 *fust*, 32 *deust*, 44

to represent the spoken language is impossible to decide. It is tempting to think that they may. In a text which, unlike most anti-feminist works, illustrates its point with typical and specific domestic situations, to use an inappropriate construction would seem uncharacteristic and self-defeating. In any case, the usage of the *Quinze Joyes* is paralleled in other texts. In the *Cent Nouvelles* the imperfect subjunctive, whether of indifferent or refractory verbs, occurs almost exclusively in dialogue, and, for each example, the same construction appears in Antoine Vérard's edition of 1486. We thus have two texts which show a modernising tendency in the case of the imperfect subjunctive A, but no such tendency here.

Cent Nouvelles, p. 58, M'amye, si j'*eusse* temps et lieu, je vous diroye telle chose que vous seriez bien contente.

p. 133, se je le *sceusse*, je ne le demandasse pas.

p. 140, Si j'en *eusse* comme aultresfoiz ay eu, je luy querroye tantost une femme.

p. 222, s'il y fust il vous *feist* bonne chere.[11]

Saintré has three examples of the subjunctive, all in dialogue.

p. 20, se je l'*eusse*, je le diroye voullentiers.

p. 398, je cuide bien et suis certaine que, si il se *trouvast* armé, que tel y a, qui de luy se mocque, qui n'y gaigneroit riens.[12]

The *Ovide moralisé* has nine examples, seven of them in dialogue.

p. 301, Et pensez, Paris, que se mon mary ne se *fiast* bien en moy, il m'eust bien laissé pour moy garder plus fortes gardes que je n'ay.

p. 71, de nuyt l'empestroit et attachoit comme l'en *feïst* une autre vache.[13]

And *Alixandre l'Orphelin* five examples, of which two are in dialogue.

p. 2, se tout le monde païens et crestiens *venissent* icy a ost banie, je ne doubteroie leur esfors de nulle riens.

---

voulisse, 106 *convenist*, 61 *amasse mieulx*; examples not in dialogue, pp. 78 *fussent – si fussent*, 90 *fust*, 27 *fust – si peust*, 115 *deussent*, 2, 38 *voulist*, 80 *voulissent*, 53, 54, 68 *vallist mieulx*, 52 *amast mieulx*, 83 *feist volontiers*.

11 Cf., refractory verbs, pp. 140 *si fusse – fust*, 164 *si peusse – eschapperoit*, 164 *si peusse – seroit*, 244 *si fust – feroye*, 263 *si fust – seroie*; and, the only example not in dialogue, 46 *voluntiers decelast – si osoit* (V., v. *declarast – si osast*).

12 Cf. p. 134 *se ne fust*.

13 Cf., dialogue, pp. 95 *peussiez avoir attendu*, 170 *feïst – se te fusses offert*, 175 *si fussiez – seroit*, 175 *feust – se puissons* (= *peüssions*?), 210 *deüst*, 219 *deüsse*; and, narrative, p. 129 *deüssent*.

p. 26, et a juré . . . que se il *tenist* Morgain en point . . . , jamais ne s'*entre-
meïst* de nul chevalier engingner.

p. 43 et se nul *venist* avant qui me demandast . . . , je luy responderoie.[14]

Elsewhere we find occasional examples of the subjunctive.

Nouvelles inédites du XVe siècle, p. 11, dialogue, point ne se *feist* se j'y peusse
remedier.

p. 40, Et se elles se aymassent, leur honneur *gardassent* et leurs armes.

Jehan de Paris, p. 32, dialogue, ce il ne *fust* bien saige, il n'eust sceu. . . .

After this, the use of the imperfect subjunctive by Christine de
Pisan or Alain Chartier is not in itself a characteristic of their elaborate
and Latinised prose style (if it was, it would surely be more common).

Livre de la Paix, p. 71, Trop lui *ennuyast* estre poursuivis longuement d'une
chose.

Quadrilogue invectif, p. 32, se tous ceulx qui a ce se soubtillent *joignissent*
ensemble leurs entendemens . . . , ilz *gaignassent* a la prosperité. . . .

From examples such as these it is reasonable to draw a number of
conclusions about the usage of the fifteenth century contrary to those
of M. Wagner.—That the subjunctive, while the minority construction,
is neither rare nor restricted to refractory verbs. That, unless it is an
accident that several texts use the subjunctive in dialogue (an accident
which repeats itself in the following century), and unless a host of
different constructions are archaisms simply because they are less
common than others, the imperfect subjunctive does not behave like
an archaism. And that verse usage, even if we accept that considerations
of rhyme, alliteration, etc., can be influential, is not to be dismissed as
unrepresentative, since it is not different from the usage of prose. It is
perhaps a relief to think that the style of certain verse texts which
might seem racy does not have to be judged by M. Wagner's criterion:
'Disons-le net: les quelques exemples de: *Se + imparfait subjonctif
B–C* . . . *imparfait subjonctif* B–C que nous relevons dans les textes du
XVe siècle sont les rappels d'un âge révolu, les échos d'une ancienne
syntaxe que connaissent seuls les lettrés' (p. 405). For instance *Pathelin*,
which has seven examples of the subjunctive, four with indifferent
verbs.

v. 603, Qui me *paiast*, je m'en *allasse*.

v. 826, se j'*eusse* aide, je vous *liasse*.

14 Cf., dialogue, p. 10 *se peüssez*; and, narrative, p. 30 *voluntiers eussent*.

v. 880, Au moins qu'il me baillast ung gage
          ou mon argent, je m'en *allasse*.
v. 1593,   se je *trouvasse*
          ung sergent, je te *fisse* prendre.[15]

And Villon, who has thirteen, seven of them with indifferent verbs.

Test., v. 121, Se, pour ma mort, le bien publique
              D'aucune chose vaulsist mieulx,
              A mourir comme ung homme inique
              Je me *jujasse*.
v. 960, Je m'en *risse*, se tant peusse maschier Lors.
v. 1780, S'elle *eust* le chant 'Marionnette' . . . ,
          Elle *allast* bien a la moustarde.
v. 1958, S'il *sceust* jouer a ung tripot,
          Il *eust* de moy le Trou Perrete.[16]

We could expect rhyme, alliteration, etc., to cause the imperfect
subjunctive to be used more often in verse than in prose. In fact I do
not know of a fifteenth century work which is really extravagant in
its use of the subjunctive. I have noted thirty instances of the subjunctive in Charles d'Orléans, nine with indifferent verbs;[17] but this
proportion bears comparison with that in the *Quinze Joyes* (Rouen

15 Cf. vv. 666, 1355 *peussiez*, 975 *fust*.
       With *Pathelin* cf. *Le Recueil Trepperel*, I, *Sotties*, *Trote Menu*, vv. 15 *eusse*, 88
    se fussions; II, *Farces*, *Sermon nouveau*, vv. 18 *fust*, 70 *fussiés*; *Beaucoup veoir*, v. 9
    fusse – si puisse; *Le Savetier*, vv. 23 *se eusse – baisasse volontiers*, 56 *si fussent –*
    passeroient. (The editors attribute these works to the last twenty years of the
    fifteenth century.)
16 Cf. *Test.*, vv. 1228 *si fust – eust*, 1572 *fissent*, 1988 *feisse*; and, refactory verbs,
    144 *si peusse – feusse*, 1571 *fussent*, 1956 *voulentiers beusse*; *Poésies diverses*, VIII,
    v. 97 *feusse*; X, v. 21 *se peusse*; XVI, v. 97 *feusse*.
       In three further examples the value of the imperfect subjunctive is uncertain.
    Test., v. 201 'se j'eusse estudié . . . , j'*eusse* (A or BC?) maison et couche molle';
    cf. v. 1486; *Poésies diverses*, XIV, v. 26.
17 Indifferent verbs, *Ballades*, IV, v. 10 *oseroit – si eust*; VII, v. 14 *si eusse – lairoye*;
    XXV, vv. 19 *si fust – eusse*, 25 *si avoye – meisse*; *Chansons*, XXV, v. 1 *se eusse*;
    Rondeaux, XII, v. 13 *parlasse – si feusse*; LXXX, v. 2 *si peusse – donnasse*; CLXXIV,
    v. 9 *si fust – eusse*; CCLIX, v. 11 *se peusse – parlasse*.
       Refractory verbs, *Retenue*, v. 253 *deusses*; *Ballades*, X, v. 5 *mieulx vaulsist*;
    XIX, v. 8 *aymasse mieulx*; XXV, v. 9 *deusse*; CXVII, v. 14 *deust*; *Chansons*, XXVIII,
    v. 12 *si fust*; XLII, v. 5 *aymasse mieulx*; XLVIII, v. 12 *fust*; LV, v. 11 *peust*; *Com-*
    plaintes, V, v. 15 *se feussiez*; *Rondeaux*, L, v. 6 *vaulzist mieulx*; LXXXVII, v. 1
    si fust; XCV, v. 9 *mieulx me fust*; CLXX, v. 9 *mieulx amassent*; CCLXXXVI, v. 5
    amasse mieulx; CCCXXVII, v. 12 *deust*.

ms.), which has thirty-five instances of the subjunctive, six with indifferent verbs.

During the sixteenth century the use of the imperfect subjunctive in prose works is comparatively uncommon, but not as exceptional as is thought (p. 478).

> *Loyal Serviteur*, pp. 218–19, toutesfois je suis vierge, et ne feiz jamais mal de mon corps ne avons pas voulenté d'em faire si je n'y *feusse* contraincte.
>
> p. 231, Sire, si j'eusse fuy, je ne *fusse* pas icy.
>
> *Grand Parangon*, p. 266, *Célestine*, Car sy elle *fust* encore en vie, je ne *fisse* pas beaucop de choses que je fais.
>
> Sala, *Tristan*, p. 127, je l'*achevasse* voluntiers plustost aujourd'huy que demain.
>
> Despériers, *Nouvelles Récreations*, Si j'eusse esté un sot, je ne *fusse* pas où je suis.
>
> *Cymbalum*, il me semble que, si cela *fust*, vous feriez choses plus merveilleuses. (Both examples in *Phrases hypothétiques*, p. 344 n. 2.)
>
> Rabelais, p. 41, *Gargantua*, Si je montois aussi bien comme j'avalle, je *feusse* pieçà hault en l'aer.
>
> p. 249, *Pantagruel*, O compaing, si je *montasse* aussi bien comme je avalle, je *fusse* desja . . .
>
> p. 480, *Tiers Livre*, Dea! si je *oasse* [*sic*] jurer quelque petit coup en cappe, cela me soulageroit d'autant.
>
> p. 653, *Quart Livre*, Dea! s'il *jectast* vin bon . . . , cela seroit tollérable aulcunement.[18]

I do not know of a sixteenth century author later than Rabelais who uses the imperfect subjunctive in a subordinate introduced by *si*, or in both clauses of a hypothetical system. Also, the use of an indifferent verb (*montasse*, *jectast*) in the subordinate seems uncommon in the sixteenth century before Rabelais (two examples of *si + avoir* are referred to below, n. 20). On the other hand, eight out of nine examples in Rabelais occur in dialogue, as do all the earlier examples in the sixteenth century, plus six out of the eight I have noted in the *Heptaméron*. And there is no support for the view that in Rabelais the imperfect subjunctive is used facetiously (p. 406), since it is used in one of his letters—a serious request for money.

> p. 1016, Monseigneur, si venant icy M. de Saint-Ayl eust eu la commodité de vous saluer à son partement, je ne *fusse* de présent en telle nécessité et anxiété.

18 Cf. pp. 416, 459 *si feust*, 517 *si feussent*, 657 *feussent*.

This example is typical of later usage, the subjunctive of *être* and *devoir* continuing into the seventeenth century.[19]

> *Heptaméron*, pp. 167–8, Car, quant il vous eust pleu me favoriser, comme celles qui ne vous sont si proches que moy, je *feusse* maintenant mariée autant à vostre honneur que au myen.
>
> p. 405, si ce n'estoit le doubte que je faictz s'il est vray ou non, vous *fussiez* desja au fond de l'eaue.[20]
>
> Brantôme, *Dames galantes*, p. 34, l'on en *deust* dire de mesmes de plusieurs marys.
>
> p. 344, si je fusse estée bien fine et bien advisée . . . , je ne *fusse* pas maintenant en ceste paine.
>
> Montaigne, *Essais*, p. 111, Mais en les maniant et repassant [*sc.* telles imaginations], au long aller, on les apprivoise sans doubte. Autrement de ma part je *fusse* en continuelle frayeur et frenesie.
>
> p. 714, Je *desirasse* d'aucuns Princes que je connois, qu'ils en fussent plus espargnans et justes dispensateurs.
>
> p. 1119, Je les *visse* volontiers deviser, promener, et soupper!
>
> p. 1237, Si j'avois des enfans masles, je leur *desirasse* volontiers ma fortune.

M. Wagner does not distinguish between the usage of the fifteenth and sixteenth centuries, for in his view both show us nothing more than archaic examples which become gradually rarer. Yet, if the examples quoted reflect the usage of the sixteenth century, there are two significant differences. Firstly, few verbs are attested in the subjunctive during the sixteenth century. Of these none is common except *être*, and only one other verb—*devoir*—is attested more than twice. Secondly, a change occurs before the middle of the century. The imperfect subjunctive tends not to be used in both clauses of a hypothetical system, or in the subordinate alone, but to be restricted to the principal. (However, this restriction of use is not absolute. Haase, §66 A, observes that Malherbe—but Malherbe alone—uses *si* with the imperfect subjunctive.) Such differences stand out against earlier usage and suggest that the obsolescence of the imperfect sub-

---

19 A. Haase, *Syntaxe française du XVIIe siècle.* §66 A.

20 Cf., dialogue, pp. 122, 371 *fusse*, 307 *fussions*, 343 *deussent*; narrative, pp. 350–1 *fussent*, 375 *deussent*; *Satyre Ménippée*, p. 8 *fusse*.

   Needless to say, the subjunctive occurs in verse as well, e.g. Marot, *L'Enfer*, *si fust*; Me *Pierre Faifeu*, pp. 16, v. 237 *fust*, 112, v. 98 *si peust – fust*; Scève, *Délie*, 433, 437, *deust*; but perhaps most interestingly in dramatic verse, e.g. *Pionnier de Seurdre*, v. 336 *fusse*; *Recueil Trepperel*, I, *Feste des Roys*, vv. 5 *si eust*, 262 *deussions*; *Sots 'escornez'*, v. 33 *fusses*; *Sots ecclésiastiques*, vv. 116 *fisse*, 287 *voulsisse*, 328 *si eusse – fusse*; II, *Saincte Caquette*, v. 179 *faulsist*.

junctive is not observable earlier than the sixteenth century, and is a gradual process even at this date. The use of the subjunctive in a principal clause, to judge from Montaigne's *desirasse*, seems to remain free to some extent, and, to judge from the preponderance of examples in dialogue, or in the first and second persons, may persist in the spoken language.

In comparison, the usage of the fifteenth century still seems to be productive. M. Wagner denies it this quality (even in the twelfth century) on the grounds that it is restricted to the refractory verbs that resist the spread of *si* + imperfect indicative – conditional. But this is not so, and his list of refractory verbs needs to be examined. *Aimer mieux*, or rather the fixed expression *j'amasse mieux*, and *vaulsist mieux* can be considered refractory if, as seems to be the case, the corresponding conditional forms are less frequent. *Etre* is common in the subjunctive, and certainly not limited to the fixed expressions (*se*) *ne fust*, for which there is also no usual equivalent in the indicative. *Pouvoir*, *devoir* and *vouloir*—the last two occurring chiefly in a principal clause —are not uncommon in the subjunctive. But most often they, and *être* when used in free constructions, are not refractory (pp. 412 ff.). Why the modal auxiliaries should continue to be used in the subjunctive is not explained very clearly. M. Wagner says that it is because, by their intrinsic sense, they admit polite, discreet attenuations of meaning which the imperfect subjunctive can provide (p. 411). If this is so, why is the subjunctive used in only a small proportion of cases? But he points out that the conditional can attenuate as well (p. 433), and that the capacity for attenuation is not inherent in the imperfect subjunctive (p. 438). To support his view he remarks that these verbs resist the conditional more frequently and later than other verbs, but this is not quite exact. While *devoir* survives the longest, the most frequent verb by far in the fifteenth and sixteenth centuries is *être*, even when its use in fixed expressions is discounted. The other verbs of M. Wagner's list do not qualify as refractory, because they are illustrated by too few of his examples for a refractory tendency to be apparent, thus: *convenir*, two examples; *falloir*, one; *voir*, one; *cuider*, none; *oser*, one; *demander*, none; *dire*, one; *chaloir*, one. Finally, the view that *volontiers* exerts a refractory influence is questionable. It is not difficult to add to M. Wagner's examples of (*volontiers*) *alasse*, *donnasse* (two, pp. 346-7), e.g., fifteenth century, *eussent*, *beusse*, *baisasse*, *feist*, *decelast* (var. *declarast*); sixteenth century, *achevasse*, *desirasse*, *visse* (all these examples have been referred to already). But when *aller, avoir, faire* and, of course, many other verbs can occur in the subjunctive without *volontiers*, and when there are more examples of the conditional with *volontiers*,[21] the connection between the adverb and the subjunctive seems illusory.

Except perhaps in the case of the fixed expressions, the concept of refractory verbs is unable to account for the occurrence of the imperfect subjunctive in the fifteenth or sixteenth centuries. The evidence we have invites a simpler explanation—that the imperfect subjunctive is a minority construction, perhaps becoming gradually less common, but still used freely in a small proportion of hypothetical sentences as an exact alternative to the imperfect indicative and conditional; if it is more common and lasts longer in the case of certain verbs, this is because these verbs are more common anyway, the proportion of subjunctive and indicative remaining roughly the same with all verbs. The imperfect subjunctive appears to be an exact alternative to the imperfect indicative and conditional because, apart from frequency of use, it is impossible to perceive a difference between the two constructions, semantic or stylistic, or, in the case of dialogue, regional or social.[22]

21 Examples of *volontiers* + conditional: fifteenth century, *Quinze Joyes*, p. 82 *s'emploieroit*; *Saintré*, pp. 20 *diroye*, 134 *verroye*; *Ovide moralisé*, p. 326 *sauroye*; *Comte d'Artois*, p. 48 *diroye*; Villon, *Test.*, v. 194 *ameroie*; Ch. d'Orléans, *Ballades*, xv, v. 13 *auroye*; xxxvii, v. 13 *feroit*; xcviii, v. 12 *feroye*; ci, v. 29 *feroient*; *Chansons*, xxxix, v. 1 *embleroye*, xlvii, v. 3 *vouldroye*; sixteenth century, Rabelais, pp. 40 *laverois*, 370 *prirois*; *Heptaméron*, p. 335 *demanderois*; Marguerite de Navarre, *Lettres inédites*, No. 98 *iroit*; La Boétie, *Servitude volontaire*, p. 155 *irois*: Montaigne, *Essais*, pp. 164 *dirois*, 315 *demanderois*, 1187 *donrrois*; Brantôme, *Dames galantes*, pp. 178 *desirerois*, 226 *alleguerois*, 384 *descrirois*, 442 *dirois*.

22 Many of the examples already quoted show how difficult it is to detect the touch of old-fashioned elegance which M. Wagner attributes to the imperfect subjunctive at the end of the fourteenth century. The following show that it is impossible. *Pathelin*, v. 666, 'Se *peussiez* esclarcir ma merde, maistre Jehan?' (the question mark, which seems popular with editors, is not needed); Villon, *Test.*, v. 1988, 'Je *feisse* pour eulx petz et rotes'; *Saincte Caquette*, v. 179, 'Il me *faulsist* aller pisser'.

For the sixteenth century A. Sechehaye, 'L'Imparfait du subjonctif et ses concurrents dans les hypothétiques normales en français,' *Rom. Forsch.*, xix (1901), pp. 321–406, considers that the imperfect subjunctive is predominantly a feature of popular usage. 'Dans le langage populaire notre imparfait du subjonctif semble donc avoir vécu davantage que dans le langage plus châtié des humanistes et des lettrés de la Renaissance . . . Nous voyons que ce sont des auteurs comme Marot, Rabelais, Marguerite de Valois et Montaigne,

The fact that the imperfect subjunctive is a good deal more common in the fifteenth century than M. Wagner recognises probably affects certain of his opinions on earlier usage. Regarding the origin of the construction, unless the usage of the fifteenth century is a phenomenal departure from earlier usage, the imperfect subjunctive hardly seems to be the learned creation that M. Wagner sees it as; in any case, this theory is unacceptable as it stands.[23] Regarding Old French usage, if the subjunctive is not archaic towards the end of the Middle Ages,

---

c.-à-d. ceux de la première période ou ceux qui du temps de la Pléiade sont restés les plus fidèles à l'ancienne manière, qui offrent presque tous les exemples de l'emploi de l'imparfait du subjonctif' (p. 386). This opinion is interesting, and the fact that the imperfect subjunctive, while used generally in previous centuries, is now used only by certain authors may well be significant. But it is difficult to see a common characteristic which unites them, and Sechehaye's definition seems oversimplified. To what degree the authors mentioned reflect popular (or even spoken) usage can be only a subject for speculation. However, some social differences may exist in the usage of the early seventeenth century. Oudin remarks that, except in the case of *devoir* ('car on dit ordinairement, vous deussiez desja avoir fait, pour, vous devriez'), the use of the imperfect subjunctive is characteristic of 'nostre vulgaire' (E. Winkler, *La Doctrine grammaticale française d'après Maupas et Oudin, Beihefte zur Zeitschr. f. rom. Phil.*, XXXVIII (1912) pp. 177–8).

23 The theory that the imperfect subjunctive BC is a learned creation is sprung upon the reader four pages before the end of M. Wagner's thesis: 'il serait bon d'ajouter que *la date* à laquelle apparaît le tour (XIIe siècle) peut légitimement faire supposer qu'il a une *origine savante*.

'Nous verrons donc en lui la création tardive (postérieure de trois siècles environ à la naissance du français) d'un clerc qui, profitant d'une conjoncture grammaticale favorable, voulut pourvoir notre langue d'un type de phrase qui rappelât, *en valeur*, le type latin *denarios si haberem, eos tibi darem*' (p. 539).

Fascinating as this theory is, it receives no more discussion than the passage quoted, plus a footnote about three times as long, and raises a number of problems. What, for instance, can be the meaning of 'une conjoncture grammaticale favorable'? What can be the point of inventing a construction corresponding to the Latin construction in value but not in form when such a construction (*si* + imperfect indicative – conditional) already exists (pp. 371 n., 443)? And how can the imperfect subjunctive BC be a learned creation of the twelfth century when it is already archaic by the twelfth century and may have been discarded by everyday usage long before that (above, n. 6)? The footnote adds the qualification that this theory does not apply to *être, pouvoir, vouloir* and *devoir*, so that we may be dealing not with a learned creation but with a case of analogical extension. But this qualification fails to account for *Alexis*, v. 202, 'Se tei *ploüst*, [i]ci ne volisse estra', which elsewhere (p. 136) is admitted as a valid example of a hypothesis referring to the present.

surely it is not archaic in the twelfth century, nor is it an artificial and learned construction; in this case its continuance in successive centuries is not extraordinary, and the special circumstances to which its continuance is attributed—the refractory verbs and stylistic considerations —may have been overstated. The affective nuances which M. Wagner associates with the imperfect subjunctive—courtesy, anxiety, regret, impatience and anger—seem rather too convenient. They are varied enough to account for a large number of examples. On the other hand, it is hard to know which nuance is to be seen in many cases, and harder still to conceive how the imperfect subjunctive can itself convey nuances as different as these. If a fairly definite nuance is often perceptible, this is because of the words used, not the mood. And M. Wagner, relying, naturally enough, on a subjective interpretation of examples, makes out a case for the stylistic use of the subjunctive which cannot finally be disproved or proved. But the view that the imperfect subjunctive, used for the imperfect indicative or conditional, has always been 'un élément de style extérieur à la syntaxe des phrases hypothétiques françaises' needs to be reconsidered.

Remarks on the list of hypothetical sentences

A particularly interesting part of *Les Phrases hypothétiques* is the list of different types of construction attested in successive centuries (pp. 453 ff.), showing that the great variety of constructions possible in Old French diminishes gradually but significantly in Middle French. Inevitably, the list is not exhaustive, and I mention below a few constructions which are not noted as late as the fifteenth or sixteenth centuries, or which seem to have been misunderstood.

1 Pluperfect subjunctive – pluperfect subjunctive (sixteenth century).

Pionnier de Seurdre, v. 224
  Ne me fusse mis a cousté,
  Il m'eust rué sur le visaige.

A unique example (at this date) of a protasis in which no subordinating word is used. To be added to the list (p. 460). Comparable examples are noted for the twelfth and thirteenth centuries (pp. 455, 462, *Roland*, v. 1102, *Fust i li reis, n'i oüssom damage*). Perhaps relatable to the fixed expressions *ne fust . . . , n'eust esté . . .*

2 Imperfect indicative – *si* + pluperfect subjunctive (fifteenth and sixteenth centuries).

> *Cent Nouvelles*, pp. 241–2, ilz se vouloient entretuer, si les sergens ne fussent survenuz, qui les menèrent tous deux refroider en belle prison. (Vérard, *mais les sergens les menèrent.*)
> Brantôme, *Dames galantes*, p. 374, Les Poullonnois le voulloient retenir, s'il ne fust parti sans leur dire à Dieu.

To be added (pp. 460, 461). An unusual contaminated construction (cf. *Roland*, v. 440, *Ferir l'en volt, se n'en fust desturnet*), which is not a true hypothetical sentence, since the principal is not a consequence of the subordinate. The order of the two clauses is significant, and this case is not the same as *si* + pluperfect subjunctive – imperfect indicative (p. 254), e.g. *Saintré*, p. 227, *Se ne eusse esté bien tost secourue, vrayement je rendoye mon esperit.*
This second type, where the imperfect indicative is used for emphasis, is a proper hypothetical system, and not uncommon in the fourteenth and fifteenth centuries.

3 *Si* + present/imperfect indicative – past definite (fifteenth and sixteenth centuries).

> *Cent Nouvelles*, p. 111, Or laissez moy avoir mon tour; si je ne fays bien mon personnage, je ne fuz oncques si esbahy.
> p. 134, si Dieu vouloit prendre ma femme, jamais ne fu si eureux.

To be added (p. 474), since a variant of this type is noted for the twelfth century (p. 455), although it has been misinterpreted. The construction is elliptical. The clause in the past definite (where *ne ... oncques*, etc., is a regular feature) is not the principal, but the first term of a comparison of (in)equality, in which *si* or an expression of comparative degree allows the sense of the second term-cum-principal to be understood. Sometimes, as in Old French, the principal is expressed in a tense corresponding to that of the subordinate.

> *Alixandre l'Orphelin*, p. 38, se vous de ceste chose lui savez aider, oncques ne receüstes si bon guerredon de chose que vous feïssez comme vous avrez de ceste besoingne.

This usage seems to continue longer.

> *Heptaméron*, pp. 104–5, si Dieu le faict retourner en santé, jamais femme ne fut mieulx traictée que vous serez.

4 *Si* + imperfect indicative – imperative (fifteenth century).

Quinze Joyes, p. 84, Et s'il parloit a toy, escoute le.
p. 87, et s'il se ouffroit a te prendre, mercie l'en.
Cf. *Saintré*, pp. 119, 121; Villon, *Test.*, v. 1873.

To be added (p. 474). No examples are noted in earlier centuries.
These sentences are, so far, the earliest instances of a construction
which still occurs sometimes in Modern French.[24]

5 *Qui* + present indicative – present indicative (fifteenth and sixteenth centuries).

Cent Nouvelles, p. 216, il semble que vous soiés courroussée, qui vous voit.
(Vérard, à vous veoir.)
Cf. *Quinze Joyes*, p. 22; *Pathelin*, v. 188.
Brantôme, *Dames galantes*, p. 442, qui se veut servir de la lampe, il y faut
mettre souvant de l'huylle.
Cf. *ibid.*, p. 294; Montaigne, *Essais*, p. 687.

To be added (pp. 474, 477). An example is noted in the twelfth
century (p. 464).

6 *Qui* + imperfect indicative – imperfect indicative/conditional.
(fifteenth century).

Cent Nouvelles, p. 123, brief, qui l'oyoit, il sembloit que le monde fust
finé.
p. 58, et qui l'oyoit, elle ne le feroit pour aussi gros d'or.
Cf. *ibid.*, p. 75. On p. 56 the past definite occurs in a sentence of the same
type as 3 above.

To be added (p. 474). No earlier examples are noted. While restricted to the verb *oïr* ('à l'entendre parler'), this construction seems
to be the counterpart in past narrative to type 5.

7 *Qui* + imperfect subjunctive – imperfect indicative/conditional
(fifteenth century).

Cent Nouvelles, p. 38, Et qui a ceste heure l'oyst, mieulx luy vauldroit la
mort.
Cf. *Saintré*, p. 405, qui oïst—il sembloit.

To be added (p. 474). A comparable example (*qui veïst – sambler
poroit*) is noted in the thirteenth century (p. 469). An alternative
construction to type 6.

24 H. Sten, *Les Temps du verbe fini (indicatif) en français moderne*, Copenhagen
1952, p. 138.

8 *Si* + present/perfect subjunctive – present/future indicative (fifteenth and sixteenth centuries).

> *Saintré*, p. 120, Et se au departir de cestes armes, vostre compaignon ait le meilleur, je vueil et ordonne que, la present, lui donrrez vostre dit bracellet.
> Cf. *ibid.*, pp. 130 and (perfect subjunctive) 120, 122, 125.

To be added (pp. 475, 478). Examples are noted in previous centuries up to the fourteenth (while Sechehaye and Lerch quote several examples in the fifteenth).[25] Also occurs in the sixteenth century.

> Sala, *Tristan*, p. 107, et si le Nigromant le puisse vaincre il luy fera trancher la teste.
> Cf. p. 57. Isolated examples in Du Fail and Palissy.[26]

No one explanation. e.g. the influence of Anglo–Norman (pp. 308–9 and Sechehaye—surely inapplicable at this date anyway), or the influence of Latin (Lerch) seems able to account for all the instances of this unusual construction.

9 *Si* + imperfect subjunctive – imperfect subjunctive, present/future hypothesis (sixteenth century).

> *Recueil Trepperel*, I, 350; *Sots ecclésiastiques*, v. 328,
> se j'eusse ung eveschié
> Je fusse content.
> *Maître Pierre Faifeu*, p. 112, v. 98, S'il peust sortir de leurs mains, il fust riche.
> Cf. *Grand Parangon*, p. 266; Rabelais, p. 249, quoted above.

To be added (p. 477), since it is not noted after the fifteenth century.

10 *Si* + present indicative – *et/ou* + present subjunctive – present/future indicative (fifteenth and sixteenth centuries).

> *Quinze Joyes*, p. 90, S'il est gentil home et le prince face sa mandee et son armee, si la dame vieult il ira.
> Brantôme, *Dames galantes*, p. 130, les corps humains ne se peuvent jamais guieres bien porter si tous leurs membres et parties . . . ne font ensemblement leurs exercices . . . , et n'en facent une commune concordance.
> Cf. *ibid.*, p. 206 (*ou*).

25 Sechehaye, p. 338; E. Lerch, *Hist. frz. Syntax*, II, pp. 209–12.
26 E. Borlé, *Observations sur l'emploi des conjonctions de subordination dans la langue du XVIe siècle*, Paris, 1927, p. 94.

To be added (pp. 478, 487). This is not noted later than the four-teenth century, but in fact continues into the seventeenth (E. Gamillscheg, *Hist. frz. Syntax*, p. 731).

11 *Si* + imperfect indicative – *et* + imperfect indicative – conditional (sixteenth century).

> Brantôme, *Dames galantes*, p. 109, il en pourroit mourir si j'en disois le moindre mot et le declarois à la justice.

To be added (pp. 477, 489). Not noted after the thirteenth century. This type, and the preceding one, show that in the sixteenth century the second subordinate is not compulsorily introduced by *que* (p. 492), any more than it is in the modern language.

12 *Que* introducing a second or subsequent hypothetical subordinate. M. Wagner's implication that this use is first attested in the four-teenth century (p. 487), and his remark that it is rare at first, gaining ground towards the end of the fifteenth century and becoming productive only during the sixteenth (p. 485), need correction. It is attested from the twelfth century in the form *si* + present indicative – *et que* + present subjunctive (*a*).

Aspremont, v. 6739

> Se recreant ne vos en fas clamer
> Et que n'en puise vostre teste porter,
> Li rois me face si vilment demener
> Come laron qui est repris d'embler.

Benoît, *Ducs de Normandie*, v. 19741

> Si vers mun mandement s'orguille
> Et que isi faire neu vuille,
> J'essaierai od les Franceis
> E od Normanz e od Daneis
> Qu'il le fera.

Cf. *ibid.*, vv. 23305, 27923.

(Thirteenth century) *Barlaam en prose*, p. 550, se vous avés le piour de la desputison et ke Balaans vous sourmont, vous serés livré a tourment.

Cf. *ibid.*, p. 551, *Livres dou Tresor*, pp. 122, 123, 123, 138; *Abrejance de l'Ordre de Chevalerie* vv. 1724, 9377, 10967, Baudouin de Condé, i.267, *Prisons d'Amour* v. 12.

Si + imperfect indicative – *et que* + imperfect subjunctive (*b*) is attested from the thirteenth century.

Merlin, I, 64, se il venoient en ceste terre et que fussent par che foriest, il trouveroient Merlin.
Cf. *Abrejance*, vv. 3171, 3651.

And *si* + imperfect subjunctive – *et que* + imperfect subjunctive (*c*) from the twelfth century.

Perceval, v. 8434,
  Mais se vos laississiez cest port
  Et ensemble od mei venissiez
  Soz cel arbre et que feïssiez
  Une chose . . .
Cf. (thirteenth century) *Troie en prose*, p. 155; *Abrejance*, v. 3333.

By the fourteenth century the use of *que* is common in certain texts, e.g. *Ménagier de Paris* and *Modus et Ratio*.[27] In the fifteenth we find multiple examples in the *Vieux Coustumier de Poictou* and occasional examples in a variety of texts.[28] M. Wagner's opinion that there is an increase in the use of *que* towards the end of the fifteenth century is unsupported, since he has observed only one example for the whole century (p. 529). I have found no evidence to support it either, and until the end of the century the use of *que* seems uncommon compared to the simple co-ordination of the subordinate by *et/ou*. If this relation is reversed in the following century, it is not to the exclusion of the alternative construction, as M. Wagner says, and the use of *que* seems to be productive considerably earlier.

Two inferences can be drawn from the various constructions mentioned above. Firstly, certain of them are older than has been stated, and of the three exceptions (*si* + pluperfect indicative – conditional perfect, *si* + imperfect indicative – *et que* + imperfect subjunctive, and *si* + present indicative – *et que* + present subjunctive) to the statement that all the constructions of Modern French are attested in the twelfth,

27 *Ménagier*, type (*a*), I, 36–7, 96–7, 174, 221; II, 52, 72, 76, 295; type (*b*), I, 33, 72, 101; II, 58.
    Modus, type (*a*), I, 21–2, 27, 30, 31, 37, 39, 48, 75, 125, 135, 166, 185, etc.
28 *Vieux Coustumier*, nine examples. Also *Livre de la Paix*, p. 66; Mathieu d'Escouchy, III, 322–3; *Quinze Joyes*, p. 63 (paralleled in two other versions); *Cent Nouvelles*, p. 179 (paralleled in Vérard); Ch. d'Orléans, *Rondeaux*, XXIII, v. 8; *L'Amant rendu cordelier*, vv. 535, 1681; *Recueil Trepperel*, II, 140, *La Cène des dieux*, v. 1276.

thirteenth and fourteenth centuries (p. 490), only the first still stands. Secondly, there are more constructions in the sixteenth century than has been stated, and the process of simplification of the great variety of constructions possible in Old French has not been accomplished by this time (p. 485). The continuance of the constructions mentioned in this rapid survey, and the continuance in use of the imperfect subjunctive, both point to the same conclusion: that the process of simplification of hypothetical constructions is more gradual and more complex than a reading of *Les Phrases hypothétiques* suggests.

A. H. Diverres

Chivalry and *fin'amor* in *Le Chevalier au Lion*[1]

Among the many contributions to the study of *Le Chevalier au Lion* is a penetrating analysis of Yvain's courtship by the honorand, who demonstrates the full irony of a situation in which a lady is persuaded to marry the man who has very recently killed her husband.[2] From this study of a single episode he goes on to draw certain conclusions about Chrétien's intentions in the romance as a whole which I do not share. It may seem ungracious to take issue with a very old friend in a volume in his honour, but I venture to publish my own conclusions, some very tentative, in the belief, shared by Frederick Whitehead, that it is only by approaching a work of literature from different angles that we can hope to get closer to its author's purpose. Chrétien is describing his ideal heroes in situations which must have been very real to his public, however unreal the world in which they take place, and he is clearly preoccupied, in varying degrees according to the romance, it seems to me, with natural human love, courtesy, chivalry and knightly prowess in the social life of the courts of his day. That *Le Chevalier au Lion* reflects attitudes towards human behaviour is made plain in the prologue, in which the failure of the knights of the time to live up to the ideals of courtesy is stated.

> Mes ore i a mout po des suens [i.e. disciples of Love];
> Que a bien pres l'ont tuit leissiee,
> S'an est amors mout abeissiee;
> Car cil, qui soloient amer,

---

1 This article was written before the publication of T. Hunt's article entitled 'Tradition and originality in the prologues of Chrestien de Troyes' (*F.M.L.S.*, VIII (1972), pp. 320–44), in which an interpretation of the *sens* close to mine is given. The edition used in its preparation is that by T. B. W. Reid, Manchester, 1942. References to *Erec et Enide* are made to the C.F.M.A. edition by M. Roques.

2 'Yvain's wooing', *Medieval Miscellany presented to Eugène Vinaver . . .*, Manchester, 1965, pp. 321–36.

Se feisoient cortois clamer
Et preu et large en enorable.
Ore est amors tornee a fable
Por ce que cil, qui rien n'an santent,
Dïent qu'il aimment, mes il mantent,
Et cil fable et mançonge an font,
Qui s'an vantent et droit n'i ont.[3]

This makes it difficult to share the view that Chrétien is indulging in a purely rhetorical exercise aimed primarily at embellishing an inherited story. His adaptation of the material must surely include concerns other than literary taste and rhetorical tradition. The discussion of Chrétien's romances against the background of twelfth century aristocratic society has already been undertaken by Erich Köhler, though his attempt would appear to be over-systematised.[4] It is also one of the approaches adopted by Professor Frappier for Le Chevalier au Lion.[5] At the risk of omitting to acknowledge what I owe them both, and no doubt others, I wish to discuss briefly the role of chivalry and fin'amor in this romance. Literary historians have moved a long way since Foerster, who, in his introduction to the text, stated that it was nothing but a psychological study of human love.[6] For Professor Frappier the action centres on 'deux conceptions plus ou moins opposées, mais finalement conciliées . . . amour et chevalerie'.[7] While I agree that both elements are present in the romance, I hope to show that Chrétien lays far greater emphasis on chivalry than on love, and that there is, in fact, no real conflict between them.

Professor Frappier sees in the development of Yvain's character an 'ascension chevaleresque' from a 'prouesse égoïste et orgueilleuse' to a 'bravoure à toute épreuve . . . mise au service du droit, de la justice, de toutes les causes généreuses'.[8] At the beginning of the romance it is made clear that Yvain already possesses most of the characteristics of the ideal knight errant. Lunete decides to help him to win Laudine's hand because, in addition to his courage, determination and knightly prowess, he alone had been courteous enough to talk to her and treat

3 Lines 18–28.
4 E. Köhler, Ideal und Wirklichkeit in der höfischen Epik, Tübingen, 1956.
5 Having first appeared as part of his 'cours polygraphié' on Le Roman Breton, it was published in book form under the title of Etude sur Yvain ou le Chevalier au Lion de Chrétien de Troyes, Paris, 1969.
6 Kristian von Troyes, Der Löwenritter, Halle, 4th edn., 1912, p. xxxii, n. 1.
7 Op. cit., p. 187.
8 Op. cit., pp. 199–201.

her with due honour when, as a callow maiden, she had visited Arthur's court.[9] But pride is indeed his dominant trait, as Chrétien makes plain, and pride was one of the deadly sins that a knight must resist with all his might, since it corrupted the order of chivalry, according to Ramon Lull.[10]

The opening episode (ll. 42–722) serves more than one purpose in the narrative: it is designed to inform Yvain of the adventure of the fountain, so that he will set out in full knowledge of what it implies and will have no excuse for repeating any of the errors that Calogrenant has made through ignorance. It also provides an opportunity for depicting Yvain's pride and lack of self-control in contrast with Calogrenant's humility. Calogrenant is the butt of Kay's envious and malicious remarks to a greater extent than his cousin, yet he reacts to them with restraint, acceding graciously to Guenevere's request to hear the adventure on which he had embarked seven years earlier, though it does not redound to his credit. Yvain's response to his cousin's account is overbearing. Insensible as to whether he is humiliating Calogrenant in public, he accuses him of failing in his duty to the family honour by remaining silent for so long, and expresses his determination to avenge Calogrenant's shame. This provokes sarcastic comments from Kay, who accuses Yvain of being a braggart and challenges him to allow the court to witness his exploits against Calogrenant's victor. Showing sufficient restraint not to start a quarrel with Kay in the queen's presence, Yvain's reply is none the less as full of sarcasm as the seneschal's remarks, betraying wounded pride and deep anger. It reveals that he lacks the maturity, required of the true knight, to cultivate the necessary strength of character, charity, forbearance and patience to control his anger.[11] The others treat Kay's aggressive remarks far less seriously than Yvain, even the queen to whom he has spoken in a boorish and disrespectful manner (ll. 92–104).

---

9 Lines 1006–13. Yvain's high reputation for courtesy is also referred to by Gawain in ll. 2212–14.

10 'Y si el caballero con ser orgulloso mantiene el oficio de Caballería, fué muy otra aquella Caballería que empezó por la justicia y para sostener los humildes contra los orgullosos injustos' (*Libro de la Orden de Caballería, Parte* II, 34). Since no edition of the Catalan text is available to me, I have used a translation into modern Spanish. See R. Llull, *Obras Literarias*, ed. M. Batllori and M. Caldentey, Madrid, 1948.

11 '. . . conviene que recorra a la fortaleza, caridad, abstinencia y paciencia, que son refrenamiento de la ira y refrigerio de los trabajos que da' (R. Llull, *op. cit., Parte* VI, 15).

Yvain should not have risen to the bait dangled by a man who, throughout French romance, is largely a figure of fun, and he should have been less sensitive to the slur on the family honour, which was seen by him primarily as an attack on his own reputation.

It is at this point that Arthur appears and, learning of Calogrenant's adventure, decides to go in person to the fountain in company of his court. Yvain's chagrin knows no bounds, for he had intended to go there alone (ll. 678-9). If he accompanies the king, he fears that Kay or Gawain will request the privilege to fight the defender of the fountain, depriving him of the opportunity to do so. Is this fear justified? Since family honour is involved, it would have been difficult for Arthur to refuse a request by Yvain to challenge the defender of the fountain. The reasons for Yvain's disappointment are more complex. His desire to avenge family honour and his anger against Kay play a part, but to these must be added his desire for self-glory: he wishes to make certain that on him alone the honour of fighting Esclados will fall and that none will know whether he has succeeded or failed until their combat is over (ll. 718-22). This is why he decides to set off for the fountain without taking leave of Arthur. His precautions to ensure the secrecy of his departure and destination smack of disloyalty towards his lord and peers. He is breaking the custom of the boon, which, as Erich Köhler has convincingly shown,[12] is the conventional way at Arthur's court of granting permission to a knight to undertake an adventure. The search for glory at the expense of one's elders and betters was considered inexcusably presumptuous for a young knight in the twelfth century, as is illustrated by the rebuke given by William of Tancarville to young William Marshal, when, recently dubbed, he tried to ride ahead of more experienced knights in the battle of Drincourt in 1173.[13]

Once he has arrived at the fountain (ll. 800-906), Yvain acts in the same way as Calogrenant. He casts water on to the marble slab, though he has learnt that this action, carried out without a prior formal challenge, will be considered hostile by Esclados (ll. 491-516). Since the formal challenge before a single combat between knights is an established convention, Yvain once more knowingly breaks one of the basic rules of chivalry in his eagerness for glory. He disobeys another, when, after mortally wounding Esclados, he pursues him

---

12 'Le rôle de la "coutume" dans les romans de Chrétien de Troyes', *Romania*, LXXXI (1960), p. 391.

13 *L'Histoire de Guillaume le Maréchal*, ed. P. Meyer, I, Paris 1891, ll. 869-78.

pitilessly to the castle, in spite of his cries of distress. He has already avenged his family honour by defeating Esclados in single combat, but, still smarting under Kay's sarcasm, he feels that he needs a trophy of his victory, and his determination to obtain it overrides charity and mercy towards a wounded adversary, which were the hallmarks of chivalry.[14]

In this first part of the romance Yvain, though courageous and determined, well versed in courtesy and skilled at arms, still lacks certain characteristics essential to the perfect knight: humility, charity and *mesure* or the ability to control his anger and his thirst for glory. The extent to which his love for Laudine helps him to overcome these weaknesses will be dealt with later. However, it should be noted at this stage that Chrétien stresses the feudal relationship between the two at least as much as the courtly and matrimonial links. In his act of submission to Laudine, Yvain accepts as his principal duty towards her the defence of the fountain against all comers in terms that make him her liege man juridically as well as her lover and husband (ll. 2033–6).

Let us now pass on to what Professor Frappier calls the second stage in Yvain's development as a knight, his decision, under Gawain's influence, to attend tournaments in search of chivalry, a quest that will end in 'un dénuement spirituel',[15] and will be responsible for the break with Laudine, since he forgets to return to her at the end of the year accorded him for this purpose.

After Yvain's whirlwind courtship and marriage to Laudine and his successful defence of the fountain against Kay, whom he humiliates in front of Arthur and his jubilant court, the king accepts his hospitality for a week. While Chrétien spares only fifteen lines for Yvain's marriage to Laudine (ll. 2148–63), he devotes 150 to the celebrations laid on by Laudine for the entertainment of Arthur and his court (ll. 2320–477), a passage which is of considerable significance. Professor Frappier remarks that although he makes a distinction between true love and flirtation, 'Chrétien fait, avec bonne humeur, de larges concessions à l'hédonisme courtois'.[16] For my part, I suspect that Chrétien is less sympathetic to courtly hedonism than Professor Frappier makes

---

14 'El caballero sin caridad no puede ser sin crueldad . . . porque, si no tiene caridad a Dios y a su prójimo, ¿ . . . como tendrá misericordia de los que ha vencido que le piden merced?' (R. Llull, *op. cit.*, *Parte* vi, 5).

15 *Op. cit.*, p. 201.

16 *Op. cit.*, p. 187.

out, and that this description forms, together with the picture of
Arthur's court at the beginning of the romance, the background against
which Yvain's shortcomings until the break with Laudine are explained.

The prologue of the romance opens with a few lines describing
Arthur's court as the home of courtesy, prowess, largesse and honour,
followed by the inference that in Chrétien's own day true love is little
more than a hypocritical façade. But Arthur's court, as depicted in the
first scene, falls far short of the idealised picture. The king, a model of
chivalry according to the prologue, behaves with more than a suggestion of sloth and uxoriousness. Kay's behaviour, though in keeping
with his character throughout Chrétien's romances, and the quarrel
about etiquette accentuate this impression of a court far removed from
the ideal described in the prologue. This is emphasised later by Lunete's
statement that, apart from Yvain, none of the knights of the Round
Table, not even Arthur himself, had taken any notice of her during
her visit to the court. Further evidence of these shortcomings is to be
found in the episode of the daughters of the Seigneur de la Noire
Espine, the younger of whom fails to find either counsel or help at the
court in her predicament (ll. 4759–85). Only then will the king react
positively, asserting his authority in the name of justice as a true
medieval monarch should. It makes one wonder whether Chrétien's
purpose is not to suggest that life at court is inconducive to true
chivalry. One finds the same implicit criticism of court life in the
description of the festivities at Laudine's castle, for emphasis is laid on
the richness of the decorations and the variety of the entertainment.
So far so good; similar descriptions can be found in twelfth century
romances, including Chrétien's, without a hint of criticism. It is in
what follows that I see evidence of the unsuitability of such activities
to the knightly calling, in the social whirl attendant on the festivities,
in the flirtations between knights and ladies, particularly between
Gawain and Lunete, which will have no sequel. This is not *fin'amor*,
though Gawain will pledge his troth (ll. 2418–23). It is mere philandering, since he will forget her when he departs.

Yvain's first duty, now that he holds possessions from his wife, is to
defend them for her. But he is so dazzled by the outward trappings
of court life that he quickly succumbs to the arguments used by
Arthur's knights to persuade him to depart with them, particularly
those put forward so convincingly by Gawain (ll. 2484–538). The
arguments used are all associated with the courtly and chivalrous codes,
such as the dangers of uxoriousness and over-indulgence in pleasure

which bring about a decline in one's knightly prowess, the necessity to safeguard comradeship in arms and to strive continually for greater merit. All these arguments are valid in themselves, and Yvain is convinced by them, though misled into the belief that true chivalry is to be found at tournaments. He asks the unsuspecting Laudine for a boon which, if granted, will add to her honour and his. When she has agreed to it, as she must according to literary convention, he requests permission to accompany Arthur (not Gawain), so that he may perform at tournaments and escape the accusation of *recreantise* (ll. 2558–61). Laudine grants him leave of absence for twelve months and presents him with a ring which will protect him from harm and ensure his return, provided he does not forget her. After a tearful separation, Yvain leaves with the king and his court. The implications that this episode has for the love element will be discussed later, and I shall concentrate now on the chivalric aspect.

As many critics have noted, Gawain bears great responsibility in persuading Yvain to further his glory at tournaments rather than defend his lady's fountain against all comers as he had promised (ll. 2033–5). Throughout the romance Gawain is referred to as the model knight, yet he fails to mention service and duty in the speech summarised above. His own conduct is not above reproach. Later he will be unavailable when Lunete, to whom he had declared his love and offered his service during the festivities, is in desperate need of his help; and again when his relatives are in danger of their lives at the hands of Harpin de la Montagne. In the episode of the daughters of the Seigneur de la Noire Espine, the only one in which he happens to be present when needed, he champions an unjust cause (ll. 6346–7). It is true that in most romances an affair for Gawain is merely an exchange of verbal and physical courtesies with damsels, without any sense of permanency, and so in *Le Chevalier au Lion* he is depicted in the traditional mould. But the prominence given to his flirtation with Lunete, and its association with the description of the philandering knights and ladies, suggest that it fulfils a definite purpose in the structure of the romance. Gawain's conduct is typical of Arthur's court as depicted in this romance; he is the courtier knight *par excellence*, unrepresentative of true chivalry as exemplified by Yvain after he has recovered from his madness. I would suggest that the episode of the festivities at Laudine's castle illustrates the dangers of court life to the knight, that decadent courtesy to which Chrétien refers so disparagingly in his prologue and in which courtly gallantry masquerades as true love. The decline of chivalry under the influence of court life is affirmed by Etienne de Fougères in his *Livre des Manières*, written probably in the 1170s.

> Haute ordre fut chevalerie,
> mes or est ce trigalerie.
> Trop aiment dance et balerie
> et demener bachelerie.[17]

Though the period spent by Yvain in performing at tournaments in Gawain's company is discussed in a few lines (ll. 2670 ff.) this passage completes the picture of the corrupting influence of court life, in which tournaments play so important a part. The two knights attend tournaments wherever they are held; Yvain is the outstanding performer, while Gawain's main role is to honour him. This he does with such success that Yvain is intoxicated, to the extent of forgetting his promise to Laudine for fourteen months. The two knights rejoin Arthur's court at Chester, but instead of entering the city to pay their respects to the king they pitch their tents outside and hold court. They are such a centre of attraction that even the greatest of the knights, including the king, make their way to the camp.

The changing character of tournaments from a form of battle training to a sport in the more firmly ordered society of the twelfth century has been often noted.[18] Despite several attempts by the Church to prohibit them, from the Council of Clermont in 1130 onwards, tournaments continued to gain in popularity until they became social occasions with a strong element of pageantry. The practice of knights forming a partnership and fighting in tournaments as a pair became established. One such example is when William Marshal and Roger de Gaugi attended all the tournaments they could in northern France between 1177 and 1179, acquiring considerable renown and wealth.[19] It looks as if Chrétien viewed with misgiving this development of tournaments from a martial exercise to a spectacle in which ostentation and the spectator's adulation had become important factors, and considered that in his day they had become unsuitable for the practice of true chivalry.

---

17 Lines. 585–8. I am grateful to my colleague, Dr Anthony Lodge, for allowing me to quote from his recent, as yet unpublished, edition of this text.

18 Most recently by R. Barber, in *The Knight and Chivalry*, London, 1970, pp. 153–5.

19 *L'Histoire de Guillaume le Maréchal*, I, ll. 3381–424. This text also contains descriptions of tournaments as social occasions, e.g. ll. 3425–98.

Professor Perroy states that by the middle of the twelfth century those taking part in tournaments were so numerous that it was no longer possible for them all to be lodged in towns and castles, and so large camps were erected for the purpose.[20] C. R. B. Combellack considers that this is the situation at Chester when Yvain and Gawain pitch their tents outside the walls.

> Yvain and Gawain were not shunning Arthur; they came to Chester because he was there. Yvain might have had a second lapse of memory, but that both should forget a duty they owed the king is doubly impossible. The king's good will toward them both is proof enough in itself that they were not acting offensively toward him; he holds them both 'mout chiers' (l. 6503). I think they were unwilling to lodge in town and preferred to set up their headquarters outside because of what is a recurrent situation in Chrétien's romances, designed presumably to indicate the size and splendour of gatherings. In *Cligés* the emperor finds Cologne so crowded that more than 60,000 persons had to lodge outside. In *Lancelot*, because of the queen's presence, Nouauz is so crowded that not a fifth of those who had gathered could find lodgings in town, and more knights, including Lancelot, were lodged outside the town than in. Chester was doubtless crowded, and Yvain and Gawain had a large retinue to find lodgings for.[21]

Combellack's argument is that Chrétien wishes to show Yvain at the height of good fortune and happiness, and not on the pinnacle of *orgueil*, as proposed by Julian Harris.[22] For me, Harris's interpretation is closer to the truth. Yvain and Gawain reveal a lack of respect towards their lord which is quite contrary to the courtesy, humility and loyalty expected of a true knight. Combellack draws a false analogy with the passages from *Cligés* and *Le Chevalier de la Charrette*, for Chrétien states why the majority have to camp outside Cologne and Nouauz. No such statement is made about Chester. The detail that neither knight loses the king's goodwill carries no weight either, since Arthur's behaviour from the beginning of the romance until much later shows him to be a *roi fainéant*, presiding over a court at which false values dominate. Yvain's pride stands at its peak at this point, and it is due to his success in tournaments and the adulation showered on him. Arthur's action in going in person with his most illustrious knights to celebrate with Yvain and Gawain at their camp is the

---

20 *La Féodalité en France du Xe au XIIe siècle*, Paris, 1962, p. 53.
21 'Yvain's guilt', *S.P.*, LXVIII (1971), p. 21.
22 'The role of the lion in Chrétien de Troyes' *Yvain*', *P.M.L.A.*, LXIV (1949), p. 1147.

lionisation of a man who has won acclaim by his victories in tournaments and not by true feats of arms in battle.

In the middle of these celebrations Yvain realises for the first time that he has overstayed his leave. That he should have remembered this and not have to be reminded of it is important, and also that he should be filled with grief and shame. Now only does Laudine's messenger arrive, to accuse him of deceit and disloyalty and to announce before witnesses the formal break between her mistress and Yvain. Is it a measure of his decline that this time, unlike the day of Lunete's visit to Arthur's court, his behaviour towards the damsel is no more courteous than that of the other knights? The significance of the passage for the development of the love theme will be discussed later. It suffices now to note the similarity between the episode and the ceremony for the cancellation of a feudal contract between suzerain and vassal, in which the petitioner's case did not have to be proved nor a decree to be pronounced by a judge.[23]

We can pass quickly over Yvain's madness (ll. 2774–3041), since it has no direct bearing on Chrétien's treatment of chivalry. Brought on by his shame and despair at having broken his oath to Laudine, it reduces him to what has been interpreted as an animal state. While wandering naked through the forest Yvain succeeds in stealing a bow and five arrows which enable him to survive by hunting game. The precision of the number of arrows suggests that number symbolism is intended. The number five had many associations, but in Christian literature one came to predominate, that of the five senses, and so five frequently became the symbol of the flesh, confirming the above interpretation.[24] Yvain lives on raw venison like a predatory beast. The first sign of a gradual recovery is to be seen when he comes into contact with a hermit who, though unable to give spiritual aid, provides him with more wholesome fare. This continues until he is discovered asleep and still naked by the Dame de Noroison and her two damsels, and he is cured by the magic ointment.

Yvain's remaining adventures, which occupy over half the romance, can be dealt with more rapidly. They have been described by some critics either as his redemption or as an expiation for his crime against Laudine,[25] but it seems to me that neither interpretation is entirely

23 See M. Bloch, *Feudal Society* (trans. L. A. Manyon), London, 1961, pp. 228–30.
24 See V. C. Hopper, *Medieval Number Symbolism*, New York, 1969, p. 86.
25 E.g. J. Harris, *loc. cit.*, pp. 1146 ff.; M. Lazar, *Amour courtois et "fin'amors"* dans la littérature du XIIe siècle, Paris, 1964, p. 250.

correct. There are six adventures in all, and there is no doubt that
Yvain is increasing in prowess in each and so becoming worthier of his
lady. With one exception—the second, in the course of which he
rescues the lion—all these adventures have an important characteristic
in common, namely that Yvain goes to the aid of ladies or damsels in
distress. In the first two he is repaying a debt for services rendered,
to the Dame de Noroison for restoring him to health and to Lunete
for her earlier help in winning Laudine's hand. In the other three no
personal obligation is involved. He places himself at the ladies' service,
because that is what a true knight should do to a lady or damsel in
distress. What these adventures illustrate above all is Yvain's recognition of the true nature of chivalry, service in the cause of justice; and
so for me this part of the romance is the hero's self-discovery rather
than his redemption.

Combellack maintains that in each of these five adventures Yvain is
depicted in situations in which his fidelity to Laudine is tested.[26] I am
in entire agreement in respect of two of them, the first one and later
at the Château de Pesme Aventure, for in both the possibility of
marriage is mentioned, but I can find no evidence to support the view
that it is a feature of the other three. Chrétien's point throughout the
adventures appears to be that a knight must be of service to all ladies
in distress, while remaining the liege man of the one to whom he has
pledged his troth.

Another view of these adventures that I consider mistaken is one
expressed by Julian Harris.[27] He believes that Yvain's frequent evoca-
tions of God's aid are intended to signify that his victories are miraculous, won specifically because Yvain has received God's aid. Only the
victory over the sons of the *netun* appears to me to be in that category;
the others resemble closely the adventures of knights errant in other
romances. Yvain fails to invoke God before the break with Laudine
because he has been seeking, above all else, his own glory and purely
secular objectives. Now he has understood that a knight's prime duty
is to have faith in God, whose aid is required for the fulfilment of
obligations.

Yvain's first adventure after his recovery is the defence of the estates
of the Dame de Noroison (ll. 3038–336). The parallelism between the
situation in which Yvain and the lady find themselves and that between
Yvain and Laudine after Esclados' death is striking. Since she is called
Dame and not Demoiselle, though there is no mention of her husband,

26 *Loc. cit.*, p. 27.   27 *Loc. cit.*, pp. 1146–7.

we may assume that, like Laudine, she is a widow in need of finding a defender for her estates. The lady-in-waiting who persuades her mistress to produce the ointment to cure Yvain so that he is able to defend her estates plays a role akin to Lunete, who also stressed to Laudine her need of a champion. The similarity between the two damsels is accentuated by certain traits in common, such as their pertness. On the other hand, Yvain's behaviour is very different in the two episodes. When he was discovered by Lunete, he was obsessed by a desire for a trophy of his victory over Esclados. In his conversation with the lady-in-waiting on regaining consciousness, he asks whether he can be of service to her (ll. 3078–9), and after he has recovered his health at the castle of the Dame de Noroison he leads her men in a sortie against Count Alier and his band, who are burning and plundering her estates. He proves his prowess in a real battle in which no quarter is given, but in which he has not committed a hostile act. Yvain overtakes the defeated count; now, however, his ferocity during the pursuit of the wounded Esclados is replaced by a more chivalrous attitude towards a defeated foe. He accepts Alier's surrender on condition that peace is made on the lady's terms, and so shows that he has learnt generosity and proves his ability to have defended Laudine's fountain as he had promised to do at the time of their covenant. The defence and inheritance of estates seem to concern Chrétien deeply in Le Chevalier au Lion, for their defence is treated again in the Harpin de la Montagne episode, while the inheritance of estates is central to the final adventure in which Yvain champions the disinherited younger sister. The amount of time that a vassal should spend in defence of his lord's estate was a burning issue in the twelfth century. In earlier centuries he had been expected to be at his lord's beck and call at most times, but by the thirteenth this duty had been reduced to a fixed number of weeks in the year.[28] Here again are we witnessing Chrétien's disapproval of the weakening of certain old-established feudal obligations?

Now that his debt to the Dame de Noroison has been repaid, Chrétien asks her leave to depart, which she grants with regret. There follows the rescue of the lion, which will be dealt with when the symbolism of the animal is discussed. Followed by the faithful beast, Yvain eventually comes to Laudine's fountain (ll. 3485–769), but instead of pouring water on the marble slab he bemoans the loss of his lady through his own folly. His lamentations are overheard by Lunete,

28 See E. Perroy, op. cit., p. 56.

who has been imprisoned for treason in an adjoining chapel because of his failure to return, and who is awaiting death at the stake on the following day. Only Gawain or Yvain has the prowess to champion her cause, since it will mean engaging three adversaries, but she had not found help at Arthur's court because neither's whereabouts were known. Gawain is Lunete's obvious champion, since he had put himself at her service at Laudine's castle (ll. 2423). This is the first of the occasions on which he is absent when his help is sorely needed, giving Yvain the opportunity of standing in for him. Once more Yvain is repaying a personal debt, and not yet going to the defence of a damsel in distress exclusively out of disinterestedness and chivalry. It is in the fourth adventure (ll. 3770–4303), which Chrétien has inserted into the middle of the third, that Yvain will defend a maiden in distress to whom he has no prior obligation.[29]

Having promised to return to defend Lunete at midday on the morrow, Yvain finds shelter for the night at the castle of Gawain's brother-in-law, who, together with his family, is in mortal danger from a cruel giant, Harpin de la Montagne. Like the two giants in *Erec et Enide*, Harpin symbolises uncourtly and unchivalrous behaviour. He has devastated the estates, captured Gawain's six nephews, killing two, and intends slaughtering the others on the next morning if their sister is not handed over to him. When he has her in his power he will pass her to the oldest and lowest of his servants and turn her into a whore (ll. 3871–5, 4113–27). The damsel is therefore in peril of total dishonour. When Yvain learns of her predicament and of her father's failure to find Gawain to act as her champion he agrees to take his place, provided that the combat is held early enough to allow him to fulfil his duty to Lunete. The next morning he attends mass, the first time that this practice is mentioned. Tension rises with the delay in the giant's arrival, Yvain's growing predicament and the family's entreaties.

A deliberate contrast is drawn between Harpin's bragging and Yvain's *mesure* and humility before the combat, which almost takes on the appearance of a *psychomachia* between pride and humility. Yvain attacks the giant without a formal challenge, as a knight is entitled to do when confronted by an unchivalrous opponent, but it requires the lion's intervention for a quick victory. The adventure exemplifies the condemnation of the ill-treatment of prisoners and of the dishonour

29 On this use of the 'entrelacement' technique in embryo, see W. R. Ryding *Structure in Medieval Narrative*, The Hague, 1971, pp. 139–40. In addition to creating suspense, however, it enables Chrétien to intensify Yvain's dilemma.

of damsels when they are of noble birth. It also shows Yvain's understanding that the championing of a worthy cause is not a service for
which a knight must expect to be thanked; it is part of his duty.[30]
Yet he asks that the victory be reported to Gawain, though not to
Arthur (l. 4276), the only time that he makes this request. Yvain's
usual silence and his decision to remain *incognito* throughout can be
attributed to his humility, while his request at this point may either
be intended as a rebuke to Gawain or else be nothing more than a
way of motivating the disinherited sister's decision to go in search of
the Chevalier au Lion.

In sharp contrast with his conduct towards Laudine when he broke
faith by forgetting to return to her at the appointed time through
his fascination for court life and tournaments, Yvain, delayed though
he is by performing feats of arms in worthy causes, arrives in time to
prevent Lunete from being burnt at the stake, and so shows that he
has learnt to respect the sanctity of a promise as every knight should.
He describes the punishment as unjustified for her offence, as indeed
it appears to have been, since it was reserved for heresy and sodomy in
the thirteenth century.[31] The fact that he is defending a lady who has
been wrongly accused convinces him that God is on his side and that
right will prevail (ll. 4332–4). This gives the fight against Lunete's
accusers the character of a trial by combat, the result of which is never
in doubt, though the odds of three to one require the intervention of
the lion. What the adventure exemplifies is a knight's duty to defend
a lady against injustice of the most blatant kind, but the introduction
of the stake as a punishment for alleged treason is puzzling, though
King Mark, too, condemns Tristan and Iseut to be burnt alive. Is it
one of those anomalies occasionally found in Chrétien's romances
because he has preserved the details of his source material? If this were
the only reason, however, one would have expected him to state that
the stake was the *coutume* in Arthur's day, which is how he often
justifies patterns of behaviour and customs inconsistent with those of
his own time.[32] Another reason may be found in the events of the late

---

30 Note how Yvain pointedly refuses the act of gratitude of the mother and
   daughter, who are ordered to throw themselves at his feet by the father.
   See ll. 3957 ff.
31 See Philippe de Beaumanoir, *Les Coutumes de Beauvoisis*, ed. Beugnot, Paris,
   I, 1842, p. 413. Treason was punishable by hanging, p. 412.
32 Examples of the use of *coutume* in this way are to be found in ll. 5152 and 5155,
   and also in *Erec et Enide*, ll. 38, 44, etc. I disagree with E. Köhler's interpreta-

twelfth century, because, after the Third Lateran Council called a
crusade against heretics in 1179, there was mounting pressure for
augmenting the severity of punishments inflicted on them. During
the 1180s a number of cases of burning were recorded in France, and
the use of the stake as a form of death penalty was greatly on the
increase. Its justification was that heresy was treason against God and
that, in Roman law, treason had been one of the crimes punishable by
burning.[33] Is it an echo of this development that we have here?

The next episode is that of the daughters of the Seigneur de la
Noire Espine, interrupted about one-third of the way through by the
adventure at the Château de Pesme Aventure.[34] In the first part the
scene is set, for the elder daughter refuses to share her inheritance with
her sister, and forestalls her at Arthur's court, enlisting Gawain's
services and forcing her to go in search of the Chevalier au Lion. Since
the young sister falls ill on the way, Yvain is found by an emissary,
who begs him to reconquer the fief of a disinherited damsel, for such
an action will increase his *vaselage*.[35] Yvain's reply brooks no hesitation:

> Nenil, fet il; de reposer
> Ne se puet nus hon aloser,
> Ne je ne reposerai mie . . .[36]

This is an unequivocal declaration of a knight's duty never to rest, but
to be always ready to serve the cause of justice.

The acid test of this declaration soon comes, for that night is spent
at the Château de Pesme Aventure. Of all the adventures, this is the
one with the most puzzling features. Details such as the annual tribute

---

tion in the article mentioned in n. 12. On the possible Celtic source, see R. S.
Loomis, *Arthurian Tradition and Chrétien de Troyes*, New York, 1949, ch.
liv.

33 See M. Bévenot, 'The Inquisition and its antecedents', *Heythrop Journal*, VIII
(1967), pp. 52 ff. I am grateful to Dr L. Macfarlane for drawing my attention
to Bévenot's articles.

34 It is interesting to note how these adventures get progressively longer:
Dame de Noroison, including discovery and cure of Yvain, 2892–3323, 432
lines; Lunete part I, 3485–769, 285 lines; Harpin, 3770–4303, 534 lines;
Lunete part II, including conversation with Laudine, 4304–634, 331 lines
(parts I and II, 616 lines); Noire Espine part I, 4703–5106, 404 lines; Pesme
Aventure, 5107–770, 664 lines; Noire Espine part II, 5771–6526, 756 lines
(parts I and II, 1160 lines).

35 It seems to me that Roques' reading makes more sense than Foerster's at this
point, i.e., *enor* for *amor* in l. 5083, and my argument is based on it.

36 Lines 5095–7.

of thirty maidens suggest earlier material, incorporated rather less
successfully, it would appear, than the Joie de la Cour episode into
Erec et Enide. The conversation between Yvain and the lord of the
castle at the end of the adventure fails to elucidate its meaning, as
do those between Erec and Mabonagrain and between Enide and
Mabonagrain's lady. An atmosphere of mystery and evil prevails from
the moment of Yvain's arrival, with the apparent hostility of the
retainers, who prophesy his shame and humiliation, the courteous
warning not to proceed further from the 'dame auques d'aage', and
the evident relish of the porter at the sight of a knight going to his
doom. This is followed by the scene of the staked enclosure in which
three hundred maidens are living in conditions worse than serfdom.
Their task is to weave brocade of gold and silk thread, but, half dead
with hunger and thirst, half clad in filthy rags and paid a pittance, they
have to work long hours under threat of physical violence. This is to
be their fate until the two sons of a demon and of a woman, who are
the servants of the lord of the castle, have been defeated in battle.

Chrétien draws a sharp contrast between the sordidness of the
maidens' enclosure and the extravagant stabling of Yvain's horse
(ll. 5358–9). This contrast is further heightened when Yvain enters the
garden in which he finds the lord leading, together with his wife and
daughter, a life of affluence and idleness made possible by the wealth
created by the maidens. It is a *locus amoenus* very like the one inhabited
by Mabonagrain and his lady. There is no suggestion that the lord is
an unwilling victim of the sons of the demon, yet when they are
defeated he expresses his joy. Yvain receives a warm welcome, so
warm that Chrétien casts doubt on its sincerity. The daughter, who
is of unrivalled beauty, tends to his needs and dresses him in the finest
clothes, inducing Chrétien to express the hope that Yvain will not pay
too dearly for this attention and flattery. After a gargantuan evening
meal they continue to entertain him lavishly until he is escorted to his
bed for the night and left alone. There is no doubt that Chrétien is
laying great emphasis on the temptations to which Yvain is being
subjected here, particularly gluttony and sloth. His resistance shows
that he has learnt temperance or *mesure*, a virtue that is essential to
the true knight,[37] in contrast with his liking for luxury prior to his
break with Laudine.

37 'El caballero bien acostumbrado debe ser templado en el ardimiento, en comer
   y beber, en hablar . . . , en vestir (en que puede haber vanagloria), en gastar y
   en todas las demás cosas semejantes' (R. Llull, *op. cit.*, Parte VI, 16).

Next morning Yvain and his companion hear mass, but there is no suggestion that the lord and his family accompany them. He is prevented from leaving the castle by the lord, who politely tells him of the diabolical custom by which visiting knights must fight the two servants. In the event of his victory, Yvain will marry the daughter and acquire the estates. It is only when the lord explains that his daughter cannot marry until the sons of the *netun* have been defeated or killed that Yvain agrees. His two attempts to leave the castle, when prevented by the porter on the previous evening, and now by the lord, have puzzled many. It is certain that the first heightens the atmosphere of evil and mystery, while the second may also have the same purpose, though Yvain's haste to fulfil his obligation to the disinherited sister is also conveyed.

The combat with the two servants follows a predictable pattern, Yvain fighting on horseback throughout, his opponents on foot. Victory is won with the help of the lion, one of the servants being beheaded and the other mortally wounded by the beast. Yvain's consent to his request for mercy on acknowledging defeat is puzzling, since one would not expect a knight, who should have a burning hatred of evil, to spare such a diabolical creature. Nevertheless, I can see no alternative but that Chrétien is insisting again that justice must be tempered with mercy. After the lord, the lady and the retainers have expressed their great joy, Yvain refuses the offer of the daughter's hand and of the estates, making it clear that it is not because he disdains her but because other obligations prevent him from marrying her or any maiden. He is ready to give an undertaking to return and take the girl as his bride, should his situation change, but the angry father refuses and tells Yvain to be on his way. He rides off, preceded by the three hundred maidens and surrounded by those who had insulted him on his arrival but who now beg forgiveness. His assurance that he bears no ill-will, and that he can recollect no hostile word of theirs, pleases them greatly, and they are full of praise for his courtesy.

This adventure shows that Yvain has now reached the status of the perfect knight: brave, courteous, generous, merciful, humble, temperate, a man of God who has acquired a capacity for forgiveness akin to sanctity and, above all, a man faithful to his lady in face of temptations of the flesh and of wealth. Is Chrétien trying to symbolise a way of life in this adventure? R. S. Loomis quotes an article which seeks to show that the description of the maidens working under disgraceful conditions was reminiscent of the employment of Christian slave girls of gentle birth in silk factories of the Moslem world.[38] One might add that the two servants are 'hideus et noir' (l. 5512), epithets applicable equally to demons or to Saracen warriors. Could this adventure symbolise a crusade, on which all true knights should ideally embark once during their lifetime? Alternatively, could Chrétien be making a general criticism of the mode of life of the aristocracy of his own day, that affluent society by the standards of fifty or a hundred years earlier, and its exploitation of the 'povre gent'? The lord and lady are not deliberately wicked, they are merely lacking in moral principles and are indifferent to the lot of those less fortunate than themselves. Chrétien is perhaps stressing the moral and cultural superiority of the ideal of chivalry, which, in his view, was being encroached upon by the more materialistic values of a wealthier society. The emphasis laid on Yvain's attendance at mass in honour of the Holy Ghost before and his shame and fear during the combat (l. 5588) suggest that it symbolises a struggle between good and evil in some form. It will be remembered that the only previous occasion when Yvain's attendance at mass is mentioned is before his fight with Harpin.

The last day of the period granted by Arthur to the younger daughter of the Seigneur de la Noire Espine to find a champion has now arrived. Her elder sister, confident that no champion can be found to oppose Gawain, claims the estate in its entirety. Arthur, convinced of the right of the younger daughter's case, refuses, since the allotted time has not yet expired. That is the moment at which she and the Chevalier au Lion arrive, much to her sister's chagrin. Since their earlier attitudes are confirmed and no agreement is possible, the issue must be resolved by trial by combat. The champions, whose true identities are unknown to all, including themselves, attack. For the first time the lion does not intervene. It is an equal combat between knights, according to the rules, but with no quarter given on either side. It reaches its climax when, with the issue undecided, they retire to rest, revealing their identity to each other. This will be the moment of Yvain's supreme gesture of humility and magnanimity, in sharp contrast with his early pride, for he acknowledges defeat, though he has not been Gawain's inferior in prowess and is aware of the moral superiority of his cause. Gawain makes a reciprocal gesture, recognising the unworthiness of his cause (ll. 6345–47).

Arthur now has to resolve the dispute between the two sisters. For

38 See R. S. Loomis, *op. cit.*, p. 323.

the first time in the romance he appears as a worthy ruler in a world of true chivalry and courtesy, and is able to dispense justice with the full approval of his court. The case is not one that is black or white according to twelfth century law. At that time in France daughters had the right of inheritance to a fief in the event of there being no son. The laws of succession differed, however, according to the area; in some a law based on primogeniture was in force, in others one based on partition. In the latter case the younger children held their share of the fief as vassals of the eldest, either with or without hommage (*parage avec hommage, parage sans hommage*).[39] In the county of Champagne, according to Marc Bloch,[40] the law changed from one based on partition to one based on primogeniture in the course of the twelfth century. In this episode, therefore, Chrétien strongly supports *parage avec hommage*, by which the younger daughter inherits a part of the estate and recognises her sister as her suzerain (ll. 6438–43). This would suggest once more that he dislikes certain new practices of his day and is hankering after others which he considers to have belonged to an earlier, purer form of feudal society.

Chrétien's treatment of the theme of chivalry is now complete. The dominant thought throughout the romance is that the keynote of chivalry is selfless service in the cause of justice. Transposed to the world of courtly romance, this means service to ladies, though by implication Chrétien is thinking of service to the Church, to one's lord and to the commonweal. This is the point of view expressed in all treatises on chivalry from the twelfth century to the end of the Middle Ages.[41] But is Chrétien only concerned with the true nature of chivalry? Is the love element only incidental, introduced because he has borrowed the romance form in which romantic love between knight and lady is a convention?

Acceptance of the prologue of *Le Chevalier au Lion* at its face value makes it difficult to believe that Chrétien has used the love story merely as a framework, for in it emphasis is laid on true love as the source of courtesy, prowess, generosity and honour (ll. 22–4). It is true that the eulogy of Arthur in the opening lines does not square with the picture of life at his court prior to Yvain's break with Laudine. Nevertheless, I hope to show that the love theme is fundamental to Yvain's search for chivalry. It is introduced when Yvain perceives the grief-

39 See G. Fourquin, *Seigneurie et féodalité au moyen âge*, Paris, 1970, pp. 150–5.
40 *Feudal Society*, p. 425.
41 See, for example, R. Llull, *op. cit.*, *Parte* II, 1–36.

stricken Laudine before and during her late husband's funeral, and its courtly characteristics are self-evident. Yvain falls irrevocably in love with Laudine at first sight, because of her beauty and the pity he feels at her grief. In addition to being confined to a real prison, he is held in a *prison amoureuse* by his love for the lady.[42] Throughout the subsequent scenes Yvain behaves strictly in the tradition of the courtly lover, conscious that he cannot betray the God of Love and alive to his own unworthiness, a fear heightened by the knowledge that the lady he loves has every reason to hate him and so is doubly unattainable. When his suit is eventually accepted, his submission to Laudine is total. Kneeling before her with clasped hands, he promises to be her lifelong slave, her *verai ami* (ll. 1973 ff.).

It is the description of Yvain's feelings after the funeral that concerns us (ll. 1339–405), for it shows how his new-found love for Laudine abates his obsession with obtaining concrete proof of his victory over Esclados and the bitter disappointment experienced on realising that Esclados's death has robbed him of the opportunity of producing this evidence in order to silence Kay's sarcasm and thus salve his own pride and anger. This is the point at which the pride that has dictated his actions so far begins to weaken and to be replaced, unconsciously no doubt, by an irresistible desire to be Laudine's knight errant, with all that it implies. It is, therefore, in the courtly conception of the *service d'amour* that the stimulus for the search for true chivalry will come to Yvain. But an important characteristic of the *service d'amour* is that a knight should become a lady's *drut* only after undergoing many tests of his skill at arms and chivalrous virtues to prove his worthiness. Yet Yvain wins Laudine's hand without submitting to any test; he does not have to show that his love is inspiring in him greater courtesy and prowess. It is no doubt this realisation that makes him so susceptible to Gawain's arguments on the importance for a knight to resist uxoriousness and to give no cause for his wife to despise him. But the tournaments at which he shines do not provide tests of true chivalry that will help him to grow in courtly perfection. Laudine has married him because he has promised to defend her fountain, and this is his overriding obligation. He forgets this when he asks her permission for leave of absence, and he breaks faith with her when he overstays the year's leave that she has unwillingly granted him. It is plain that there is no question of Yvain's infidelity to Laudine. He weeps profusely as

42 See F. Whitehead, 'Yvain's wooing', *op. cit.*, p. 327.

he departs, leaves his heart behind and remains deeply in love with her throughout his absence (ll. 2625 ff.). Alone the glitter of the tournaments and the adulation of the crowd are responsible for his exceeding the agreed time limit. By so doing, he commits a heinous offence in both courtly and feudal terms by breaking faith, but Chrétien deliberately mitigates it. At the moment of his greatest triumph Yvain realises his fault of his own accord, and his shame and remorse prove that there has been no intentional betrayal on his part.[43] Then only does Laudine's messenger arrive to announce the formal break, Yvain's resultant despair culminating in a brainstorm. On his recovery, he has grasped the true nature of service, whether it be the service of chivalry or the service of love, for they are henceforth interwoven, and he sets out to prove himself worthy of his lady by performing deeds of chivalry. Throughout these adventures he remains steadfastly faithful to Laudine and is sustained by his love for her, though in two the temptation of infidelity is great. It is with Yvain's constancy, not with that of Arthur's courtiers, that Chrétien is contrasting, in the prologue, the fickleness of lovers in his own day. When Yvain returns by chance to the fountain, with its associations with Laudine, his despair nearly overwhelms him again. On meeting her after Lunete's rescue he deliberately refuses to reveal his identity, because he realises that even now, after four truly chivalrous deeds, he has not yet proved his worthiness to be her consort. It is only when he has won justice for the cause of the disinherited sister that he is satisfied. At this point we are told once more of his irrevocable love for Laudine and of his inability to go on living without her (ll. 6511-16). And so he makes a conscious decision to leave Arthur's court and to return to the fountain.

Imperious and proud, Laudine accepts Yvain on the strength of his victory over her late husband, of his reputation and high birth. She is a *châtelaine*, very conscious of her responsibilities to her estates as symbolised by the fountain. While Yvain's character develops, in a manner parallel to those of sinners such as Theophilus or Christopher who attain sanctity, Laudine's remains static, and in this respect she is totally unlike Enide, who, together with Erec, has to search for true courtesy and happiness in marriage. It is this difference that leads me to believe that Chrétien was not concerned with the conflicting claims of chivalry and marriage in *Le Chevalier au Lion* as he was in *Erec et Enide*. Laudine's relationship to Yvain is far more that of *dompna* to lover than that of

43 I disagree with Combellack's assertion that Chrétien blames Yvain's fault on Gawain (*loc. cit.*, p. 20), though the latter must bear a large share of the blame.

wife to husband. The subordination of Enide to Erec is closer to the reality of marriage in twelfth century aristocratic circles than Laudine's domination of Yvain. One is briefly told, it is true, that Esclados and Yvain had become lords of the estate on marriage (ll. 2093-4 and 2164), and this is according to twelfth century practice, but it is not reflected in Yvain's relationship with Laudine, possibly because Chrétien is not greatly interested in it. Further points in support of this view are Chrétien's dismissal of the marriage service in a few lines and of the conjugal bed in one (ll. 2148 ff.), and finally his treatment of the scene in which Laudine's messenger announces her mistress's break with Yvain. This is not the reaction of a wife but of a *dompna* who is bringing her relationship with her *drut* to an end because he has broken their solemn covenant.

Varying views have been expressed about Laudine's reasons for marrying Yvain. There can be little doubt, however, that calculation plays an important part in her decision. She quickly realises that it is to her advantage to marry her husband's killer, since he has proved the better knight and will turn out to be a more efficient defender of the fountain. She is flattered also to be courted by a king's son, and so convinces herself of her love for him. Though she accepts Yvain of her own free will, she does so for the wrong reasons. From her side, it is above all a marriage of convenience, and it is only at the moment of separation that we learn of her affection for her husband, and later of her continual anxiety during his absence. Just as Yvain should have had to prove by his prowess and conduct that he was worthy of Laudine before marriage, so she had a duty as a *dompna* to consciously instruct and encourage him in the ways of courtliness and chivalry. Nowhere are these obligations carried out, nowhere is there any sign of her spiritual superiority, and so by implication a certain blame attaches to Laudine for Yvain's continued fascination with court life and tournaments. When this has led him to be oblivious of the passage of time, her messenger accuses him of treachery and deception, without giving him the opportunity to defend himself. Laudine remains unrelenting towards Yvain until the *dénouement*, though by marrying him so soon after Esclados's death she herself has been guilty of a degree of disloyalty to her late husband's memory. How different from the feelings of the Châtelaine de Vergi towards her lover, who, she believes, has betrayed her! To the end she remains proud and imperious, and it is her pride that leads to her reconciliation with Yvain, since it prevents her from going back on her word to Lunete, to whom she

has sworn to bring about the reconciliation of the Chevalier au Lion
and his lady.

How sympathetically does Chrétien treat the character of Laudine?
The figure of the *belle dame sans merci* is one that does not appeal to
him, as already shown in *Le Chevalier de la Charrette*. The first hint of
criticism of Laudine's implacability is to be found in the eulogy of
Yvain's prowess by those watching the battle against Count Alier.

> Mout doit an amer et cherir
> Un prodome, quant an le trueve.[44]

When, after Lunete has been saved, Laudine comes face to face with
Yvain travelling incognito as the Chevalier au Lion, she utters words
so full of irony that they amount to unconscious self-condemnation
(ll. 4593–8). She is also cut down to size at the end of the romance,
where her helplessness without a champion is clearly demonstrated;
nevertheless the *dompna* has not yet found true humility. Justified as she
may have been in her anger at Yvain's breach of their courtly covenant,
she has no right to bear resentment indefinitely. She has not grasped
that understanding of human weakness and forgiveness are part of true
love. It is very grudgingly that she finally accepts Yvain's contrition
and request for mercy. Once she does, peace and harmony are brought
to 'Yvain le fin' and 's'amie chiere et fine', but how true is Professor
Frappier's view that 'le couple parfait est exalté'?[45]

It is in this context that the theme of love and hate must be studied.
It runs like a *Leitmotiv* through the romance,[46] appearing for the first
time when Chrétien states the paradox that Yvain loves the person
who hates him most (l. 1361), a point developed further in Yvain's
monologue (ll. 1428–506). The second variation of the theme is
Laudine's warning to Yvain that her love will change to hatred if he
fails to return within a year, a threat which she will carry out after
fourteen months, but without affording him the opportunity of explaining his lapse; yet he remains steadfastly true to her. The third
variation is to be found in the unjustified hatred, inspired by greed,
that the elder daughter of the Seigneur de la Noire Espine harbours
for her affectionate younger sister. One wonders whether a deliberate
parallel is not being drawn with the situation between the unrelenting
Laudine and the faithful Yvain, implying that, like the elder sister, she

---

44 Lines 3210–11.
45 *Op. cit.*, p. 24.
46 As Professor Frappier so aptly describes it, *op. cit.*, p. 194.

must learn to be generous, for Yvain has more than paid for his
fault. The fourth variation is the long digression on love and hate
and their coexistence in both Yvain and Gawain at the same time
(ll. 5998–6105). They hate each other as combatants because they do
not recognise each other, but this hatred is only superficial, since they
really love each other. Rhetorical and scholastic as this passage is, it is
unlikely that an author as concerned as Chrétien with structure and
proportion could have inserted it merely as an embellishment. Once
again, is a parallel not being drawn with the relationship between
Laudine and Yvain? She hates him because she does not know him.
She has misjudged his character on the strength of his one lapse, and
her hatred is the consequence of her pride and of her refusal to appreciate Yvain's true qualities. Of course, another possible explanation is
that Chrétien is contrasting Laudine as the *semper mutabile femina* with
the constant and faithful Yvain.

Let us now consider the significance of the lion in the romance.
Since it happens to be a character in its own right, there is sometimes
inconsistency between picturesque detail and any symbolism that may
be intended, and this makes interpretation more hazardous. The lion
must be taken at more than its face value because Yvain assumes the
pseudonym of Chevalier au Lion, and this pseudonym becomes the
title of the work. It has been variously interpreted as the symbol of
strength, courtesy, courage, nobility, gratitude, fidelity and generosity,
to name but a few. That the lion was used as a symbol of all these
during the Middle Ages is well attested, but they do not equally fit
the context here. If this is chivalry and *fin'amor*, as I have tried to
show, are not one or two interpretations more likely than the others?
The possibility of more than one significance being intended by the
author cannot be dismissed.

The resemblance with the story of Androcles and the lion was first
noted by Foerster in his introduction to his edition of the text.[47] In his
study of the treatment and development of the Androcles legend in
medieval literature,[48] A. C. Brodeur states that Petrus Damianus, in
the eleventh century, is the first to introduce the detail of the lion
being saved from the coils of a serpent. The story is usually taken by
medieval writers as illustrating fidelity developing from gratitude and,
for Professor Frappier, both gratitude and fidelity are included among

47 Kristian von Troyes, *Der Löwenritter*, p. xlvi.
48 'The grateful lion: a study in the development of medieval narrative',
  P.M.L.A., xxxix (1924), pp. 485–524.

the qualities symbolised by Yvain's lion.[49] Let us examine the part played by the lion in the romance. On leaving the Dame de Noroison, Yvain comes across the beast struggling in the coils of the serpent and goes to its rescue. The previous adventure has contained the first test of Yvain's fidelity to Laudine after their break. As shown earlier, the parallel between the situation of the Dame de Noroison and Laudine is close, while there is no difference between their desirability as matches. Yet Yvain does not consider for a moment the possibility of transferring his affections; he remains true to Laudine. The introduction of an emblem of fidelity would therefore be most appropriate at this point. In this case the serpent would probably represent temptation, as in the story of the Garden of Eden, or merely ingratitude, as suggested by W. R. Ryding.[50] Only in the combat against Gawain does the lion not intervene, possibly because when two truly chivalrous knights are involved the fight should be between them alone. It plays an active part in the other combats, against the giant Harpin de la Montagne, Lunete's three accusers and the two sons of the *netun*—that is to say, when Yvain is fighting against non-chivalrous adversaries. The lion's intervention in these cases may signify that the strength and skill required to overcome superior physical odds are inspired by Yvain's fidelity to Laudine. The atmosphere of evil pervading the Château de Pesme Aventure suggests that the lion's intervention in the battle may denote more than strength and skill inspired by fidelity to Laudine, though this adventure also provides the greatest test of Yvain's fidelity to her. Perhaps the explanation is that the lion symbolises *foi*, for the meanings of fidelity and of belief in the truths of the Christian religion are widely attested in the twelfth century.[51] Alexander Neckam, a contemporary of Chrétien, provides confirmation of the grateful lion story used to illustrate *fides* and *amor* by opening his version with the following sentence:

> Compendiose rem gestam stilo commendare libet, ut doceam quandoque bestias majoris esse *fidei* et *amoris* certioris quam sit nobilis creatura, cum dignitatis immemor efficitur.[52]

Le Chevalier au Lion does not demonstrate that a knight and his lady must find a compromise between chivalric and marital duties, as does

49 *Op. cit.*, p. 216.　　　50 *Op. cit.*, pp. 84–5.
51 See Tobler and Lommatzsch, *Altfranzösisches Wörterbuch*, Wiesbaden, III (1954), cols. 1965–71.
52 *De Naturis Rerum*, Lib. II, cap. cxlviii, Rolls Series, pp. 229 ff., as quoted by A. C. Brodeur, 'The grateful lion', *loc. cit.*, p. 495. The italics are mine.

Erec et Enide. On the contrary, Chrétien makes the point that there should be no incompatibility between true chivalry and an understanding marriage. While Chrétien shows how both Erec and Enide attain the state of courtly marital bliss, in *Le Chevalier au Lion* it is Yvain who is the more important character. It is his problem that the romance is really about: his search for the nature of true chivalry, which he eventually discovers in selfless service to those in need of help and in the cause of justice. Does this mean that *fin'amor* is unimportant? Not at all. *Fin'amor* is essential to the plot, for by falling in love at first sight with Laudine, Yvain stumbles on to the path leading to true chivalry, since he is now able to turn his mind from thoughts of vengeance and to restrain his obsessive desire to disprove the validity of Kay's wounding taunts. But he has yet to learn that, far from being the object of chivalry, self-glory is its negation, and his commitment to self-glory will be responsible for his forgetfulness and his breach of faith. Nevertheless his love for Laudine never wanes. It sustains him as he struggles along the arduous path to true chivalry, a goal attained thanks to his fidelity to his lady, an essential element of *fin'amor*. The services that he renders to the ladies and damsels in distress in the course of his adventures form part of his *service d'amour* to Laudine. Though subordinate to the chivalrous element, the love theme is closely interwoven with it and forms an integral part of the romance. If indeed it symbolises *foi*, the keystone of both chivalry and *fin'amor*, the lion provides in concrete form the close link between the chivalrous and courtly elements. Chrétien de Troyes appears throughout the romance in the guise of a moderate conservative who fears the corrupting influence of increased wealth, which was playing an ever bigger part in the lives of the secular knighthood of his day, and who hankers after the ideal of chivalry as described in the treatises of the time.[53]

53 It is interesting to note that Ramon Lull, a century later, had come to accept tournaments as an essential part of a knight's life. 'Correr en caballo bien guarnecido, jugar la lanza en las lizas, andar con armas, torneos, . . . pertenecen al officio de caballero, pues con todo esto se acostumbran a hechos de armas y a mantener la Orden de Caballería' (*op. cit., Parte* II, 10).

Ida L. Gordon

Processes of characterisation in Chaucer's *Troilus and Criseyde*

Critical studies of Chaucer's *Troilus and Criseyde* over the last century
seem to bear out, in practice at least, André Malraux's observation that
every work of art must have a different meaning for every age. So
long as the nineteenth century idea of character for its own sake in
narrative literature continued to dominate the critical attitude, critics
were content to see Chaucer's narrative in these terms—find the 'fatal
flaw' in Criseyde and all is explained. Over the last decade or two
there has been a shift of critical viewpoint. As one modern writer
puts it,

> Criticism does not interest itself much today in the old idea of character.
> Where drama is concerned we have quite stopped asking whether a character
> is 'convincing' or not, or discussing what he is 'really like'; and we more
> and more assume that the novelist, too, need not start out by making his
> characters like 'real life', but will subordinate their individuality to the
> general atmosphere and purpose of the work. We feel we should estimate
> them not in themselves but in relation to the kind of achievement the novel
> aims at. Seen in this way character becomes much less important, much more
> something for the author to manipulate to secure his main effect.[1]

No doubt this general shift of critical attitude has been a factor in the
new approach to *Troilus and Criseyde*, but other, more decisive, factors
have been at work too, notably a closer study of its literary origins
with an eye to appreciating the ways in which Chaucer has handled
his material—a process which has revealed, among other things, how
fundamentally his treatment of his narrative was influenced by his
interest in Boethius' *Consolation of Philosophy*. This revelation has
opened up whole new areas of the poem's meaning, which help to give
it coherence and significance in a way that must transfer the emphasis
from the characters *per se* to their function in the general theme of the
poem—the exploration and elaboration of the problem of love as

1 John Bayley, *The Characters of Love*, London, 1960, p. 25.

medieval philosophy saw that problem. Can we then say of Chaucer, as Eugène Vinaver says of Chrétien: '. . . it would be misleading to say that [his] purpose in introducing [his] characters . . . was to make them behave like "real people": everything they do is related to a problem and its elaboration within the work, since it is with problems that courtly poetry is concerned, not with human realities'?[2]

It is not quite so simple as that. *Troilus and Criseyde* is not a courtly romance, though Chaucer gives it something of the guise of courtly romance. And one thing that distinguishes it from the French romances is the greater attention given to the characters in proportion to that given to the action, and the more realistic depiction of their behaviour. The realism is not maintained consistently, nor is the attention given to the characters of such a kind as to make the poem into a 'story of character' as we use the term to describe a genre; but they constitute an important part of the effect of the poem. As Robert O. Payne observes, 'Chaucer's skill with dialogue, and a range of other technical skills, produces at times so strong an illusion of reality around the central characters of *Troilus and Criseyde* that it is quite possible to forget the typicality and representativeness of the characters.'[3] But the truth to life of the characters does not depend only, or even mainly, on this kind of realism. There are two kinds of characterization in the poem, one by which the persons in the story are placed for us in what we might call their public characters, and one which takes us below the surface into the more private areas of their minds and emotions. It is in the first kind mainly that Chaucer's technical skills, such as an ear for dialogue and an eye for gesture, produce at times a strong illusion of reality. In the second the realism consists not so much in creating an illusion of 'real life' as in the fidelity of the rendering of mental and emotional processes: they are recognizable as familiar human phenomena, and convincing as accounts of how the persons concerned would react in the circumstances, though the method of presentation is not usually naturalistic.

Certainly Chaucer does not present his characters to us as 'real people': far from trying to trick us into believing that he is telling a 'real' story, he constantly reminds us of its origins in 'olde bokes', and keeps before our eyes the literary processes of his own narration of it.[4] And the characterization is not simply portrayal of persons: Chaucer

2 *The Rise of Romance*, Oxford, 1971, pp. 30–1.
3 *The Key of Remembrance: a Study of Chaucer's Poetics*, New Haven, 1963, p. 182.
4 See Robert Payne, *op. cit.*, chapters 6 and 9.

would have understood the word more in its basic, literal sense as 'the marking out of the precise form of anything' (*O.E.D.*, sense 1)—the 'anything' being in this case the persons in the story as they relate to the love situation. He develops the story that he found to hand in Boccaccio's *Il Filostrato* in a series of situations in which the reactions of the characters realise, or particularise, different aspects of the problem of love, by revealing their attitudes and motives on the important issues raised. And it is in this revelation of attitude and motive that we have, at one and the same time, the elaboration of the problem of love and the characterisation at its deepest level. It usually takes the form of a discussion, either debate or internal monologue, on the issues raised; and it would not be true to describe Chaucer's use of this method as Professor Vinaver describes Chrétien's: '[he] let the characters enact a line of argument that happens to interest him, no matter what kind of characterisation, real or unreal, may emerge as a result.'[5] For when Chaucer uses his persons to enact a line of argument, he usually contrives to do it in a way that is in character with the person speaking; or, to put it in another way, he manipulates his characters to accommodate his elaboration of his theme. The realism, or otherwise, depends on how successfully he has integrated the discussions into his narrative. For example, Criseyde's reaction to her first sight of Troilus, after she knows of his love for her, is expressed in a long internal debate which reveals her cautious, circumspect and apprehensive character, and at the same time is a revelation of the kind of factors that carry most weight with her in matters of love. As an elaboration of the theme of love (a revelation of the nature of her kind of love) it sits comfortably within the narrative, despite its length. But when Chaucer puts into the mouth of Criseyde, roused from sleep by Pandarus in the middle of the night with his story of Troilus' jealousy, the arguments used by Boethius to show that worldly happiness is delusive (III, 813–36), or when he gives to Troilus, when it is decreed that Criseyde must leave Troy, the involved Boethian discussion on God's foreknowledge and man's free will (IV, 958–1078), he is using his persons more arbitrarily to develop his theme. In both passages the arguments used and the conclusions reached, especially in their limitations, are compatible with the characters of the speakers, but the discussions are unnatural in the situations, and thus are unrealistic. The difference is more a matter of narrative technique than of any real dichotomy between interest in character and interest in line of argu-

5 *Op. cit.*, p. 30.

ment. Only rarely does the one exclude, or conflict with, the other in this poem, since Chaucer is not so much promulgating his philosophical theme as analysing it in concrete human terms. The characters are completely subordinated to the theme, but, paradoxically, it is from this subordination that they gain the added dimension as characters which gives the narrative its psychological interest. For, as Robert Payne puts it, it is within 'the affective immediacy of the moral and emotional problems' that the characters are defined.[6]

Before I go on to examine the processes of this kind of definition of character, I must mention briefly some of the methods by which Chaucer places his persons for us, as individuals. The most obvious method of doing this is by explicit description, of who and what the persons are, their appearance and personal attributes. This is the method he uses in the Prologue to the *Canterbury Tales*, where it is by details of this kind, used selectively for their implications and connotations, that we come to know the pilgrims as persons and as what they signify. But it is a method he uses sparingly in *Troilus and Criseyde*, even where we might expect it, when the persons in the story are first introduced. Criseyde is the only character who is described for us on first introduction, and even then we are told only what we need to know for the part of the story that is to follow—that she is in 'gret penaunce' as the daughter of a traitor, that she is a widow and 'allone of any frende' in whom she can confide, and that she is surpassingly beautiful. Troilus is never introduced to us: we meet him casually, as it might be in real life, leading his 'yonge knyghtes' up and down in the temple, taking stock of the ladies and mocking at lovers. Pandarus too is brought in without description, and we are told little about him directly at any time, except that he is the uncle of Criseyde and friend of Troilus, and an unsuccessful lover himself. Yet, oddly enough, there are set descriptions of both Troilus and Criseyde in the last book (v, 806–40), after a stanza describing Diomede. Both appearance and personal qualities are mentioned, and, except for the reference to Criseyde's 'slydynge corage' (which we are about to see in action), the descriptions seem out of place so late in the story. Chaucer has taken the details for them from sources other than Boccaccio,[7] and it may be that this is one of the places where his pastiche method of composition has betrayed him, for in these sources the story does not

6 *Op. cit.*, p. 182.

7 See R. K. Root's edition of *Troilus and Criseyde*, Princeton, N.J., 1926, notes to ll. 799–840, pp. 541–5.

begin until this point, after Briseida has been sent to the Greek camp. Whatever the explanation, these set descriptions in the last book have little value as characterisation. They are mainly eulogistic, and, coming so near the end of the story, they read almost like obituaries.

For the most part Chaucer uses direct descriptions of his persons more tellingly—either they are significant as revelations of character, or they contribute immediately to the action of the story. An example of the former is the description of Criseyde's appearance and demeanour in the first scene in the temple (I, 178–82), which conveys, with admirable economy, a first impression of that combination of apprehensiveness and decorous self-control which is to characterise her behaviour throughout. And an example of the latter is the description of Troilus as he rides past Criseyde's house on his return from battle (II, 624–48)—besides conveying a picture of him as a typical courtly knight the description helps us to share the impact he is making on Criseyde as she watches from her window. Pandarus' appearance is never described, but emphasis is given to his physical actions and gestures; and it is partly because he *moves* more than the other characters that he comes more alive as a 'real person'. But at the same time his actions and gestures become a way of impressing on us both his 'bisynesse' and the element of 'game' in the part he plays. And his speech, both content and style, contributes to this impression. For Chaucer uses style of speech, to some extent, to define his persons: where Pandarus tends to a lively, colloquial manner of speech, with plenty of homely sayings and analogies, Troilus tends to a more formal, elaborate style. But neither uses his style consistently, and, on the whole, style of speech relates more to situation than to character: Pandarus uses elaborate rhetoric when it suits his purpose of persuasion or protestation, and Troilus can be blunt enough on occasion—as when he replies to Pandarus' vociferous efforts to rouse him from his inertia, 'frende, though that I stylle lye, / I am nat deef' (I, 752–3). Criseyde's style of speech, perhaps in keeping with her character, tends to vary with the company she is in, or, again, with the situation: for example, her usually restrained style gives way to highly emotional rhetoric when she is protesting her intention to be true to Troilus, in the fourth book (757–98).

All these processes of characterisation show us the persons objectively, from an external viewpoint. For giving us a deeper and fuller insight into the springs of their behaviour Chaucer shows them to us either subjectively, through their own self-consciousness expressed in their words and thoughts, or, more obliquely, through the medium of his irony, either to make those words and thoughts reveal more than the persons themselves realise, or in the form of ambiguous comment by the narrator, who similarly gives away more than he appears to be doing. For it is the kind of irony that entails, and must surely have helped to develop, the imaginative power of seeing through the eyes of its victims, entering their mental and emotional worlds. And it is in these areas of the characterisation that we can see most clearly how Chaucer manipulates his characters in the interests of his theme. The beginnings of the process lie in the changes he makes in the characters that he had found in Boccaccio's version of the story. We can take Troilus as an example. His transformation from a young man experienced in love affairs to one who has hitherto scorned love has often been cited as evidence of Chaucer's intention to depict him as a 'purer' lover than his prototype. But that is not the effect the transformation has: in the immediate context Troilus' scorn of lovers is seen as folly, since all it did was to provoke the god of love to prove the power of his arrows, when he suddenly 'hitte hym atte fulle', as he set eyes on Criseyde in the temple (I, 206-10). This provides the occasion for Chaucer's comment (in his role of narrator), 'O blynde world, O blynde entencioun! . . .' (I, 211-59), which is both a comment on Troilus' blindness and a general warning, directed to the audience, on the folly of scorning (deriding, or underrating) the power of sexual love, since all mankind is subject to it by natural law. But at the same time, by an ingenious play on words and syntax, it is also a warning to scorn (disdain) the kind of (sexual) love that can so easily enslave to itself the freedom of the heart,

> For evere it was, and evere it shal byfalle,
> That love is he that alle thing may bynde;
> For may no man fordo the lawe of kynde.   [I, 236-8]

The problem of reconciling these two natural laws, of sexual love and universal love, which Chaucer's irony puts to us so neatly in this passage, is central to his philosophical theme, and he has manipulated the character of Troilus in a way that enables him to put that problem also in human terms: Troilus becomes an *exemplum* both of the 'natural law' of sexual love and of its power to enslave the freedom of the heart in a way that puts it outside the bond of universal love, which is the 'lawe of kynde'. And it is this role of *exemplum* that gives to Troilus' character its psychological interest. For by making his subjection to the god of love into his first experience of sexual attraction, Chaucer is able to introduce with naturalness the analysis of his reactions to that experience, and of the processes by which his desire develops into passion. At this stage the processes can be seen as the familiar, at times amusing, stages through which a young man passes in the grip of his first infatuation; and the excesses are offset by the beneficial effect of love in making him more gentle and kindly (I, 1079-85). The fact that the processes by which his desire develops into passion conform exactly to the processes of *cupiditas*, as defined by the theologians, is not obtrusive at this stage of the story. Its significance becomes clearer later, when the infatuation hardens into an obsessive passion, deadening to everything but itself. Similarly, the more idealistic attitude that Troilus adopts to love—which is another of the changes Chaucer makes in his character, a natural consequence of the initial change by which his love for Criseyde becomes his first love— likewise enables Chaucer to elaborate his philosophical theme. For Troilus' idealistic attitude to love expresses itself at its strongest in the two great hymns to Love in the third book (1254-74 and 1744-71), and Chaucer's irony uses these hymns to subject Troilus' own love to a comparison it cannot bear, by the use of language that is applicable only to a higher kind of love—the universal love that binds all things in a holy bond of harmony. To the modern mind, which does not share so unquestioningly the Christian view of the order of nature, and is more ready to accept that each one of us may have his own way of apprehending love, the irony of putting these hymns into Troilus' mouth as he lay in bed with his mistress may not be as clear as it would be to a medieval audience. But the medieval view which Chaucer is putting to us permits us to believe that Troilus is aspiring to the universal love his hymns extol—he cannot 'fordo the lawe of kynde' which plants that aspiration in him, though he is deluded in believing his own passion could ever be a part of the holy bond of universal love. The disparity between Troilus' idealistic concept of love and the reality of his own love, which his hymns reveal, contributes to the significance of Troilus, both on the philosophical level (as an *exemplum* of misdirected love) and on the human, or psychological, level. For the kind of self-delusion they reveal in Troilus is a familiar one—the kind that operates to make us rationalise our motives and attitudes into something finer than they are when they fall below our ideals. And both the idealism and the self-delusion are in keeping with the character of Troilus as Chaucer depicts it. For example, his capacity for self-delusion is seen also in his 'passiveness', which stems from his view that what happens to him always comes from the outside—from the inescapable power of the god of love, from Fortune, from 'necessitee', never from his own volition.

That Chaucer took a different view of Troilus' 'passiveness', however, is revealed by his irony, notably in the talk between Pandarus and Troilus, after Pandarus has successfully contrived the first meeting between Troilus and Criseyde and is taking stock of the situation:

> For the have I bigonne a gamen pleye
> Which that I nevere don shal eft for other,
> Although he were a thousand fold my brother.
>
> That is to seye, for the am I bicomen,
> Bitwixen game and ernest, swich a meene
> As maken wommen unto men to comen;
> Thou woost thi selven what I wolde meene . . .   [III, 250–6]

But he takes God to witness that he is not doing it 'for coveitise', only to curtail the distress for which, it seemed to him, Troilus was nearly dying (III, 260–3).

Here, again, Chaucer has manipulated his character in the interest of his theme, and again the effect is to make the character more complex and interesting. It was not usual for a go-between in medieval story to announce so clearly what he was doing, and when Chaucer chose to make his go-between do so he gave him the opportunity to explain his motives. This adds complexity and interest to his character, since the motives are mixed—a sincere concern for Troilus and a relish in the 'game' of acting as go-between. But at the same time his speech raises in passing, the question whether the concern for Troilus alters the nature of what he is doing. And this is the question that Chaucer puts more obliquely, but also more pointedly, in Troilus' reply to this part of Pandarus' speech:

>   me thoughte, by thi speche,
>   That this which thou me doost for compaignie,
>   I sholde wene it were a bauderye.
>   I am nat wood, al if I lewed be;
>   It is nat so, that woot I wel, parde.   [III, 395–9]

For, he adds, one who goes on such an errand for gold or riches—call him what you will, but what Pandarus is doing should be called

'gentilesse, / Compassioun, and felawship, and trist': the distinction
should be made—

> for wide wher is wist,
> How that ther is diversite required
> Bytwixen thynges like, as I have lered.   [III, 404–6]

But the distinction between like things which Troilus has 'learnt' must
be the formal logical distinction between likeness and identity of substance; and far from proving that what Pandarus is doing for Troilus
is not 'bauderye', such a distinction proves just the opposite: it is
essentially 'bauderye', whatever may be the motive. And Chaucer
underlines the point, with an emphasis unusual in this poem, when
Troilus follows up his spurious 'proof' with an offer to do the like
for Pandarus by procuring for him his sister Polixene, Cassandra,
Helen 'or any of the frape'. Nowhere is the discrepancy between
Troilus' idealism and his behaviour so strongly highlighted by Chaucer's irony, and nowhere is his 'passiveness' so clearly shown to be an
illusion. There was no need for irony in Pandarus' speech, because
Pandarus himself, as Chaucer depicts him, is too much of a realist to
be under any delusion about what he is doing and too amoral to feel
a need to veil its true nature. Troilus can elevate 'bauderye' into
'gentilesse' in a speech which betrays his eagerness for Pandarus to
complete his office—he ends his speech with the plea, 'Parforme it out;
for now is moste nede.' It is in this way that Chaucer has manipulated
his characters to enable him to put to us the moral issue that Pandarus'
part in the action raises in relation both to himself and to Troilus.

It is because the characters are manipulated always in the interests
of the theme that attempts to explain the action directly in terms of the
qualities of character of the actors have always been unsatisfactory. For
example, G. L. Kittredge's view—'As Cressida is at the beginning, such
she is to the end; amorous, gentle, affectionate, and charming altogether,
but fatally impressionable and yielding'[8]—fails to explain either her
resistance to Pandarus' efforts to bring her quickly into Troilus' arms,
or the firmness with which she counters Troilus' suggestions for keeping her, when it is decreed that she must leave Troy. But the problem
of Criseyde is really a problem created by the efforts to explain her
behaviour primarily in terms of her character, for it is not Chaucer's
method to make the character of his persons determine their behaviour,
but rather the other way round. Or, to put it more precisely, the

8 *Chaucer and his Poetry*, Cambridge, 1915, p. 135.

difference of his characters from their prototypes is the result, not the cause, of his different treatment of the story. When he chose to elaborate the story into a series of situations in which the reactions of his persons reveal their attitudes and motives in relation to the issues raised by the situation, the effect was to impart a greater depth and fullness to the characterisation of those persons. But to connect their reactions to the theme or problem with which his poem is concerned, without imparting a too serious tone of didacticism to his narrative, he employs oblique and devious methods. The seeming inconsistencies in Criseyde's behaviour disappear if we are alert to these oblique and devious methods. The difficulty of understanding Criseyde really hinges on the question whether, like her prototype, she was prone to love too lightly, since this is what the account of her surrender to Diomede's wooing would suggest, yet the account of her behaviour in the first love episode would seem to deny. And this is the very question the narrator puts to us, obliquely, in the part of the narrative most relevant—the part which follows immediately on Criseyde's first sight of Troilus, after she has learnt of his love for her, when he rides past her window on his return from battle:

> Criseyda gan al his chere aspien,
> And leet it so softe in hire herte synke,
> That to hire self she seyde: 'who yaf me drynke?'   [II, 649–51]

And she blushed at her own thought, remembering that this was the man her uncle swore would die unless she had pity on him, and she quickly pulled in her head:

> And gan to caste and rollen up and down
> Withinne hire thought his excellent prowesse,
> And his estat, and also his renown,
> His wit, his shap, and ek his gentilesse;
> But moost hire favour was, for his distresse
> Was al for hire, and thought it was a routhe
> To sleen swich oon, if that he mente trouthe.   [II, 659–65]

It is at this point that the narrator intervenes to defend her from those malicious tongues that might 'jangle thus':

> This was a sodeyn love: how myghte it be
> That she so lightly loved Troilus
> Right for the firste syghte, ye parde?   [II, 667–9]

Yet who had suggested that Criseyde loved Troilus at first sight, unless it was the narrator himself in the foregoing account? And the terms in which he goes on to refute the charge, or try to clear up what he pretends to feel may have been a misunderstanding, are themselves ironically misleading:

> For I sey nat that she so sodeynly
> Yaf hym hire love, but that she gan enclyne
> To like hym first, and I have told you whi;
> And after that, his manhood and his pyne
> Made love withinne hire for to myne;
> For which, by proces and by good servyse,
> He gat hire love, and in no sodeyn wyse.   [II, 673–9]

What Charles Muscatine has called 'a pointed contradiction between narrative and dramatic action'[9] here is, however, less a contradiction than a typical piece of Chaucerian prevarication. For there has been a subtle shift of position on the narrator's part from the idea of loving at first sight to that of 'giving' or 'getting' love. Criseyde's exclamation, 'who yaf me drynke?', like Lavinia's in *Eneas*, certainly implied that she was smitten with love for Troilus at first sight, but it is true, as the narrator says, that she did not 'give' him her love, suddenly, in the sense of yielding to her inclinations. Criseyde's behaviour throughout is consistent and in character if we realise the distinction that Chaucer is making here with unobtrusive irony—a distinction which the subsequent behaviour of Criseyde confirms, between falling in love and 'giving' her love: it is completely compatible with Chaucer's picture of Criseyde that, for her, the two do not necessarily go together. For Troilus, falling in love had led quickly to a complete surrender of his will to his passion: for Criseyde, it raised considerations, practical and otherwise, as to how a love affair would affect her position and her happiness—considerations which throw light upon both her character and the nature of her love, in the same way that Troilus' surrender to his passion had done. In each case the process of putting the moral and emotional problem becomes also a process of characterisation.

It was awareness of the difficulties of explaining the action primarily in terms of character that led Arthur Mizener, in his study of Criseyde, to his hypothesis 'that for Chaucer a character consisted in a group of unchanging fundamental qualities, and that the relation between such a character and the events of the narrative was one of congruence rather than of cause and effect', his view being that 'the arrangement of [Chaucer's] narrative was determined primarily by a desire to develop

9 *Chaucer and the French Tradition*, Berkeley and Los Angeles, 1964, p. 154.

fully the dramatic possibilites of the action, not by a desire to reveal
the characters of the personages in the narrative by making motivation
the significant aspect of it'.[10] There is one episode in the narrative
which might seem to support Mizener's hypothesis, and that is in
the bedroom scene, cited by Mizener, where Pandaras comes in to
Criseyde with his 'cock and bull story about Orestes'. Mizener challenges the view that Chaucer 'makes it clear that Criseyde sees through
Pandar when, while inviting her to his house for supper, he implies that
Troilus is out of town'; for 'if Criseyde's action through the events of
the night at Pandar's house must be explained in terms of a Criseyde
who knew all along that Pandar was manœuvring her into Troilus'
arms, then her attitude, when Pandar comes in with his tale of
Troilus' jealousy, must be put down to pure hypocrisy. Can anyone
read this last passage and believe that Chaucer meant Criseyde to
appear hypocritical in her protestations?'[11] The answer, of course, is no.
Yet the evidence suggests that she may have seen through Pandarus
when he invited her to his house, and it would have been surprising if
she had not. She had already been tricked by him once into a meeting
with Troilus, at the end of which he had promised to arrange another
meeting at his house. And after he has lied (not 'implied') to her that
Troilus is out of town, when he invites her to his house, the narrator
remarks that his 'auctour' does not make it quite clear whether she
thought he was speaking the truth or not (III, 575–8). Since the whole
episode is Chaucer's own invention, the appeal to his author must
surely be the ironist's way of suggesting that she may not have believed
him. And when, after she has agreed to go with him, she begs him
to beware of gossips and be careful whom he brings there (582–6), it
seems clear that she has her suspicions. So there is an inconsistency in
the narrative here: it is stretching credulity too far to expect us to
accept that a Criseyde already suspicious would have believed Pandarus' story of Troilus' jealousy, which he was using to induce her to
admit Troilus into her room. But while it may be true that this scene
was necessary to complete the action (as Mizener says), this does not
explain the inconsistency, which lies in the attitudes of Criseyde: the
action could easily have been completed, without inconsistency, by
making the account of her reaction to Pandarus' story as ironical as

10 'Character and action in the case of Criseyde', in *Chaucer, Modern Essays in
Criticism*, London, 1959, p. 350 (reprinted from *P.M.L.A.*, LIV (1939), pp.
65–81).
11 *Ibid.*, p. 357.

the account of her reaction to his invitation. But this would not have allowed her speech on 'fals felicitee' (813–36), since this required that she should believe the story of Troilus' jealousy. And it is in this speech, I believe, that we have the explanation of the discrepancy in the narration: Chaucer sacrifices consistency here, as well as dramatic plausibility, in the interests of his philosophical theme. In the same way he sacrifices dramatic plausibility when he gives to Troilus his painfully long and laboured discussion on the problem of God's foreknowledge and man's free will, when he is in despair at the thought of losing Criseyde.

He does not often have to do this: his technical skill is such that the elaboration of his theme sits easily within the narrative, with the help of the lyrics and the narrator's comments. And what makes the achievement possible is that he has chosen a story that lends itself well as an *exemplum* of his theme, and that he has exploited its poten-tialities in that direction by subtle changes in his characters. We have seen something of how this process works in the characterisation of Troilus. And it is by a similar process of exploitation in the interests of his theme that Criseyde becomes a less bold and sensual, more cir-cumspect and decorous character than her prototype: what is initially a change in her character, as seen when we first meet her in the temple, opens the way for her hesitations about embarking on a love affair with Troilus, which Chaucer uses as a medium through which he elaborates his theme. And these transformations in turn make room for the expansion and elaboration of the role of Pandarus, who, as the uncle, instead of the cousin, of Criseyde, assumes a greater authority and plays a larger part, in helping to overcome her reluctance and in contriving plans to bring her eventually into Troilus' arms in a way that satisfies both her caution and her sense of decorum—she is absolved from taking any initiative. And here again the transformation is part of a process by which Pandarus is brought into closer relation with the theme of the poem. For his greater contribution to the action is matched by his contribution as a sententious but shrewd commen-tator, whose clearer view often serves to reveal Troilus' blindness (as when he rebukes Troilus for blaming Fortune for his afflictions, by explaining to him the Boethian concept of Fortune). But the limitations of his practical wisdom are seen when the crisis comes; all that he can suggest to help Troilus, when he is faced with the prospect of losing Criseyde, is to forget her and 'love an other lady swete', and, when that fails, 'Go ravysshe hire' (IV, 489 and 530).

This brings us to a final point about Chaucer's methods of characterisation: there is no development of character in the sense of the character changing under the impact of experience. What changes is the light in which the characters are to be seen. And it is by this change of light that the characters themselves become an intrinsic part of Chaucer's theme, as *exempla*. What was benevolent, practical but unscrupulous efficiency in Pandarus at the beginning is still benevolent and practical when the crisis comes, but his lack of scruples can be seen now as opportunism in all its ugliness, and his practicality as inadequate. Criseyde's gentle circumspection, which adds to her charm when she is hesitating to give way to the pressures Pandarus is putting on her, is less charming when she makes her crucial decision to remain in the Greek camp for the same kind of reasons that moved her to make the similar crucial decision not to dismiss the idea of Troilus as a lover. Troilus' passion for Criseyde, in the beginning a young man's first blind infatuation, is seen at the end as a pathetic obsession. But if the end is implicit in the beginning in this way, it is not simply in terms of qualities of character. Far from asking us to believe (as W. C. Curry, with his coinage of the term Nature-as-Destiny, suggests)[12] that, given the characters of the persons as they are established in the beginning, they had to behave as they did, Chaucer is careful to indicate at each important turn of events that a deliberate decision is made by the person concerned, generally after a debate on the matter, in some form or other. And it is these decisions that determine their subsequent behaviour. The debates connect their attitudes and motives to their actions in a relation of cause and effect which is only partly a matter of character *per se*: moral choice in various forms comes into it too, with all the psychological, emotional, and circumstantial factors that are involved in questions of moral responsibility, factors to which Chaucer gives full attention. For what he is demonstrating, through the medium of his persons, is what medieval thought realised (and modern thought is belatedly rediscovering)—that the problems of love are ultimately moral problems,[13] however much they may be complicated by other factors, such as physical and circumstantial pressures.

This is not to say that Chaucer's purpose in writing his poem was a moralistic one, for who can say with confidence what has triggered off a work of art? It could be that, when his interest in medieval

12 *Chaucer and the Medieval Sciences*, 2nd edn, London, 1960, pp. 244 ff.
13 See D. W. Robertson, *A Preface to Chaucer*, Princeton, N.J., and London, 1963, p. 462 and *passim*.

philosophy (and more particularly Boethian philosophy) suggested to him the possibility of retelling in this different way the story he knew from Boccaccio's version, it was the challenge the task offered to a poet of his temper that was the real inspiration. For the impression his narrative leaves with us is that his concern with the theme of love is not so much that of a moralist as of a philosopher. Certainly he chooses to tell his story with a wit that makes the moralistic message unobtrusive and depicts his persons with such wide human understanding that they retain our sympathy even while his irony reveals their failures in love.

G. B. Gybbon-Monypenny

Guillaume de Machaut's erotic 'autobiography': precedents for the form of the *Voir-Dit*

The *Voir-Dit*, if not the latest, is certainly the most elaborately developed of a small number of medieval works which, while they appear
to have no direct links with each other and differ greatly, have sufficient
in common to constitute a genre. This genre I would call the 'erotic
pseudo-autobiography'. It is an account by a poet, usually in verse,
of an episode or episodes of his own supposed love life, into which are
interpolated a number of his own lyric compositions. The songs are
said to have been composed in connection with the love affair described, and the narrative serves, among other things, to explain their
genesis. While critics have given some consideration to the question
of antecedents for the form in individual cases, there has not, as far
as I know, been any awareness of or attempt to consider the genre as
a whole.[1] This is understandable, given the fact that these works are
spread over four languages and more than a century. I am not about
to suggest that there is a common source for the form of all these
works; it seems more probable that this is a case of polygenesis, that
poets of different backgrounds and character arrived coincidentally at
the same formal concept. But whereas the *Frauendienst*, the *Vita Nuova*
and the *Libro de buen amor* appear to be unique and without parallel
or precedent in their respective languages, the *Voir-Dit* has a closely
contemporary imitation in the *Espinette amoureuse* of Jean Froissart.
Furthermore, as I hope to show, one can trace through the previous
150 years of French narrative poetry a succession of formal developments which suggest that these two examples of the genre are the
products of a process of evolution. I propose, therefore, to look first
at each of these 'erotic autobiographies' in turn, in order to clarify
both the parallels and the differences, and then to describe those formal

---

1 Except for my own comments in 'Autobiography in the *Libro de buen amor* in
the light of some literary comparisons', *Bulletin of Hispanic Studies*, XXXVIII
(1957), pp. 63–78, especially pp. 70–4. The present study is a development
from those comments.

developments which seem to me to lead up logically to the concept of the 'erotic pseudo-autobiography' as the *Voir-Dit* embodies it.

The *Voir-Dit* is a lengthy poem, apparently composed *c.* 1363, in the conventional octosyllabic couplets of French narrative verse.[2] It narrates Machaut's love affair with a young girl of noble family whose name, as Paris worked it out from the *engin* at the end, was Peronne d'Armentières. The lovers exchange both lyric poems and letters, which are quoted in full—some sixty poems (*virelais, rondeaux, ballades,* etc.) and forty-six letters in prose. Paris regarded the *Voir-Dit* as literal autobiography and believed that he had identified Peronne as a real person (pp. xxiii–xxvi); he accepted, therefore, not only that the love affair occurred as Machaut described it, but that the poems and letters attributed by Machaut to Peronne were actually composed by her and that the *Voir-Dit* was begun during the course of the affair in order to commemorate their love and to incorporate the evidence of that love in 'their' book.[3] Later critics have been more sceptical, or more cautious, but it appears to be generally accepted that the *Voir-Dit* contains genuinely autobiographical elements.[4] This is largely attributable to the realism with which Machaut identifies his protagonist with himself: middle-aged, beset with infirmities (especially

2 Guillaume de Machaut, *Le Livre du Voir-Dit*, ed. Paulin Paris, Paris (Société des bibliophiles françois), 1875. For the date, see Paris's 'Notice', pp. xxviii–xxxi. Fourrier, in his edition of the *Espinette amoureuse* (see n. 5 below), p. 34, gives the date of the *Voir-Dit* as 1364, without giving grounds for this statement.

   Paris's edition arrives at a total of 9,037 lines of narrative and lyric verse for the *Voir-Dit*, but this results from a printer's error: line numbers are given for the first line on each page only and from p. 272 to p. 273 the total jumps from 6,084 to 6,704, an obvious error for 6,104. The error is perpetuated through the rest of the text, so that an extra 600 lines are accidentally counted in.

3 See *Voir-Dit*, ll. 422 ff., where Machaut names the book for the first time and declares '. . . celle pour qui Amours veille / vuet que je mete en ce VOIR-DIT / tout ce qu'ay pour li fait & dit / et tout ce qu'elle a pour moi fait, / sans rien celer qui face au fait'. The progress of the book is frequently referred to in the letters, especially from letter XXI on.

4 See especially G. A. Hanf, 'Über Guillaume de Machauts' *Voir-Dit*', *Zeitschrift für romanische Philologie*, XXII (1898), pp. 145–96; V. Chichmaref, *Les Poésies lyriques de Machaut*, Paris, 1909, p. liv; Guillaume de Machaut, *Oeuvres*, ed. E. Hoepffner, Paris (S.A.T.F.), 1908–21, I, pp. xl–xli; J. Bédier and P. Hazard, *Histoire de la littérature française*, re-edited by P. Martino, Paris, 1948–49, I, p. 115; R. Bossuat, *Histoire littéraire française*, I, *Le Moyen Âge*, Paris, 1931, p. 361, etc.; W. Eichelberg, *Dichtung und Wahrheit in Machauts 'Voir-Dit'*, Düren, 1935.

gout) and full of uncertainties as a lover, at the beck and call of his real-life patron the Duke of Normandy (ll. 3151 ff.), fussing over the details of composition or referring to his own works (e.g. letter VI, where he writes of his *Morpheus*). To the effect of authenticity conveyed by this identification of protagonist and author can be added a number of touches of realism in parts of the narrative where facts are not likely to be verifiable: e.g. in the love scenes, as in Machaut's description of the temptation provided by Peronne's physical nearness (ll. 2224 ff.) or Peronne's exasperation at Machaut's fussing over her lack of discretion about their love (ll. 2364 ff.); or in background details, such as their visit to a fair (ll. 3365 ff.), where they are found somewhere to rest by a drunken *sergent d'armes*, or Machaut's request to Peronne to date her letters in future because he has difficulty sorting them out for inclusion in the book (letter XXVII).

Against this incidental realism one must set much that is unrealistic. Leaving on one side the question of how far the lovers' behaviour is derived from literary models and conventions, one can point to such unrealistic passages as the constant interchange of lyric compositions between them while Machaut is riding towards Peronne's house, with no indication of how they could compose and transmit their songs in this instantaneous fashion (see ll. 1535 ff., 1679 ff. and also 2160 ff.). Again, while the use of allegorical figures could at times be regarded as the metaphorical presentation of states of mind (e.g. the appearance of Douls-Pensers at l. 329 or the visits of Honte and Esperance at ll. 1944 ff.), when Machaut tells us that he has promised Esperance a Lay d'Esperance as an 'amende' for his shortcomings (ll. 3963 ff.) or describes this encounter with Esperance to Peronne in realistic terms (letter XXI), it is difficult to accept that this is meant to be either a literal account of the facts or an attempt to achieve psychological realism through allegory.

To establish the balance between truth and fiction in the *Voir-Dit* would call for detailed examination such as cannot be attempted here. The point I wish to make is that the same question mark hangs over all the works that belong to the genre. This arises logically from the fact that each author identifies the protagonist with himself both as the lover in the story and as the composer not only of the songs but of the narrative itself. There is thus a minimum of truth in that the author/ protagonist actually composed the songs and the story, while at the other extreme there is in every case at least some degree of fiction, some things which cannot literally be true.

It is not surprising that Froissart, whom Fourrier calls 'le disciple et continuateur [de Machaut]', should, in the *Espinette amoureuse*, have created a work which shares many of the formal characteristics of the *Voir-Dit*.[5] Fourrier dates the *Voir-Dit* at 1364 and the *Espinette* at 1370 (pp. 30–4). The *Espinette* tells of Froissart's youthful love for 'Marguerite', interpolating fourteen of his own lyric compositions (some 1,400 lines out of a total of nearly 4,200). The incidental realism is less substantial than in the *Voir-Dit*, but Froissart links the story to such events in his career as his first visit to England (ll. 2383 ff.), with a stormy Channel crossing (ll. 2507 ff.), and an earlier editor, Scheler, and a subsequent biographer, Shears, accepted the *Espinette* as a basically true story.[6] But there are also such allegorical scenes as his meeting with Venus and other goddesses (ll. 339 ff.) and it is clear that the *Espinette* is, sometimes at least, neither factual biography nor realistic fiction.

I propose to discuss the other works in chronological order. Ulrich von Lichtenstein's *Frauendienst* is dated by scholars at about 1255.[7] It is a long work (approaching 15,000 lines of octosyllabic verse) which recounts Ulrich's two love affairs: the first lasts for a number of years from the time when, in his teens, he serves the lady as a page until, after a final quarrel, he decides to break off his service (st. 1365); the second, deliberately sought (st. 1384 ff.), appears still to continue at the end of the poem. Ulrich also describes his participation in jousts and tournaments, which involve him in lengthy travels. He interpolates fifty-eight of his own songs, as well as three *Büchlein* or rhymed love letters

5 Jean Froissart, *L'Espinette amoureuse*, ed. A. Fourrier, Paris, 1963. See introduction, p. 34: 'La conception même de l'*Espinette amoureuse* dérive en droite ligne de Machaut . . .'

6 Jean Froissart, *Poésies*, ed. A. Scheler, Brussels, 1870–72, I, p. xxii; F. S. Shears, *Froissart, Chronicler and Poet*, London 1930, especially pp. 7 and 204–5. Froissart did, of course, write autobiographically in the *Débat du Cheval et du Lévrier* and the *Dit du Florin*. On the other hand, touches of incidental realism, far from revealing the autobiographical nature of a work, may prove to have a literary origin: Froissart describes his lady's pulling his hair in passing as a sign of reproof (*Espinette*, ll. 3787 ff.); this 'realistic' detail also occurs in the *Frauendienst*, st. 134, where Ulrich's lady pulls his hair sharply as he helps her dismount, as a rebuke for his not having the nerve to speak to her. Are both authors reporting the same actual experience, did they invent coincidentally the same touch of realism, or is this a 'topos' of feminine behaviour in medieval romance?

7 Ulrich von Lichtenstein, *Frauendienst*, ed. R. Bechstein, Leipzig, 1888; *U. v. L's Service of Ladies*, trans. (in condensed form) by J. W. Thomas, Chapel Hill (University of North Carolina Studies in the Germanic Languages and Literatures, No. 63), 1969.

and two letters in prose. Ulrich appears to wish that these three activities, love service, jousting and the composition of songs, should be seen as three facets of the life of a true knight.

The identification of the protagonist with Ulrich's historical self is supported by his bringing in two historical events, the marriage of the daughter of Prince Leopold in 1222, on which occasion Ulrich is knighted, and the death of Frederick, Duke of Austria and Styria, at the battle of the Leitha in 1246, and by the inclusion of the names of historical persons as rivals in the jousts, etc.

In the case of the *Frauendienst* the issue has been not only how much of the work is truth and how much is fiction, but whether it is meant as a serious presentation of the ideals of chivalry and courtly love (as, for example, Bechstein, Neumann and McFarland have thought), or whether it is a sly burlesque of courtly literature (as Becker and, more recently, Thomas have claimed).[8] It is difficult to judge how far episodes which today seem irremediably comic (such as Ulrich's jousting tour dressed as a woman and calling himself the goddess Venus, or his visit to his lady's castle disguised as a leper, when he has to endure a series of mishaps and indignities that remind one of the *fabliaux*) were meant by the author or would be seen by his contemporaries as comic. Whatever interpretation is given to Ulrich's narrative, it must be one that can be reconciled with the obvious seriousness with which he publishes such a large selection of his lyric poetry.

Scholars generally seem to have thought that there was no identifiable source of inspiration for what M. F. Richey called Ulrich's 'interesting and unique experiment' (*Essays . . .*, p. 7). Thomas con-

---

8 See R. Becker, *Wahrheit und Dichtung in Ulrichs von Lichtenstein 'Frauendienst'*, Halle, 1888; F. Neumann, 'Ulrichs von Lichtenstein *Frauendienst*: Dichtung und Leben', *Zeitschrift für Deutschkunde*, XL (1926), pp. 373 ff.; M. F. Richey, *Essays on the Medieval German Love Lyric*, Oxford, 1943; A. H. Touber, 'Der literarische Charakter von Ulrichs von Lichtenstein *Frauendienst*', *Neophilologus*, LI (1967), pp. 253–62; Timothy McFarland, 'Ulrich von Lichtenstein and the autobiographical narrative form', in *Probleme mittelhochdeutscher Erzählformen. Marburger Colloquium, 1969*, Berlin, 1972, pp. 178–96; J. W. Thomas, '*Parzival* as a source for *Frauendienst*', *Modern Language Notes*, LXXXVII (1972), pp. 419–32.

McFarland appears to think, without giving reasons for his view, that the tournament of Friesach and the 'Venusfahrt' actually took place (p. 188); Thomas regards them as fictitious (*Service of Ladies*, pp. 16–19 and 27–8). He also argues that the imprisonment of Ulrich in his own castle for a year by robber barons (sts. 1696–730) is fictitious (*Service . . .*, p. 21).

cludes that Ulrich had no definite model for the autobiographical
form, though he thinks that he may have been influenced by Provençal
song collections which contain biographies of the troubadours and
also by works such as the *De consolatione philosophiae* (*Service of Ladies*,
pp. 36–7). McFarland thinks that Ulrich could have been influenced
by the self-depiction of poets such as Walther von der Vogelweide in
lyric poetry or Wolfram von Eschenbach in the *Parzival*, but the only
work prior to 1300 in which he finds the same basic formal characteristics is Dante's *Vita Nuova* ('Autobiographical narrative form',
especially p. 186 and section 11).

There are, of course, as McFarland recognises, vast differences
between the *Frauendienst* and the *Vita Nuova*, and there can hardly be
any question of Dante having read Ulrich. But in terms of what constitutes an erotic pseudo-autobiography the parallel is justified. The
Vita Nuova describes Dante's love for Beatrice from the time when he
first saw her at the age of nine to the period following her untimely
death, when, after being distracted from his grief for a while by a
donna gentile, he returns to full devotion to Beatrice's memory and
then resolves to write no more about her until he is better fitted to do
so. The external events described are few and briefly indicated, most
of the narrative being devoted to Dante's visions and states of mind;
it is cast in the form of introductions to the thirty-one *sonetti* and
canzoni which Dante selected and ordered for inclusion, with often a
very close correspondence in terms of content between introduction
and song. Each song is also accompanied by a brief commentary on
how it is divided into its parts.

Again, the protagonist of the work is clearly Dante himself, and in
consequence there has inevitably been discussion as to the balance
between truth and fiction, the most obvious question being the existence and the identity of Beatrice. The relationship between the
circumstances under which the songs were originally composed and
the account of them which Dante gives in the *Vita Nuova* is clearly
much less susceptible of proof, as are the thoughts, emotions and
visions he describes. But critics generally appear to accept that the
Vita Nuova has a factual basis.[9]

9 Dante Alighieri, *Vita Nuova*, ed. K. McKenzie, London, 1921, pp. vii ff.;
  Umberto Cosmo, *Handbook to Dante Studies*, trans. D. Moore, Oxford, 1950,
  ch. iv, especially pp. 38–49. An exceptional view appears to be that of Carl
  Stange, *Beatrice in Dantes Jugenddichtung*, Göttingen, 1959, who regards the
  Vita Nuova as pure allegory, with no biographical content—see *Studi Dante-
  schi*, XXXVIII (1961), p. 373.

The question of where Dante found the inspiration for the form of the *Vita Nuova* has also remained a matter for speculation. Two main sources for the concept of a prose narrative and commentaries written round the author's own lyric poems have been suggested: the *prosimetrum* form, which can be traced back to Menippus and whose most significant example is Boethius's *De consolatione philosophiae*, and the biographies and *razos* which accompany the songs of Provençal troubadours in some thirteenth century song collections, notably those of Bertrand de Born, a poet well known to Dante. Neither suggestion seems wholly satisfactory: the essence of the *prosimetrum* is that prose and verse alternate in a continuous flow of narrative or discussion and the verse cannot stand on its own as independent poetry, whereas in the *Vita Nuova* the songs were originally independent and were only subsequently organised into a consecutive series linked by prose commentary. In favour of the *razo* theory is Dante's use of the term *ragione* to describe his narrative sections or commentaries (e.g. before the sonnet 'Videro li occhi miei . . .' and the two following sonnets). But, as Zingarelli pointed out, the *razos* occur in the mss. without organic plan or logical sequence and are often by different hands, so that the careful structure of the *Vita Nuova* cannot have been inspired by them.

The Spanish Arabist, Asín Palacios, suggested as a source for the *Convivio* the Arabic philosopher Ibn 'Arabi's *Treasure of Lovers*, where philosophical chapters are headed by poems, whose content is discussed in the ensuing prose. Asín appears, however, to overlook the fact that Dante had already evolved the idea of prose commentaries on his own poems in the *Vita Nuova* (and he himself reminds his readers of the *Vita Nuova* at the start of the *Convivio*—*trattato* I, cap. i), at a period when the likelihood of his having come across Arabic philosophy is remote.[10]

The essence of the *Vita Nuova* is the poet's desire to provide an explanation of how he came to write a number of lyric poems, selecting and ordering them and relating them to specific experiences, as well as providing a technical commentary for each poem. For all their lack

10 See Pio Rajna, 'Lo schema della *Vita Nuova*', *Biblioteca delle Scuole Italiane*, II (June 1890); Miguel Asín Palacios, *La escatología musulmana en la 'Divina Comedia'*, Madrid, 1919, pp. 339 ff.; S. Santangelo, *Dante e i trovatori provenzali*, Catania, 1921, pp. 15–30; J. R. Reinhard, 'The literary background of the *Chantefable*', *Speculum*, I (1926), pp. 157–69, especially p. 167; Nicola Zingarelli, *La vita, i tempi e la opera di Dante* [*Storia letteraria d'Italia*, III], Milan, etc., 1931, *Parte prima*, cap. xiii, pp. 278–309; Domenico di Robertis, *Il libro della 'Vita Nuova'*, Florence, 1961, *cap.* i, especially pp. 18–19.

of organic unity, the Provençal biographies and *razos* come nearest to
that idea.

The *Libro de buen amor* differs from the other erotic pseudo-auto-
biographies in several respects, both as to form and content. Unlike
Machaut, Froissart, Ulrich and Dante, Juan Ruiz is totally unknown
apart from this one work and the *Libro* contains no references to outside events, so that the protagonist cannot be identified with a historically authenticated figure and we do not know whether the name 'Juan
Ruiz, Arcipreste de Hita' (sts. 19 and 575) is genuine.[11] It is clear,
however, from the way in which he digresses to topics that interest
him as author that he makes no distinction between the protagonist
and himself. But whereas Dante and Machaut, for example, identify
their protagonists totally with themselves in the sense that, however
much fiction there may be in their works, that is how they see themselves and wish to be seen, Juan Ruiz treats his protagonist with objective irony, presenting him as an ambiguous figure showing the duality
of man's nature, doomed to the frustrating pursuit of the will-o'-the-
wisp of sexual love while continually aware that he should be pursuing
the love of God. That we are not intended to take all the Archpriest's
adventures as genuine autobiography is clear from the fact that Juan
Ruiz not only borrows the most fully treated of his amorous experiences from the well known 'comedy' *Pamphilus* but expressly acknowledges his debt (sts. 891 and 909). The allegorical debate with the god
of love which precedes it borrows extensively from the *Ars amatoria*,
and this debt is also acknowledged, though in less direct fashion (sts. 429,
446 and 612). The Archpriest's adventures in the *sierra* (sts. 950–1042)
are centred upon four songs in which Juan Ruiz's public might well
recognise the echo of the *pastorela* tradition. This autobiography was
to be seen to be fictional.

The character and function of the interpolated songs are also different. Four are devotional songs, two 'Joys of Mary' (sts. 20–43) and

---

11 Juan Ruiz, *Libro de buen amor*, edited with English prose translation by Raymond S. Willis, Princeton, N.J., 1972. Regarding the author's identity, L. G.
Moffat, 'The evidence of early mentions of the Archpriest of Hita or of his
work', *Modern Language Notes*, LXXV (1960), pp. 33–44 (especially pp. 41 and
43), suggests that the name 'Juan Ruiz' may, like the American 'John Doe', be
merely the equivalent of 'Everyman'. In a paper read at the first International
Congress on the Archpriest of Hita (Madrid, June 1972) Emilio Sáez and José
Trenchs produced evidence of the existence of a certain Juan Ruiz de Cisneros,
a protégé of Cardinal Gil de Albornoz, who might have held the office of
Archpriest of Hita, though there was no clear evidence of this.

two 'Passions of Jesus Christ' (sts. 1046–66), having no direct connection with the Archpriest's love life. Four songs are the above-mentioned *pastorela*-type *cantigas de serrana*—and here Juan Ruiz plays a series of variations by altering the relationship between the songs and their narrative introductions.[12] The remaining song (sts. 115–20) forms the centrepiece of the Archpriest's second, abortive love affair; together with its narrative framework it records with wry humour and sacrilegious punning a disastrous failure—not the celebration of love but the deflation of amorous pretensions.

A phenomenon which has yet to be explained is the indication by the author at several places that a song is to follow, where no song appears in the text: in five cases (sts. 80, 104, 171, 915, 1319) the author tells us that he sent them to the lady in question in the course of his wooing and in two (sts. 947, 1507) he says that they were written to express his feelings at the outcome of an affair. Were these songs present in the mss., the *Libro's* resemblance to the *Frauendienst* and the *Voir-Dit* would be considerably strengthened; but, though he promises them, Juan Ruiz gives us no love songs.[13]

The *Libro de buen amor* is as unique in Spanish literature as the *Frauendienst* is in German, and suggestions concerning the source for its form have been more wide-ranging. The opinion of so authoritative a figure as Menéndez y Pelayo that it was useless to look for a source may well have inhibited speculation on that score for a number of years; but earlier Ferdinand Wolf had pointed to the Oriental frame story as the ultimate source, and it was to this line of thought that Américo Castro returned dramatically in his epoch-making *España en su historia*, published in 1948. He saw the structure of the *Libro* as derived from the Arabic genre of the *maqamat*, which allowed for the interpolation of digressions and passages of verse into a framework of

12 See R. B. Tate, 'Adventures in the *sierra*', in *'Libro de buen amor' Studies*, ed. G. B. Gybbon-Monypenny, London, 1970, pp. 219–29.

13 Two of the mss., the Gayoso and the Salamanca, have, after what is clearly the formal ending of the work (st. 1634), a miscellany of songs with no linking narrative between. Three are common to both mss. (a fourth probably was, but is missing from G because of a *lacuna*), six are found in S only and two in G only. These songs have no obvious connection with the *Libro*, but no critic has seen fit to doubt that they are by Juan Ruiz—even though he himself invites any qualified person ('si bien trobar sopiere', st. 1629) to add or alter anything he chooses. Though Ulrich also invites whoever will to write in any songs which he, Ulrich, may compose in future (*Frauendienst*, st, 1847), there is no hint that he would welcome contributions from others.

episodes related to a single protagonist; he thought the immediate
source for Juan Ruiz was the treatise on love called *The Dove's Neck-
ring* by the eleventh century philosopher Ibn Hazm of Cordoba (which
Castro inaccurately termed a *maqamat*), in which several autobiographical episodes are recounted and a good deal of verse is interpolated. María Rosa Lida de Malkiel, who in an early study (1940)
had seen the autobiographical form of the *Libro* as arising out of the
preacher's tradition of using an exemplary 'I', advanced the view in
1959 that Juan Ruiz's inspiration was not the Arabic *maqamat* but the
derivative form of it developed by Spanish Jews, the immediate source
being *The Book of Delightful Instruction* by the twelfth century Barcelona
Jew Ibn Sabara, a work whose autobiographical framework is a
device enabling the author to range over any topics that interest him,
though it contains no stories of the author's love life. Both Castro and
Lida were able to point to parallels of theme and topic between the
Libro and the work they identified as its model. But there is no firm
evidence that any part of the *Libro* is derived from Arabic or Hebrew
literary sources (as opposed to any knowledge of their customs and
received notions which Juan Ruiz might have gleaned from their
continued presence in Spanish cities in his day). More recently Francisco
Rico has taken a fresh look at the medieval Latin tradition and has
postulated that Juan Ruiz's model was the pseudo-Ovidian *De Vetula*,
which is cast in autobiographical form, with various interpolated
didactic digressions and which presents similar situations and topics to
those found in the *Libro*. The clear evidence of Juan Ruiz's familiarity
with the Ovidian tradition greatly strengthens the case, in Rico's
view.[14]

I hope that the foregoing survey, brief and superficial though it is,
establishes my claim that the works I have discussed have enough
features in common to constitute a genre. Attempts by scholars to

14 Ferdinand J. Wolf, *Historia de las literaturas castellana y portuguesa*, translated by M. de Unamuno, Madrid, undated, p. 154; M. Menéndez y Pelayo,
Historia de la poesía castellana en la Edad Media, Madrid, 1911–16, I, ch. v,
especially p. 309; Américo Castro, *España en su historia*, Buenos Aires, 1948,
ch. ix, especially pp. 402 ff. (later versions of this book modify but do not
substantially alter Castro's thesis); María Rosa Lida de Malkiel, 'Notas para la
interpretación, influencia, fuentes y texto del *Libro de buen amor*', *Revista
de filología hispánica*, II (1940), pp. 105–50, and 'Nuevas notas para la interpretación del *Libro de buen amor*', *Nueva revista de filología hispánica*, XIII (1959), pp.
17–82; Francisco Rico, 'Sobre el origen de la autobiografía en el *Libro de buen
amor*', *Anuario de estudios medievales*, IV (1967), pp. 301–26.

explain the nature and provenance of these works individually, in apparent unawareness of the existence of similar works, have been inconclusive. Recognition that they belong to a genre does not, of course, immediately solve the problem: as I said at the beginning, the lack of links between the individual works (with the exception of the *Voir-Dit* and the *Espinette amoureuse*) suggests that each was arrived at by a separate path. But recognition of the genre helps to isolate the essential features which define the form, and this should clarify the issue for each individual work. For example, the superficial resemblance between the *Vita Nuova* and the *prosimetrum* seems less significant than the fact that Dante was writing an explanation of independent and independently composed lyric poems.

I now hope to show that in the case of the *Voir-Dit* and the *Espinette amoureuse* the incorporation of independent songs into a narrative is the fundamental factor, the starting point from which the genre developed. To begin with, we find that both Machaut and Froissart adopted this practice in other works of rather different nature. Machaut incorporated lyric poems in two erotic allegories, the *Remède de Fortune* (written, according to Hoepffner, before 1342) and the *Fonteinne amoureuse* (c. 1360–61).[15] The former is a didactic allegory in the customary vision form, into which Machaut interpolates a series of his own songs, each representing a different form, as he points out: 'un dit qu'on claimme "lai"' (l. 430), 'un dit qu'on appelle "complainte"' (l. 901), etc. Hoepffner considered (p. xxxvi) that these songs were specially composed for the *Remède*. In the *Fonteinne amoureuse* Machaut overhears a lover's complaints, makes contact with him and goes walking with him to discuss his love situation; they fall asleep at a fountain and both have the same allegorical dream. The lyrical interpolations consist of the 'Complainte de l'amant' overheard by Machaut (ll. 235–1034), a 'Confort de l'amant' sung by the lady in the dream (ll. 2207–526) and a final *rondel* sung by the lover (ll. 2825 ff.). Froissart interpolated songs into his early poem, the *Paradys d'amour*, in which he imagines himself appearing before the god of love at his court and being crowned by his lady with a 'chapelet' as a reward for his songs, six of which are included, including the well known *balade*, sung at his lady's request and with various allegorical figures sitting round, 'sus toutes fleurs j'aime la margherite' (ll. 1627–53). In the *Prison amoureuse* Froissart repeats the basic formula of the *Espinette*, but

15 Machaut, *Oeuvres*, II and III; for Hoepffner's discussion of these works, see II, pp. i–liv, and III, pp. xx–xlii.

reduces his own role to that of observer and counsellor, the protagonist-
lover being his friend 'Rose' (Wenceslas, Duke of Bohemia). Both
songs and letters are incorporated; the songs which are here attributed
to 'Rose' are elsewhere given as Froissart's own. In the *Méliador*, a
30,000-line *roman d'adventures* in the old Arthurian vein, he included
nearly eighty songs on the pretext that they are composed and sung
by various characters in the story while travelling and so forth.[16]

Thus for Machaut and Froissart the idea of interpolating songs into
a narrative poem is not inseparable from, not does it appear to grow
out of, the concept of an erotic autobiography. It is, rather, the other
way round. The combination of narrative and lyric verse was clearly
capable of being, and had in fact been, exploited in a number of ways.
In this respect the *Méliador* is particularly interesting, for not only does
Froissart revert to a theme of a bygone age but he also revives what
proves to be the first way in which the combination was tried.

Jean Renart's *Roman de la Rose ou de Guillaume de Dôle* has been
dated variously between *c.* 1200 and 1228.[17] The traditional plot of the
enterprising heroine who clears her name so that she can marry the
prince by tricking her slanderer into proving himself a liar is worked
out in a comparatively realistic contemporary setting. Renart interpolates songs at forty-eight places in the courses of the 5,655 lines of
the poem. Each song is introduced as being sung by a character or a
group in the course of the story. The unique ms. gives varying amounts
of the song quoted, usually a refrain or a stanza, but presumably
Renart intended that the whole song should actually be performed at
the point where it occurs and, as the songs were well known (most can
be identified in contemporary *chansonniers* and some are by well known
troubadours such as Jaufré Rudel or Gace Brulé),[18] he himself may
have written down only enough for the song to be identified. In his

16 Froissart, *Poésies*, I, pp. 1–52 and 211–347; *Méliador*, ed. A. Longnon, Paris
    (S.A.T.F.), 1895–99.
17 Jean Renart, *Roman de la Rose ou de Guillaume de Dôle*, ed. Félix Lecoy, Paris
    (C.F.M.A.), 1962. Lecoy dates the *Dôle* at 1228 (pp. vi–viii); G. Servois,
    editor of the S.A.T.F. edition (1893), suggested *c.* 1200; Rita Lejeune-Dehousse,
    L'Oeuvre de Jean Renart, Liège and Paris, 1935, pp. 73–82, arrives at 1208–18;
    in her edition of the *Dôle*, Paris (1936), p. xiii, she gives 1212–13; C. Mattioli,
    'Sulla datazione del *Guillaume de Dôle*', *Cultura Neolatina*, XXV (1965), pp. 91–
    112, argues for 1200–11.
18 See Lecoy, introduction, pp. xxii–xxix; Lecoy describes only forty-six songs,
    but one quotation (ll. 1335–67) is of an epic *laisse* and the song quoted at
    ll. 2514 ff. is the same as that quoted at ll. 295 ff.

preamble Renart makes three claims: firstly, that this insertion of 'chans et sons' into the *roman* is a new thing (l. 12); secondly, that his listeners will be saved from boredom because the singing of the songs will relieve the monotony of the recited narrative verse:

> Ja nuls n'iert de l'oïr lassez
> car, s'en vieult, l'en i chante et lit,
> et s'est fez par si grand delit
> que tuit cil s'en esjoïront
> qui chanter et lire l'orront,
> qu'il lor sera nouviaus toz jors.   [ll. 18–23]

and, thirdly, that he has made such a skilful selection from the *chansonniers* that people will think he must have written the words of the song himself:

> . . . s'est avis a chascun et samble
> que cil qui a fet le romans
> qu'il trovast toz les moz des chans,
> si afierent a ceuls del conte.   [ll. 26–9]

The validity of the last claim is, perhaps, best left to the reader's judgement, as Lecoy suggests (Introduction, p. xxii). More pertinent here is that the songs are clearly introduced in order to be performed during the recital of the narrative verse. That this was really the novelty that Renart claims is supported by the fact that in the *Galeran de Bretagne*, a slightly earlier work attributed by some to Renart (Lecoy, Introduction, p. v), a character is made to sing at several points, but either the song is not quoted (e.g. at ll. 2277 ff., 2297 ff.) or else the lines quoted rhyme with the surrounding narrative verse (ll. 6972 ff.), which indicates that in the *Galeran* the idea of having the song actually performed has not yet emerged.[19]

Whether or not such performaces of the *Dôle* as Renart envisaged ever took place, as a literary form it set a lasting fashion. It was almost immediately imitated, both in its plot and in the introduction of songs, by Gerbert de Montreuil in the *Roman de la Violette*.[20] Gerbert intro-

---

19 *Galeran de Bretagne*, ed. L. Foulet, Paris (C.F.M.A.), 1925. In the first instance the author gives the theme of the lay (ll 2303 ff.); in the second the reaction of the listeners is dwelt upon (ll. 6981 ff.). It was not haste to get on with the story that prevented him from quoting the songs.

20 Gerbert de Montreuil, *Roman de la Violette*, ed. D. L. Buffum, Paris (S.A.T.F.), 1928.

duces some forty songs from the contemporary *chansonniers* in the same fashion and he makes the same boasts in his preamble about the attractiveness of this new concept and the appropriateness of the songs to their context:

> Et s'est li contes biaus et gens
> que je vous voel dire et conter;
> car on i peut lire et chanter,
> et si est si bien accordans
> li cans au dit, les entendans
> en trai à garant qui di voir   [ll. 36–41]

Often no more than a line is quoted, rarely more than a stanza, but presumably Gerbert also intended that the songs should be sung in full during the performance of the work.

Buffum gives a list of twenty other works in which he indicates that Renart's device was imitated (p. lxxxiii, n.). This list, which I reproduce here, has been referred to by subsequent critics as though it were definitive:[21] *Cléomadés, Méliacin,* le *Châtelain de Coucy,* la *Châtelaine de St. Gilles,* les *Tournois de Chauvency,* le *Jeu de Robin et Marion,* le *Lai d'Aristote,* la *Poire, Renard le Nouvel,* la *Prison d'amour,* la *Cour de Paradis,* le *Salut d'amour,* la *Complainte douteuse,* l'*Espinette amoureuse,* le *Paradis d'amour,* le *Voir-Dit, Mariage des Sept Arts et des Sept Vertus, Traduction d'Ovide,* le *Mariage de Fauvel,* le *Roman de Renard.*

Not all these, however, can be described as narrative poems with independent lyric poems interpolated. The *Châtelaine de St Gilles* has a refrain at the end of each seven-line stanza, which carries on the sense of the stanza and does not constitute an independent song; the *Jeu de Robin et Marion* is a dialogue piece (Langlois calls it 'une pastorale dramatique'—edn., p. vi) with popular refrains interspersed; the *Saluts d'amour* and the *Complainte douteuse* are not narrative poems (the former is a direct plea to the poet's beloved, in which a refrain from a song is quoted at the end of each stanza, forming part of the sense of the whole, while the latter is a complaint addressed to Amours in *laisses* of octosyllabic couplets, interspersed with passages in lyric form which also carry on the sense of the poem); the *Mariage des Sept Arts,* in the version in Alexandrine quatrains, has Musique singing a refrain at the end of stanzas 38, 39, 43 and 44 and one complete song at the

---

21 E.g. by Lecoy, *Dôle,* p. xxiii, n. 1; by Delbouille in his edition of the *Châtelain de Couci* (see n. 26 below), p. lxiii, n. 1; by Lejeune-Dehousse, *L'Oeuvres . . . ,* p. 372, n. 3.

end; Baudouin de Condé's *Prison d'amour* has forty-nine refrains quoted, usually of two lines, which provide a summing up of or comment upon the situation, with no sign that the whole song was to be performed; one ms. of the *Roman de Fauvel* has an interpolated description of the marriage in which there are lyric insertions, but Långfors does not, unfortunately, print them.[22] Whether or not any of these seven very varied works owes its form to the influence of the *Guillaume de Dôle*, they are irrelevant from our point of view because the developments which concern us are along the lines of the interruption of the narrative by complete and independent songs. In this respect there are important omissions from Buffum's list: not only the *Remède de Fortune* and *Fonteinne amoureuse* of Machaut and the *Prison amoureuse* and *Méliador* of Froissart, which I have mentioned, but also the *Dit de la Panthère* of Nicole de Margival, to which I shall return.

Renart's precedent is followed without modification in the *Cléomadès* and the *Méliacin*, late thirteenth century *romans d'aventures* based on the magic horse theme: in the former, popular songs of the time are put into the mouths of the heroine and her companions as they wait for the hero, the songs appearing in two small groups: the *Méliacin* remains unpublished, but E. Stengel's publication of the twenty-four songs in their immediate contexts shows that the procedure is unchanged.[23] The same is true of the *Lai d'Aristote*, the *Romanz de la Poire*, the *Tournoi de Chauvency* and the *Renard le Nouvel*; but in each case there is some innovation as regards the characters who are made to sing.[24] In the *Lai d'Aristote* there is also a skilful use of the device

22 *Châtelaine de St Gilles*, in *Recueil général et complet des Fabliaux des XIIIe et XIVe siècles*, ed. A. de Montaiglon, Paris, 1872–90, I, pp. 135–46; *Jeu de Robin et Marion*, by Adam le Bossu, ed. E. Langlois, Paris (C.F.M.A.), 1924; *Salus d'amours*, in *Nouveau Recueil de contes, dits, fabliaux*, etc., ed. A. Jubinal, Paris, 1839–42, II, pp. 235–41; *La Complainte douteuse, Nouveau Recueil . . .*, II, pp. 242–56; *Mariage des Sept Arts*, ed. A. Långfors, Paris (C.F.M.A.), 1923; *Mariage de Fauvel*, see *Roman de Fauvel*, ed. A. Långfors, Paris (S.A.T.F.), 1919, appendix; Baudouin de Condé, *Li Prison d'amours*, in *Dits et Contes de B. de C. et de son Fils Jean de Condé*, ed. A. Scheler, Brussels, 1866, I, pp. 267–377.

23 Adenès le Rois, *Li Roumans de Cléomadès*, ed. A. van Hasselt, Brussels, 1865–66; E. Stengel, 'Die altfranzösischen Liedercitate aus Girardins d'Amiens *Conte du cheval de fust*', *Zeitschrift für romanische Philologie*, X (1886), pp. 460–76.

24 *Lai d'Aristote*, in *Recueil général . . .*, V, pp. 243–62; Messire Thibault, *Li Romanz de la Poire*, ed F. Stehlich, Halle, 1881; Jacques Bretel, *Le Tournoi de Chauvency*, ed. M. Delbouille, Liège and Paris, 1932; *Roman de Renard et le Renart le Nouvel*, ed. D. M. Méon, Paris, 1826. In the last case three of the

as a constructive element in the plot: Alexander's mistress sets out to seduce Aristotle as a revenge for his disapproval of her; she appears scantily clad before his cell, singing seductive songs. The first three songs serve to attract Aristotle's attention and to turn his thoughts in a sensual direction; the fourth is sung while the girl rides triumphantly on the back of the besotted philosopher. In the *Renart le Nouvel* the characters are animals, and various beasts are made to sing love songs (genuine love songs of the period) at the court of their king, obviously parodying the courtly *roman*. The *Poire* is an erotic allegory after the manner of the *Roman de la Rose* and has no 'real-life' characters apart from the poet and the beloved; Thibaut chooses to place songs in the mouths of his allegorical symbols: Courtoisie (ll. 885 ff.), Noblece (ll. 948 ff.), Douz Regard (ll. 1421 ff.) and so on. Apart from the question of the appropriateness of the song to the qualities symbolised by the singer, Thibaut's idea marks a step away from the logic and the realism of Renart's device. Lecoy points out the realistic nature of the contemporary setting in which Renart develops his fairy-tale plot (*Dôle*, pp. xiii ff.), with secondary figures bearing actual names of the period and many aspects of social behaviour accurately reflected. To put songs into the mouths of his noble and royal personages was also, surely, realistic: singing must have been a favourite pastime at social gatherings. This is borne out by the *Tournoi de Chauvency*. Composed by Jacques Bretel in or about the year 1285, it is an account in verse of a series of jousts and a tournament which were apparently held in that year. Many of the personages described as taking part, either in the lists or in the social gatherings attended in the evenings by the ladies and by those knights who were still fit after the day's jousting, can be identified as historical figures.[25] Bretel depicts these personages as singing, as the knights make their way to and from the lists or, more especially, after the evening meal. The tournament presumably took place in reality; but we cannot know whether Bretel was reporting the facts or using his imagination when, for example, he tells us that the Comtesse de Chiny started off the after-dinner dancing with the song 'Mal dehait ait qui ne vient en la dance' (ll. 1348 ff.) and that a certain Simon de Monclin was the first to reply in song (ll. 1360 ff.). We must

---

mss. give musical settings, which indicates that, although only a line of the song is quoted and it rhymes with the preceding introductory line, the songs were intended to be sung (see Méon, I, pp. ix ff.).

25 See Delbouille, *Tournoi* . . . . introduction, section XIII, 'Les Personnages historiques'.

assume, however, that he knew that to ascribe such behaviour to them would not displease his patrons. In a sense he is reversing Renart's procedure by making real-life persons behave like characters in a 'society' romance. But in both cases the behaviour reflects what was socially normal.

Closely contemporary to the *Tournoi de Chauvency* and, according to Delbouille, to some extent indebted to it is the *Roman du Chastelain de Couci et de la Dame de Fayel*, by a certain Jakemés, whom some scholars have thought to be Bretel himself.[26] Delbouille claims that Jakemés borrows whole passages from the *Tournoi* when describing a fictitious tournament at which his hero distinguishes himself (*Chastelain* . . . , pp. xlvi ff., especially lviii–lx). It might be assumed, therefore, that he also got from Bretel the idea of interpolating songs into his *roman*. But his particular innovation owes nothing to Bretel's example. His hero, Renault, Châtelain de Couci, is a poet as well as a knight-at-arms, who, after a protracted love affair with the Dame de Fayel, is tricked by her jealous husband into enrolling for Richard Coeur-de-Lion's crusade and dies from the effects of a poisoned arrow while being brought home from the Holy Land. In the course of this story he is inspired to compose seven songs and these are quoted in full at the appropriate places. Thus the songs cease to be a purely decorative element designed to relieve the monotony of narrative verse: they are integrated into the story and the story functions in part as an explanation of how they came to be written. Though Jakemés introduces three further songs, as being sung by other characters (echoing Renart's device still), a total of ten songs in a *roman* of 8,266 lines is sparing as compared with Bretel's thirty-five in the 4,563 lines of the *Tournoi*. Jakemés's deliberate passing over of an opportunity to introduce further songs at one point suggests that he did not regard the introduction of songs as important for its own sake:

Quant ot dit ceste chancon chi,
si recommenca a canter
une autre dame de coer gai.
Dire ne compter ne vous sai
les cancons que on y canta,
car je croi c'on ne vit pieca
fieste de caroller plus gente . . .   [ll. 3865–72]

26 Jakemés, *Roman du Chastelain de Couci et de la Dame de Fayel*, ed. J. E. Matzke and M. Delbouille, Paris (S.A.T.F.), 1936.

But the most interesting point about Jakemés's creation is that there really was a Châtelain de Couci, a certain Gui de Thourotte, *châtelain* from 1186 to 1203, who went on the third and fourth crusades and who eventually died on an expedition to the Holy Land. Furthermore, a number of songs in the *chansonniers* are attributed to a 'Châtelain de Couci' and four of those borrowed by Jakemés are thus attributed; of the other three, two are anonymous and one is found only in the *roman*. It seems reasonable to suppose that Jakemés had grounds for believing that all seven were by the real *châtelain* and that, had he found more songs attributed to him, he would have used them too.

The love story Jakemés tells is obviously fiction: the final episode, for instance, in which the Sire de Fayel intercepts the *châtelain*'s embalmed heart and has it served up to the Dame at a banquet, is a well known folk-lore theme (see Delbouille's introduction, pp. xlvi ff.). But Jakemés built his fictional structure on a foundation of what to him was apparently historical fact: namely the identification of the author of the seven songs with the author who died in the Holy Land. A fictional love story written round the songs of a real-life poet is a long step towards the concept of the *Frauendienst* or the *Voir-Dit*; the missing ingredient is the author's choice of himself as protagonist.

This ingredient is supplied by Nicole de Margival in his *Dit de la Panthère*, composed about the turn of the fourteenth century.[27] Margival's poem is mainly a dream allegory in the *Roman de la Rose* tradition, but with the attention concentrated on the discussions about love between the author and the god and goddess of love. Margival was not the first poet to interpolate songs into an allegory, as we have seen from the *Poire*, but his use of the device is more sophisticated than Thibaut's. The first of the ten interpolations is a *dit* which the poet recites to Dous-Penser, Esperance and Souvenirs to explain his desire (ll. 825–966); the next three are stanzas from songs by Adam de la Halle which Margival quotes to show Venus that her advice to be *hardis* in wooing does not have Adam's support (ll. 1073–81, 1086–95 and 1100–7); the fifth is a *dit* which Venus hands Margival so that he may offer it to the beloved (ll. 1152–210); the next three are quotations by Venus from songs by Adam about the folly of doubt and

27 Nicole de Margival, *Dit de la Panthère d'amours*, ed. H. A. Todd, Paris (S.A.T.F.), 1883. Todd gives the *terminus a quo* as 1290 (death of Drouart de la Vache, from whom Margival borrows) and the *terminus ad quem* as 1328 (death of Clémence of Hungary, who possessed copies of the *Panthère*); see introduction, pp. xxvi–xxvii.

despair (ll. 1518–28, 1543–60 and 1571–9); the ninth is a song by Adam which Margival quotes to Venus in praise of the state of love (ll. 1590–1629); the last is a *dit* which Amour gives Margival to present to the beloved (ll. 1744–865). The interpolations form a large part of the allegory: the quotations from Adam are used to make didactic points, almost as a preacher might quote from the *auctoritates*, while the three *dits*, clearly Margival's own, may have been composed specially for the *Panthère*, though they are straightforward love poems and could well stand independently.

In the allegory the use of the first person is, of course, conventional and didactic rather than personal, so that the identification of author and protagonist is not significant. But Margival adds an epilogue in which he contrasts the ideal conclusion to the affair expressed in the dream (the *panthère* is persuaded by Pitié, Bone Volontez and Grace to grant her *Merci* to the poet) with the reality: so far the lady has not shown him *Merci*. But he resolves to continue in her service and explains the reasons for his love and its effects upon him. These reflections serve to introduce five of his own songs, which he quotes in full. This first part of the epilogue ends with a *chant royal* by Adam de la Halle, quoted to show how humility in love leads to pessimism. Turning to address his lady directly, he pleads for her kindness, and this leads to the introduction of three further songs directed at her: the first describes the sentiments he would like her to express towards him; the second, the reaction which he would in that case experience; the third, after expressing gratitude to Amour for what love has brought him, makes a final plea to the lady for her *Merci*.

This epilogue, as Hoepffner noted,[28] resembles the *Vita Nuova* in its provision of a commentary around a group of the author's songs, relating them to his own love affair (whether true or fictional). But there is no history of the affair from its inception, as is the case with the other erotic autobiographies, nor are there any of the external details which characterise the *Voir-Dit* or the *Frauendienst*. Nevertheless, the *Panthère* provides a logical link, if one were needed, between the *Châtelain de Couci* and the *Voir-Dit*, between the romance built round the songs of a long-dead poet and the romance built round the poet's own songs.

The existence of the *Frauendienst*, composed more than a century earlier and apparently without there having been previous experiments

---

28 E. Hoepffner, 'Les Poésies lyriques du *Dit de la Panthère* de Nicole de Margival', *Romania*, LIII (1920), especially pp. 210 and 216.

to build upon, provides a warning against taking it for granted that the *Voir-Dit* needs to be explained as the end product of a series of formal developments such as I have described. But, given the existence of such a series of developments in a literary tradition with which Machaut must have been reasonably familiar (the *Méliador* shows that his pupil Froissart knew Renart's idea in its original form), it seems unreasonable to assume that he owed nothing to the experiments of earlier poets.

T. E. Hope

Gallicisms in Dante's *Divina Commedia*: a stylistic problem?

Quel che pende dal nero ceffo è Bruto
—vedi come si storce! e non fa motto! [Inferno, xxxiv 65-6]

I am not the first to observe with dismay how Dante fidgets uncomfortably upon his hard golden throne at the apex of the Italian literary establishment, how frequently Dante the poet suffers at the hands of Dante the Sage, the purveyor of precepts. Many a verse of the *Divina Commedia* has become so memorable, so timeless that it lives a life of its own, with a spatial and temporal autonomy so firmly established that its original context of time and place both within Dante's work and within his life seems to add but little to its essential meaning and may even appear to diminish it.

The lines cited above, which I should like to take as a starting-point for this tentative inquiry into a lesser known aspect of Dante's vocabulary, are also memorable, but in the simpler and more primitive sense that they are remembered by anyone who has read the *Divina Commedia*. And in remembering these two verses one recalls precisely their position within the narrative scheme of the work and the poignancy of the emotion which seethes around them. Yet despite their familiarity I wonder how many readers of Dante are aware that in these verses—which come at the climax of the focal and most intensely dramatic scene of the *Inferno*, at one of the high points of Dante's artistic creation and therefore of Italian literature—the most striking word, *ceffo*, is a borrowing from the *langue d'oïl*? And of those who are indeed aware that *ceffo* is an adaptation of Old French, *chef*, *chief*, how many have felt it worth while to consider what the intrusion of this *xénisme* might imply—or whether its status was for Dante that of a foreign word at all? Certainly Dante's earliest commentators felt that *ceffo* required to be glossed; not, as I see it, because the word had become obscure or archaic during the short period between Dante and Francesco da Buti, but quite the contrary—because the term was unfamiliar either on account of its register, or its novelty, or both. Some recent editors of

Dante also mention it in a philological footnote, perhaps to remark
upon the semantic difference between Dante's words and the French
original. But for the most part those who set their sights at the higher
academic levels choose to pass over the verse in silence, either because
they take a knowledge of these etymological details for granted or
because they assume that such knowledge is irrelevant to their purpose
as literary commentators.

They may be right. Much depends on what one understands by
'loan word' or 'linguistic borrowing'; whether, for instance, one thinks
that a lexical sign only merits the name of loan word when something
of its original form or sense remains to link it with the extraneous
system, or whether one continues with equanimity to use the same
global term when the lexical element was borrowed at a more or less
distant date in the past and has since become fully accepted into the
vocabulary of the receiving language. No one denies that Dante made
use of a number of words which originated in Northern French or
Provençal, even if, as Parodi claimed, 'è certo che Dante si mostra
meno corrivo a valersi di forme straniere che non siano di solito i suoi
contemporanei'.[1] It is widely assumed that gallicisms in the *Divina
Commedia*, like those of many another writer of the Duecento and the
Trecento, are part of the common fund of words in literary and spoken
usage at that time, with perhaps a slight individual variation such as
that tentatively defined by Migliorini in the *Storia della lingua italiana*,
p. 193, with reference to one or two observations made by Schiaffini
in an article written as long ago as 1928.

It is, of course, true that many of the borrowings from the *langue
d'oïl* and the *langue d'oc* which formed part and parcel of the lexical
resources available to Dante and his contemporaries were of long and
respectable standing, even in his day. Most terms relating to feudalism
are old enough for the lexicologist to wonder whether they should be
classified as gallicisms, borrowings from Romance or borrowings
direct from the Germanic superstrata, especially Frankish and Lango-
bard.[2] Latin's position as a universal intermediary for 'serious', official
or bureaucratic writing sometimes helps the historical lexicologist,

1 E. G. Parodi, 'La rima e i vocaboli in rima nella *Divina Commedia*', *Bull. Soc.
Dant.*, III (1896), pp. 81–156; repr. in Parodi, *Lingua e letteratura: studi di
teoria linguistica e di storia dell'italiano antico*, Venice, 1957, pp. 203–84. The
reference here is to the *Ling. e lett.* edition, p. 274.

2 The reader is referred to my own brief survey of the problem, *Lexical Borrowing in the Romance Languages* (1971), I, pp. 66–73.

sometimes hinders him in his quest for the true dating of a neologism. It is clear, for example, that a good deal of feudal and legal terminology —two semantic categories which have obvious affinities on the extra-linguistic plane—developed in Latin and was normally current in that language rather than in any Romance idiom; and that ultimately these terms reached French and Italian independently from the same primal source. Occasionally, however, the presence of a Latin equivalent attested earlier may be very helpful indeed to the etymologist if it bears formal traces of French, as in Low Latin *scuerius*, 1105 in the *Liberatio Orientis*, which cannot be construed as a form of the Latin military term *scutarius*, attested from the reign of Constantine, but must rather be interpreted as a reflex of the Old French word *escuiier* clothed in Latin garb to meet the needs of the writer, suggesting strongly that the French borrowing rather than the Latin form *scutarius* was uppermost in the mind of the Italian or Norman–Italian clerk who was composing the work, and that presumably it was also familiar to those who read him.[3]

As with English, many gallicisms entered Italian through Norman intermediaries. Here again one suspects that the actual volume of borrowings from the late eleventh century onward was much greater than the information now available to us would suggest. It is reasonable to suppose that such was the case, and any Romance etymologist would agree. The mere handful of attestations in the few Italian texts remaining from the twelfth century cannot adequately reflect the amount of lexical contacts which must have taken place at that time. In chronological terms, many of the borrowings from French which for lack of earlier attestations we are obliged to ascribe to the thirteenth century must have been current in the language anything up to a century or even a century and a half earlier, though exactly when, in what register, and still more in what dialect we shall probably never know.

It follows that in Dante's day quite a large number of what one might consider to be typical medieval gallicisms must have been accepted into different levels of usage for three, four or even five generations.

Nevertheless it is also undoubtedly true that some of them were borrowed more recently, nearer to Dante's lifetime. If many of the gallicisms which first appear in texts of the Duecento should by rights

3 See R. R. Bezzola, *Abbozzo di una storia dei gallicismi italiani nei primi secoli*, Heidelberg, 1925, p. 114 and notes.

belong to the previous century, it remains true that the impact of medieval French upon European languages in general was appreciably greater in the thirteenth century than in the earlier period. This is so of French loan words in English, which are excellently documented and where there is a clear distinction to be made between the original Anglo–Norman importations and words from Central French, which rise to a peak during the course of the thirteenth century. One supposes that something very similar happened in Italy, for the *external* or *imposed* motives for lexical contact referable to the dominant position of French culture in its many guises applied to Italy and the Italian language in just the same way as it did to England and to Middle English; while the *internal* or *induced* aspect of borrowing also offers a parallel in terms of the close political involvement which existed (Charles d'Anjou and his court; conflicts with the Holy See) as well as in the economic ambitions of a commercially sophisticated Italy which looked to France for markets and a suitable terrain for its banking and handling operations.[4]

In attempting to envisage what Dante's attitude towards these words of foreign ancestry might have been it is relevant also to recall what Parodi said about the poet's 'moderato arcaismo', harking back to 'l'uso toscano di poco più che una generazione innanzi alla sua';[5] that is to say, contemporary with the outstanding writers of the mid-century, including Iacopone da Todi (1230–1306), Guittone d'Arezzo (1230–94) and Brunetto Latini (1220–94), all three of whom stand high on the lists of those in whose works the Duecento gallicisms as a whole are first attested, and who willingly press into service words of Northern French provenance already current in their day. There is thus a reasonable possibility, to put it no more strongly, that a number of the sixty or seventy words of Northern French origin in the *Divina Commedia* were of recent introduction when Dante acquired his mastery of language, or, better, at that period to which Dante was inclined to turn when seeking for norms of linguistic usage, according to Parodi's judgement. To put it in lexicological terms, some of the gallicisms Dante uses may still have been in the *interim period* that elapses between the time when a neologism is coined or imported from another idiom and its definitive acceptance into the language.[6] This interval may

4 For an explanation of the terms *external* (*imposed*) and *internal* (*induced*) referring to lexical borrowing *vide* Hope, *op. cit. supra*, II, pp. 722–4, 733.
5 Parodi, *op. cit.*, p. 253.
6 For an explanation of the term *interim period* see Hope, *op. cit.*, pp. 609–11.

cover a number of years; a word may attain a measure of currency only to lose favour and be launched a second time or a third time, usually in slightly different circumstances. The period is one of experimentation and of tentative confrontation with the semantic pattern that already exists; it is also one in which the stylistic or expressive potential of the word is enhanced because it may be used to form novel collocations. The new term may participate in imagery with greater impact because it is at liberty to inspire and retain new aesthetic or emotive connotations; in brief, it has not yet found its feet in terms of either form or meaning and therefore is imbued with a greater suggestive force, a greater power to stimulate the imagination of both author and audience, and in particular to spur the reader to co-operate positively in the twofold process of literary creation.

Apart from its relevance to *langue* and the fund of linguistic signs available to the creative artist who uses the medium of language at any given time, the concept of *interim period* has an individual or idiosyncratic application to the linguistic habits of a given individual—a dichotomy which in stylistic corresponds to the descriptivism of Bally and his long line of followers on the one hand and the differing approaches of individual or genetic stylisticians on the other. As a rule an individual tends to use a word with the connotations it acquired for him when he first availed himself of it earlier in life. One would not need to venture too far into the land of surmise to suppose that for Dante much of his sense of linguistic register as well of emotive and aesthetic connotation was acquired at the time of his pupil-and-scholar relationship with Brunetto Latini, whose feeling for the French language and literary competence in that idiom are well known. We are therefore led to conclude that although it is hard to date early gallicisms with any degree of accuracy, for the reasons already mentioned, many of the sixty-odd words of French origin which appear in the *Divina Commedia* are genuinely attributable to a period earlier in the thirteenth century, as their first attestations available to us seem to indicate. A certain number of them are found already in the Sicilian school: *cangiare* (*Inf.* II, 38; III, 101, etc.), *obblio* (*Purg.* X, 90, Par. X, 60), *sire* (eight examples), *diffendere* in the sense of 'forbid' (*Inf.* XV, 27), *motto* (ten examples) and *alleggiare* (*Inf.* XXII, 22), also used figuratively by Dante as generally by his predecessors (*alleggiar la via*, *Purg.* XII, 14), the latter current outside the Sicilian ambit in Angiolieri and Fr. da Barberino. But these are very much a minority (the reader will note that I am speaking of loan words which may be traced back more particularly to Northern French, not Provençal). It is instructive to check through a glossary based on the Sicilian school like Panvini's[7] and notice how few of Dante's gallicisms from the *langue d'oïl* appear there. As one would expect, some of the rest—of the majority group, that is—are found in Brunetto Latini, among them *avvantaggio* (*Par.* XXVI, 31; two other examples read *vantaggio*) and *diffalta* (*Purg.* XXVIII, 94 and 95, meaning 'sin'; *Par.* IX, 52, implying 'broken faith, betrayal'). Iacopone precedes Dante in using *abbandonare, addobbare, reame* and *retaggio* (in the form *ereditaggio*), though all these may have been current earlier in the restricted feudal sense. *Volentiere* (*-i*) is in Guittone before Dante (ten examples, including two of *volontieri*). *Cisterna, Inf.* XXXIII in the sense of 'well', fig., 'spring, fountain' in *Purg.* XXXI, 141, is found in Dino Compagni and Bono Giamboni, Dante's near contemporaries, while the latter also uses *bolgia* (eleven examples in the *Divina Commedia*), *leggiero* (ten examples) and *sentiero* (seven examples). There is a large group of Dante's gallicisms which first appear in the romances and epics of the later thirteenth century closely associated with Northern France: *arnese* in the *Novellino* and *I Fatti di Cesare*, though Dante uses it with the idiosyncratic meaning of 'fortress' (*Inf.* XX, 70) as well as the more usual generic sense of 'equipment' (*Purg.* XXIX, 52; but used even here in a rather unusual context to designate collectively the seven torches or candelabra used to illuminate the actors in the 'pageant' preceding Beatrice's triumph); *gaggio* (*Par.* VI, 118) in the same two sources, together with Dante da Maiano; *bordello* in the *Novellino* and the *Fiore*; *dama* in the most of the French-inspired texts as well as in the *Tristano Riccardiano* and the *Fiore*; *assembrare, bias(i)mo, biasimare* and *mestiere*, equally well attested in an extremely wide range of texts both native and foreign in their affilia-tions. The words common to the *Fiore* and Dante (cf. also *giubbetto* and *corsiero, -e*) have a particular interest for those who are convinced that Durante and Dante are one and the same person.

But there is still more cogent evidence to suggest that some at least of Dante's gallicisms may have been recent innovations in the language and therefore still in their *interim period* at the time when the *Divina Commedia* was composed. Quite a number of the Old French borrow-ings in Dante's poem are in fact the very first attestations of these words that have yet been brought to light by lexicologists. *Ceffo* itself is one of them; so is *acceffare* 'to fasten upon, seize in the jaws', referring

---

7 B. Panvini, *Le rime della scuola siciliana*, II, *Glossario* (*Bibl. dell' Archivum Romanicum*, LXXII), Florence, 1962–64.

to a dog worrying a hare (*Inf.* XXIII, 18). Others are *alluminare, bastardo, brogliare, burro, cordigliero, lai, rivera* meaning 'river'—the complete list into the 'teens. We are obliged, naturally, to treat these first attestations as no more than provisional, for at any moment some earlier example may be found. But the lexical facts as they stand at present are suggestive, even though they can never be conclusive; and they imply that if the great Florentine was 'mildly archaic' at some levels of linguistic usage (always assuming that this judgement is a sound one) he can when he wishes be very much a man of his own time as far as lexis is concerned. A word like *ceffo* may, of course, have been current in the spoken language before Dante enshrined it in a work of literature. The same applies to most of his other 'first' examples, together with a goodly number of those which have already been mentioned, where Dante exploits lexical conventions already estab-lished. In the case of *ceffo* the pejorative shift from 'head' to 'muzzle' implies a certain period of usage for the semantic restriction to take place and the specialised application to become established. Dante's propensity for basing his images and other heightened forms of literary statement upon practical, down-to-earth concepts is too well known to require any emphasis on my part; I merely note with interest that in this particular his employment of Old French loan words is closely similar to that of the native Italian lexicon. Lest this may seem some-thing of a *vérité de Lapalisse,* let me add that Dante's borrowings from Provençal, in harmony with those of his contemporaries from that language, are typically of quite a different nature. Duecento and Trecento Provençalisms have a strongly literary connotation which arises from the aesthetic associations traditionally attached to the words themselves: they are 'literary terms' in their own right, a farrago of stylistically charged neologisms which is cherished and handed down with remarkably little wastage or substitution to Petrarch and beyond. Except for one or two examples like *vallea, lai* or *fiordaliso* which have innate expressive values at the phonostylistic or lexicostylistic (seman-tic) level, Dante's borrowings are remarkably un-literary—almost paradoxically so, at first sight. Whatever their stylistic motivation may be, it is at any rate very different in nature from that of the Provençal elements. This is why it is important to draw a distinction between the contribution of the *langue d'oïl* and that of the *langue d'oc* when seeking to evaluate the influence of foreign idioms upon the literary norms of medieval Italian. The impact of the *langue d'oc* upon thirteenth century Italian is well documented, having attracted the attention of scholars for several decades (though it would do no harm to bring some of their findings up to date); that of the *langue d'oïl*, on the other hand, has remained uncodified.

We can also usefully take cognisance at this stage of the fact that many of the words we have before us, particularly the 'first attestations', appear in those passages of the poem which consist of direct speech. To put it another way, many of Dante's borrowings, as well as being in themselves typically 'spoken' or everyday words, are actually used as such by the characters in his poetic drama. One of them, *alluminare* (*Purg*, XI, 81) appears in direct speech while seeming at the same time to hint at words spoken and feelings shared on a previous occasion, so that what superficially is a neutral, concrete artisan's term—to illuminate a manuscript—becomes in Dante's hands the agent by which a complex and subtle play of emotion is evoked. Several other matter-of-fact gallicisms turn up in similarly affective contexts; but we must not anticipate what rightly belongs to a later stage in our exposé.

Scholars who discuss Dante's versification have always devoted a good deal of attention to his choice of rhymes. Not infrequently their appreciation takes a form which comes near to that of an *apologia* in which the writer seeks to explain or, better, to explain away the poet's use of alternative and anomalous forms, regionalisms, nonce words and personal coinages to eke out his rhymes (or so it seems to the casual observer). Parodi's venerable article of 1896 cited earlier was one of the surveys composed in this defensive spirit, though, as one would expect, its upshot was to vindicate the poet on all counts. Parodi's approach concerns us here because he gives *vocaboli stranieri* a place, though a minor one, among the potentially offending words, and a number of those he draws attention to appear in our own list of confirmed gallicisms (*cennamella, diffalta, giuggiare, ostello* and *villa* meaning 'city', for instance). The view that Dante uses such ecoticisms as appear in the *Divina Commedia* in the same way as the other anomalistic items— solely to meet the exigencies of rhyme—is very widely held even nowadays; one hears it discussed among colleagues. Yet even a superficial assessment will show that the accusation has no substance. It is perhaps convenient that *giuggia* (*Purg*, XX, 48) fits in well with *aduggia* and especially with *Bruggia*; but one could hardly have a more accommodating list of place names to ring the changes on (v. 46)! And as Zingarelli pointed out long ago, the man who is using *giuggiare* instead of *giudicare* is after all a 'Frenchman', Hugues Capet.[8] The notorious *flailli* (*Par.* xx, 14), with its varying manuscript tradition, uncertain French etymon (*flavel*? *flaiel*?) and possible Sicilian intermediary, is no easy way out for a rhymester; on the contrary, its egregious form poses a deliberate metrical conundrum—which the author neatly answers with *lapilli* and *squilli*. Actually, few of the gallicisms at the rhyme are words of this kind. They usually display a pattern which can be readily paralleled in native vocabulary, e.g. well attested suffixes or other easily matched morphemes: cf. *avvantaggio, oltraggio, ostello, bastardi, roccia, roggio, vallea, rivera, motto, arnese, ancora* and many another equally amenable example.

Dante's use of alternative cognates from different dialects or from Italian and an (ultimately) foreign source has been strongly deprecated. One concurs with Migliorini that 'Dante approfitta volentieri della possibilità di servirsi di un quadrisillabo oppure di un trisillabo anche se questa non sia la ragione esclusiva'[9] and agrees that pairs like *cambiare–cangiare, lampada–lampa* are not infrequently found; but even here one must tread warily. I part company with Migliorini when he avers that 'manicare e manducare sono usati promiscuamente con mangiare'.[10] What of

> O tu che mostri per sí bestial segno
> odio sovra colui che tu ti mangi . . .

where the gallicism alone can hope to convey something of the crunch of tooth on bone, the ravening yet unnatural hunger of this dreadful scene, and to express the loathing of him who beholds it? Here the verb *mangiare* has become as much a *bestial segno* as the act it denotes. *Manducare* would never do in this context. It is a gentle contadino of a word.

A wise man will steer clear of any passively critical assessment of Dante's technique as a versifier, certainly when seeking for diagnostics to characterise the *mots voyageurs* which find their way into his literary masterpiece. A metrical conjuncture which would present itself to lesser writers as a problem to tackle and overcome as best they might

8 I note that Sapegno considers the detail worth taking up: 'È un gallicismo . . . non comune, entrato nella lingua poetica con Guittone: in Dante compare in quest'unico caso e, messo in bocca a un francese, potrebbe essere una nota di colore locale, secondo un procedimento consueto nella tecnica dei narratori' (*La Nuova Italia* edn., Turin, 1967, p. 220).

9 Bruno Migliorini, *Storia della lingua italiana*, Florence, 1961, p. 190.

10 *Ibid.*

becomes for Dante an opportunity to display boldness and virtuosity. We may therefore find acceptable Parodi's conclusion:

> Nella sua imaginazione meravigliosamente plastica e . . . rudemente originale, egli vuole la rima vigorosa ed audace, che s'adatti ai muscoli del suo pensiero, come una maglia, e che lo atteggi così, da renderlo quasi sensibile alla vista ed al tatto; e se la rima non si pieghi di buona voglia, egli cerca altrove il suo vocabolo o ne foggia uno nuovo . . .[11]

with the important proviso that when loan words are involved the rhyme seems in no way to be recalcitrant, but malleable and subservient to the craftsman's ends. Where the word does something other than slot easily into his verse its function is a gainful one: it stands out by reason of the positive stylistic contribution it makes.

There is another mistaken impression which we can usefully correct before passing on to the words which are crucial to our inquiry: that Dante's gallicisms appear *only* at the rhyme and not at random elsewhere in the line. This is a fallacy which can easily be dispelled by a simple statistical exercise, yet it persists. I have heard Italian philologists maintain quite confidently that it is so. An analysis for exploratory purposes of twenty words chosen indiscriminately gave the following result: (a) total number of occurrences in the *Divina Commedia*, 91, i.e. a theoretical average of 4·55 attestations per word; (b) number of occurrences in non-final positions with the line, 46; (c) number of occurrences at the rhyme, 45.

A corpus of twenty words is very small, as for that matter is the total number of gallicisms involved when viewed in proportion to Dante's vocabulary as a whole, so anything one may deduce from it can be no more than a hint. Yet a further analysis of the sample seems to adumbrate one or two other patterns which are worth our consideration.

In the first place the proportion 46: 45, while it proves that words do occur readily elsewhere in the line, still shows a marked preference for the final position. The contention that gallicisms are found in the rhyme is therefore justified in the spirit though not in the letter. My guess is that a truly even distribution might show something like three or four to one in favour of a medial or initial position. Admittedly it is hard to decide what a random distribution means in proportional terms,[12] but this ratio may be taken as a reasonable theoretical average

11 *Ling. e lett.*, p. 215.
12 The main difficulties are prosodic, because the stress pattern and number of syllables in a word may limit its possible positions within a verse, and struc-

to measure from. Secondly, the words seem to fall into two contrasting groups which form what one might call a polarity. Six of them are found on seven or more occasions during the course of the *Commedia*; in fact the total number of occurrences for these six words is seventy-one, an average of more than ten times per word. Moreover, this group accounts for nearly three-quarters of the initial and medial examples. The details are as follows (the first figure of the ratio indicates occurrences at the rhyme, the second figure occurrences elsewhere):

	Ratio	*Totals*	
sentiero	4 : 3		
sire	3 : 5		
volentier(i)	2 : 8		
motto	7 : 3	Rhyme	29
bolgia	1 : 10	Elsewhere	42
abbandonare	12 : 13		71

Note that the two words which seem to run counter to the trend of the others, *abbandonare* and *motto* (actually *far motto* in almost every case: cf. my opening quotation) are attested in forms which are prosodically more suitable to appear at the end of the verse.

On the opposite side of the polarity is a larger group of gallicisms attested either twice or once only, and these are far more likely to appear at the rhyme, thus:

	Ratio	*Totals*	
addobbare	1 : 0		
acceffare	1 : 0		
giuggiare	1 : 0		
lamps	1 : 0		
alluminare	1 : 1		
avvantaggiare	1 : 1		
rampognare	1 : 1		
retaggio	1 : 1		
approcciare	2 : 0	Rhyme	12
arnese	2 : 0	Elsewhere	6
alleggiare	0 : 2		18

tural, since lexical items are not free to take up every theoretically available position within a given structure, so the number of 'possible' positions is notably fewer than the average number of words the verses contain. These collocational limitations differ from one lexical item to another.

Only three words fall between these extremes, (*av*)*vantaggio*, *allumare* and *biasmo*, attested three, four and five times respectively, four at the rhyme and eight elsewhere.

For me the important thing about these figures is that they confirm precisely the impression I had gained intuitively while revolving in my mind the problem of Dante's loan words as a whole; and this is the construction I should like to put upon them.

In the first group, which is perhaps better exemplified elsewhere than in this sample, one might more readily expect to find the borrowings which have passed their *interim period* and have become fully accepted into the language. Those attested in something approaching the average proportion (rhyme versus non-rhyme) might be considered most typical of this group. The adverb *ancor*(*a*), which in the opinion of most etymologists owes something to an extraneous influence, though the degree of interference involved is open to dispute, is found on somewhat more than a hundred occasions, of which about one in four are at the rhyme. If my surmise is correct these words are in principle less likely to possess a *valeur stylistique* than the other, larger group which is also signally represented in the rest of the borrowed vocabulary. This majority group of rarely attested words— almost all the relevant ones appear on one or two occasions only[13]— is responsible for the supposition that gallicisms appear exclusively at the rhyme. They are found at the rhyme because that is the most emphatic position, and one where any stylistic aura the word may possess can best be exploited, not because they are needed to help the poet complete his terzinas. One of the borrowed words appears in what is the supreme strategic position afforded by Dante's chosen metre, the final verse, the curtain line, as it were, of a canto. I am sure all readers of Dante will agree that in

Io fei *giubbetto* a me delle mie case   [*Inf.* XIII, 151]

the gallicism contributes worthily to one of the most shocking and dramatic lines of the *Inferno*, where the horror and criminality of self-murder are set in a matrix of utter finality and despair. The dark brutality of a borrowed word evokes the one, inspired prosody the other. I might add that *giubbetto's* expressive power is not diminished

---

13 Others which appear once only in the *Commedia* are *bastardo*, *bersaglio*, *biasimare*, *bordello*, *brogliare*, *burro*, *cennamella*, *cordigliero*, *corsiere*, *gabbo*, *giubbetto*, *leuto*, *schifo*; and twice only: *ceffo*, *cisterna*, *fiordaliso*, *lai*, *mastino*, *vallea*, *veltro*.

but heightened by the fact that it is a *hapax* in Dante and a rare word in Italian before Dante's time, to the extent that Francesco da Buti has to explain to his less informed readers what it means, that 'questo giubbetto è vocabolo francesco e significa luogo della forche'.[14]

Novelty, rarity, dramatic intensity of context, key position in the line —what other attributes can we discover to complete our picture of Dante's typical gallicism? One, affectivity, has been hinted at though not overtly identified in most of the verses we have cited from the *Commedia* so far. Almost all the words which concern us appear in contexts where powerful emotions are portrayed, and where strong feelings are inspired in the reader. The emotions are essentially those which attend upon tragedy, fear, horror, hatred, wrath, moral indignation and a little pity, gradually giving way to the expression of joy, love and ineffable peace of mind which accompany the certitude of divine intervention and ultimate salvation; but the gallicisms on the whole are more appropriate to the first *phasis* than the second. Not that Dante's borrowings are all either pejorative or neutral; occasionally a word is beautiful in itself (*cennamella*) and used to animate concepts which are intrinsically beautiful:

> Quante il villan ch'al poggio si riposa
>   nel tempo che colui che'l mondo schiara
>   la faccia sua a noi tien meno ascosa
> come la mosca cede a la zanzara,
>   vede lucciole giú per la *vallea* . . .   [*Inf.* XXVI, 25–9]

But we must not forget the matter to which the simile refers, nor fail to notice the next gallicism, this time an ugly one, which brings us sharply down from Arcadia not only to earth but to the pit of Hell:

> Di tante fiamme tutta resplendea
>   l'ottava *bolgia*, sí com'io m'accorsi
>   tosto che fui la 've 'l fondo parea.   [*Ibid.*, 31–3]

Lai, which passes for a *trouvaille* of Dante's, in the *Commedia* has an elegiac if not frankly tragic resonance; the lays which the nightingale sings are sad ones (*Purg.* IX, 13), and those of the cranes (*Inf.* V, 46) provide a comparison with which to describe the lament of the Lustful

---

14 *Grande dizionario della lingua italiana* (S. Battaglia), s.v. *giubbetto*.

who go *traendo guai* as they are borne along and buffeted by the *aere maligno*, the everlasting wind. Even mellifluous *fiordaliso*, though it graces the heads of the four-and-twenty elders (*Purg.* XXIX, 83) is used on the other occasion by Hugues Capet to denote the French faction in the opprobrious *Attentat d'Anagni* (*Purg.* XX, 86).

But pejoratives are thicker on the ground. Mystic, symbolic *veltro* has its antithesis in *mastino* 'mastiff', a fierce, cruel animal seen hunting a thief (*Inf.* XXI, 44), or used as an epithet to characterise two hell-hounds in human shape, the Black Guelph noblemen Malatesta da Verrucchio and his son. We have already had cause to refer to *acceffare* and *ceffo*, which with *mastino*, *corsiero* and *veltro* provide further resources for Dante's celebrated animal imagery. Where there is crime and punishment there are also recrimination and invective: *rampognare* joins the older gallicism *biasimare* to extend the vocabulary of odium and reproof (a 'dynamic' conceptual field which, being by nature hyperbolical, requires frequent refurbishing: Dante also uses *riprendere*; *rinfacciare* may be a little later, in Domenico Cavalca, but *rimproverare* is already in Iacopone, and *rimprocciare* probably dates from the time of Brunetto Latini). Words which fall within this semantic area are still better exemplified in the laments and denunciations through which much of the passion of the *Commedia* is unleashed, as Guido del Duca's

> Oh Romagnuoli tornati in bastardi!   [*Purg.* XIV, 99]

or Dante himself, reaching down for language bitter and vulgar enough to castigate his native land with, a land that was formerly the sojourn of all that was noble; now

> Non donna di provincie, ma bordello!   [Purg. VI, 79]

Except for the metonymic use of *fiordaliso* just cited and the remote possibility of local colour in Capet's speech, there is no internal evidence to suggest that any of our words gain stylistic momentum or acquire meaningfulness within the literary context of the poem because of their continuing association with French—apart from one outstanding exception: that of the verb *alluminare* in the limited technical sense we referred to a little while ago (the second attestation of *alluminare* is a different lexical item, synonymous with *allumare*—*Purg.* XXII, 66). It will be recalled that Dante expressly identifies the word as a gallicism in the scene on the first cornice of Purgatory, that of the

proud, when he addresses the renowned miniaturist Oderisi da
Gubbio in what one assumes are strongly approbatory terms:

'Oh!' diss'io lui 'non sei tu Oderisi,
l'onor d'Agobbio e l'onor di quell'arte
ch'alluminar chiamata è in Parisi?'   [*Purg.* XI, 79–81]

Superficially straightforward, the reference in reality is one of the
abiding minor enigmas of Dantean exegesis. Is the poet merely 'indulging in a little display of his knowledge of the right technical phrase',[15]
as many think, or has he some purpose more closely integrated with
the narrative or the mood of the canto? Dante does enjoy displaying
his technical knowledge, or rather exploiting it in a number of medi-
tated and artistically productive ways. But I feel that Professor Sapegno
is nearer the mark when he says that 'tutta la frase deve avere, nell'inten-
zione di Dante, un significato allusivo: compiaciuto ricordo di lontane
conversazioni, fra artisti, sui segreti del mestiere . . .? Certo è che tutto
l'episodio vive in questo clima di reminiscenze fra uomini . . .'[16] If,
as seems likely, Dante did actually meet Oderisi about the year 1270
I think the deeper meaning of the allusion may well rest upon the
precise connotation at that time of *alluminare* as opposed to the traditional term *miniare*, its exact synonym, on the face of things. What if
Dante were insisting, gently but purposefully, upon Oderisi's use of
alluminare instead of *miniare* because the consciously French word was
beginning to usurp the place of the homely term in the mouths of
those miniaturists who considered themselves highly placed in the
hierarchy of their craft? Artists', tradesmen's and professional usage in
the European languages abounds in such 'ameliorations', today as in
former times. Might not some such act of craftsman's snobbery on
Oderisi's part—perhaps something he said to Dante—be the reason
why he is chosen to appear as one out of only three actual people who
represent the sin of pride (the rest are biblical or mythological names)?
It might be objected that this would imply a malicious act by Dante,
however mild his irony might be. But we have already seen Virgil's
protégé in a similar role. Just as the poet goes through Antenora 'perco-
tendo . . . altrui le gote' (*Inf.* XXXII, 89) *either by will, fate or chance*,[17] so
here he more temperately acts as an agent of retributive justice in

15 Dorothy L. Sayers, *Dante: The Divine Comedy*, II, *Purgatory*, Harmondsworth,
    1955, p. 156.
16 *Ed. cit.*, p. 123, n. 81.
17 See *ibid.*, vv. 76–8: 'Se voler fu o destino o fortuna, / non so; ma, passeggiando
    tra le teste / forte percossi il piè nel viso ad una.' The italics are mine.

reminding Oderisi of his pride through a circumstantial detail. The
interpretation renders all the more telling Oderisi's reply—a reply
which is humble yet dignified; and, if truth were told, a little too
detached and didactic to evince that warm intimacy between fellow
artists which some have professed to recognise in the scene.

Moreover the fact that Dante's contemporaries would also be
aware of the 'socio-linguistic' standing of *alluminare* would turn the
remarks from an unfathomable personal reminiscence between two
men into an *exemplum* accessible to the poet's audience at the mere
cost of using perceptively the linguistic clue they had to hand. If this
gloss is correct it carries the implication that Dante's readers were
aware that at least one gallicism possessed semantic overtones (potentially stylistic, under the rubric of *valeurs évocatives*) attributable to its
foreign origin. And what was true of one gallicism could conceivably
have been true of others.

I have already let it be known more than once that Dante's gallicisms
are 'rare' words in the sense that most of them require to be explained
by his near-contemporary fourteenth century commentators. This
point needs to be amplified because it relates to a crucial aspect of
Dante's borrowings which we cannot afford to pass unnoticed. That
the words are uncommon in the literary language of the late thirteenth
and early fourteenth centuries is perfectly correct. Yet they are not in
themselves uncommon terms in the sense of representing concepts
which are bizarre, alien or hermetic. The very opposite is true. They
denote things or activities (but mainly *things*) which are so much a part
of real life that one wonders why some of them came to be derived
from a foreign source at all; in fact many of them were eventually
accepted as lexical items of moderately high frequency in the language.
Many examples have been cited already; words like *mangiare, sentiero,
bastardo, giallo, burro, roccia, ostello, oltraggio, cisterna*. Not that Dante's
choice of French borrowings is unique; concrete and comparatively
high frequency terms are fairly common in gallicisms up to and including the fourteenth century, common enough to be considered a typical
trait of words from that source: cf. *villaggio, paniere, foraggio, forgia,
celliere, formaggio* and numerous others of the same stamp which are
not part of the lexicon of the *Commedia* but which also refer to material,
everyday things. They are words which are bound up essentially with
the human being and his immediate environment.

The significance of these 'homely' gallicisms is that they provide
Dante with the stuff of his imagery, in particular those wide-angled

yet material and especially visual similes which are such an important part of his poetic *afflatus*. Thus one of the money-bags cumbering the tormented usurers is emblazoned with a coat of arms

come sangue rossa,
mostrando un'oca bianca piú che *burro*   [*Inf.* xvii, 63]

Italy, ravaged by civil strife, is an inn or mansion of grief:

Ahi serva Italia, di dolore *ostello*!   [*Purg.* vi, 76

while Master Adam the coiner, bloated with dropsy, appears first to Dante's horrified eyes as

. . . un fatto a guisa di *leuto*   [*Inf.* xxx, 49]

These transfers and others like them have always been given their due as the very choicest wines of Dante's poetic feast. Critics have discussed their vintage and extolled it in many a rapturous line, and some have been perceptive enough to remark upon the subtlety of its blend. Let us not forget to add, if only to keep the accounts straight, that a small but surely not insignificant portion of the *must* was pressed in France.

We are now, I think, as close to bringing the different factors of Dante's French-inspired vocabulary together under one roof as we can ever expect to be. The subject does not fit convincingly under a single rubric: it possesses different dimensions according to whether one is considering the intrinsic excellence of Dante's poem as a work of art or its status as a monument of engaged literature.

Firstly, as we have just seen, the borrowed lexicon adds a new resource to Dante's imagery and in doing so contributes in its minor way to his poetic achievement in the *Commedia*. Almost all the gallicisms we have examined which have a stylistic potential (to which one pointer seems to be the frequency of each word's occurrences and its strategic placing within the verse) appear as the key element in an image, and some of these images are among the most evocative that Dante ever composed. Whether their success is due in any measure to the words' ultimate foreign origin I leave the reader to judge for himself, recalling only that what matters here is not whether they retain any expressive or evocative connotations they had in French, but whether as borrowed neologisms they are sufficiently recent to be stylistically generative in their new environment.

S M L L—M

From the second standpoint Dante's gallicisms may be seen to have
what I should like to call a hermeneutic or exemplary value. They
stand in a similar relation to the existing literary medium as do the
varying dialectal forms and the different registers that Dante employs.
In their own way they illustrate the principle that the *volgare illustre*
must be acceptable to those who use all sorts, levels and tones of
language. But the gallicisms, as I see it, do not represent an argotic or
restricted language confined to a minority of speakers upon which
Dante has drawn, nor yet a register—a 'polite' one, possibly—which
speakers of the *lingua dell'uso* could call on if they wished. It seems to
me that the gallicisms are part of the Italian language as Dante himself
knew it, actually used within his own experience by a broad band of
the social classes he was familiar with. During the thirteenth century
the influence of France on Italy and of French on Italian remained of
great moment, because of new contacts of the kind Dante himself
was on occasions involved in and because of the working out of
powerful linguistic influences already established, mainly Norman,
which dated from previous centuries. It looks as if Dante was being
deliberately realistic which he gave *entrée* to his borrowed words. One
has the impression that he just lifted them from everyday use, without
fear or favour. Speaking of Franciscans Dante's contemporaries used
the familiar name given to the monks of the order in France, *cordeliers*.
What more natural than that Guido da Montfeltro should say

Io fui hom d'arme, e poi fui cordigliero?   [*Inf.* XXVII, 67]

Yet before Dante no writer seems to have made this simple, productive
concession to the linguistic state of things. If he does not happen literally to call a spade a spade, he certainly calls butter butter and a
brothel a brothel. Would it be too imaginative to suggest that Dante
was aware of the French ingredient in the modern life he lived in, that
he neither revered nor resented it, but felt himself strong enough to
come to terms with it and look towards the future, leaving the
gallicisms to stand as a token of his confident belief in the Italian
language?

Finally it is a matter of significance that Dante's borrowings readily
appear at points where the level of style requires to be deliberately
lowered, not merely to gain a stylistic effect of bathos, but because
there is a danger that the language will rise *pari passu* with the emotion
it portrays to a pitch of rhetorical intensity which would not befit the
middling level of style which the author has chosen to write in, a style

which is that of the *commedia*, the comedy, as he has taken the trouble
to tell us in the only overt stage direction he has left for his dramatic poem. It is a Divine Comedy, not an Epic of the Immortal
Soul.

Precisely why Dante chose to compose his great work in the *mediocris stylus* does not immediately concern us here, though we cannot fail
to appreciate how right he was to do so. English enthusiasts of Dante
note with admiration how the 'mediocre' style enabled him to avoid
a trap Milton fell headlong into, with his insistence upon a sustained
tragica conjugatio, the lofty tragic or epic diction that makes a god out
of his Devil and an unbending puritan out of his God. Dante's *mediocris
stylus* is strategically unassailable; it covers all fronts from a single
position. If in the *Inferno* any of his sinners reach up to tug at the hem
of human sympathy he deftly plucks them down by means of a brutal,
vulgar or disabusing image to a level where humanity cannot reach
them. Conversely the *Paradiso* gains immeasurably through its stylistic
restraint, humility and demotic homeliness, which bring even the
highest truths, the visions of death and the after-life down within the
grasp of ordinary mortals.

Quite frequently this *damping* or *lenitive* function is performed by a
borrowed word. Consider, for example, the pregnant understatement
of the image based on *ostello*, appearing as it does at the crisis of
Dante's longest and most impassioned tirade. Or the example cited
above of *burro*, whose reality helps to bring the punishment of the
burning sand ominously close to everyday life, thwarting any attempt
to seek refuge in distance or detachment. Or the third example, *liuto*,
which serves to emphasise the grotesque inhumanity of the fraudulent,
making them fit to be jeered at but not a source of amusement: a
spectacle to be gazed upon, but without pity, like the wretched,
ridiculous *homunculi* in Bosch's *Hell of the Musicians*.

This 'damping' process is nowhere seen more clearly than at the
climax of the *Inferno*. Dante, sensitive to the expectations of his
audience as well as to the demands of his narrative, does not fail to
appreciate how great is the task that awaits him, and also the risk he
runs as regards sheer plausibility and conviction when handling such a
subject. For even a Dante is incapable of evoking, literally, the spectacle of total sin, any more than he is able to figure forth the Godhead
in a form directly accessible to the senses.

The 'stylistic damping' begins in the very prospectus, so to speak,
for the trip to Cocytus, where a commonplace and probably rather

vulgar gallicism, *pigliare a gabbo* (O.F. *prendre a gab*), is followed by
words taken from a child's nursery language:

> ... che non è impresa da *pigliare a gabbo*
>   discriver fondo a tutto l'universo,
>   né da lingua che chiami mamma e babbo   [*Inf.* xxxii, 7–9]

And so the description of nether Hell continues, with highly emotive
and potentially tragic passages partially mitigated from time to time
by the insertion of a falling cadence, a banal or casual line, until the
time comes for the poet to cut the knot of his story and rescue his
hearers, so to speak, from the pinnacle of emotion on which they have
been placed. As everyone knows, he does this by a final *escamotage*,
erasing the masque of the damned souls in a few quick lines, and
bringing us back from a dream to watch two men, alone, climbing
their way back up to the night air.

The very last line before the malefic vision fades and is swallowed up
in reality is the one cited at the beginning of this paper. And one word,
ceffo, a rhetorically ignoble term, gives the cue to this sudden *dégringo-
lade* which is also the *dénouement* of the first cantica. It is virtually the
last of the strongly emotive words, though the canto has still seventy
lines to run. Before verse 65 the description was heightened by every
expressive and affective resource Dante's language could provide; but
from that point onwards the narrative is drastically abridged; already
Cassius is no more than glimpsed as the picture melts away, and the
lines immediately following usher in the epilogue:

> Ma la notte risurge, e oramai
> è da partir, ché tutto avem veduto ...   [*Inf.* xxxiv, 68–9]

Elspeth M. Kennedy

The role of the supernatural in the first part of the Old French prose *Lancelot*

Arthurian romance without any marvels would be like *Alice in Wonderland* without any wonders, but the attitude of some of the medieval authors towards these marvels was at times rather ambivalent. Even in the twelfth century one can sense a certain reserve towards the non-Christian supernatural in some of the French romances, and in a thirteenth century French romance such as the prose *Lancelot* the tension between the requirements of the traditional Arthurian supernatural and the tendency towards rationalisation and explanation, characteristic of the move from verse to prose, becomes more marked. The author of the first part of the prose *Lancelot*,[1] which deals with Lancelot's adventures from childhood up to his achievement of a seat at the Round Table, inherited a strong tradition of the supernatural from his twelfth century sources, and it is the handling of this tradition in a thirteenth century prose romance which I propose to examine.

It is generally recognised that in most of Chrétien de Troyes' romances marvels, usually with a Celtic flavour, are not just used (as often happens in the *Romans d'Antiquité*) as a kind of adornment, giving exotic colour to the poem, but are given quite an important role in the structure of the work. It is usually only the hero who comes into close contact with the marvellous and has these strange adventures, and this serves to indicate that he has special qualities as a knight and is destined to perform great deeds. No external force directs these marvels; the essence of the art of a skilful writer of Arthurian romance such as Chrétien de Troyes is that marvels should appear just to happen without logical reason, but that at the same time these strange adventures should serve a structural purpose in that they are used to test the hero and to reveal his quality. In Chrétien there is usually a coherence at the courtly level, a *sen*, the logical exposition of some idea of love

---

1 Volume III of H. O. Sommer's edition of the *Vulgate Version of the Arthurian Romances*, Washington, D.C., 1910.

or chivalry, but an incoherence—I believe, often deliberate—at the supernatural level.[2] This can be seen in two of the main sources of the prose *Lancelot, le Chevalier de la Charrete* and *le Conte del Graal.* In the first of these Chrétien uses a twelfth century tradition of the abduction and rescue of Guinevere, which still has a few hints of a journey into the Otherworld or the Land of the Dead, to illustrate a theme of courtly love. It is this courtly *sen*, an exploration of the nature of love and its relationship with chivalry, which predominates and provides the logical structure of the romance. The supernatural elements are not to be found so much in any of the characters themselves as in the traditional magic devices: the perilous bed on which Lancelot insists on lying, the slab which only he can raise, the sword bridge which he crosses (whereas Gauvain nearly drowns when he tries to cross the other strange bridge), the magic ring worn by Lancelot—all these help to reveal Lancelot's special qualities as a hero, and the power of love as a source of inspiration. Chrétien also uses more subtle means to suggest the special character of his Arthurian world, a world which mixes glimpses of twelfth century aristocratic life with a hint of magic in the background. He does this by using a narrative technique characterised by a skilful withholding of explanations. Thus the mysterious opening of the adventure, the obscure past of Lancelot, just hinted at in the allusion to his fairy upbringing, the unexplained gaps in the narrative, the references to Gorre as the kingdom from which no one returns (alongside a quite prosaic portrayal of some very ordinary prisoners of Gorre), the occasional suggestions of a link between the rescuer of Guinevere and a more universal saviour, all these may be echoes of myth, as some scholars have suggested,[3] but here are used as a deliberate literary device in a work which has its own logical structure and is rooted in twelfth century French courtly ideas.

In *le Conte del Graal*, which is also an important source for a number of themes and episodes in the prose *Lancelot,* Chrétien uses a similar technique. There is a continuous courtly theme of education in chivalry, and many of the adventures are at an ordinary earthly level, but the heroes, Perceval and Gauvain, are given a special quality through their

---

2 Cf. J. Fourquet, 'Le Rapport entre l'œuvre et la source chez Chrétien de Troyes et le problème des sources bretonnes', *Romance Philology,* IX (1955), pp. 298–312. See also E. Vinaver, *The Rise of Romance,* Oxford, 1971, pp. 33–52.

3 See J. Frappier, *Chrétien de Troyes,* Paris, 1957, pp. 136–7, for a discussion of the importance of mythical elements in *le Chevalier de la Charrete.*

periodic contact with the supernatural. The stages of Perceval's progress in chivalry towards a deeper understanding of its meaning are marked by scenes in which he also learns a little more about the mysteries of the Grail, but there is no continuous thread at the supernatural level, and magic has a strictly controlled part to play.

However, the author of the prose *Lancelot* would also have been familiar with Arthurian romances where the *sen* was not important, where there was a proliferation of marvels and where the same careful balance between the courtly and the magical was lacking. Such a text would seem to have been the lost French source of the *Lanzelet* of Ulrich von Zatzikhoven, a romance which abounds in incoherences and contradictions at every level, but which is important for the study of the prose *Lancelot*, as it contains quite a detailed account of Lancelot's fairy childhood in a lake, one which is similar in broad outline to that to be found in the prose *Lancelot*.

The other main sources of the prose *Lancelot* were the Arthurian chronicles from which the author drew the 'historical' material for the setting of the Lancelot story within the Arthurian kingdom, but in which he would also have found powerful elements of magic. Not only do the chronicles give an account of Arthur's mysterious end, when he is borne away by Morgan le Fay and her companions to Avalon, but they also present a figure who is much closer to being a truly supernatural creature with strange powers than any character in Chrétien. This more than human figure is Merlin, with his mysterious origins—a child without an earthly father, born of an incubus and a girl—and his powerful way with stones.[4] Although Merlin does use his powers mainly for good in Geoffrey of Monmouth and in Wace, he is not yet firmly Christianised; he has not yet been transformed into the redeemed Antichrist of Robert de Boron, and it is an unredeemed Merlin who is to prove a powerful source of magic in the first part of the prose *Lancelot*. The chronicles offered, therefore, quite a heady combination of 'history' and magic, and it is on this, as well as on the *merveilles* of Chrétien de Troyes and on the fairy childhood of the twelfth century Lancelot tradition, that the author of the first part of the prose *Lancelot* draws in his creation of a new kind of Arthurian world. This world presents a fascinating combination of the two inter-twining traditions of chronicle and romance, a combination which often reveals an interesting ambivalence with regard to the *merveilleux*.

4 It is Merlin, according to Geoffrey of Monmouth and to Wace, who by mysterious means brings Stonehenge over from Ireland.

In spite of this choice of an Arthurian setting and of a hero firmly
linked to a fairy and watery upbringing—for Lancelot cannot be
Lancelot without a lake—the writer seems to have found it difficult
to accept magical happenings as a matter of course. Not only does he
show the characteristic tendency of prose romance to explain events
which Chrétien would have left mysterious, but he also has a strongly
feudal conception of the Arthurian world. Every single adventure
undertaken by any of Arthur's knights concerns the redressing of some
wrong done to one of Arthur's vassals, and in each case the feudal link
is strongly emphasised.[5] Lancelot's own father becomes a vassal of
Arthur, and the king is severely criticised for not righting the wrong
done to his vassal. The weirdest situations will again and again be
finally explained as the result of wars between Arthur's vassals and
those of rival kings, or of problems over marriages in lands over
which Arthur is suzerain. Typical of the author's approach to the non-
Christian supernatural, from whatever source, is his description of the
goddess Diana, whose name—significantly enough, in view of her
association in the Middle Ages with magic arts—had been given to
the lake into which Lancelot is carried by the Lady of the Lake. The
writer explains that Diana was Queen of Sicily at the time of the good
author Virgil and was a lady who loved hunting, but was regarded as
a goddess by the ignorant people:

> Li lais estoit apelés des le tans as paiens li lais Dyanes. Dyane fu roine de
> Secile et regna au tans Virgile le boin auctor. Si l'apeloient la fole gent
> mescreans qui lors estoit pour diuesse. Et ch'estoit la dame del monde qui
> plus amoit deduit de bois, et toutejour aloit chachier; et pour che l'ape-
> loient li mescreant la diuesse del bois.[6]

How could such a rationalising attitude be reconciled with the mysterious adventures demanded by the conventions of Arthurian
romance? I would suggest that the author found part of the solution
in Merlin, who, although mentioned only three times in this branch
of the cycle,[7] could provide a 'rational' explanation in thirteenth century terms for nearly all the necessary marvels, as an examination of
the magic elements in Sommer III will show.

There is, in fact, very little marvellous in this part of the romance,
compared with most of the other branches of the cycle or with

---

5 See E. M. Kennedy, 'King Arthur in the first part of the prose *Lancelot*',
Medieval Miscellany presented to E. Vinaver, Manchester, 1965, p. 189.
6 Sommer, III, p. 8.   7 *Ibid.*, pp. 19–21, 270, 275.

Arthurian romance in general. Only Lancelot has any supernatural adventures; the other knights just have earthly ones, however strange and inexplicable they may appear at first sight. And even Lancelot does not have many adventures involving enchantments. The main marvel is the adventure of the Dolorous Guard, the one which he has to achieve before he can learn his name—a theme already to be found in the *Lanzelet*. The first part of this adventure, in spite of references to the strange customs of the castle, is chiefly straightforward fighting (admittedly on Lancelot's side with the help of special shields which increase his strength), although the crashing down of a bronze figure does foretell the capture of the castle. Then comes the scene in the cemetery which closely resembles one in Chrétien's *Chevalier de la Charrette*, a scene in which the tombstones are mysteriously inscribed with the names of the knights of the Round Table who will lie there. But not only does this come *after* Lancelot has conquered the castle, instead of being used to show that he is the predestined hero (as happens in Chrétien), but also a great deal of the writing on the tombs is done by ordinary human means to mislead King Arthur and to force him to stay in the castle.[8] The mystic aura of predestination surrounding the figure of Lancelot in this particular scene in Chrétien's poem has therefore been considerably diminished by the prose romance. However, the enchantments of the Dolorous Guard form an important element in the story: it is made quite clear that it is Lancelot who is to put an end to them, and the scene in which he does so contains the most undiluted *merveilleux* of the whole of the first part of the prose *Lancelot*. But it is a *merveilleux* with a curious autonomy, as if governed by its own internal mechanism (a trend already to be found in the *Romans d'Antiquité* and in Chrétien).[9] The lord of the castle himself is presented on a purely human plane, and the enchantments do not appear to depend upon him, although it is said that if he had been captured he would have been able to *descovrir* the enchantments and thus bring peace to the castle.[10] It is Lancelot, however, who achieves this by fighting his way through darkness and stench, past deep abysses and strange bronze figures which rain down blows, until he finally reaches the key and opens the chest which contains these

8 *Ibid.*, p. 155.
9 See E. Faral, *Recherches sur les sources latines des contes et romans courtois du moyen âge*, Paris, 1913, pp. 307–88, and F. Schürr, *Das altfranzösische Epos*, Munich, 1926, pp. 312–15.
10 Sommer, III, p. 153.

enchantments. The explanation of the marvels in the chest itself represents a characteristic combination of mechanical wonders and diabolical forces. It has pipes coming out of it rather like an organ, pipes which produce strange noises as if devils were inside; and indeed, as the author says, 'Et por voir si estoient il deable.'[11]

The important point for us is that Lancelot is able to achieve the adventure of the Dolorous Guard only with the help of the Lady of the Lake, who supplies him with the magic shields to increase his strength. And indeed all the *merveilleux* connected with Lancelot in the story seems to come from his association with the Lady of the Lake. It is through her that he is brought up in a lake, even if by the thirteenth century it is only the semblance of one, so that Lancelot, unlike Lanzelet, does not have to rely upon mermen for his training in the use of arms, and can learn to ride before he leaves the domain of the Lady of the Lake. It is she who gives him a ring with the magic power to lay bare enchantments, just as in Chrétien.[12] Not only does she send him magic shields, but she also sends Guinevere the shield with the gap between the two lovers which closes of itself when Lancelot and Guinevere's love is consummated, a shield which has other wonderful properties, as it helps to cure Lancelot's madness. Not only does the Lady of the Lake do all this for Lancelot, but she also uses special powers to rescue his cousins, Lionel and Bohort. Her damsel puts magic wreaths on their heads and transforms them into greyhounds to get them away safely. Throughout the story it is her damsels appearing at court or in the middle of battles, bearing strange shields or mysterious messages, who provide much of the necessary Arthurianly magical flavour to the story. The author makes it clear that it is because she is a fairy that she can do these things, but he is not prepared to accept a fairy into his Arthurian kingdom without some form of explanation. One might expect her to be presented as a being from another world who, neither angel nor devil, has by her nature more than human gifts, but this is not the prose *Lancelot's* conception of a fairy. What are, in fact, the supernatural powers of the Lady of the Lake? She has some knowledge of the future, although this is not very greatly emphasised except in so far as Lancelot's career is concerned.[13]

---

11 Sommer, III, p. 192.

12 *Ibid.*, p. 123, and Chrétien de Troyes, *le Chevalier de la Charrete* ed. M. Roques, Paris (C.F.M.A.), 1958, ll. 2336–55.

13 The Lady of the Lake's outstanding quality, like the fairy protectress in *le Chevalier de la Charrete*, is her ability to give Lancelot help whenever he needs

She also has some remarkable possessions, almost like a series of mechanical aids or gadgets, such as the shields she gives Lancelot, or the wreaths which are used to transform Lancelot's cousins into the semblance of greyhounds and the greyhounds into the semblance of children when the two boys are being rescued from Claudas, who has taken their land and is keeping them in prison. She has the ability to transform, but—as was often traditional in magic—only the outward semblance of things, not their nature. She is not really able to live under water, but only brings up Lancelot in the semblance of a lake; her land is protected by the appearance of water, that is all.[14] Similarly, with the changing of the greyhounds into children and vice versa, it is only in the eyes of the beholders that this seems to happen, not in the eyes of the children themselves, nor, presumably, in those of the dogs. This is linked with the use of the word *descovrir* in connection with both the transformation of Lionel and Bohort[15] and the enchantments of the Dolorous Guard.[16] In the same way, the door wrought of air by Camille, the Saxon maiden with a knowledge of magic, cannot withstand the power of the shield, but is revealed to be only air.[17] Once these spells are laid bare, are shown to be unreal, they no longer exist. Otherwise, apart from these accomplishments, the Lady of the Lake seems to be quite normal and has a perfectly ordinary *ami*, just like anyone else.[18] She is never shown using unusual methods of transport, she comes by ship and horse with Lancelot to Arthur's court; she may sometimes arrive unexpectedly, but she never just materialises, nor does she vanish, but takes her leave politely and goes away in the usual manner.

There is therefore nothing intrinsically superhuman about her, for to be a fairy, according to the first part of the prose *Lancelot*, it is enough to study, to have the right books or the right teacher. The Lady of the Lake did not by her nature know spells; the author would probably not have considered this respectable or at all suitable for the protectress of Lancelot, for it might imply ties of kinship with the powers of darkness, with the devil. It is therefore made quite clear

---

it, no matter where he is. In Chrétien Lancelot asks for help (ll. 2342–4), but in the prose *Lancelot* the Lady of the Lake knows, without any appeal from Lancelot, whenever her assistance is required. See, for example, her sudden appearance when Lancelot is suffering from madness (Sommer, III, p. 416).

14 Sommer, III, p. 22.

15 *Ibid.*, p. 57.   16 *Ibid.*, p. 153.

17 *Ibid.*, p. 424.   18 *Ibid.*, p. 118.

near the beginning of the story that she took a course in magic with Merlin, an unpleasant Merlin, who could be shut up without the Lady of the Lake losing her virtue, and it was from him that she learnt all her magic accomplishments. Merlin, therefore, is the ultimate source of almost every marvellous occurrence in this part of the prose *Lancelot*, and the author, right at the beginning of his narrative, explains Merlin's knowledge in a way rationally acceptable to the thirteenth century by giving an account of his birth: he is the result of a casual love affair between a devil and a girl, he was never baptised, was false and disloyal and inherited from his father all the knowledge which can come from the devil.[19] Note that here we have quite a different account of the birth of Merlin from that to be found in the *Merlin* of Robert de Boron,[20] a prose version of which was later incorporated in the second branch of the Vulgate cycle (Sommer II). Robert de Boron needed a virtuous Merlin, the product of a foiled plot to create an Antichrist, a Merlin who had been baptised and was worthy to be a prophet of the Holy Grail. In Sommer III a wicked Merlin is needed so that the Lady of the Lake can learn from him and then shut him up for life without being blamed for it; because Merlin, as the representative of the diabolical element in magic, is imprisoned and his pupil is virtuous, the Lady of the Lake's gifts are not dangerous.

There is very little *merveilleux* outside the events which I have mentioned. Camille, the Saxon maiden who captures Arthur, has some knowledge of magic, but like the Lady of the Lake she relies upon study and she is helpless once her books are burnt.[21] Galehot is described as *fiex de la Bele Jaiande*,[22] but has no supernatural characteristics; Arthur has dreams and visions,[23] but these are given a Christian significance, like many of Charlemagne's visions in the *Roland*. Agravain is anointed with a mysterious ointment as a punishment by two damsels, but the emphasis is on the medical side throughout the episode.[24]

19 Sommer, III, p. 19.
20 See Robert de Boron, *le Roman de l'Estoire dou Graal*, ed. W. A. Nitze, Paris (C.F.M.A.), 1927, pp. 126–30, for the surviving fragment of the verse text.
21 Sommer, III, p. 427.
22 *Ibid.*, p. 201. Other giants in the prose *Lancelot* are large and uncouth but not particularly mysterious. Dwarves are cantankerous and often treacherous, but no emphasis is given to the supernatural associations attributed to them in some medieval romances.
23 Sommer, III, p. 199, for Arthur's visions, pp. 200 and 220–3 for their interpretation.   24 Sommer, III, pp. 316–17.

Gauvain inherits one strange quality from earlier verse romance: his strength waxes and wanes with the sun,[25] but apart from that there is nothing unearthly about him or his adventures. He tries and fails to raise the tombstone with Lancelot's name underneath it, but undertakes no other marvellous adventure, nor do any of Arthur's knights. Indeed there are not (apart from the Dolorous Guard) any supernatural adventures to be undertaken, for the main role of the knights is to see that justice on a human plane is done in Arthur's kingdom, that ladies are not forced to marry against their will, that knights are not wrongfully condemned for treachery. Only Lancelot, through the Lady of the Lake and ultimately through Merlin, has direct contact with the supernatural.

The account of Merlin's birth and imprisonment, therefore, serves an important purpose, out of all proportion to its length, as a rationalisation, an explanation of nearly all the magic elements in the romance. It is self-contained, although linked up in time by a brief reference to events lying outside Sommer III, that is to say to the deceiving of the Duke of Tintagel by Uther, Merlin and Ulfin when they contrived the visit of Uther in the form of the Duke to the Duchess the night that Arthur was engendered.[26]

However, while the author uses Merlin to explain away some of the mystery in this part of the work, he also uses two unexplained and at first sight rather puzzling allusions to Merlin to remind us of the mysterious aspect of the Arthurian world and to set the more natural events which form the great bulk of the story in the right context of the *merveilleux*. The first allusion occurs in a description of the land of Sorelois. The author describes how Galehot won the land in battle from King Gloier and then goes on to explain that it was an island which could now only be reached by two *felons passages*. Formerly there had been many ways of going there, but at the time when Merlin prophesied the adventures which were to come, King Lohoz, father of Gloier, had the two bridges made and all the others were destroyed. These two were to remain the only means of access as long as the adventures lasted.[27] The allusion serves both to explain why there are

25 *Ibid.*, pp. 293–4. The *First Perceval Continuation* describes the waxing and waning of Gauvain's strength in relation to the sun. See *The Continuations of the Old French Perceval Romance of Chrétien de Troyes*, ed. W. Roach, III, part I, Philadelphia, 1952, pp. 404–5.
26 Cf. Wace, *le Roman de Brut*, ed. I. Arnold, Paris (S.A.T.F.), 1938, ll. 8681–736, and Sommer, II, pp. 64–8.
27 Sommer, III, pp. 269–70.

only two ways into Sorelois and to give the quest for Lancelot, who is now hidden in Sorelois, the appropriate more-than-ordinary flavour. The author combines a 'historical' explanation of Galehot's possession to Sorelois in terms of concrete 'reality' with an explanation of the difficulty of access which reminds us that this is Arthurian romance, in which strange adventures happen. The reference is not necessarily to any text which contains a history of Lohoz and Gloier or an account of the *aventures*. It fits in the context of the Arthurian kingdom, as seen in the chronicles, where there are constant wars between rival kings on the frontiers of the kingdom, and of the Arthurian kingdom as seen in Chrétien de Troyes' *Chevalier de la Charrete*, where dangerous bridges did exist and were connected with mysterious adventures.

The second reference to Merlin occurs in a passage describing how Gauvain and his companions set out on a quest for Lancelot. Gauvain pauses to give his companions advice at 'une piere qui a non li perons Merlin, la ou Merlins ochist les .ii. encanteors'.[28] Again, the allusion serves to remind us that this is a quest in an Arthurian world in which strange things happen, without the author being obliged to scatter enchanted castles everywhere, so that he is able to reserve them for the first great achievement of his hero, the capture of the Dolorous Guard and the bringing to an end of its enchantments. On an earlier quest for Lancelot an allusion to the quest for the Grail (as though it were an adventure which had already happened in the past) is introduced by Gauvain to emphasise the importance of their quest and to invest it with a special aura: 'la plus haute queste qui onques fust aprés celi del Graal'.[29]

These allusions, left hanging, as it were, in the text, are, I believe, part of the author's special technique and fit into a whole system of references along three main themes: firstly, the time of the adventures, represented by Merlin, with his associations with magic and prophecy, but without, in Sommer III, any link with the Grail; secondly, the Grail, which is a theme both spiritual and *aventureus*, represented in the text by allusions to Joseph of Arimathea,[30] to Perceval[31] and to the

---

28 Sommer, III, p. 275.   29 *Ibid.*, p. 226.
30 *Ibid.*, pp. 117, 140, 222.
31 In the list of the three most beautiful women (Sommer, III, p. 29) most mss., although not B.M. Add. 10293, used by Sommer, name one of them as the sister of Perlesvaus or Perceval, 'celui qui vit apertement les granz mervoilles del Graal et acompli lo Siege Perilleus de la Table Reonde' (B.N. fr. 768, f. 12d). See E. M. Kennedy, 'The scribe as editor', *Mélanges de langue et de*

Grail quest itself as an example of a great quest which had happened in the past; thirdly, the 'historical' theme, Arthur as king, and his wars with the barons and the Saxons.[32] The references under the first two headings allude to events in the past. Merlin is connected with the beginning of the *aventures*. The incident with the *perron* and the enchanters, whatever it may have been, happened well before the story started. Merlin is not used in Sommer III to prophecy events to come, that is, events in the future in relation to the narrative; rather is he a link with a marvellous past. The Grail references too in Sommer III seem to be allusions to the past, reminders of another remarkable manifestation of the Arthurian world. Under the third heading, 'historical' references, the allusions are either to the past or to contemporary events. Those referring to the past are used to give the story, as it were, an 'historical' basis, to provide an explanation for the present situation. The allusions to events contemporary with the story are often incomplete, but serve to show that the characters have an existence outside this particular narrative, and that the adventures belong to a whole complex of events of which we are told only part.

Chrétien too employs a technique of incomplete allusions, broken threads, gaps in the narrative, even cross-references to another of his romances (as, for example, the allusions in *Yvain* to events in *le Chevalier de la Charrete*,[33] but for a rather different purpose. He uses it as a method of creating suspense, keeping the reader guessing, so that in his Lancelot romance the main character appears from nowhere, vanishes again and is only seen at intervals in the first part of the romance. In the prose *Lancelot* (Sommer III), however, the main threads of the narrative are followed through remorselessly. We always know where Lancelot is and what he has been doing, even when practically the whole of Arthur's court are out looking for him. But those references to other adventures, which are never followed up or fully explained, serve to set the prose *Lancelot* in a network of adventures, to give it a deeper perspective in space and time, and to place it in relation to the main themes of Arthurian romance.

Some of these fragmentary allusions may, therefore (as, for example,

---

littérature du moyen âge et de la renaissance offerts à Jean Frappier, Geneva, 1970, I, p. 527. See also A. Micha, 'La tradition manuscrite du *Lancelot* en prose', *Romania*, LXXXV (1964), pp. 297–8.

32 See 'King Arthur in the first part of the prose *Lancelot*', p. 191.

33 Chrétien de Troyes, *le Chevalier au Lion* (*Yvain*), ed. M. Roques, Paris (C.F.M.A.), 1960, ll. 3692–709, 3912–28 and 4734–9.

two of the Merlin ones), be an appeal to the imagination rather than a precise reference to an actual text, but they all fit in with an already existing context of Arthurian romance. As far as Merlin and King Arthur as a 'historical' figure are concerned, this context is provided by Wace and Geoffrey of Monmouth; for the Grail the background seems to be that of both Chrétien's *Perceval* and Robert de Boron's *Joseph*. All these allusions seem to be inspired by the desire to give the Lancelot story an authenticity—that is, an Arthurian authenticity—to show it as forming part of the accepted pattern of the Arthurian world, with its three main strands, the historical, the magical and the spiritual —Arthur, Merlin and the Grail. The main interests of the author seem to lie in the presentation of an idea of chivalry through the person of Lancelot, a conception of chivalry in which the inspiration of love has to play its part, but in which the role a knight can play in helping the king to see that his vassals receive proper justice within his kingdom is given far greater emphasis. Lancelot's magical associations are therefore treated with great discretion, and handled in such a way that they enhance his status within the Arthurian convention without interfering too much with a more rational, if perhaps not very realistic, presentation of knighthood. And both the magical and the historical allusions which have been discussed above play an important part in achieving this effect and in presenting the Lancelot story in Sommer III not as an isolated romance in a shadowy setting but as one part of a whole complex of adventures, taking place in an Arthurian world which has its own 'reality' as well as its magical quality existing outside the individual work.

R. A. Lodge
On the 'character' of Renart in Branch I

My aim in this essay is to discuss some of the ideas put forward some
twenty years ago by P. Jonin in an article entitled 'Les Animaux et leur
vie psychologique dans le *Roman de Renart* (Branche I)'.[1] It seems to
me that Jonin's quest in that article for psychological realism in
Branch I of the *Renart* deflected him from what constitutes the essential
coherence underpinning the actions of Renart; it also forced him to
neglect important changes in the conception of Renart from one part
of the branch to another. I shall argue that in the earlier sections—I
proper and Ia—the authors offer us primarily, not a realistically portrayed individual human psyche, but a parody of the epic–chivalric
hero. In Ib the role of parody in the conception of Renart becomes
less important, but even here it is the comedy of situation which
matters rather than the presentation of a full-blooded, lifelike character.
Jonin's article, in fact, discussed all the main characters of the branch,
but space here restricts us to a consideration of Renart alone.

Jonin's approach to the *Renart* belongs to a long critical tradition
going back to the early nineteenth century. The first modern readers
of the text, notably J. Grimm,[2] saw it as a specimen of primitive
popular literature and as *Naturpoesie*. They delighted in its apparent
freedom from literary convention, in the vividness of its evocation of
the natural world, in the psychological veracity of its characters. As
well as playing down the obscenity of the text, nineteenth century
critics favourable to the *Renart* tended to diminish the importance of
parody and burlesque, presumably feeling that art which is at only one
stage removed from folk-lore feeds not upon art but upon 'nature'.
Moreover, their thinking about the *Renart* was also coloured by current
political notions. The text was admired as one of the earliest pieces of
middle-class literature and Renart hailed as a middle-class champion

---

1 *Annales de la Faculté des Lettres d'Aix*, xxv (1951), pp. 63–81. Like Jonin, the
   edition of the text to which we refer is that of M. Roques, *Le Roman de
   Renart*, Paris (C.F.M.A.), 1948.   2 *Reinhart Fuchs*, Berlin, 1834.

against the traditional aristocracy—he became a forerunner of the
eighteenth century freethinker, irreverent towards the political and
religious establishment and disdainful of the ignorance and stupidity of
the peasants. Although this critical edifice did not go unchallenged in
the nineteenth century—P. Paris uttered protestations in favour of
learned origins in the 1860s[3]—the folk-lore–naturalist thesis remained
predominant, culminating in the work of L. Sudre.[4] It was not seriously
undermined until the great study published by L. Foulet in 1914.[5]

Foulet brought about the Copernican revolution in *Renart* studies
with his assertion of the bookishness of the *Renart*. This undoubtedly
forced a sizable wedge into the Romantic critical edifice. However,
Foulet himself did not force the wedge far enough to cause the whole
structure to crumble. Half a century later critics have managed to
accommodate his ideas with some surviving pre-Foulet critical attitudes. For instance, some modern critics still see the text as mildly
subversive and they persist in considering Renart as a mischievous
freethinker: J. Flinn maintains that although the earliest branches of
the *Renart* are mainly comic, the germs of real discontent are present
and play a progressively more important role as the genre develops.[6]
J. Dufournet actually describes Renart as a *libre-penseur*.[7] Furthermore,
and more pertinent to the subject of this essay, although Foulet forced
scholars to ascribe greater importance to the role of parody, many
modern critics are loath to accept that this extends right down to the
very conception of the characters—they are loath to give up the idea
that the basic coherence underlying the behaviour is anything other
than a realistically portrayed human psyche. Bossuat sees the originality
of the *Renart* in the subtleness and veracity of the characters: 'Dans la
fable antique, le goupil n'est qu'un animal rusé; mais pour les conteurs
de Renard, s'il garde l'aspect extérieur de l'animal, il est doué d'un
esprit plus subtil et d'une psychologie plus nuancée.'[8] These sentiments
are echoed by B. Beck[9] and J. Dufournet, and it is this tradition of

---

3 *Les Aventures de maître Renart et d'Ysengrin son compère mises en nouveau langage,
   racontées dans un nouvel ordre et suivies de nouvelles recherches sur le Roman de
   Renart*, Paris, 1861.
4 *Les Sources du Roman de Renart*, Paris, 1892.
5 *Le Roman de Renard*, Paris, 1914 (Bibl. de l'Ecole des Hautes Etudes, fasc. 211).
6 *Le Roman de Renart dans la littérature française et dans les littératures étrangères au
   moyen-âge*, Toronto, 1963, p. 156.
7 *Le Roman de Renart*, Paris, 1970, p. 47.
8 *Le Roman de Renard*, Paris, 1957, p. 95.
9 'Roman de Renart', *Tableau de la littérature française*, Paris, 1962, I, pp. 76–83.

criticism to which Jonin's article belongs. These post-Foulet critics have, as it were, divided up the disputed territory—parody and burlesque are conceded a domain in the style and in the feudal institutions so faithfully reproduced by the text;[10] observed nature, however, retains its position not only in the depiction of the countryside but also in the realistic psychology of the central animal characters. This partition is made explicit in the very chapter division of Bossuat's book, one chapter being devoted to 'La Peinture des personnages' and a separate one to 'La Parodie et la satire'.

The purpose of Jonin's article was to show that in all the absurd fantasy of the half-animal and half-human world of the *Renart* there was a constant, and that that constant was not allegorical *senefiance* but the psychological veracity of the central characters. Jonin schematised the anthropomorphism of the characters by seeing them basically as men dressed in the skins of beasts—'Or ce peuple, animal par la forme reste humain par le fond. Ces interférences d'humanité et d'animalité accentuent la fantaisie de l'ouvrage et en rehaussent la bigarrure sans nuire à l'analyse morale.'[11] It was the acuteness of the *analyse morale* (which I take to mean 'study of character') which raised the text above the level of later parts of the *Renart* tradition like *Renart le Nouvel*, where the characters are flat personifications. The most convincing characters of Branch I were those with the most convincing human minds. On the one hand we have those 'êtres bien vivants', Renart, Isengrin and Brun; on the other those 'qui manquent de force et de vie individuelle',[12] Fière, Hersent, Chantecler, Pinte. These characters are burlesque or semi-allegorical.

Renart, according to Jonin, is the character endowed with the most interesting and most complex psyche. His behaviour is analysed under two distinctly modern heads—the *portrait moral* and the *portrait intellectuel*. Under the heading *moral* Jonin places examples of Renart's lying, hypocrisy, cruelty and pride. Observing that all these characteristics are unfavourable, he tries to exonerate Renart from some of the responsibility for them by asserting the role of the fox's instinct.

10 The accuracy and authenticity with which the text reproduces details of feudal, legal and political institutions have been studied by J. Graven, *Le Procès criminel du Roman de Renart: Etude du droit criminel féodal au XIIe siècle*, Geneva, 1950, and more recently in an unpublished M.A. thesis presented to Leeds University by C. D. Peel, 'Feudal institutions and vocabulary in the *Roman de Renart*', 1969.

11 Jonin, *art. cit.*, p. 81.   12 *Ibid.*, p. 82.

Under the heading *intellectuel* Jonin describes Renart's cunning, his intelligence and his cynicism. Jonin fears the sadist in Renart but admires the freethinker. From this examination he concludes that Renart possesses a 'caractère dense, complexe mais aussi cohérent et construit, avec dans cette construction juste assez de lézardes pour en garantir la vérité'.[13] Summing up on the same page about the portrayal of the animals as a whole, he says, 'Si parfois l'allégorie vit encore en eux, elle est loin cependant de se présenter comme la condition première de leur être. Ils vivent d'une existence si pleine et si indépendante qu'on ne saurait dire exactement quelle idée, quelle institution ou quel personnage ils symbolisent.' Despite the absurdity of the animal–human mixture, the coherence of the central characters of Branch I is underpinned by naturalistic psychology.

Let us begin our reappraisal of Jonin's thesis with a resumé of the main events in what Jonin loosely terms Branch I, that is, volume I of Roques' edition. This branch is in fact a composite work consisting of a core text and two independent continuations denominated by E. Martin I, Ia and Ib. Foulet estimated their dates of composition as 1179, 1190–95 and *c.* 1200 respectively.[14]

I   (ll. 1–458) Debates at court on Renart's rape of Hersent, terminated by the arrival of the body of Coupée.

    (ll. 459–736) Brun's unsuccessful embassy to Maupertuis to deliver the summons.

    (ll. 737–937) Tibert's unsuccessful embassy to Maupertuis.

    (ll. 938–1220) Grinbert's successful embassy.

    (ll. 1221–520) Renart's trial and reprieve.

    (ll. 1521–678) His repudiation of the King and flight.

Ia   (ll. 1679–960) The siege of Maupertuis, the tying of the tails, the rape of the Queen and the capture of Renart.

    (ll. 1961–2260) Hermeline's intervention and Renart's second reprieve, followed by the untimely arrival of the body of Pelé and Renart's flight.

Ib   (ll. 2261–660) Renart's disguise and the emasculation of Isengrin.

    (ll. 2661–798) The lechery of Hersent.

    (ll. 2799–920) The fickleness of Hermeline.

    (ll. 2921–3052) Renart's trap for Poincet and his expulsion of the women.

13 Jonin, *art. cit.*, p. 82.
14 Foulet, *op. cit.*, pp. 108, 358.

(ll. 3053–256) The women's brawl, terminated by Renart's reconcilation with Hermeline.

Jonin's concentration on the 'mind' of Renart seems to me to have almost totally blinded him to changes in the conception of Renart which become discernible over the three branches he considered, particularly between I–Ia on the one hand and Ib on the other. Renart does not change his crafty nature, but whereas in the earlier parts he is a creature of fantasy and his animality is essential to mark the contrast with the dignified human role he fills, in the last section his animality is much less important. It is true that there are slight differences of tone between I proper and Ia,[15] but the basic conception of Renart is the same in both. However, when we arrive at Ib the whole perspective of the piece changes from that of a feud of national importance to that of domestic squabbles. The author of Ib uses Renart's banishment at the end of Ia (or I) only as a pretext for the theme of the fugitive and the disguise in dye. Thereafter he rarely invokes the context of feudality, not even when Renart returns to Maupertuis and reveals his identity. Renart ceases to fulfil the role of the feudal baron to take up that of the ordinary *mari cocu*. We leave the mock epic to enter the realm of the *fabliau*. Humour now lies much less in the animality of the characters and in parody of the feudal court and its ethos. Let us consider the two sections separately.

If we consider Renart's actions closely, in I proper and in Ia, it emerges that the portrayal of Renart's 'mind' is not quite as convincing as Jonin would have it. The author's attempts at motivation, if they occur at all, are only superficial. Many of Renart's actions are quite inexplicable in psychological terms. Why, for instance, does Renart tremble at the sight of the King's seal when Grinbert delivers the third and final summons?

Li lechierres tranble et fremist;
par grant paor le seel brise,
voit que la letre li devise,
si soupira au premier mot:
bien sot dire ce que i ot.   [ll. 1008–12]

Nothing indicates that Renart's fear is anything but genuine, so we are forced to ask: why does he here suddenly come to dread the wrath of the King and allow himself to come to court, but then after his

15 These have been examined by Foulet, *op. cit.*, pp. 355 ff.

reprieve intentionally and with great bravado incur the greater wrath of
the King by repudiating him and his court (ll. 1571 ff.)? It is hard to
find an explanation even in the twisted psychology of Renart. We
have to admit with Gaston Paris[16] that Renart's humble *volte-face* with
Grinbert is not consistent with his usual rebelliousness. Psychologically
it is not plausible. However, in my view the author was not primarily
interested in psychological realism. The reason why Renart comes to
court is simply that the author needs him there if he is to offer his
audience the spectacle of the smooth talker at court, and if he is to
develop his central theme of the arch-traitor in action, this time
betraying the trust even of his just and merciful king. The motif of
the King's seal and Renart's fear on seeing it are a superficial gesture
on the part of the author to justify a surprising change of tack by
Renart. They are no more than a gesture, however, and Renart's temporary fear is forgotten as soon as its immediate purpose has been
fulfilled. For our author the moral (and comic) spectacle takes precedence over psychological realism.

Then, if we look at other actions by Renart in Branch I proper and
in Ia, we find that most of his crimes—for example, the tricking of
Tibert—are purely gratuitous. We can look for implicit motivation for
them as Jonin does, but if we do we are likely to be left with Jonin's
limp conclusions—namely that Renart commits his crimes through the
fox's instinct for hunting, or (more usually) because he is a sadistic
pervert: 'Cet amour du mensonge va si loin que Renart devient un
véritable sadique de la tromperie. Il éprouve un plaisir pervers non
seulement à faire le mal, mais aussi à se le rappeler,'[17] and 'il tue pour
le plaisir et il étrangle Pelé le rat dont la mort ne peut lui être profit-
able'.[18] Jonin is not alone among modern critics in seeing Renart as a
sadist,[19] but such an explanation for Renart's actions is surely a solution

16 'Le Roman de Renart' in Mélanges de littérature française du moyen âge, Paris, 1912,
    p. 411.   17 Art. cit., p. 64.
18 Art. cit., p. 65. In the case of Renart's killing of Pelé in a scuffle after the episode
    of the tying of the tails in Ia (ll. 1953–60), Jonin's invention of a motive for
    Renart is quite spurious, for the text gives no indication that Renart killed
    for reasons other than self-defence. In fact the reason for the killing is quite
    simple and has nothing to do with Renart's psyche—the author needed a body
    if he was to repeat the motif of the timely arrival of a corpse on a bier, an imita-
    tion of the Coupée episode of Branch I proper.
19 J. Dufournet approvingly quotes B. Beck on the cover of his edition: 'Renart
    ne se montre pas féroce uniquement pour assurer sa subsistance, mais aussi
    pour le plaisir. C'est un devancier de Valmont et du marquis de Sade.'

of despair. It is an admission that the author, if he ever intended to give us a profound insight into the mind of his protagonist, has not carried out his task successfully.

We shall approach the intentions of the twelfth century author more closely if we read Renart's actions primarily as moral symbols, rather than as symptoms of a psychological condition. We are entitled to read them as symptoms if we like—indeed, Jonin was quite right to assert that Renart is not the flat, lifeless personification he later becomes at the hands of Jacquemart Gielée; the animal characters do have a sort of autonomy and life of their own; once we accept the conventions of the piece we *can* visualise Renart's existence in his fantastic world. However, we should not mistake the accidental for the essential. The basic coherence underlying Renart's actions, in Branches I proper and Ia at least, is an abstract set of values. The basis of Renart's 'character' is allegorical and not an individual psyche.

The *Roman de Renart* ought to be seen in the perspective of the Bestiary and the *Physiologus*, where 'the various versions are more concerned with the alleged properties of the animals than with accurate description'.[20] There is little motivation behind the actions of the characters in the *Renart*, there is little evolution in their character because the characters are conceived of as immutable essences. Noble reprieves Renart on two occasions in I proper and Ia, and on the second occasion at least (l. 2138) we raise our eyebrows at his gullibility. Faced with the need to save Renart in the nick of time for the sake of the next episode, the author of Ia tries to motivate the King's clemency with Noble's desire for the ransom money offered by Hermeline. However, at least part of the explanation for the King's magnanimity lies in the fact that it is his property always to have mercy, always to be just and (as his name tells us) always to be noble. Brun twice allows Renart to lure him into a trap in II–Va and into the same trap in I proper. Again, we marvel that the character has not learnt his lesson, but it is the property of the Bear to love honey above anything else. Similarly it is the property of Renart to be devious and treacherous—the questions of why Renart possesses this property and what are the psychological correlations between its manifestations do not arise.

H. R. Jauss has argued convincingly that the characters of the *Roman de Renart* are distinguished from one another not by virtue of their

20 W. T. H. Jackson, *The Literature of the Middle Ages*, New York, 1960, p.329.

possessing individual psychological make-ups, but in accordance with
the principle which he terms *Einzig-Artigkeit*:

> Die Einzig-Artigkeit der Tierfiguren ist indes von der 'einmaligen, unver-
> wechselbaren Artung' des Individuums prinzipiell zu unterscheiden. In
> Renart z.B. stellt sich das Füchsische des Fuchses im Unterschied zu dem
> Wölfischen des Wolfes und nicht der Charakter eines ganz bestimmten
> Fuchses dar: indem sich seine Gestalt als Quasi-Individuum entwickelt,
> 'setzt sich hierin gerade das Arthafte durch'.[21]

Jauss goes on to point out that the *Roman* offers by and large only one
named representative of each species and that the authors take care not
to kill off the name-bearer. A second representative of each species is
introduced with a name only if there has to be a death—in the branches
we are considering here, this is the treatment meted out to Coupée
and to Poincet. The female characters do not constitute an exception
to the rule because male and female form an indissoluble pair, and
perhaps also because women are conceived of first and foremost not
as animal types but as female types cast in the anti-feminist mould.
Consequently the difference between the characters of the *Roman* is
embodied primarily in the difference between the species. As Gaston
Paris once wrote, 'Renard . . . n'est pas un certain goupil, ni Isengrin
un certain loup, dont on nous raconte telle histoire: c'est le goupil,
c'est le loup, et les aventures qu'on leur prête caractérisent les rapports
constants qui résultent de leur nature.'[22] The creatures contain in themselves the particular and the general. The essential distinguishing characteristic of Renart is his foxiness, and the author does not need to
individualise further. Renart is not, as Jonin would have it, an individual
man with all his quirks and foibles dressed in the skin of a fox. He is
foxy through and through. He is the epitome of foxiness, the ultimate
embodiment of the hypocrite and deceiver.

If we look at the conception of Renart in I–Ia we shall find that the
authors do in fact go further than this. Although they do not seek to
particularise his individual characteristics in psychological terms, they
do particularise the type of treachery which he embodies. Whereas the
Aesopic fox represented a general, timeless notion of cunning and
deviousness, the fox of *Renart* I–Ia embodies treachery defined in
specifically feudal terms. Renart's treachery, and indeed his other

---

21 *Untersuchungen zur mittelalterlichen Tierdichtung*, Tübingen, 1959, (*Z.R.P.I*,
Beihaft 100), p. 202.
22 Quoted by Jauss, *op. cit.*, p. 202.

characteristics too, are in my opinion defined in contrast to the feudal ideal of chivalry. Whereas Renart's *raison d'être* is treachery and deceit, the keystone of the whole feudal and chivalric ideal was loyalty and the sanctity of the oath. As J.-C. Payen remarks, 'le parjure est le crime le plus anti-chevaleresque qui soit'.[23] Etienne de Fougères insists upon this quality of loyalty when he equates orders of knighthood with the monastic orders:

> Menbrer li deit, et cel sovent
> qu'en leialté ust son jovent
> plus que nul moigne de covent.
> L'espee prist par tel covent
> que il ne triche ne ne mente
> ne tricherie ne consente.   [*Livre des Manières*,[24] ll. 598–603]

The knight should keep his word to everyone, but especially to his feudal lord. A glance at Branch I proper shows that it relates three great betrayals by Renart, and that these betrayals are arranged in a progression. Firstly, Renart tricks his enemy Brun: in a knight, underhand dealing of this sort was reprehensible enough, but then he employs a similar trick upon his ally Tibert—see l. 491. Finally and *pour comble* Renart betrays his natural lord, Noble. His speech in his own defence at the King's court (ll. 1235–308) is, as Noble observes (l. 1317), a masterful piece of oratory, but not a word of it is sincere. It epitomises the performance of the smooth talker, the flatterer at court. Despite the overwhelming desire of the Court of Peers to hang Renart for his crimes (l. 1408), Noble exercises his prerogative of reprieve after the intercession of Renart's kinsman Grinbert (l. 1450) —on condition that he cease all anti-social acts forthwith and that he set off on a pilgrimage to the Holy Land. Renart promises compliance but immediately breaks faith, making amorous overtures to the Queen, attacking Couart the hare and finally publicly renouncing his pilgrimage and mocking the King and his court (ll. 1571–84). Renart is a traitor and a consummate liar.

Renart acts with treachery and deceit perhaps because he lacks that other essential knightly quality *prouesse*. Renart demonstrates great resourcefulness and an endless capacity for exploiting the foibles of others, but he is far from being manly and courageous. As we have

23 *Le Moyen Age*, I, *Des Origines à 1300*, Paris, 1970, p. 26.
24 Ed. J. Kremer, *Ausgaben und Abhandlungen*, xxxix (1887), Marburg. I have myself produced a new edition of the text which is contained in an unpublished Ph.D. thesis in Manchester University.

seen, he trembles with fear at the sight of the King's seal. He refuses
to face the danger presented by the court like a man; he seeks to
extricate himself from threatening situations by flight or by deceit and
underhand means. A real knight fights with his sword, not with a
crooked tongue. Moreover Renart is a bully. He preys on the weak
and defenceless, fouling Isengrin's cubs, stealing their food, murdering
hens and raping women—not only Hersent but also the Queen herself.
In the earlier branches at least he never takes on creatures of his own
size in a fair fight. Many of Renart's actions are thus a direct contradiction of the main functions of chivalry, which was the upholding
of justice and the defence of the weak:

> Chevalier deit espee prendre
> por justisier et por defendre [= place under ban]
> cels qui d'els funt les autres pleindre:
> force et ravine deit esteindre.   [*Livre des Manières*, ll. 537–40]

Renart is a renegade who refuses to submit to the laws of feudal
society. He is full of that other unknightly quality *orgueil*. The only
thing for which Renart shows any genuine love or respect is his own
castle and *maisnie*. In Branch I proper Renart utters the knight's fare-
well to his *maisnie* as he is about to leave for the court with Grinbert:

> Et Renart, quant vint au matin,
> laissa sa fame et ses anfanz;
> au departir fut li diaus granz.
> Congiè a pris de sa mainie:
> 'Enfanz, fait il, gentil lignie,
> que qu'il de moi daie avenir,
> pansez de mon chastel tenir
> contre contes et contre rois,
> que vos ne troverez des mois
> conte, prince, ne chastelaine,
> qui vos forface une chastaigne.
> Qant vos avrez le pont levé,
> ne serez la por nul grevé.'   ll. 1126–38]

In Ib, ll. 2921–6, Renart is greatly saddened by the dilapidated state
into which his castle has fallen during his banishment. It would be
reasonable to see Renart as representing the relatively insubordinate
and unruly knights of twelfth century France. Renart's pride also
appears in his boasting. His confession to Grinbert (ll. 1048–114) is
nothing but a boastful account of his own misdeeds. The theme of
Renart standing on a high place mocking his discomfited enemies

below occurs frequently—in I proper, ll. 1573–84, in Ia, ll. 1710–70, and
in Ib, ll. 3020–34, as well as in Pierre de Saint Cloud.[25]
   Another of the requirements of knighthood was the defence of the
Holy Church. In Branch I Renart does not in fact attack the Church,
but he certainly shows none of the monkish piety required of a knight
in that first quotation we drew from Etienne de Fougères. Indeed,
Renart turns on its head the whole ideal of the monk's (and knight's)
loyalty when, apprehensive about his forthcoming visit to court, he
makes this heavily ironic statement to Grinbert:

'Diex! quar fuse or moines randuz
a Cluigni ou a Clere vaus:
mes je sant moignes a si fax
que je criem ne me mesavaigne,
se je faz tant moignes devaine.'   [ll. 1030–4]

Renart's religion is cant hypocrisy. As we have just seen, his confession
is a boastful account of his misdeeds. His prayers (ll. 1147–62 and
2273–90) are breathed only in time of adversity. Here, as in the burial
of Coupée, the parody of Church rites can easily strike the uninitiated
modern reader as sacrilegious.
   As well as the political and religious aspects of chivalry, the courtly
ideal is also parodied in the actions of Renart. Renart holds a strong
attraction for women—in Pierre de Saint Cloud Hersent had willingly
connived in her own seduction, and in Branch I–Ia Fière gave Renart
gifts on two occasions, before he raped her (l. 1513) *and after* (l. 1979).
The reason for this attraction may well lie in the affinity of the creatures
involved: women in the *Renart*, like Renart himself, are devious and
mendacious. Renart's relationship with Fière is a clear parody of the
courtly situation. The external aspects of courtliness are reproduced
accurately—Fière is a high-born lady in a position echoing that of
Guinevere. Even Jonin concedes that 'par son attitude, par sa conduite
la lionne ressemble à la dame courtoise au point qu'elle semble en être
la parodie'.[26] Renart's courtship of her involves the ritual love talk
(ll. 1503–12) and the giving of a ring (l. 1513). However, as this noble
image is built up it is simultaneously deflated by huge incongruities.
In addition to the permanent incongruity of the lofty personages being
in fact animals, we learn that the relationship between the 'courtly
lovers' is an animal one of carnality and lust. The secret visit of the

25 Ed. M. Roques, Paris (C.F.M.A.), 1955, ll. 7167–96.
26 *Art. cit.*, p. 73.

lover to the lady is reduced to a scene of rape—reminiscent of the
rutting in a gully we saw between Renart and Hersent in Pierre de
Saint Cloud. Dame Fière is a creature of great lechery, and Renart for
his part is the antithesis of the *fin amant*. His request for Fière's ring
is accompanied by a promise of the obscene reward *he* will give *her*:

> Sachiez, se vos le me donez
> bien vos sara guerredonez
> et donrai vos de mes joiaus
> tant que vaura bien .c. aniaus.   [ll. 1509–12]

Predictably, he is the opposite of faithful and true:

> La roïne l'annel li tent;
> Renart par grant amor le prent.
> Entre ses danz basset a dist:
> 'Par mon chief, quiconques nel vit
> l'annel, certes le conperra:
> ja nule riens ne l'en garra.'   [ll. 1513–18]

Here Renart not only demonstrates his insincerity to his lady but he
also shows that he is seducing the Queen as a conscious act of treachery
against Noble—a point about which he has the effrontery to remind
Noble later (ll. 1764–70).

It seems to me, then, that Renart's actions in I–Ia represent so
systematically the antithesis of the knightly virtues that we should be
justified in seeing the author's desire to invert the chivalric code as the
mainspring of Renart's 'character'. It is the moral attributes of the anti-
knight which form the basis of his 'character', not a coherent and
realistically observed psyche. The one does not completely exclude the
other, but the former enjoys precedence. The authors do give certain
details in the portrayal of Renart which seem to have been *pris sur le
vif*, but they do so merely as an embellishment. They do not invite us
to proceed from there inductively to the construction of some hypothetical psyche. In this part of the *Renart* parody operates not only
with the style and setting of the 'aristocratic' genres—the nature of
which has been elucidated by several scholars, Bossuat in particular—
but also with the very notion of the epic–chivalric hero. This part of
the *Roman* is fundamentally burlesque and in its fantasy world psychological realism is largely irrelevant.

If we now turn briefly to Ib we shall find that the conception of the
'character' of Renart is somewhat different. The role of parody is
reduced. The humour relies much less on the incongruity of animals

playing out dignified human roles. Indeed, on the one hand human roles here are substantially less dignified—Renart spends most of the story disguised as an Anglo-Norman *trouvère*, Isengrin enters the *vilain's* barn like a common thief and emerges literally emasculated, and the two wives are thrown on to the street to swear and brawl like sluts. On the other hand, reminders of the animality of the characters are rare—the author contents himself with the occasional perfunctory reference to *poue* instead of to *main*, to *beste* instead of to *home*, to *taisniere* instead of to *maison*. Furthermore, in earlier branches, whenever the animals came into contact with humans (always peasants, the lowest order of humanity) they cast off their human garbs and reverted entirely to their animal physiognomy. In Ib, however, when Renart meets the *teinturier* he speaks to him in human language. One feels, then, that in Ib the comedy would lose little if all the characters were human. The burlesque fantasy world of I–Ia has gone.

Moreover the whole perspective of the piece has been narrowed. The focus has shifted from debates of national importance in the King's court to domestic squabbles in the conjugal bed. The author of Ib is not interested in the great political problems of the age. He is more preoccupied with sex and the nature of women. The humour of the text relies mainly on the traditional *fabliau* motifs of sex and anti-feminism, trickery, mistaken identity, *quiproquo*, irony, language jokes and so on. As Foulet said, 'nous nous éloignons de l'épopée, et c'est le point de vue et la manière du fabliau qui dominent de plus en plus'.[27] The role played by parody is here reduced more or less to that which it plays in the *fabliaux*.

In Ib, therefore, Renart can no longer be seen essentially as a parody of the perfect knight. He does inherit some of the specifically un-knightly qualities he possessed in I–Ia—he shows the same religious hypocrisy when he prays for divine protection in his banishment (ll. 2273–90 and 2361–70); he shows the same *orgueil* when he mocks his defeated foe (ll. 3020–34). He is still devious and treacherous, to be sure, but his treachery now lacks its previous menacing resonance. His victims no longer stand for anything other than themselves. His crimes are less gratuitous than before: now he tricks only those who have directly threatened or wronged him—the *teinturier*, Isengrin, Poincet and the lecherous and unfaithful women. We can no longer say that the fundamental coherence underlying Renart's actions is the antithesis of the knightly virtues. Perhaps, then, the Jonin approach, seeking

27 *Op. cit.*, p. 356.

lifelike psychology, might well be applicable here where it was not earlier. Even here, however, the author fails to give us a profound study of Renart's character. The only part of Renart's personality which the author explores is his capacity for deception. Like the authors of the *fabliaux*, the author is not interested in the characters of the tricksters and the tricked, he is primarily concerned with exploiting the comedy of trickery in action. The comedy is one not of parody, nor of character but of situation. The author was simply seeking to amuse his audience with the spectacle of the supreme trickster at work —a trickster so well endowed that he can outwit even women, generally invincible in the *fabliaux*:

> Bien sorent [Hermeline and Hersent] qu'engennies furent
> quant au parler le reconurent,
> mais grant mervoille lor est prisse
> ou si faite coulor a prise.   [ll. 3099–102]

In this essay we have tried to show that the authors of the branches of the *Renart* contained in Roques I were not uniform in their treatment of their central character, and that at no time was it their prime endeavour to endow him with an individual and realistic psyche, as Jonin suggests. In I–Ia Renart is fundamentally a creature of fantasy and parody, whereas in Ib he is the epitome of the foxy and cunning man, closely akin to the social types found in the *fabliaux*, but without the specific reference to the chivalric ethos found in I proper. Most critics agree that Branch I proper is perhaps the greatest of the branches of Renart. We would maintain that this is the case not in spite of the burlesque quality of the text but because of it. We have tried to show that in Branch I–Ia the essence of Renart's 'character' is parody of an abstract set of values. As Hodgart has shown,[28] Renart can be seen as the feudal version of the trickster of folklore, the breaker of all the taboos of medieval social life, the inversion of the noble and lofty aspirations of the age. This does not make him a subversive precursor of revolution, any more than the participants in the medieval asses' masses were harbingers of the Reformation. It is possible to parody something one loves without hating it, and periodic releases of tension can be cathartic. Moreover the antithesis offered by the *Renart* is simply a reversed mirror of the thesis—it does not transcend the thesis or contest its validity. Renart is the hero of the piece, but his actions can be seen only as an example in negative—in an inverted way

28 See M. Hodgart, *Satire*, London, 1969, pp. 23 ff.

the text presents us with a serious discussion of the problems of chivalry and feudality. Thus the burlesque quality of the style and of the underlying ethos places these branches of the *Renart*, at least, squarely alongside the 'aristocratic' and conservative literature of the day.

However, Renart is not a flat personification, a mere symbol of unknightliness. Part of the greatness of Branch I lies in the author's success in creating a new comic world of fantasy in which we *can* visualise the existence of characters like Renart, Isengrin and the rest. As Jonin showed, Renart does possess a certain degree of autonomy: up to a point his psychology *is* coherent and credible. But it is so only enough to stave off our total unbelief, not to sustain the close scrutiny of the psychologist for its own sake. We are in the presence of both a *sensus allegoricus* and a *sensus litteralis*. It is a question of priorities. We have tried to show that it is primarily the *sensus allegoricus* which forms the 'essential' coherence underpinning Renart's actions and we find confirmation in the fact that the medievals themselves had no doubt about what was 'essential' with Renart—Jacquemart Gielée's *Renart le Nouvel* extracted the 'essence' and turned Renart into pure allegory. He also produced a turgid poem.

Faith Lyons

Some notes on the *Roman de la Rose*— the golden chain and other topics in Jean de Meun

The golden chain

Nature's confession (ed. Lecoy, III, ll. 16699–9375) contains some of the most vigorous and skilful writing in the *Roman*. Her speech has been praised for its encyclopedic knowledge or blamed for its digressions. Overlooked by Langlois and misunderstood by G. Paré, one image, that of the golden chain of the elements, 'la chaene dorée' (l. 16756) has attracted the attention of the *Roman*'s latest editor, M. Lecoy (I, p. xix, n. 1). For G. Paré, symbolising the heavens and Aristotle's fifth essence, the chain is distinct from the four elements of the sublunary world: 'Par "la chaîne dorée", entendons l'ensemble des astres, la voûte céleste qui entoure la terre, région des quatre éléments' (*Les Idées et les lettres au XIIIe siècle*, 1947, p. 216). However, Jean's text speaks of the bond that entwines and ties together the warring elements. In the words of Nature, she holds this chain, at the divine behest:

> Si gart, tant m'a Dex honoree,
> la bele chaene dorée
> qui les .IIII elements enlace. .
> et me bailla toutes les choses
> qui sunt en la chaene ancloses.   [ll. 16755–7 and 16759–60]

Later Nature tells of the influence of the heavenly bodies upon the sublunary world,

> sur les particulieres choses
> qui sunt es elements ancloses.   [ll. 17480–1]

The chain is thus equated with the elements so that Paré's interpretation is erroneous. The chain binding the elements occurs both in Jean de Meun and in his source, Alain de Lille's *De Planctu Naturae*. Indeed, the Latin text is quoted by Lecoy in his note to line 16756 (III, p. 164). Alain speaks here of chains in the plural and without the qualifying word 'golden'. I suggest that Jean may have recalled the mention of a single and a golden chain in a later passage of the *De Planctu* where Largitas says to Nature that she is linked to her through close relationship by the golden chain of love,

> me tibi aurea dilectionis catena
> connectit   [ed. T. Wright, Rolls Series, LIX, II, 1876, p. 516]

The late Rosamund Tuve noted the cosmological theories which appear in the *Roman* concerning the creation and nature of the universe. She made a special study of Jean de Meun's reference to 'the physical theory of the separation and reconciliation of the elements' in her article 'A medieval commonplace in Spenser's cosmology' (*Studies in Philology*, XXX (1933), pp. 138–9), where parallel passages are also quoted from the *De Planctu* (her p. 142). However, if one compares not the common theory but artistic purpose and poetic atmosphere, the divergences between Jean and Alain are great. The *Roman* gives a different role to Nature where the tools with which she works in her forge are the sexual symbols of the anvil and the hammer. Nature's role in the *De Planctu* is less functional and more sublime. Similarly Jean de Meun uses the golden chain in a context that is entirely physical, and devoid of any spiritual feeling.

Students of cosmology are, of course, familiar with the doctrine of Macrobius as expressed in his commentary on Cicero's dream of Scipio. In Book I, chapter vi [24], Macrobius explains how the elements were bound together with an unbreakable chain, earth and fire being held together by the two means of air and water. Macrobius gives as his authority Plato's *Timaeus*, 31b–32c. But in his history of cosmological doctrines, *Le Système du Monde*, II, pp. 481–2, Duhem points out that in speaking of the mingling of a common quality, e.g. coldness shared by water and earth, Macrobius here refers not so much to the *Timaeus* itself as to the developments given Plato's thought by Chalcidius in his Late Latin commentary. Macrobius expands his description of the unbroken chain of the universe in Book I, chapter xiv [15], and he then calls it 'golden', *Homeri catena aurea*. It reaches from the supreme God down to the earth. The allusion to Homer derives from the *Iliad*, VIII, 19, where God orders the golden chain to hang from the sky down to the earth.

In the twelfth century William of Conches, in his still unpublished *Glosae super Macrobium*, associates this golden chain with Jacob's ladder in Genesis. William of Conches, the Chartrian teacher, has also evoked

Homer's chain in his own commentary on the Latin *Timaeus*, 35a, where Plato's Demiurge creates the World Soul. Writing of the third intermediate kind of existence, William comments '*Tercium* in aurea catena Homeri' (*Glosae super Platonem*, ed. E. Jeauneau, 1965, p. 149). Even if unfamiliar with William of Conches, medieval readers of Macrobius and of Chalcidius could have made similar inferences about the cosmological union of the highest with the lowest. Two other well known twelfth century thinkers use the image of the chain in their writing about creation. One is Bernardus Silvestris in his myth of creation, the *De Mundi Universitate*. Speaking of the world or mega-cosm, he says 'Mundus enim quiddam continuum, et in ea catena nihil vel dissipabile vel abruptem' (ed. C. S. Barach and J. Wrobel, 1876, p. 31, IV, 79–80). This chain must surely correspond with what Pierre Lévêque has termed a general allegory of the bonds of the universe, mysteriously thrown around all things in the world. Later Bernardus, speaking of man or the microcosm, uses the image of the golden chain to link the highest with the lowest, as in Macrobius, Book I, xiv [15], when he writes as follows:

> In lunari enim limite, ubi aureae homini quasi medietas est catenae superioris inferiorisque mundi vidilicet umbilicus, spirituum numerus ad milia circumfusus populosae more civitatis laetabundus occurrit. [p. 47, VII, 1–3]

This golden chain, like an umbilical cord, seems to correspond with what Pierre Lévêque has characterised as the chain of the spiritual powers of the universe. A twelfth century Cistercian mystic, Isaac de l'Etoile, in his treatise on the soul, compares its various qualities—sense, imagination, reason, intelligence—with the four elements of earth, water, air and fire (Migne, P.L. 194, 1885c). Then he writes of the harmonious linking of the elements, and of the soul's corresponding qualities, in a golden chain, *catena aurea poetiae*, that reaches from the heights down to the depths. He appears here to be adapting to Chris-tian thought both the chains described in Macrobius.

Jean de Meun considers the golden chain of the elements only in relation to the physical universe. As a secondary creator, his allegorical figure, Nature, knows that man's reason and immortal soul are the divine handiwork alone. This consideration is manifest when she adapts from the Latin *Timaeus* the speech of the Demiurge to the inferior gods (ed. Lecoy, III, ll. 19047–82). Nature's role as creator is therein limited to the realm of the corruptible (ll. 19059–61). In all these so-called borrowings Jean de Meun consciously joins traditional

commonplaces to a singularly distinctive view of the world and of
life.

Necessity and free will

Nature in her confession has much to say about necessity and free
will. In the main section of her discourse on this topic (ll. 17071–468)
the arguments are based on the well known fifth book of the *Consolation of Philosophy* by Boethius. In his notes to the recent edition of the
Roman (III, p. 168) M. Lecoy remarks that Jean de Meun has simplified
Boethius somewhat. However, I believe a brief survey of what immediately precedes and follows this discourse in the *Roman* will help to
explain Jean's shift of emphasis. Nature tells how the instability natural
to the elements provokes corruption and death (ll. 16951–7028). Some
untimely deaths are due to accident and some to suicide. Fate is held
responsible, though Nature observes that man's reason may be able to
check disaster (ll. 17045–70). In this way the theme of death leads to the
topic of free will. Yet Nature tires of this topic before she has ex-
hausted it (ll. 17697–706). Indeed, she finally admits she would never
have spoken of free will except to forestall any pleading by disobedient
man, who might maintain in his own defence that necessity domi-
nates human actions (ll. 17707–32). Since the disobedience of mankind to Nature's laws—a theme found originally in the *De Planctu*
—is of importance, Nature declares that free will is very relevant
to her confession,

> Mes il affiert a ma matiere.   [l. 17709]

How then is free will dealt with in the *Roman*? God's foreknowledge
and man's free will must coexist, while divine foreknowledge of all
events is asserted. Necessity could threaten the ethical life of mankind,
since reward of good deeds and punishment of crimes would be vain
(ll. 17081–94). In Boethius these moral issues do not arise till the end
of Prose iii in Book v. In the *Roman* they are spoken of at once, necessity being fundamental to mankind's guilt or innocence in Jean de
Meun. In favour of necessity Nature at once mentions an argument
based on the convertibility of truth and necessity. To forecast the
fulfilment of some possible event is to state a truth. But, when concerned with a possible event, it is at once objected that necessity is only
a relative or conditional necessity (ll. 17175–208). Boethius himself
felt uneasy about man's free will, since to him divine precognition must

exist independently of past and future events, i.e. without causation. Otherwise God's foreknowledge would be caused by such events, which is not admissible. The problem of causation also bulks large in the *Roman* (ll. 17256–9 and 17351–4).

In the *Consolation* it is Boethius himself who puts the arguments against free will in Book v, Prose iii, whereas it is Philosophy who presents counter-arguments in favour of free will in Book v, Prose vi. In adapting this dialogue to his own purposes, Jean changes the order of ideas and foreshortens the arguments in his source. The questioner's arguments in Book v, Prose iii, contain a logical weakness. A sits down and B sees him sitting. A's sitting necessarily makes B's opinion true, but also B's opinion is necessarily true because A sits. Boethius asserts there is a common necessity. Lecoy in his edition (III, p. 169) says the argument based on logical convertibility (all that is true is necessary, all that is necessary is true) is not in Boethius. But I find the same answer in both texts, though in Book v, Prose vi, it is given by Philosophy, and in Jean's poem (ll. 17191–208) by Nature. The reply in Boethius objects that an act like that of a man walking is possible— that is, one of relative or conditional necessity, Jean's 'necessité en regart' (l. 17198)—whereas an event like the setting of the sun is certain—that is, one of absolute or causal necessity, 'necessité simple' (l. 17199). Jean de Meun places his very similar though less developed argument at the beginning of the discourse on necessity and free will. On the other hand, Boethius reserves it for the last words of Philosophy. However, Boethius makes the distinction between two kinds of necessity lead on to the notion of time, which for God is an eternal present. On the other hand, Jean, after making the same kind of distinction, inserts arguments firstly against divine precognition with causation, and secondly in favour of God's foreknowledge without causation, concluding that divine omniscience exercises no constraint upon human action. It is only after these arguments that the *Roman* ends with an answer, as in the *Consolation*, which is that time for God is an eternal present. In conclusion, by his positioning of the main arguments in favour of free will and by his curtailing of arguments opposed to it, Jean has used his source to reinforce Nature's case against the guilty disobedience of mankind. Jean reveals himself here as a writer without the lofty imagination of Boethius and Alain de Lille, but he does show qualities of good sense, inventiveness and curiosity.

The phoenix

In the symbolical portrait of Nature traced by Alain de Lille's *De Planctu* the phoenix figures on her dress, with the swan, the peacock and other birds. Of the phoenix we are told only how it resurrects miraculously in another:

> Illic phoenix, in se mortuus,
> redivivus in alio, quodam Naturae
> miraculo, se sua morte a mortuis
> suscitabat.   [ed. T. S. Wright, Rolls Series, LIX, ii, p. 438]

The *Roman* retains nothing of this portrait of Nature. However, when Jean represented her working at the forge to replace the living things destroyed by Death, he may have recalled the image of the phoenix in the *De Planctu*.[1] In any case, Jean uses the phoenix to symbolise Nature overcoming Death, which catches hold of individuals. One individual will always escape, and thus the common form, the species, always survives. This truth is embodied by the phoenix:

> et par le fenix bien le senble,
> qu'il n'an peut estre .ii. ansenble.   [ll. 15945-6]

Already in the twelfth century two Old French romances known to me contain a similar tag. In Chrétien's *Cligés* the peerless beauty of the heroine, Fenice, is compared with the phoenix, of which there could only be a single one alive on earth at any one time. She is rightly named Fenice because her beauty is unique:

> Car si con fenix li oisiax
> Est sor toz les autres plus biax,
> Ne estre n'an pot c'uns ansanble,
> Ice Fenyce me resanble:
> N'ot de biauté nule paroille.   [ed. Micha, 1957, ll. 2687-91]

Nature could never create her like again (ll. 2692-4). As for the poet, to describe her adequately remains beyond his powers (ll. 2695-705). We must note the striking trait about the phoenix, of which it is said

---

1 I owe to the kindness of Mr Henry Bodenham additional references to the phoenix in Alexander Neckam's late twelfth century *De naturis rerum* (ed. T. Wright, Rolls Series, XXXIV (1863), pp. 84-6 and pp. 377-8), particularly the following lines:

> Parvulus in lucem prodit phoenix novus haeres;
> Has natura potens fertque refertque vices.

that only a single one can live on earth at a given time, 'estre n'an pot c'uns ansanble' (l. 2689). This same trait occurs in *Partonopeu de Blois*, where the down of a wonderful pillow is made of phoenix feathers:

> Li duns en fu tos de fenis,
> D'un oisel qui molt est soltis;
> Sa nature mervelle samble,
> Car ja n'en ert que uns ensamble.   [ed. Gildea, 1967, I, ll. 1397-400]

Again we are told that there never will be but one such bird. Unlike *Cligés*, a long development is added about the phoenix and fire, with the funeral pyre from the ashes of which emerges another bird once the first is consumed in the flames (ll. 1401-22). The thirteenth century romance *Galeran* describes at length a marvellous pillow with a detail about the feathers seemingly based on the *Partonopeu* passage:

> S'en fu la plume prise en Ynde
> D'un oysel qu'on clame fenis:
> C'est ung oysel par qui ja nis
> N'est fait que d'un seul, ce me semble,
> Car estre n'en puet qu'un ensemble.   [ed. Foulet, 1925, ll 464-8]

In Jean de Meun the treatment is quite different, since, far from being a picturesque detail, the phoenix illustrates a main point in the poem's argument. Paré's book, which I have already quoted above, puts all this clearly (pp. 56-7). Death destroys Nature's work, but the birth of new individuals maintains a sort of immortality. The perennial nature of the species or 'forme comune' is symbolised by the phoenix. Even when consumed in the fire, it keeps its universal form so that either a second phoenix replaces it or else perhaps the original phoenix is resurrected. Thus the species can never disappear from the earth (ed. Lecoy, III, ll. 15935-74). No other Old French poet has turned the legend of the phoenix into a coherent piece of thought. It is true that in Philippe de Thaun's *Bestiaire* the phoenix represents the resurrected Christ, but mostly the usual details describing the bird's nature are without significance for Christian thought (ed. E. Walberg, 1900, pp. 81-5). On the other hand, in the *Roman* alone even the rhyming 'ensemble' and 'semble', a tag which appears elsewhere, is given real meaning and ceases to be a commonplace. The slight modification 'n'an peut estre .ii. ansenble' (ed. Lecoy, III, l. 15946) relates a mere detail more closely to a general truth. The fixed phrase 'n'est qu'uns

ensemble' probably originated in some Old French bestiary. It appears
in Guillaume le Clerc's *Bestiaire* (ed. Reinsch, 1892) where no creature
is like the phoenix, of which there can be only a single one:

> Cist oisel est toz dis sanz per:
> Car ja nen ert fors un ensemble
> Ne nul altre ne li resemble.   [ll. 742–4]

Guillaume le Clerc's text, dated 1210, serves to bring out the superior
quality of the later writer Jean de Meun who handles general truths in
unique fashion, however time-worn his material.

Ian Michael

The Spanish *Perceforest*: a recent discovery

In September 1971 I was allowed entry into the Biblioteca de Palacio in Madrid in order to further my research on the *Libro de Alexandre*. The catalogue of this rich collection of books and manuscripts, except for the holdings relating to Latin America and a few other specialities, remains unpublished and, to a considerable extent, unexamined, since readers are not permitted direct access to the card file index. I held the faint but inextinguishable hope of coming across one of the two lost mss. of the *Alexandre*, the ms. known to have been in the monastery of Bugedo in the seventeenth century, or the ms. quoted by Gutierre Díez de Games in the fifteenth century. By writing various headings on slips of paper ('Alejandro', 'Gonzalo de Berceo', 'Juan Lorenzo de Astorga', 'Libro', 'Poema' and, finally, 'Historia'), I managed to prevail upon the Librarian's most helpful assistant to allow me to see the relevant index cards. Needless to say, I did not find either of the lost *Alexandre* mss., but I did discover, among other interesting material, the ms. now numbered Palacio ms. 266–7, 2 vols. in folio, paper (Sign. ant. 2–D–2; VII–F–5), and entitled *Primera y segunda parte / Dela antigua y moral Historia del noble Rey / Persefores, y del esforçado Gadifer su her / mano, Reyes de Inglaterra y Escoçia. / Traduçida de la lengua Fran / çesa en la nuestra Cas / tellana por Fer / nando de / Mena*. To the best of my knowledge, the existence in the Biblioteca de Palacio of this Spanish version of the French *Perceforest* has not been noticed previously by any scholar, nor have I found it listed in any of the standard bibliographical works.[1]

The two tomes appear to have been rebound, in Spanish buckram, in the late eighteenth century. The hand seems to date from the latter part of the sixteenth century, the text having been quite roughly but

1 The substance of the present article was contained in a lecture I delivered to the International Arthurian Society at its tenth congress, held at Nantes on 22 August 1972. The article is here published with the express permission of the Consejero Delegado Gerente of the Patrimonio Nacional, Jefatura del Estado Español.

for the most part legibly written, with various cancellations, alterations and corrections, on paper which contains some watermarks. The folios measure approximately 220 mm. × 315 mm. The hand appears to be the same throughout, apart from the actual folios 6–15 of the first tome, which have been rewritten in a later hand and inserted to replace the folios originally numbered 4–33, which, apparently, were torn out; the sense, however, is continuous.[2] Discounting the guard leaves, the first tome now contains 258 folios: the title page, one folio of prologue, and 256 folios of text, but, as the pagination and signatures make clear, this tome must originally have contained 278 folios (the missing thirty folios having been recopied in a very small hand on the ten replacement folios, which themselves bear arabic page numbers upside down in the bottom right recto and left verso corners in an order which suggests that they were blanks intended for some other work left uncompleted). The second tome contains 230 folios: the title page and 229 folios of text. This title page bears some scribblings, which seem to read 'dios mio. yo confieso que no meres/co la tiera que piso. y que soy inme/rito. del bien que me haseis / (El capitan paredes) / yn dey nomine amen et (?) benditisi (?) muy a mi costa y saber (?)', and the notation 'Sal 2ª. Est 9. Cax. 5º.'[3]

Despite the fact that the title page of the first tome indicates that only the first and second of the six parts of the French *Perceforest* are to be found in the Spanish version, the two tomes of the Spanish ms. end with a similar phrase which suggests that there was more to follow. Part I ends (ms. 266, f. 258v):

> y se metio conellos por la espesa floresta diziendo que no sosegaria hasta hallarle muerto o bibo. donde la dexa la historia hasta su tp̃o.—deograçias—. finis:— traduzida por fernando de Mena en toledo. acabada año de 1573 [*the 3 is blotched*] en diez de Mayo—de lo poco vienen alo mucho—*etc.*[4]

Part II ends (ms. 267, f. 230v):

> Quando los dos caballeros tuvieron señalado el dia yel lugar donde hazer su batalla salto cada vno sobre su cavallo y selanço en la floresta vno hazia vna parte y otro hazia otra ala claridad de la luna que jamas el caballero estraño

2 A third hand, similar to, but not the same as, the second hand, and chrono-logically earlier than it, appears in ms. 266, last seven lines of f. 124v and first twenty-eight lines of f. 125r, and in ms. 267, bottom of f. 4v to top of 5r.

3 I am indebted to Professor Harvey L. Sharrer, who has checked and verified my collation of the folios and signatures of the ms. and who has thrown light on a number of difficult readings; his suggestions have been incorporated into the transcriptions of the *Persefores* given here.

4 This ending does not correspond to the end of Part I of the French versions,

los pudo detener a que quedassen el vno conel otro—antes se fueron por la espessura adelante y el caballero estraño se quedo a la puerta del templo [durmiendo *cancelled*] donde los dexa la historia hasta su tp̄o—finis. laus deo. traduzida por fer^do de mena acabola en primero de abril 1576 años.[5]

The similarity of these *explicits* at an interval of almost three years would seem to imply that further parts of the Spanish version existed, since what we have corresponds to something less than a third of the French original. On 31 July 1972 Señorita Doña Matilde López Serrano, Director of the Biblioteca de Palacio, very kindly undertook a search at my request to see if further tomes might exist; she found nothing, however. I searched also the catalogue of the library of the Real Academia de la Historia and the Biblioteca Nacional in Madrid, as

---

because the Spanish translator omitted part of one episode and the whole of another. Part II of the Spanish version, however, begins exactly as the second part of the French: ms. 267, f. 2*r*, '. . . Capitulo primero de vn razonamiento q̄ hizo el Rey Gadifer de Escoçia a sus caballeros tocante ala buena gouernaçion y poliçia de su Reyno—.'; cf. printed ed. [P], Paris, 1528, II, 1*r*, col. a, 'Du parlement que le Roy Gadiffer descosse ent a ses Cheualiers / touchant le gouuernement et police de son Royaulme. Chapitre premier.'

5 This corresponds, though not exactly, to the end of Part II in the French versions, cf. Bibliothèque Nationale ms. 346 [A], f. 423*r*, col. b, 'Quant la journee fut affiee des ii preux [f. 423*v*, col. *a*] chevaliers ilz se alerent departir lun de lautre. Sy prist chacun son cheval et monterent sus et sen alerent lun a ung lez et lautre a lautre Et le chevalier estrange qui les avoit departiz a celle fois demoura a la chappelle car oncques ne les peult retenir ne faire demourer lun avecques lautre aincois sen ala chacun en la grant forest descendre la ou il luy pleut le mieux navrez et debrisiez durement. mais a tant se taist lystoire deulx deux Et retourne [*ms. holed*] parler des xii chevaliers qui les veux de lermite mirent a fin a leur honneur—cy fine le deuxiesme volume de percheforest.'; and cf. printed ed. [P], Paris, 1528, II, 153*r*, col. b, 'Quāt la journée fut afiee des deux preux cheualiers ilz se allerent deptir lung del autre. Si prindrēt chascun son cheual & mōterēt sus et sen allerent lung a vng coste et lautre a lautre. Et le cheualier qui les auoit departys a celle fois demoura a la chappelle: Car oncques ne les peut retenir ne faire demourer lung auesques lautre: aincois sen alla chascun descendre en la grant forest la ou il luy pleut le mieulx / naure et debrise durement. Mais atant se taist lhystoire a parler deulx / et retourne a racompter des douze Cheualiers / qui les veux de lhermite misrent a fin a leur honneur. ℂ Cy fine le Deuxiesme Volume du noble Roy Perceforest.' The Spanish is closer to French ms. A: 'caballero estraño' / 'chevalier estrange' (P 'cheualier'), but these French versions do not contain an equivalent for 'ala claridad de la luna' (though it might possibly have been a misunderstanding of 'lun a ung lez'). I am most grateful to Mrs Jane Taylor for providing me with the extracts from the French ms.

well as that of the library of the University of Salamanca, where a
number of important mss. were returned from the Biblioteca de
Palacio in 1953–54, but in vain.

On 20 October 1972, however, I learned from Madrid that Doña
Matilde and Doña Justa Moreno Garbayo had recognised the old signature notation on the title page of the second tome (Sal 2ª. Est 9.
Cax. 5⁰) as belonging to the library of the Conde de Gondomar (1567–
1626), after having matched it with the signature in another ms. from
his famous library at the Casa del Sol, Valladolid, which is also preserved in the Biblioteca de Palacio. This important piece of information
led me to the inventory of Gondomar's books and manuscripts drawn
up in 1623 and now to be found in the Biblioteca Nacional; a list of the
mss. in the inventory was published by Manuel Serrano y Sanz in
1903.⁶ Serrano (p. 297) has the following entry:

> HISTORIA del Rey de Inglaterra Persefores y Gadifer su hermano, traduc.
> por Fernando de Mena de frances en Castellano. F⁰. 2. volum.

He did not make any comment on this entry, nor did he note that
this ms. still survived in the Palacio library, but he mentioned the fate
of Gondomar's collection and the characteristic signatures of its mss.:

> La biblioteca del Conde de Gondomar, aunque ya muy saqueada, fue adqui-
> rida por Carlos IV hacia el año 1785; muchos de sus manuscritos se hallan
> en las Bibliotecas Real, Nacional y de la Academia de la Historia. Son
> fáciles de reconocer por las signaturas escritas en letra gruesa; una de ellas
> (Bibl. Nac. R. 378, *Viage a Turquia*) dice así: SAL. 2ª EST. 12. CAX. 6⁰.
> [p. 65, n. 1]

Further information on the dispersal of Gondomar's library is given
by Richard Ford:

> The *Casa del Sol*, opposite to San Gregorio, with a fine portal, and now a
> barrack for recruits! was the house of Diego Sarmiento de Acuña, the
> celebrated Conde de Gondomar, ambassador of Philip IV. [*sic*] to James I.,
> and by whom he was led by the nose [. . .]; his library of 15,000 vols was
> one of the earliest and finest ever formed in Spain. It contained most curious
> English literature, collected in London when Shakespere was living. The

6 See Bibl. Nac ms. 13593–4, *olim* Uu. 46–7 (2 vols., fol.), *Indice y inventario
de los libros que ay en la libreria de Don Diego Sarmiento de Acuña, Conde de
Gondomar, en su casa en Valladolid, hecho a ultimo de Abril del año de 1625.* . . .
Serrano's list, 'Libros manuscritos o de mano [de la Biblioteca del Conde de
Gondomar]', is in *Revista de archivos, bibliotecas y museos*, 3ª época, VIII (1903),
pp. 65–8, 222–8, 295–300, and is taken from Bibl. Nac. ms. 13594, 163 ff.

Marquis of Malpica, the heir, sold the whole to Charles IV., but as his Majesty did not pay—*cosas de España*—some 1600 volumes were kept back, and left at Valladolid to the care of the bricklayer! who looked after the house, these books soon disappeared. The portion which was sent to Madrid contains the secret correspondence of Gondomar during his embassy in England [. . .]. This buried mine of Shaksperian period, which clamors for a Collier, lies unexplored in the private library of the crown of Madrid.[7]

It is clear, therefore, that the *Persefores* ms. had been acquired by Gondomar by the year 1623, forty-seven years after the date of the second tome, and that he possessed only the two parts which are still extant. The ms. then passed from Valladolid to the Biblioteca de Palacio *c.* 1785, in the reign of Charles IV, whose *ex libris* is to be found inside the cover of both tomes. It will be very difficult to discover from whom Gondomar obtained the work.

The difficulties of undertaking even a preliminary collation of the Spanish version with the extant French versions have been considerable. First, the rules of the Biblioteca de Palacio do not permit complete microfilms to be taken of mss. held there; second, there is no modern published edition of the French text. There is, however, a long summary of the plot published by L.-F. Flûtre, a valuable analysis and study by Jeanne Lods, and, most recently, an excellent edition of the two manuscript traditions, with variants, and a study of most of the first part by Jane Taylor in her regrettably still unpublished Oxford doctoral thesis.[8] Mrs Taylor has most generously allowed me to reproduce here the stemma she has drawn up for the French versions, and she has helped me to present the very partial and provisional collation which follows.

7 *A Handbook for Travellers in Spain*, 3rd edn., London, 1855, II, p. 581. Some of Gondomar's letters have since been published: *Cinco cartas político-literarias de D. Diego Sarmiento de Acuña, primer Conde de Gondomar . . .*, Madrid, 1869, and *Documentos inéditos para la historia de España: Correspondencia oficial de don Diego Sarmiento de Acuña, Conde de Gondomar*, Madrid, 1936–45.

8 L.-F. Flûtre, 'Etudes sur le roman de *Perceforêt*', *Romania*, LXX (1948–49), pp. 474–522; LXXI (1950), pp. 374–92 and 482–508; LXXIV (1953), pp. 44–102; LXXXVIII (1967), pp. 475–508; LXXXIX (1968), pp. 355—86; XC (1969), pp. 341–70; XCI (1970), pp. 189–226; Jeanne Lods, *Le Roman de Perceforest (origines, composition, caractères, valeur et influence)*, Paris, 1951, and *Les Pièces lyriques du roman de Perceforest*, Paris, 1953; Mrs Taylor's thesis was presented to the University of Oxford in 1970.

Stemma of French versions of 'Perceforest' drawn by Jane Taylor

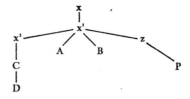

A Bibliothèque Nationale ms. 345–8.
B Bibliothèque Nationale ms. 106–9.
C Bibliothèque de l'Arsenal ms. 3483–94.
D British Museum Royal ms. 15.E.v, 19.E.iii, and 19.E.ii.
P printed edition: *La Treselegante, Delicieuse, Melliflue et tresplaisante Hystoire du tresnoble, victorieux et excellentissime roy Perceforest, Roy de la grande Bretaigne, fundateur du Franc palais et du temple du souverain dieu, & c. Le second—le sixiesme et dernier volume des anciennes croniques Dangleterre, & c.* 6 vols. G.L. N. Cousteau, pour Galiot du pre: Paris, 1528. fol. [British Museum 85.1.5, and G.10556, 57 (two copies); Bodleian Library, Douce P 20–2]. The edition of 1531 (Paris, E. Gormontius) is a reprinting of the first.

Sample collation of the Spanish ms. with the French versions

Spanish, f. 3*r*: Y aviendo puesto en su subjeçion los mas poderosos del. puso su yndignaçion sobre la gran babilonia y sus soberbios habitadores aquien por mandamientos y mensajes jamas pudo traer asu dominio. por lo qual juro de nos sossegar hasta aver la conquistado y metido debaxo de sus poderosas leyes

A Quant le gentil roy Alexandre eut mis tous les plus puissans d'Orient en sa subjection, car par mandement de menaces ne les peult a luy attraire, adonq dist il que jamais n'auroit repos si l'auroit par force a luy submise

B Quant le gentil roy Alixandre eut mis tous les plus poissans d'Orient en sa subjection, sus Babilon mist son indignation, car par mandement de manaisses ne le peult a lui attraire. Adont dist il que jamais n'auroit aucun repoz se l'auroit par force a luy submise

C and D Quant le victorieux Alexandre eust mis a son obeissance tous les plus puissans d'Orient, il se anima sur la cité de Babilione, pour ce que par menaces ne autrement ne la pouoit attraire a lui. Adont jura que jamais n'auroit repos si l'auroit soubmise a lui

P Quant le gentil roy Alexandre eut mis en sa subiection tous les plus
puissans Dorient / il mist son indignation sur Babilōne / lesquelz
par mandemēs ne peut a luy attraire. Et alors il iura et dist que
iamais nauroit repos iusques a ce que il leust submise a luy

[*A has scribal omission, B has 'mandement de manaisses', C and D have
'se anima', P has no equivalent for 'y mensajes'; Spanish mistranslates,
apparently, 'luy' as 'leyes': here B is nearest, followed by P*]

Spanish, f. 2r: en compañia de muchas señoras y de muchos grandes de
França.

A il y eut grant plenté de nobles princes de l'une partie et de l'autre
B grant *omitted*

P se trouuerent grant nombre de princes et barons tant dune part q̄
dautre

[*since 'grandes' is a reasonable translation of 'barons', P is marginally better*]

Spanish, f. 3v: sus desbaratadas gentes

A sa gent qui estoit desbaretee
B ses gens qui estoient departis
P ses gens

[*A is best*]

Spanish f. 3v: se fue para el blandiendo vna gruessa lança conla qual
le hirio por medio del cuerpo tan poderosamente que le tendio
muerto por tr̄ra

A et le fiert de son glaive parmy le corps sy le jette mort
B et le fery; sy chut mort par terre
P & le frappa de son glaive p̄my le corps vng tel coup quil le gecta
mort par terre

[*P is best*]

Spanish, f. 3v: gran daño y lastima por que no quedaua en Vida otro
mejor que el

A dommaige et pitié, car pou demoura de meilleurs en vie
B dommage pou remainst de meilleur chevallier en vie
P dommage et pitie / car il ny en demoura point de meilleur en vie

[*A and P are best*]

Spanish, f. *3v*: y caminando el gentil Rey

A Le gentil Roy Alexandre chevaulchoit
B Le noble roy a.
P Le gentil roy Alexandre cheuauchoit

[*A and P are best*]

Spanish, f. *4r*: Quando el Rey Alexandre oyo al buen hombre

A Quant le gentil roy eut oy parler Cassanus
B *omits* gentil
P Quant le gentil roy Alexandre eut ainsi ouy parler le preud'homme
   Cassanus

[*P is best*]

Spanish, f. *5r*: y por otra parte el gentil prinçipe que sabia hazer toda
   honrra y cortesia

A Et le gentil prince qui sçavoit tout honneur
B Et pareillement le noble prince qui reluisoit en toute honneur
P et dautre coste le gentil prince qui scauoit tout hōneur

[*P is best*]

Even from this preliminary collation it is clear that the Spanish
version often, but not always, coincides with P and sometimes with A,
but occasionally it is nearer B (it coincides least with C and D). It is
therefore not in the same position as the Italian translation, printed at
Venice in 1556–58 in six books, which, according to Vaganay, was
based on P.[9] Provisionally we might hazard that the Spanish translator
made use either of P plus x^1 or z or a ms. descended in that line, or
such a ms. alone. It is certain that he made very extensive omissions,
the purpose of which seems to have been to remove the more tan-
gential material in the French original in order to concentrate on the
main lines of the story; by the 1570s it is not, of course, surprising to
find a considerable disintegration of what Eugène Vinaver has called
'the complex moving tapestry of interlocked themes, a structure which
reaches its acme in the prose fiction of the last three centuries of the

9 Hugues Vaganay, 'Attraverso il Cinquecento: III, *Il Parsaforesto* Livres I et
   V', *Rivista delle bibliotheche e degli archivi*, XVI (1905), pp. 11–15, at pp.
   14–15.

Middle Ages'.[10] Although late, the Spanish version will no doubt be
of interest to those studying the French *Perceforest*, because it does not
correspond exactly to any of the extant French texts.

At least one of the alterations in the Spanish version suggests that
the Palacio ms. is not a scribal copy but a draft written by Mena
himself:

Spanish, f. 3*v*: con abundançia de [viandas *cancelled*] bastimentos de los
   quales tenian neçessidad
P garniz de victailles en grant habondāce dont lost auoit mestier

It seems more probable that the translator crossed out *viandas* and
wrote *bastimentos*, perhaps thinking that the latter was less of a gallicism,
than that a mere copyist would have had a stylistic qualm of this sort.
However, Harvey L. Sharrer of the University of California at Santa
Barbara and I, who are jointly preparing an edition of the Spanish
text, will wish to examine all the evidence before committing our-
selves on this point.

Of the translator, Fernando de Mena, we know very little, except that
he also translated Heliodorus' *Historia Aethiopica*, known in Spanish as
Los amores de Teágenes y Cariclea. Mena's translation of that work was
published in Alcalá de Henares in 1587, and four further editions
followed: Barcelona, 1614; Madrid, 1615; Paris, 1616; Madrid, 1787.
In the opinion of the modern editor of Mena's *Amores*, Francisco
López Estrada,[11] he used the Latin translation of Heliodorus made by
the Pole StanislavWarschewiczki in 1534, but also had before him the
French translation of Jacques Amyot, Bishop of Auxerre, which was
published in Paris in 1547, 1549 and 1559, and possibly the Italian
translation published in Venice in 1556. Mena's translation of the first
two parts of the *Perceforest* therefore antedates his published translation
of Heliodorus' work by eleven years. He may well have undertaken
the *Persefores* for some noble patron in Toledo, and it would not be
surprising if the work had some use in the education of the children of
the nobility, for, as Sir Walter Scott remarked, 'Even the sagacious
Catharine of Medicis considered the romance of Perceforest as the
work best qualified to form the manners and amuse the leisure of a

---

10 Eugène Vinaver, *The Rise of Romance*, Oxford, 1971, p. 138.
11 *Historia etiópica de los amores de Teágenes y Cariclea*, edición y prólogo de
  Francisco López Estrada, Madrid, 1954.

young prince; since she impressed on Charles IX the necessity of
studying it with attention.'

The Spanish biographies list two persons called Fernando de Mena
in the sixteenth century: our translator, from, or writing in, Toledo,
of whom nothing else is known, except that he claims to have been
helped in his translation of Heliodorus by the great Flemish humanist
Andreas Schott and that that translation was first published in Alcalá;
and a *licenciado* of the University of Alcalá, who took two examinations
in medicine on 29 October and 23 November 1543, a fact recorded
by the *Universidad de Alcalá, Prueba de curso de 1540 a 1555*, tome 476f,
f. 86*v* and 87*r* (now preserved in the Archivo Histórico Nacional,
Madrid). This physician was born in Socuéllamos (Ciudad Real)
c. 1520, and he became professor of medicine at Alcalá. Philip II later
made him chief royal physician, and he published a number of works
on medicine, mainly commentaries in Latin on Galen: *Liber de ratione
permiscendi medicamenta, quae passim medicis veniunt in vsum, dum morbis
medentur*, Alcalá, 1555; *Commentaria nuper edita, in libros de sanguinis
missione, & purgatione Claudij Galeni Pergameni*, Alcalá, 1558; *Methodus
febrium omnium et earum symptomatum curatoria; Hispaniae medicis potis-
simum ex usu . . .* , Antwerp, 1658.

We still know too little to decide whether the translator and the
professor of medicine were quite distinct persons, or whether the professor with the royal appointment provided his noble patients with the
proper bedside reading as well as the proper bedside manner; he may
have thought, with Caxton in his *Boke of y*ᵉ *ordre of Chyvalry*: 'Rede
the noble Volumes of Saynt Graal, of Lancelot, of Galaad, of Trystram,
of Perseforest, of Percyval, of Gawayn and many mo: ther shall y see
Manhode, Curtoyse and Gentylnes.'

Note. Since the above was written, Professor Sharrer has examined two eighteenth century inventories of the Gondomar library at Valladolid. The first is
preserved as Palacio ms. 2618 (*sign. ant.* IV-C-1, *olim* Gondomar Sal 2ª Est. 17
Cax. 3⁰) and bears the title *Indice de la Biblioteca de Gondomar en 1769*. It was
prepared in the library for checking purposes in that year and lists the *Persefores*
on ff. 202*v*–3*r*, revealing that the ms. was then still bound in parchment but
that it had been moved from the ninth to the first shelf in the second room
in Gondomar's library. The second inventory was made by Juan Bautista
Muñoz, probably between April 1781 and the end of 1783 while he was
working at Simancas, thus only three or four years before the *Persefores* ms.
was removed from Valladolid to Madrid. This inventory is preserved in the
Academia de la Historia, Madrid, as ms. 9/4855 (*olim* A/120), and on f. 31*r*
ists the *Persefores* as bound in parchment.

Cedric E. Pickford

Sir Tristrem, Sir Walter Scott and Thomas

I was first made aware of the existence of the poem *Sir Tristrem* when, in the session 1946–47, I was a member of Dr Whitehead's special subject class on the 'Old French romances of Tristan'. During the course of the following session, when I was once more working under Frederick Whitehead's guidance, I was fortunate enough to see on the shelves of a Manchester second-hand book shop a copy of the 1819 printing of Sir Walter Scott's edition of the romance. That book has ever since been a treasured possession and a tangible reminder of the interest which Dr Whitehead's inspired teaching provoked. In presenting the following observations on *Sir Tristrem* I should like to offer them as a tribute to a man whose teaching not only opened new windows on medieval literature, but whose scholarship, humanity and warmth have been a valuable example and encouragement for me.

When, in the early years of the nineteenth century, Walter Scott, Esquire, member of the Faculty of Advocates in Edinburgh since 1792, and from 1799 sheriff-depute of Selkirkshire, turned to literature and writing as a 'staff and not a crutch', he made a name for himself as a poet whose subject matter was the local history of the Scottish border. The first two volumes of the *Minstrelsy of the Scottish Border* were published in 1802. While working on this theme the poet decided to incorporate into his anthology the thirteenth century English verse romance *Sir Tristrem*. The manuscript in which the romance is preserved was, Scott tells us, 'presented to the Faculty of Advocates in 1744, by Alexander Boswell of Auchinleck'.[1] It is from this owner that ms. Advocates' Library (W.4.1.) is usually named, and it is doubtless Scott's membership of the Faculty of Advocates that gave him the opportunity to familiarise himself with this text.

It is interesting to observe how he approached this romance as its

1 *Sir Tristrem, a metrical romance of the thirteenth century by Thomas of Erceldoune, called the Rhymer, edited from the Auchinleck MS by Walter Scott, Esq.,* Edinburgh and London, 4th edn., 1819, p. cviii.

editor. He corresponded with various antiquarians, e.g. Ellis, Ritson, Francis Douce and Richard Heber, during the years in which he was preparing the edition. Writing to George Ellis on 27 March 1801, he says:

> I enclose the first sheet of Sir Tristrem, that you may not so much rely upon my opinion as upon that which a specimen of the style and versification may enable your better judgment to form for itself . . . These pages are transcribed by Leyden, an excellent young man, of uncommon talents, patronised by Heber, and who is of the utmost assistance to my literary undertakings.[2]

Thus Scott employed a young minister–surgeon to do the day-to-day work of transcription from the original manuscript. Scott was clearly more interested in the historical and literary problems of the text, which he was anxious to make known to his friends. Writing later in the same spring to George Ellis, he sent him an analysis of the text, with the comment that the author, 'Philo Tomas, whoever he was, must surely have been an Englishman'.[3] Again, after expressing impatience that his duties as quartermaster to a regiment of volunteer cavalry were taking him from his work of editing: 'Where do you read that Sir Tristrem weighed out hay and corn; that Sir Lancelot du Lac distributed billets; or that any Knight of the Round Table condescended to higgle about a truss of straw?', he returns to the problem of elucidating the text: 'I am in utter despair about some of the hunting terms in Sir Tristrem'.[4] The correspondence with Ellis bore fruit towards the end of the year 1801.

> I have to acknowledge, with the deepest sense of gratitude, the beautiful analysis of Mr Douce's Fragments, which throw great light upon the romance of Sir Tristrem. In arranging that, I have anticipated your judicious hint, by dividing it into three parts, where the story seems naturally to pause, and preferring an accurate argument, referring to the stanzas as numbered.[5]

This is the earliest record we have in *Tristan* criticism to the Douce fragments of the *Tristan* of Thomas and the *Folie Tristan* of Oxford.

2   *The Letters of Sir Walter Scott, 1787–1807*, Edited by H. J. C. Grierson, London, 1932, p. 111.
3   *Letters, ed. cit.*, p. 112 (20 April 1801).
4   *Letters* (to George Ellis), *ed. cit.*, pp. 114–15 (11 May 1801).
5   *Letters* (to George Ellis), *ed. cit.*, pp. 123–4 (7 December 1801).

Ellis's advice is both valuable and practical. Scott's presentation of the text is certainly very readable in its numbered stanzas, divided into three 'Fyttes', each of which is preceded by a clear and full summary of the narrative.

By this time Scott was aware of the problem of the relationship between the text he was editing and the French verse fragments. In order to acquaint himself the better with these problems, to which he added that of the Celtic romances, he consulted the Welsh antiquary and lexicographer William Owen.

> I have been . . . engaged in . . . an edition of an ancient metrical romance called *Sir Tristrem* . . . which announces itself to be a composition of Thomas the Rymer of Ercildoune who flourished in the end of the 12th century. This poem is essentially different in all its parts from the Voluminous ffrench Romance in prose bearing the same title, but it resembles very nearly in the conduct of the story of *ffrench metrical romance* of which I have a copy and which is obviously much more ancient than that in prose and as you doubtless are well aware that all the celebrated ffrench romances were originally composed in Rhime. The Romance is obviously of *Celtic* extraction; but there occurs a curious query in solving which I venture to hope for Mr Owen's Assistance. Did the Minstrel of the Scottish Borders borrow his subject from the Normans who might have picked it up in Amorica among other traditions of Wales? Or are we entitled to suppose that Thomas of Erceldoune, residing very near to Silva Caledonia and other districts of Scotland long possessed by the Cumraig, collected his materials from the Celtic traditions which must have continued to float for a length of time through the countries which they had so long inhabited?[6]

We shall return to Scott's views on this matter in due course: suffice it to say now that Owen's reply was unhelpful—giving a fanciful description of the 'Mabinogion' or 'Juvenilities' and mentioning the existence of Trystan in the Triads. Scott again consulted Owen later in the same year on the place names. He states that the names of all the personages seem to him to be British—Morgan, Rowland Riis, Urgan, Ysoude or Yseult, Caer-Leon—Brengwain-Meriadote. Only Ermonie 'stumbles' him—does it mean the land opposite Mona (Anglesey)?[7] On these grounds Scott argues that the text he is editing is not an adaptation from something in a 'ffrench' dress but is originally British.

These hastily expressed thoughts are no doubt prompted by the

6 *Letters, ed. cit.*, p. 148 (15 July 1802).
7 *Letters, ed. cit.*, p. 167 (22 December 1802).

desire to publish—in April 1803 he writes to James Balantyne to advertise Sir Tristrem:

> To the Minstrelsy I mean this note to be added by way of an advertisement:—
> 'In the press, and will speedily be published, The Lay of the Last Minstrel,
> by Walter Scott, Esq., Editor of the Minstrelsy of the Scottish Border.
> Also Sir Tristrem, a Metrical Romance, by Thomas of Ercildoune, called
> the Rhymer, edited from an ancient MS. with an introduction and Notes,
> by Walter Scott, Esq.'[8]

Despite this notice, in May 1803 Scott was still hoping to find spare moments to resume Sir Tristrem. In November 1803 Ellis was still asking, 'Where is Tristrem?' Should it not form the fourth volume of the *Minstrelsy*? In truth Scott's work was delayed, since a visit to London had enabled him to make a detour and see the library of Francis Douce. In March 1804, however, Scott was able to write to Ellis to inform him that he would shortly receive a copy of Sir Tristrem.[9]

Scott's edition is, then, a work over which he had taken considerable pains. He consulted friends and colleagues in order to prepare his commentary, and he studied carefully all the texts to which he could gain access—'Tristrem shared this fate, and his short story was swelled into a large folio now before me, beautifully printed in 1514'[10]—and he also refers to the Duke of Roxburghe's manuscript copy as well as one in the National Library of Paris, and probably many others.[11]

But despite Scott's knowledge of the French prose romances—and his very astute reassessment of their relationship to the verse romances —his approach to Sir Tristrem was in some ways unscholarly. Despite his careful annotation of the text, and his very erudite observations, he saw the work as forming part of a local literary tradition—part of the minstrelsy of the Scottish border. In his enthusiasm to claim the poem for his own part of the world, he makes enthusiastic and rash statements: 'I am determined, not only that my *Tomas* shall be the author of Tristrem, but that he shall be the author of Hornchild also.'[12] And adds, 'I must, however, read over the romance before I can make my arrangements.'

8 *Letters*, p. 183 (21 April 1803).
9 *Letters*, p. 214 (19 March 1804).
10 *Letters*, p. 211 (27 January 1804, to Rev. R. Polwhele).
11 *Ibid*.
12 *Letters, ed. cit.*, p. 215 (19 March 1804, to George Ellis).

Scholarly integrity gives way to local pride, and, not content with claiming the work for the Borders, Scott fills in the missing last section by composing himself the concluding strophes in the Middle English. A far cry from Didron's advice—'ne restaurer à aucun prix'. In fairness to Walter Scott, one must say that his contribution does make a good conclusion and is in keeping with the rest—a literary *tour de force* which has the great merit of making the poem more enjoyable to a wider circle of readers.

Thus sandwiched between the *Minstrelsy* and the *Lay of the Last Minstrel*, *Sir Tristrem* acquired—or at least, was found to invest itself with—Scottish characteristics. To such an extent that when it was next published by a new editor in Great Britain it appeared in the series of the Scottish Text Society.[13] Throughout the introduction the editor, G. P. McNeill, describes the text as the 'Scottish version of the story of Tristrem'. The locating of the poem is based on the bald statement 'The language of the poem is such as was written towards the close of the thirteenth century in the north of England and the south of Scotland',[14] which is presumably taken from the linguistic comments made by the earlier German editor of the text, E. Kölbing.[15]

The pattern of argument seems to be as follows:

1 A certain Thomas is named in the poem, as well as the little township of Erceldoune (modern Earlston).
2 Scott, and others, attributed the poem to Thomas of Erceldoune, or Thomas the Rhymer, a thirteenth century border poet.
3 Since Thomas of Erceldoune is the author, and is a north-countryman, the language of the text must be northern.
4 Any non-northern forms can be explained by assuming the existence of a non-northern copyist.

It is in some ways fortunate that the poem had such a renowned figure as Scott as its first editor; in other ways it has been overshadowed by Scott's personality. It is curious that his antiquarian enthusiasm led Scott to attribute the work to the legendary Thomas of Erceldoune when, in his introduction, he says of the manuscript:

Many circumstances lead us to conclude that the MS. has been written in an Anglo-Norman convent. That it has been compiled in England there can

13 *Sir Tristrem*, ed. George P. McNeill, Edinburgh and London, 1886 (Scottish Text Society, 8).   14 *Ed. cit.*, p. xxxiii.
15 *Sir Tristrem, mit Einleitung, Anmerkungen und Glossar, Herausgegeben von Eugen Kölbing*, Heilbronn, 1883.

be little doubt. Every poem, which has a particular local reference, concerns South Britain, alone . . . On the other hand, not a word is to be
found in the collection relating particularly to Scottish affairs.[16]

This paragraph states clearly the cause for the English origin of the
manuscript at least, if not of the poem. Though Scott, because of a
strong local enthusiasm, did not follow his own lead, so to speak, the
point which he made has, some century and a half later, been taken
up by two American scholars. In a brief article published in 1941
Bertram Vogel concluded his linguistic study by declaring:

> It may well be that, after all, the author of *Sir Tristrem* was, in reality, a
> cosmopolitan Londoner, who perhaps spent part of his youth in the North,
> but who, at any rate, was familiar not only with the Northern dialect, but
> also with Northern literary tradition.[17]

In the following year Laura Hibbard Loomis considered the Auchinleck manuscript as a whole: her study is a most interesting one, for
she demonstrates, in my view convincingly, that this manuscript was
not simply the work of London scribes but is a volume that could
perhaps best be described as a collection of Middle English verse in a
form which was expressly devised for this volume. In short, it could
be called an up-to-date anthology of English romances specially
brought together by a man who was almost certainly the 'director' of
a London 'bookshop'.[18]

The position of the *Sir Tristrem* in this collection of forty items is
not out of line with the other works in it, for extant French texts still
exist for all but five of the romances. Many of the romances refer to
their source as a *boke* or a *geste*—that is to say, to a written source. The
Sir Tristrem refers explicitly to a written source: 'As we finde in scrite'
(ed. McNeill, v. 1944; ed. Scott, fytte second, st. LXXV), a clear echo,
if not a direct translation of the French formula 'Si com nos trovons
en escrit'.

It is doubtful whether, after the appearance of Bédier's remarkable
edition and reconstruction of the *Tristan* of Thomas, any scholar
would consider that the Middle English poem was anything other than

16 *Sir Tristrem*, ed. W. Scott, 4th ed., p. cviii.
17 Bertram Vogel, 'The dialect of *Sir Tristrem*', *Journal of English and German
    Philology*, XL (1941), pp. 538–44, especially pp. 543–4.
18 Laura Hibbard Loomis, 'The Auchinleck manuscript and a possible London
    bookshop of 1330–40' *Publications of the Modern Language Association of
    America*, LVII (1942), pp. 595–627.

an adaptation of the French verse romance whose author names himself as Thomas.[19] Bédier describes the *Sir Tristrem* as 'un poème composé dans le Nord de l'Angleterre, en 1294 au plus tôt, en 1330 au plus tard.'[20] He simply accepts the linguistic arguments of Eugen Kölbing. There is no longer any controversy on this matter, but it does seem to me that in the discussion *Sir Tristrem* has suffered from the enthusiasm of the Scots on the one hand, and from the critical judgements of Continental scholars on the other.

Thus Bédier opens his account of Sir Tristrem by referring to Kölbing's judgement, in these terms: 'Tout est dit sur l'étrangeté et l'incoherence du poème anglais. A quoi bon les décrire?'[21] He then quotes M. Bossert's excuses for 'son obscurité, ses contre-sens, ses non-sens' (*Thomas* II, p. 87). The only value *Sir Tristrem* has for Bédier is that of a battered, ill-conceived and wrong-headedly executed adaptation which may throw some light, under the strict control of other versions, on the lost portions of the poem of Thomas. Otherwise the value of *Sir Tristrem* alone is 'négligeable' (*Thomas* I, p. 26), or worse, e.g. the variants offered of the Roald episode are 'si vraiment singuliers qu'il paraît inutile de les discuter' (*Thomas* I, p. 31), or, towards the end of the poem, 'Le récit de E [*Sir Tristrem*] est d'ailleurs, comme il arrive souvent, incompréhensible' (*Thomas* I, p. 343).

These devastating observations are, on the rarest of occasions, slightly tempered. In the episode of the *Harp and the Rote*, some of the variants are described as 'non dépourvus parfois de valeur poétique', but Bédier refuses to list these possible good points—they are dismissed thus: 'nous renvoyons à l'étude de Kölbing, mais nous nous dispensons de les noter ici' (*Thomas* I, p. 175).

To what extent are these strictures justified? Is *Sir Tristrem* really of such poor quality? To answer these questions would require a full collation of the Middle English with those passages of the French original which are extant. This task has in a sense already been carried out by Bédier in that his edition does indicate carefully the equivalent passages in the texts. From this we notice first of all that the English text often presents a shortened version—thus vv. 2575–600 are the equivalent of the fifty-two lines of the Cambridge fragment[22] and

---

19 *Le Roman de Tristan par Thomas, poème du XIIe siècle publié par Joseph Bédier* Paris (Société des anciens textes français), I, 1902; II, 1905.

20 *Thomas*, I, p. iii.   21 *Thomas*, II, p. 86.

22 *Les Fragments du roman de Tristan, poème du XIIe siècle, par Thomas, édités avec commentaire par B. H. Wind*, Leiden, 1950, pp. 63–5.

perhaps more significantly the 940 lines of the first Sneyd fragment are reduced to some sixty lines (vv. 2640–705).

This is achieved by cutting out most of the psychological analysis and concentrating on the most brief outline of the narrative of the marriage of Tristan and Yseult aux Blanches Mains. Again, the equivalent of the extant 256 lines of the Turin fragment of the Salle aux Images and the daring water episodes is in the Middle English text lines 2839–71. Wherever precise passages of the English text are set against the surviving French fragments, it is clear that the English poem is very much a shortened version.

For Bédier 'less meant worse', but in the case of the *Sir Tristrem* is this conclusion justifiable?

Some years ago, Professor T. C. Rumble made a plea for the reconsideration of the poem.[23] He argued that it was a reasonably successful effort to present the romance in a manner which was appropriate to its English audience. Professor Rumble's article has not received all the attention which it merits, and on this side of the Atlantic scholars have continued to show indifference towards the poem. It is regrettable that the romance is not more widely known,[24] for then one could perhaps appreciate more of its qualities.

To 'reduce' a French romance into English does not necessarily destroy it—witness Malory's great contribution to English literature. To prepare a shortened version of a narrative is a worthy and on occasion valuable and successful exercise, as one sees in the case of the *Tristan* itself, which is twice summarised—the *version commune* in the *Folie Tristan de Berne* and the version of Thomas in the *Folie Tristan d'Oxford*. But the *Sir Tristrem* is not presented as a condensed narrative in the context of an episode of the Tristan romance—it is itself an independent work.

To argue simply that 'less means worse' is to refuse to consider the text itself and the reasons which may lie behind its very existence. As far as the text alone is concerned, it must not be assumed that all is poor and weak. The narrative has its high points: the author does not always shorten. Indeed, he lingers over the hunting scenes and takes

---

23 T. C. Rumble, 'The Middle English *Sir Tristrem*: towards a reappraisal', *Comparative Literature*, XI (1959), pp. 221–8.

24 The edition prepared in 1963 by Charles Edward Long, '*Sir Tristrem*, edited from the photostats of the ms. collated with previous editions and provided with introduction and notes', as a doctoral dissertation for the University of Arkansas (B.B.S.I.A., XVI [1964] No. 110), seems not to have been published.

no fewer than fifty-five lines (or five stanzas) to describe the procedure to be adopted when a stag is slain, how it is to be quartered and what rituals are to be observed. Apart from demonstrating this cynegetic interest of either the translator or his public, such a passage serves to demonstrate that one is not in the presence of a mere summary. The author excels when presenting conversations and disputes. The speech of the porter to Roland, who, in poor clothing, is unrecognisable, is a lively example:

> Cherl, go away,
> Other Y schal the smite,
> What dostow here al day.   [st. LVII, vv. 520–622]

Again, all the scenes of combat are related with vigour—perhaps best represented by the patriotic cry in the account of the fight of Tristrem against the Morholt:

> God help Tristrem the Knight!
> He faught for Ingland.   [st. XCIV, vv. 1033–4]

The duel between Tristrem and the giant Beliagog is once more told with a wealth of colourful description (vv. 2772 ff.).

Similarly, the author seems to take pleasure—and he certainly gives pleasure—by emphasising details of everyday life that throw light on character. An instance must suffice, namely his careful reference to money, whether it be the offer of payment made by Rohant to a palmer who was to guide him:

> And readily gaf him sa,
> Of wel gode moné,
> Ten schillings and ma.   [st. LVI, vv. 611–14]

which echoes the palmer's own reference to a gift of ten shillings from Tristrem:

> He gave me ten schilling.   [st. LV, v. 605]

This extends to an interest in gaming, and the poet lingers over Tristrem's game of chess with a Norse sea captain for a stake of twenty shillings a game, and how Tristrem won a total of a hundred pounds. Echoes of international chess championships! (St. XXVIII–XXXI, vv. 297–340.)

The verse form chosen by the poet has been almost universally assailed. Was he more interested in the intricacies of a somewhat restrictive form than in the tale he was telling? Whereas it is true that the form is somewhat involved, and, I would concede, perhaps rather too light to bear the weight of the romance, it is also the case that the writer can handle it well. The use of the stanzaic form could well be described as experimental. Several romances in the Auchinleck manuscript are in stanzaic form, and the work has been called the 'fountain head' of this style. Perhaps the innovation was not particularly successful, but at the very least this use of the form does demonstrate the willingness of the author of *Sir Tristrem* to break new ground.

These and similar points are, in some sense, a far cry from Thomas, and his Tristan to which the English poet refers on occasion (vv. 10, 412, 2787). The long courtly passages are greatly reduced, the psychological reflections are expressed succinctly, and instead pride of place is given to fighting, hunting and wagering! Little wonder then, in some ways, that French critics, seizing upon these points and the fact that the stanza form is somewhat light to bear the burden of the story, have failed to appreciate the vigorous narrative qualities, and the simple forthrightness of this English version.

In speaking of the English version one must not fail to enquire why it exists. Clearly a reading or listening public which could easily follow French would have no immediate need to read or hear *Sir Tristrem*. In other words, the audience or patron for which this and similar poems were written was of a quite different class from the readers of Thomas or the prose *Tristan*. They must have been basically monolingual, knowing little or no French, and having perhaps only a slight awareness of the existence of French or other versions of the story. The compiler of the Auchinleck manuscript was not an earlier Caxton who provided for an audience now of English, now of French speakers. His book was a presentation of French work to an audience ignorant of that tongue. *Sir Tristrem*, like other romances in this volume, has considerable value in that it sheds light upon the literary tastes of a public which is eager to have acquaintance with the vigorous action of the Tristan story, but which has little patience with psychological niceties. A public concerned with cleverness of form, and which delighted in simple everyday human occurrences. In short, one could see the *Sir Tristrem* as an interesting social document as well as a literary curiosity. It is both these things, but it is also a fresh retelling of a great story, presented simply and directly, and in this bicentenary year of Scott's birth it is fitting to hope that once again the romance which he first brought to our notice should receive the attention which it deserves.

T. B. W. Reid

A note on homonymic convergence: *aimer/esmer*

Though Whitehead published comparatively little concerning linguistics in general, as contrasted with the linguistic situation of the individual author or scribe of a specific text, he had strong convictions about acceptable methods in the study of language, and strong feelings about certain schools. Brought up in the philological tradition of Waters, Miss Pope and Ewert, he was critical of many of the claims of descriptive linguistics. Nor did every kind of diachronistic linguistics meet with his approval: the school of Gilliéron, in spite of its concentration on the mind and circumstances of the individual speaker, also aroused his suspicion. This was no doubt largely because of the alogical, impressionistic and even histrionic character of the expositions of Gilliéron and some of his followers such as John Orr, especially in their applications of the doctrine of the 'homonymic collision';[1] and it led to Whitehead's uncompromising declaration to the Strasbourg congress in 1962 that 'la collision homonymique est une méthode d'explication à laquelle la dialectologie a constamment recours, mais que la sémantique historique trouve sans utilité'.[2] In the particular instance he was discussing on this occasion, the replacement in Middle French of *nouer* 'to swim' by *nager*, which in Old French had meant 'to row (a boat)', he rejected the explanation of the disappearance of *nouer* 'to swim' by its homophony with *nouer* 'to knot, tie';[3] and he

---

1 John Orr, 'On homonymics', in *Studies in French Language and Mediaeval Literature presented to Professor Mildred K. Pope*, Manchester, 1939, pp. 253–97, repr. in *Words and Sounds in English and French*, Oxford, 1953, pp. 91–133, with additional notes, pp. 134–40 (subsequent references are to the reprinted version).

2 *Xe Congrès international de linguistique et philologie romanes: Actes*, ed. G. Straka, Paris, 1965, I, p. 230.

3 This explanation is adopted by W. von Wartburg, *Französisches etymologisches Wörterbuch*, VII, Basel, 1955, p. 65, and by J. Dubois and H. Mitterand in their revision, *Nouveau Dictionnaire étymologique et historique*, Paris, 1964,

maintained that irrespective of the existence of *nouer* 'to knot', *nouer* 'to swim' would have given way to *nager* for intrinsic semantic reasons, the lively image being preferred, as in so many other cases, to the colourless objective term.

Instances of phonetic convergence resulting in two originally quite distinct words becoming homonyms, like *NOTARE and NODARE both giving Old French *noer*, are, of course, common in French as in other languages. There is general agreement that in many cases this formal identity has no perceptible influence on the subsequent evolution of the words, but that in others a very variable degree of coalescence of meaning takes place; it is also fairly widely believed since Gilliéron's time that where the phonetic convergence brings together two words which have contrasted senses and yet belong to the same general field of activity, it sometimes results in the elimination of at least one of the words.[4] What remains in doubt, however, is to which of these three classes the actual pairs of homophonous words should be allocated. Orr sees in the history of both French and English a considerable number of instances not merely of coalescence but of elimination: I have some personal justification for suggesting that in these matters Rectus, the Dr Watson of his dialogue 'On homonymics', allows himself to be much too easily convinced by the forensic eloquence of Orthos. There are indeed some fairly clear cases of semantic coalescence. There can be no doubt, for example, that the Modern French meaning of *souffreteux*, which was originally the adjective of *sofraite* 'lack, (de)privation, poverty', is due to its formal association, since the disappearance of *sofraite* and the verb *sofraindre*, with the historically unrelated verb *souffrir*. Again, in Modern English certain recurrent irregularities of spelling indicate a degree of coalescence or at least contamination in pairs of homonyms such as *hoard/horde, rein/reign, flair/flare*; newspapers and periodicals in particular provide frequent examples like 'filling the country with hoards of tax-collectors', 'Hitler . . . was the incarnation of the little man's worst nature given free reign', 'the Welsh flare for the poetical turn of phrase'. Even

---

of A. Dauzat's *Dictionnaire étymologique de la langue française*. Orr, however, implies that the homonymy which led to the disappearance of *noer* 'to swim' was with *noier* 'to drown' (*Words and Sounds*, p. 104).

4 As in the notorious case of the Gascon dialects where GALLUM 'cock' and CATTUM 'cat' both evolved phonetically to *gat*, and the first disappeared (J. Gilliéron and M. Roques in *Revue de philologie française et de littérature*, XXIV (1910), pp. 278 ff.).

where the fact of the association is obvious, however, its nature and cause often remain obscure (are hoards of gold now more familiar than the Golden Horde, and the notion of government than that of horsemanship? has the sense of *flair*, having been extended from 'discernment' to 'gift', acquired an element of flamboyance?). In many other cases of homonymy any judgement about a possible semantic coalescence or association depends on a purely subjective impression. As for the complete elimination of one of the words involved in a 'homonymic clash', it is probably impossible ever to state *a priori* that in a given linguistic system a given pair of meanings are related in such a way as to make homonymy of the words that carry them intolerable (how does one define and measure meaning? what constitutes identity of field of activity? is homonymy equally intolerable in all registers or to all speakers?); it is only *a posteriori*, when one of the words shows signs of obsolescence, that the homonymy may be suspected of being responsible—and even then it is rarely possible to attain anything approaching proof.

This is why the declaration of Orthos, 'You are emphatically not entitled to forget the complexities of the whole linguistic situation, in so far as you can reconstitute them' (*Words and Sounds*, p. 116), innocuous or even commendable as it may seem at first sight, is in its context methodologically misleading. If a given linguistic change— such as the disappearance of Old French *noer* 'to swim'—can be explained by a formal or material cause which can be shown to have operated similarly in parallel cases, the fact that a homonymy existed is no proof that this homonymy contributed in any way to the change. The particular case to which Orthos's statement is applied is the replacement of Old French *am-* as the weak stem of the verb from AMARE by *aim-* in Modern French, and the suggestion of Rectus which it contradicts is that this replacement is sufficiently accounted for by the analogical influence of the strong stem *aim-*. This is in fact what had traditionally been considered to be the cause of the change; an exactly similar generalisation of the strong stem has taken place in other verbs with vocalic alternation where no homonymic influence has been suggested (*plorer → pleurer; noier → nier, proisier → priser; enoier → ennuyer; enveer → envoyer*, etc.). It is nevertheless maintained by Gilliéron, Orr and others that an essential element in the ancestry of Modern French *aimer* is the Old French verb *esmer* ← ÆSTIMARE.[5]

5 J. Gilliéron, *Généalogie des mots qui désignent l'abeille*, Paris, 1918, pp. 267–73; J. Orr, *art. cit.* and 'Le français *aimer*', *Mélanges Mario Roques*, I, Paris, 1951,

Neither Gilliéron, Orr nor McMillan is very specific about the semantic
side of this alleged convergence; but it would appear that the senses
involved (*esmer* had also others which are not relevant here) can be
reduced to three groups: (1) 'to love (a person)'; (2) 'to esteem, value
highly, like (a person or thing)'; (3) 'to estimate, appraise, judge the
value of (a thing, or less usually a person)'. The first of these senses
clearly derives from AMARE and remains associated with *amer* → *aimer*;
the third derives from ÆSTIMARE and is expressed in Old French by
esmer, supplemented from Middle French by the learned form *estimer*.
It is the second group of senses that *esmer* is most usually alleged to
have bequeathed to *aimer*.[6] It may be noted that these senses do not
seem to have been attached in Latin to either AMARE or ÆSTIMARE, but
would often have been expressed by DILIGERE; with the disappearance
of DILIGERE, however, it might be expected *a priori* that they would fall
within the extended scope of AMARE (less probably of ÆSTIMARE).

From a Modern French point of view, it is easy enough to envisage
homonymy between *aimer* and *e(s)mer*, between *j'aime* and *j'e(s)me*,
etc. Since the influence of *esmer* is credited with having caused (or at
any rate contributed to) the replacement of weak forms such as *amer*,
amez, etc., by *aimer*, *aimez*, etc., one might expect that influence to
have been exerted at the time when this replacement took place. As
far as the evidence of spelling goes, however, the generalisation of the
stem *aim-* does not seem to have begun until the fifteenth century (it
is only partially carried through in the mss. and early editions of
Villon), and was not complete until well on in the sixteenth; but by
that time the verb *esmer*, as a distinct entity, was obsolescent if not
obsolete,[7] and was certainly in no position to exert any influence on a
common verb such as *amer/aimer*. To this objection Orr's reply appears

217–27, repr. in *Words and Sounds*, pp. 141–53; D. McMillan, 'Remarques sur
esmer–aimer', *Travaux de linguistique et de littérature publiés par le Centre de
philologie et de littérature romanes de l'Université de Strasbourg*, IX, 1 (1971), pp.
209–28. The same view is adopted by I. Iordan and J. Orr, *An Introduction to
Romance Linguistics*, London, 1937, pp. 167–8; P. Gardette, in *Revue de
linguistique romane*, XXVII (1963), p. 487; A. Dauzat, J. Dubois and H. Mitterand, *Nouveau Dictionnaire étymologique*, s.v. *estimer*. It is rejected by G.
Millardet, *Linguistique et dialectologie romanes*, Paris, 1923, p. 393; W. von
Wartburg, *Französisches etymologisches Wörterbuch*, I, Bonn, 1928, p. 46;
C. A. Robson in *French Studies*, VIII (1954), pp. 57–8.

6 *Words and Sounds*, pp. 115–16, 144–9; but see below, p. 236.

7 Huguet's *Dictionnaire de la langue française du seizième siècle* contains only
three examples of the verb *esmer*, all from the same work.

to be that it is quite irrelevant, because the collision or coalescence of the French representatives of AMARE and ÆSTIMARE had in fact taken place very much earlier, at a date not specified but necessarily before the end of the eleventh century; for we are told that in two passages in the *Roland*, *Jo ne vus aim nïent* 306/327 and *Jo vus aim mult* 635, it is not AMARE but ÆSTIMARE that is represented by *aim* (*Words and Sounds*, pp. 144–5). Acceptance of this view would mean that the spelling distinction in Old French texts between *aim-* and *esm-* must be denied all significance as regards meaning: either of these spellings might in principle be used for the single verb meaning 'to love', 'to like' and 'to estimate'.[8]

Such a position is based on the assumed phonetic resemblance between the strong forms of Old French *amer*, such as (*il*) *aime*, and the corresponding forms of Old French *esmer*, such as (*il*) *esme*.[9] But was this resemblance really close enough to cause, or even to encourage, any confusion? The strong stem in forms like AMAT developed through /ãim/ to /ɛ̃im/ and then /ɛ̃m/, a stage reached in some regions in the twelfth century but in others not until very much later.[10] The strong stem in forms like ÆSTIMAT developed to /ɛzm/, which had lost its /z/ by the end of the eleventh century (Pope, §377); it is probable that the vowel, on coming thus late into contact with an intervocalic nasal consonant, would not be nasalised,[11] but even if it was, the /ɛ̃/ would in most regions have been promptly lowered to /ã/ as in *feme*,

8 It would then have to be by sheer coincidence that in Old French texts the spelling *aim-* is nearly always associated with sense 1, 'to love', AMARE, and the spelling *esm-* with sense 3, 'to estimate, appraise, judge', ÆSTIMARE, while none of the examples with the spelling *esm-* in the dictionaries of Godefroy, III, pp. 494–5, or Tobler–Lommatzsch, III, cols. 1115–17, shows anything approaching the sense 2, 'to esteem, value highly, like', which would seem to form the only possible common ground between the two Latin verbs.

9 Gilliéron, *op. cit.*, pp. 267–8; Orr, *Words and Sounds*, p. 113.

10 M. K. Pope, *From Latin to Modern French*, Manchester, 1934, §§467–9. As evidence for the reduction of the diphthong in *aime* McMillan (*art. cit.*, p. 217) cites Pope, §529, and the fact that in the *Roland* words like *faire*, *repaire*, etc., appear in assonances in /ɛ–ə/; but all this relates only to oral vowels and is therefore irrelevant to the pronunciation of the nasal diphthong in Old French *aime*.

11 According to P. Fouché, *Phonétique historique du français*, II, Paris, 1958, pp. 357–9, a vowel in this situation was nasalised in the course of the eleventh century after the fall of the /z/. The only evidence he cites, however, is the presence of *blasme* in *Rol.* 1082 in a laisse in nasal /ã–ə/. This is in fact a quite isolated instance. Elsewhere in the text *blasme* assonates only in oral /a–ə/ (ll. 1346, 1718), and similarly *pasme(n)t* (ll. 1348, 1988, 2273); though

geme, etc. (Pope, §§447–50). On either hypothesis, there would seem to have been no stage in the early history of the language at which there could have been homophony between forms from ÆSTIMAT, etc., with stem /ɛzm/, then /em/ or possibly /ãm/, and forms from AMAT, etc., with stem /ãim/, then /ɛ̃im/ and /ɛ̃m/; homophony could have arisen only in the sixteenth century with the denasalisation of nasal vowels before intervocalic nasal consonants. It must be remembered, too, that in the Old French period proper, to which the coalescence is ascribed, the very limited phonetic resemblance we have noted did not even apply to all the strong persons of the verbs, but only to five of them, the pres. indic. 2, 3 and 6, pres. subj. 6 and imper. 2. In the other four strong persons, the forms of *esmer* must have been clearly distinguished throughout that period from those of *amer*, even if the tonic vowel is assumed to have been similar, by the presence of the post-tonic supporting vowel /ə/ in pres. indic. and subj. 1 *esme*, pres. subj. 2 *esmes* and and 3 *esme(t)*, contrasting with *aim*, *ains*, *aint* respectively: forms in *esm-* without this vowel, and forms in *aim-* with an analogical post-tonic /ə/, do not seem to be attested in any Continental text earlier than the fourteenth century.

If, then, homonymy between corresponding forms of the Old French representatives of the two Latin verbs seems to be excluded as far as the nine strong persons are concerned, could it have arisen—more unexpectedly at first sight—in the numerous weak forms? The weak stem from AMARE was throughout the relevant period /ãm/; that from ÆSTIMARE was, like the strong stem, /ɛzm/, then /em/, in which, as we have seen, the vowel does not appear to have been nasalised, at any rate down to the date of the *Roland*. If it did later nasalise, there would indeed have been homonymy between the weak forms of the two verbs, both having the stem /ãm/. This hypothesis, however, finds no support in the spellings used in medieval texts; for there the stem written *am-* continued to be associated with the senses 'to love, to like', and the stem written *esm-* with the sense 'to estimate, appraise', with only minimal traces of possible semantic confusion.[12]

---

no form of the verb *esmer* appears in assonance, the phonetically similar word *pesme* assonates six times, always in oral /ɛ–ə/ and /ai–ə/ (ll. 56, 813, 2122, 2919, 3304, 3404), and the only assonance in which *resne* appears is oral /ɛ–ə/ (l. 1290).

12 According to Tobler–Lommatzsch, I, col. 343, *amer* in certain uses 'mit acc. des Objektes und des Preises' is 'zum Teil viell. vermengt mit *esmer*'. In the three examples cited under this heading, e.g. 'Amis, volez la chievre vendre?'— 'Oïl, sire, se vos volez.'—'Frere, dites que vos l'amez Et por combien je

A special importance seems to be attributed by the 'homonymists' to the alleged ambiguity of the forms of the pres. indic. 1 of *amer/esmer*. As we have seen, Orr maintains that in *Jo ne vus aim nïent* and *Jo vus aim mult* (*Rol.* 306/327 and 635) the meaning of the verb is not 'love' but 'esteem', a meaning derived from ÆSTIMARE; but *aim* cannot here be scribal for *esme*, which would be metrically impossible in both lines. The phonetic contact between certain other forms of the verbs from AMARE and ÆSTIMARE respectively, which is assumed to have given rise to the 'double valeur du mot *aimer*' (*Words and Sounds*, p. 145), must therefore be pushed back far enough into the past to enable this double value to have been extended to all parts of the verb by the date of composition of the *Roland*—that is, to a date when homophony or even marked phonetic resemblance between any of the parts of the representative of AMARE and the corresponding parts of the representative of ÆSTIMARE is hardly conceivable. If, then, the *aim* of the *Roland* passages means anything other than 'love',[13] it cannot be because of any formal influence of the verb ÆSTIMARE → *esmer*. Nor does it seem possible to accept Orr's ingenious and seductive interpretation of the famous words of Cordelia (Cordeïlle) to her father (Leir) in Wace's *Brut*, which for Orr constitute 'the perfect proof of the fusion of *esmer* and *aimer*' (*Words and Sounds*, p. 114):[14]

> Mes peres iés, jo aim tant tei
> Come jo mun pere amer dei.
> E pur faire tei plus certein,
> Tant as, tant vals e jo tant t'aim.[15]

---

l'averai' (Méon, I, p. 199 = *Trubert*, ed. Ulrich, l. 236), the verb is undoubtedly to be identified as *asmer*, a well known by-form of *esmer* (cf. Tobler—Lommatzsch, III, 1116), or reduced form of *aesmer*, used here in the unambiguous sense of 'to appraise, value'; if the verb stem in these examples had been written *esm-* no one would have thought of associating them with the verb *amer*. In the immediately preceding section of the article *amer* a number of examples are cited under the heading 'wert halten (einen Besitz), Wert legen auf'; this rendering might suggest a semantic influence of *esmer*, but in fact all the examples (mainly involving the locution *amer sa vie*) come clearly under *amer* 'to love'.

13 For the sense of *aim* in *Rol.* 306/327 see G. S. Burgess, *Contribution à l'étude du vocabulaire pré-courtois*, Geneva, 1970, p. 144, quoting also G. F. Jones, *The Ethos of the Song of Roland*, Baltimore, 1963.

14 Orr's interpretation is accepted as definitive by M. D. Legge, *Anglo–Norman Literature and its Background*, Oxford, 1963, p. 199 and n. 1, and by D. McMillan, *art. cit.*, p. 223, n. 35.

15 Ed. I. Arnold, Paris (S.A.T.F.), 1938, ll. 1739–43.

The last line of Cordelia's speech consists of a well attested Old French proverb (Morawski, 2283); in her use of it the verb *aim* had traditionally been understood in the obvious sense of 'love', all the more so because the words are spoken in reply to the question Lear had put to each of his daughters: *jo vuil saveir Cumbien tu m'aimes* 1687–8; *Fille, di, combien m'aimes tu?* 1704. According to Orr, however, the meaning of the proverb was 'So much you have, so much you're worth, of such a price you are to me' (*Words and Sounds*, p. 115), the verb *aim* being semantically if not phonetically[16] the representative of ÆSTIMO; the whole point of Cordelia's use of the proverb, and the reason for Lear's anger, is in Orr's view the pun or play on the 'double sense' of *aim*. This, he says, displays the dramatic skill of Wace, who is in this episode 'a good deal more convincing than Geoffrey of Monmouth, and even Shakespeare' (*Words and Sounds*, p. 114); and McMillan goes still farther in declaring that while Geoffrey's version of the proverb, *Quantum habes, tantum vales, tantumque te diligo* (II, xi), 'ne signifie pas grand'chose', Wace's use of it 'donne à cette scène une portée et une raison d'être qui manquent entièrement à Geoffroy de Monmouth, à Holinshed et même à Shakespeare' (*art. cit.*, p. 223, n. 35). Even if we could overlook the phonetic difficulty, however, and assume that *aim* could nevertheless stand for *esme*, this is open to other objections. The translation offered for *jo tant t'aim*, 'of such a price you are to me', would form a tautology with *tant vals*, 'so much you're worth'; it would also imply that the spelling *aim-* could be used not only for sense 2 above, 'to esteem, value highly, like', where semantic contact with AMARE was possible, but also for sense 3, 'to appraise, judge the value of', of which no other example with this spelling has been adduced. It must be remembered, too, that Wace

---

16 As we have seen (pp. 233–4 above), the phonetic difference between *aim* and *esme* was very considerable in twelfth century French generally; it was perhaps still greater in the language of Wace, in which /ãi/ was not levelled to /ɛ̃i/ (ed. Arnold, I, pp. xix f.), so that the forms must have been respectively /ãin/ and /ɛmə/. It may be worth noting that the *aim* of the proverb is regularly found in rhyme with words whose tonic vowel comes from Latin *a* tonic free before *m* or *n*: so in *Brut* 1742 and *An Anglo-Norman 'Brut'*, ed. Bell, 1250 (: *certein*); Gautier d'Arras, *Ille et Galeron*, ed. Cowper, 1017 (: *aim* ← HAMUM); Chardri, *Petit Plet*, ed. Merrilees, 1642 (: *mein* ← MANUM); Beaumanoir, *Fole Larguece*, ed. Suchier, II, p. 257 (: *reclaim*). Once more, then, we are asked to believe that the verb has retained its forms phonetically representing AMARE but has acquired the senses of the phonetically different forms representing ÆSTIMARE.

was translating Geoffrey, who had used the verb *diligo*; Orr's account
of the matter requires us to assume that Geoffrey was familiar with the
Old French proverb but either misunderstood the true force of *aim* or
despaired of rendering it in Latin, and that Wace, reading Geoffrey's
text, had the perspicacity to recognise and restore the original form of
the proverb, and the dramatic skill to turn the ambiguity to account.
It is surely much more probable that there is no play on words in
Wace's text; that what both Geoffrey and Wace, both Lear and
Cordelia, understand by the final verb of the proverb is 'love';[17] and
that what shocks Lear is not the last clause in particular but simply
Cordelia's failure to exaggerate her affection, combined with her
flippancy in concluding with a 'common saw'.

There may, however, be an element of ambiguity in the use of the
proverb, not indeed in the sense of *aim*, but in that of *tant*. In some
contexts closely related to the proverb *tant* has clearly its temporal
value, the implication being '*As long as* you are rich, *so long* do I love
you', or, in the terms of an English proverb which goes back at least
to 1474, *Love lasteth as longe as the money endurith* (Caxton, cited in
Oxford Dictionary of English Proverbs, p. 390). This value appears also
in several passages of Wace's Cordelia story, such as Lear's lament
about Fortune:

> *Tant cum* jo fui alques mananz
> *Tant* oi jo parenz e serganz;
> E *des que* jo, las! apovri,
> Amis, parenz, serganz perdi.   [1931-4]

> Bien me dist veir ma mendre fille,
> Que jo blasmoe, Cordeïlle,
> Ki dist que *tant cum* jo avreie
> *Tant* preisiez, *tant* amez sereie.   [1937-40; cf. 1943-8]

> Or me sunt mes filles faillies
> Ke dunc esteient mes amies,
> Ke m'amoent sur tute rien
> *Tant cum* jo oi alques de bien.   [1955-8]

17 Or possibly with some weakening of force 'esteem'. The verb *aim* is replaced
by *pris* in some thirteenth century versions of the proverb, such as Rutebeuf,
Voie de paradis 654 (ed. Jubinal, II, 194) and three proverb collections cited by
Morawski as variants to 2283; cf. the proverb *Tant a home tant est prisé*
(Morawski, 2281).

The same is true of the context of Chardri's use of the proverb; speaking of false friends, the Youth says:

> . . . il vus faudrunt al grant busoin.
> Ceo est le amisté de mein en mein:
> Tant as, tant vaus, e tant vus aim.
> De teus en averez vus assez,
> *Deske* les eez ben espruvez;
> Amis vus serrunt deskes en terre
> *Tant cum* vus lur porrer nul ben fere.   [*Petit Plet*, 1640–6]

The temporal interpretation is also possible in the passages in Gautier d'Arras and Beaumanoir, though here it does not positively impose itself. If, however, *tant* is to be taken as implying in any degree the temporal notion of 'so long', the most probable sense of *aim* will always be 'love'.

It would seem, then, that many of the arguments put forward in favour of the hypothesis of a homonymic convergence of AMARE → *amer* → *aimer* and ÆSTIMARE → *esmer* → *émer* are invalid. It does not, of course, follow that no kind of semantic contact between the verbs ever took place; in particular, it is probable that in the negative derivatives, especially those incorporating the prefix AD-, there was some confusion in Old French between *des(a)amer* and *desaesmer* and between *mes(a)amer* and *mesaesmer* (cf. *Words and Sounds*, pp. 150–3; McMillan, *art. cit.*, p. 223, n. 35). In most respects, however, it would appear that Modern French *aimer* is in form and sense the descendant of Latin AMARE and of AMARE only.

W. Rothwell

Appearance and reality in Anglo-Norman

It is a truism to say that Anglo-Norman spelling is often arbitrary, even more arbitrary than that usually found in the Continental varieties of medieval French. Yet so conditioned are we—humble readers and learned editors alike—to trust in the phonetic 'laws' of the neo-grammarians that it may come as a shock to realise just how often these can lead us astray in our interpretation of Anglo-Norman texts. The purpose of the present article is to illustrate by reference to a wide variety of Anglo-Norman material the kind of gross error of sense that has been perpetrated in the past by scholars who have failed to realise that the only sure guide in this labyrinth of meaning is the thread of context. Study of the phonology of a verse text will usually produce a reasonably coherent picture of the sound values of the language used, but orthography, especially in a prose text where there is no rhyme to provide clues to pronunciation, does not lend itself to this kind of systematic treatment, giving no clear pattern, but only what appears to be a random assortment of oddities. This is particularly true of late prose texts, composed when the divergence of Anglo-Norman from Continental French had become wide. In texts of this type examples abound of cases where an editor's silence on a strange form not only betrays his own ignorance but leaves the reader bereft of the necessary guidance he has a right to expect.

To start with the simplest of cases: on occasion an editor will fail to make a distinction in his text between *u* and *v*, as in the following instances from the Herbert version of the *Ancrene Riwle*:

nostre bien qest si tenue. noz pecchez qe sunt [si] multz   [p. 119][1]

meaues paroles. porteurs maures et tenures afferent a recluse   [p. 52]

The words *tenue* and *tenures* here need to be read as *tenve* and *tenvres*,[2] the sense in the first case being 'slight', 'unsubstantial' and in the second

---

1 *The French Text of the Ancrene Riwle*, ed. J. A. Herbert, Early English Text Society, No. 219, 1944.   2 See Godefroy, VII, pp. 683-4.

'mild', 'unassuming' (of behaviour—*porture*). The *Mirror of Justices*[3] similarly uses the verb formed from *tenvres-tenvrer*—but spells it *tenurer*:

> E Billing dist qe rasture pur tenurer los de la teste & leveure
> descarde del teste [est] mahaim [p. 25]

Billing's judgement here is that whilst the loss of molar teeth, ears, etc., does not constitute mayhem, abrasion of the skull with consequent thinning of the bone (*tenvrer l'os*) does constitute this offence. Conversely, when the editor of *Femina*[4] comes to deal with the section on animal and bird noises, he prints this:

> Lyon romyt, greve graile

The difficulty of the form *greve* disappears if we read *greue*, as in the manuscript, this being simply an Anglo-Norman form of the modern French *grue* 'crane'.

More frequent and usually far more confusing is editorial failure to distinguish correctly between *n* on the one hand and *u* or *v* on the other. In many manuscripts the difference between these characters can be very slight indeed, and it would be idle to claim that medieval scribes never confused them. Yet whether the confusion is scribal or editorial in origin is beside the point: it is the clear duty of the editor to present to his reader an intelligible text, or, if he chooses to print his manuscript in its raw state, to interpret and elucidate for his reader any scribal vagaries. Time and again, however, this type of confusion is allowed to stand in Anglo-Norman texts, uncorrected and unexplained. Although a number of such errors can be spotted without difficulty—*peals lannes* for *lanues* on p. 90 of the *Domesday de Gippewyz*,[5] *peaux launes* (p. 198) and *hastinesse* for *hastivesse* (p. 96) are transparent enough, as is *chaitifneté* in v. 527 of *Le Sermon en Vers*[6] and *sa lance braule* for *branle* in the *Ancrene Riwle*[7] (p. 44), *braulissement* for *branlissement* (*ibid.*, p. 271)—others may very well disconcert the reader. In the first version of the *Ancrene Riwle* we read that the religious orders

> moustrent et crient qil ount tout ensemble vn amour et vne voluntee
> chescun antiele come altre [p. 9]

3 Ed. W. J. Whittaker, Selden Society, vii, 1895.
4 Ed. W. A. Wright, Roxburghe Club, 1909, p. 6.
5 In *The Black Book of the Admiralty*, ii, ed. T. Twiss, Rolls Series, 1871–76.
6 *Le Roman des Romans et le Sermon en Vers*, ed. F. J. Tanquerey, Paris, 1922.
7 The Herbert version of the *Ancrene Riwle* will be referred to hereafter as *Ancrene*[1] to distinguish it from *The French Text of the Ancrene Riwle*, ed. W. H. Trethewey, Early English Text Society, No. 240, 1958 (referred to as *Ancrene*[2]).

The reading here should surely be *autiele* rather than *antiele*. The second Anglo-Norman version of this text contains a mysterious *jeune* which ceases to cause difficulty when read as *jeuue*, an insular form of the modern French *joue* 'cheek':

> Celui fet il ke solitaries est e ki silence tient ueut contre le ferur offrir la
> ieune [p. 241]

Further cases of similar errors are to be found in *Dermot and the Earl*:

> E les chanz e les larriz
> Erent convers de occiz[8]

The correct reading here must be *couvers*, not *convers*. Less obvious, however, are two other cases from the same text:

> Milis de Cogan tost yuaus
> Le dreit chemin ver Finglas
> . . .
> S'en est turné [vv. 1916–19]
>
> S'en est alé tost iuanz
> Al rei anglés [vv. 263–4]

The solution to the difficulty here lies in reading *ynaus* and *inauz* for *yuaus* and *iuanz* respectively. *Inaus* is the nominative singular form of *inal*, an Anglo-Norman variant of the more usual continental *isnel*, meaning 'quick', 'quickly'. A further instance of the same error is provided by the edition of the Anglo-Norman *Vitas Patrum*, where *gaudies* is allowed to stand for *gandies* 'tricks, wiles':

> Kar tel labur uncore suffrir ne purras,
> Ne l'engin del deble, ne ses gaudies,
> Ne ses temptatiuns[9]

Mention of the Devil would perhaps be sufficient to give the reader a lead to the correct interpretation of this word, but he would need a wider acquaintance with Old French to be able to spot a form of *estovoir* behind the *estent* of this next example from Bibbesworth:

> E cil qui trop laumbei au quer
> Sovent li estent escouper[10]

8 Ed. G. H. Orpen, Oxford, 1892.
9 B. A. O'Connor, *Henri d'Arci's Vitas Patrum*, Washington, D.C., 1949, vv. 5939–41.
10 *Le Tretiz de Langage*, ed. A. Owen, Paris, 1929, vv. 1091–2.

The section concerned deals with the various French words for clearing the nose and throat, so that any idea that our *estent* can be the usual present tense of *estendre* is excluded. It is in fact a form of the more usual *estuet* 'it is necessary', although this does not figure in the glossary.

In the case of the Anglo-Norman versions of the *Ancrene Riwle* published by the Early English Text Society a number of confusions are caused by the society's method of edition, by which the manuscript is simply reproduced in print without even the correct separation of words being attempted (as in the example quoted earlier). This results in absurdities such as the following being allowed to puzzle the ordinary reader without any scholarly justification:

un savoner qe ne porte fors savon et anguilles   [*Ancrene*[1], p. 124]

Une povere savonier ke ne porte riens fors savon e cheitifves anguilles
                                                                [*Ancrene*[2], p. 237]

This poor man peddling his soap is surely more likely to have 'needles' (*auguilles*) as part of his household wares than 'eels' (*anguilles*). Again, this second version contains a tricky passage about the anger of woman:

Ire de femme si cum ire de la leuve, ceo est de la leunesse   [p. 217]

Unless the reader is looking out for the confusion of *n* and *v*, he is liable to take *leunesse* as 'lioness' in view of the well attested *leun* for 'lion'. In fact, however, it must mean 'she-wolf', i.e. *leuvesse*. The form *leuve* occurring in the same sentence, together with *lovesse* (p. 217) and *leusse* (var. *levesse*) (p. 218) found in close proximity support the reading *leuvesse*; it is the editor's function to bring this evidence together and present it to his reader. It might also have been pointed out in the edition of the Anglo-Norman version that the Middle English version reads *wulvene* at this point.

Sometimes other factors are added to the simple confusion of *n* with *u/v* to make correct identification and interpretation more difficult. In a passage from *La Estoire de seint Aedward le Rei* there is inadvertent failure to join parts of a word wrongly divided by the scribe. The text as printed runs thus:

Fame tes vertuz descuvre
Ke Deus en tere pur vus uvre,
E ne devet, beus reis gentilz,
Vos vertuz partir en niz[11]

11 Ed. H. R. Luard, Rolls Series, 1858.

It is difficult to attach any satisfactory meaning to these lines as they stand, but if we read *enviz* in place *en niz* in the last line the sense becomes clear. *Enviz* means 'reluctantly', 'against one's will', so that the general tenor of the passage is now that Edward the Confessor is being urged to use his God-given powers of healing in order to restore the sight of one of his servants and to use these powers willingly, in a generous spirit and not grudgingly.

A somewhat different kind of problem is posed when the confusion of *n* with *u/v* is coupled with an unusual substitution, as in this case arising in the *Reliquiae Antiquae*:

> Mut fut petit le sorys,
> Kaunt ele entra e[n] mun cervere
>
> . . .
>
> Kant ele denea de mun blé[12]

The general context of the mouse taking corn would lead one to give the meaning of 'garner', 'barn' to *cervere*, even though at first sight the form may cause difficulty. Once it is recognised, however, that there is a misreading or miscopying of *v* for *n* (i.e. *cernere*) allied to the use of *c* for *g* not unknown elsewhere in Anglo-Norman (e.g. *courde* for *gourde* in a manuscript of the *Manuel des Pechés*[13]) it may be seen that we are really dealing with an aberrant form of *gernere* 'garner'.

A final example of the difficulties caused by an editor's failure to distinguish correctly between *n* and *u/v* may be taken from the difficult *Traité* of Bibbesworth mentioned above. In the passage already referred to the author gives a list of the various actions involved in clearing the passages of the throat and nose:

> Ausi ad il tusser e escouper,
> Ruper, vomer e esternuer   [vv. 1087–8]

Manuscript B then runs on, however:

> Lamberer e lanreer . . .

A little farther on this same manuscript repeats this second verb in slightly changed form *lanrerer*, whilst ms. C gives a form in *u*:

> E cil laureye proprement

12 Ed. T. Wright, London, 1845, I, p. 107.
13 'Courdes esteit le fruit apelé (*sc.* in Palestine) in ms. B, f. 22*v*a; cf. 'Gurdes est le frut apelé' printed in Furnivall's edition v. 2580.

Both these verbs need explanation. In the case of *lamberer*—omitted from the glossary, incidentally—the editor has already printed a form *laumbei* (ind. pres. 3) in line 1091, together with a Middle English gloss *wamblez*, the meaning being 'to retch' ('Neigung zum Erbrechen haben' as Schellenberg says).[14] This verb, however, interests us less at the moment than the strange *lanreer*, *lanrerer*, *laureye* forms, where there is clearly a confusion between *n* and *u*. The editor omits the first two of these from her glossary, but translates the third form, under the infinitive *laureyer*, as 'avoir le hoquet'. Godefroy, Tobler and Schellenberg all omit reference to this verb, so that it is not possible to say whether the correct form is *lanr-* or *laur-*, even though we may be sure that we are dealing with the same verb in all three cases.

Closely allied to this confusion of *n* with *u/v* is the misreading of minims. This produces strange forms liable to befog the reader who has not access to the manuscript upon which an edition is based. In the second version of the *Ancrene Riwle* already referred to above there occurs a strange form—*limeines*:

> Li chaliz ki fu fundu el fu . . . , et puis par tant de martels e par tant de
> limeines si noblement ovré el hanap Dampnedeu   [p. 8]

The variants—as so often—point to the correct solution here, giving *limeures* and *lui meures*. The meaning is 'filing, polishing', the form *limeure* being a noun derived from *limer* 'to file'. Further confirmation of this is to be found both in the Herbert version—*por tant de cops et froture* (p. 199)—and in the Middle English version, which reads: '. . . so monie duntes & frotunges'. Whether the base manuscript reads *limeines* or not, the form should not be simply set down in print without either emendation or a note of interpretation.

In the *Glasgow Glossary*[15] there appears an unusual herb:

> hec limestica, limesche

Neither the Latin nor the French strikes a chord until one reads the minims differently to produce *luvestica* and *luvesche*, the English 'lovage'. Similarly, in the Owen edition of Bibbesworth referred to above, the editor's reading *limower* (v. 867) is blatantly wrong. The text is giving the French for various parts of a cart:

> En lymons (gloss: 'thilles') veet li limower (gloss: 'thille hors')

14 'Bemerkungen zum Traité des Walter von Bibbesworth', diss, Berlin, 1933.
15 Paul Meyer, *Documents manuscrits de l'ancienne littérature de la France*, Paris, 1871, p. 123.

One might have expected the form *lymons* ('shafts') and the *lymoner* (gloss: 'thilke hors') printed only a few lines below (v. 878) to alert the editor to the fact that *limower* can be nothing but *limouner*—a horse that works between the shafts of a cart, hence 'cart-horse'. Yet again, in the *Manuel des Pechez* we read this:

En vduiesce sa vie meneit[16]

Only by reading the minims correctly to give *udivesce* ('idleness') can good sense be obtained. Finally, although the modern editor of the *Vitas Patrum* is given the form *larecinusement* in v. 2969 of his text, he prints in both text and glossary a mysterious *larcemissement* (v. 218) that needs only a different reading of minims to give the more normal *larcenussement*.

Similar in kind to the confusion of *n* with *u/v* is that sometimes occurring between *f* and *s*. These two characters are often so alike in medieval manuscripts as to be distinguishable only with difficulty, yet this cannot be taken in any way as an excuse for printing forms which have no meaning, even if the reader may be able to make the necessary substitution on his own. In the *Anonimalle Chronicle, foudres* is clearly to be read for the printed *soudres*:

hidous soudres, grisyls et nayves[17]

just as in this passage from Britton the ship's bottom—*founz*—must be read for *sounz*:

les marchaundises . . . gisauntes au sounz[18]

Difficulties of a different order are liable to arise in Anglo-Norman from an editor's failure to divide words correctly. In No. 31 of Kjellman's edition of the *Miracles de la seinte Vierge*[19] we read of attempts to help a woman who has lost her reason:

En mutes maneres la confortent,
De herbes, de charmes, d'enchantement,
Mes tut ne vaut mie un flur de glent   [vv. 72–4]

The editor glosses *glent* as modern French 'gland', presumably having seen flowering acorns! *Flur d'eglent* 'wild rose' would make, perhaps,

16 Ed. F. J. Furnivall, London, 1901–03, v. 4164.
17 Ed. V. H. Galbraith, Manchester, 1970, p. 46.
18 Ed. F. M. Nichols, Oxford, 1865, I, p. 16.
19 Paris and Uppsala, 1922.

better sense. A *Vie de sainte Marguerite* edition by F. Spencer[20] contains
a similar example of bad word division, although in this case the editor
had before his eyes a Latin source which ought to have been sufficient
to preserve him from error. The Anglo-Norman text runs thus:

> Enclin ka ta oreillie, me dolurs me leschez
> Ke cil ne me charnissent qui vers moy sunt si fer   [vv. 130–1]

The Latin has at this point *ut mitigentur plage mee*, so that, given the
Anglo-Norman propensity for aphetic forms and the evidence of
charnissent for *e(s)charnissent* in v. 131, it would seem reasonable to read
m'eleschez in v. 130 and to understand this as an insular form of the
imperative of *eslegier* 'to alleviate'. Sometimes this failure to divide
words correctly can result in the creation of ghost words. If we may
return to Kjellman's edition of the *Miracles* in order to illustrate this
point, we find in the glossary a verb *coster* with the meaning 'aller à
côté de, suivre de près'. The passage where this verb occurs describes
the arrival of the Virgin accompanied by her retinue:

> Este vus ke fu menee
> La treshaute duce reine
> Des angeles, . . .
> Les patriarches les costoint,
> Les prophetes l'acoudeint . . .   [No 36, vv. 79–87]

Kjellman is aware that *les costoint* poses a problem, since he takes up
the question of the plural verb on p. 328 of his edition, but he advances
no solution to the difficulty, failing to see that the key is provided by
l'acoudeint in the next line. This failure is all the stranger to understand
because Kjellman comments on p. xcl of his introduction on the confusion of prefixes in Anglo-Norman. All that has happened in this
instance is that the scribe has written *les costoint* instead of *l'escostoint*;
enough examples exist of the use of *es-* for etymological *ad-*[21] to make
escoster a perfectly natural Anglo-Norman form of *accoster* 'to accompany, escort'. If this reading is accepted, the syntactical problem of a
plural pronoun referring to the Virgin disappears.

Similar cases arise in the Anglo-Norman version of *Boeve de Haum-*

20 *Mod. Lang. Notes*, v (1890), vv. 130–1.
21 *Esbraser* for *abraser*, *esprendre* for *apprendre*, etc. See 'Rectus vindicatus?' in
   History and Structure of French: Essays in Honour of Professor T. B. W. Reid,
   Oxford, 1972, pp. 203–22.

tone[22] and the *Proverbes du Vilain*.[23] In the former we find an apparent past participle *demoné*:

> ne donasse le vailant de un dener demoné   [(ms. D) (v. 1060)]

Later in the poem, however, there occurs *moné* instead of *demoné* in the same locution:

> jeo n'en averai le vailant de un dener moné   [v. 2840]

In his glossary the editor lists both *demoné* and *moné* as past participles with the translation 'geprägt'. It might be wiser, however, to read *de moné* in v. 1060, interpreting *moné* both here and in the later instance not as a past participle but rather as a perfectly normal Anglo-Norman form of the noun usually found on the Continent as *moneie*, bearing in mind the modern English form 'money'. In similar fashion the editor of the *Proverbes du Vilain* prints this:

> meuz valt maloir, que prester e crungeir   [(var. nungeir) (No. 59)]

Comparison of this with Morawski's compilation of similar proverbs from Continental sources[24] can eliminate two different errors here. Morawski's Nos. 70 and 2104 read as follows:

> Ki preste ne jot, ke demande mal ot
> Qui preste ne jot, qui ne preste mal ot

In the first place the Continental *ne jot* in both cases would reinforce the temptation to use the variant reading *nungeir* (instead of the mysterious *crungeir*) in the Anglo-Norman text, and, secondly, the Continental separation of *mal* and *ot* would lead to the reading *mal oir* in the insular text, thus giving perfectly good sense:

> meuz valt mal oir que prester e nun geir

'It is better to be reviled (for not lending) than to lend and not be repaid (not enjoy one's goods).'

Up to now the examples dealt with have fallen into one of a limited number of categories, but there exist in Anglo-Norman many cases where a purely arbitrary spelling may lead the reader into error unless he is prepared to let context and sense be his main criteria for judging meaning without undue regard to the 'rules' of phonology as thought

22 Ed. A. Stimming, Halle, 1899.
23 Ed. E. Stengel, *Zeitschrift für französische Sprache und Literatur*, XXI (1899) pp. 1–21.
24 *Proverbes français antérieurs au XVe siècle*, Paris, (C.F.M.A.), 1925.

to apply on the Continent. To take first a very simple example: *fel* 'base, treacherous' is the stock epithet applied to hundreds of villains in medieval French epic and romance, yet here is *Alienor, cunpaigne sire Edward* writing *a sun lel et fel sire Johan de Lundres* . . .[25] The meaning here is clearly quite the reverse of the normal Old French one and is to be found in scores of Anglo-Norman writings. Phonetically, of course, we are dealing with the reduction of a diphthong, as in the case of *lel* also, but, given that the product of the Latin *fidelem* is found in at least fifteen forms in Anglo-Norman, this knowledge is of more theoretical than practical use to the ordinary reader.

Since Anglo-Norman is perhaps the most unruly of all the varieties of medieval French, it may be worth while to examine a number of such cases in order to demonstrate the extent to which the reader needs to abandon the traditional 'rules' of phonology if he wishes to understand insular texts. Examples where the reduction of diphthongs may cause difficulty spring immediately to mind following upon the cases of *fel* and *lel*. This latter word, for instance, has a parallel adverbial form *leument*, which has nothing to do with its usual Continental sense of 'easily', 'lightly':

a mes cumanz tant leument obeir *S Auban*[26]

A better illustration of the triumph of sense and context over phonology in Anglo-Norman might be *lange*, which, in addition to the usual Continental meaning of 'cloth, is also found as an alternative form of both *langue* 'tongue' and *loenge* 'praise':

A li loenges lange sone
A ki loenges sanz lange done[27]

Glorie, lange e digneté[28]

Or again, the student of Old French confronted with the form *poveraile* would in all probability interpret it automatically as a collective noun formed on the adjective *povre*, as in this quotation from Godefroy (VI, p. 361):

Mieus amons nous assez les ames
Des chevaliers, des beles dames,
Que de vilains ne de povraille.

25 *Royal Letters*, ed. W. W. Shirley, Rolls Series, 1862–60, II, p. 298.
26 Ed. A. R. Harden, Anglo-Norman Text Society, XIX, 1968.
27 Pierre d'Abernun, *The Miracles of Saint Richard*, Portland ms. I.c.l., vv. 952–3.
28 *Le Evangel translaté de latin en franceys*, in *Seven More Poems by Nicholas Bozon*, ed. Sister M. Amelia (Klenke), New York, 1951, v. 679.

In the *Rotuli Parliamentorum*,[29] however, this word is a variant—
aberrant?—spelling of what is elsewhere in the same text spelt as
puraille, purale (i.e. 'perambulation'):

> qe la chartre de forest soit *tenu* . . . , saunz qe la poveraile qi fuist chivache
> . . . estoise si come ele est chivache et enchartre   [p. 121]

Cf.

> Crepilgate qi est deins la puraille de la citee   [p. 136]

> nusaunces qi de deins la dite purale serront trouez   [p. 141]

The editors could have contributed to the understanding of these
phrases, of course, had they added accents to mark off the *-é* endings
from those with unaccented final *-e*.

Other simple cases drawn from widely differing sources may suffice
to show that this kind of aberrant spelling is not confined to just one
or two texts but is to be reckoned with as a standard feature of Anglo-
Norman. In Trivet's *Chronicle* we read that:

> Esdre avoit poer del roi . . . de lower les coustages des princes[30]

where *lower* must be interpreted not etymologically as a product of
laudare or *locare* but simply as an odd form of *lever* 'to raise, levy'.
Similarly, no one could misinterpret *suffire* in this sentence from the
Life of St Modwenna:

> Certes ne puet nul quer suffire
> Lur grant travail, lur [grief] martire[31]

Faced with the phrase *pur saver verité* in an Anglo-Norman text it
would be quite natural to assume that the infinitive *saver*—as so often—
represented the Continental *saveir* 'to know' with reduction of the
ei diphthong to simple *e*. The text from which this comes—the *Merure
de seinte Eglise*[32]—goes on, however, to read *e dampner fausté* (l. 564),
thus proving that *saver* is here an Anglo-Norman form of *sauver*,
not of *saveir*: the reduction is of *au* to *a*, not of *ei* to *e*. On the other

29 Ed. H. G. Richardson and J. O. Sayles, Camden Society, 1953.
30 'The Anglo-Norman Chronicle of Nicholas Trivet', ed. A. Rutherford, diss.,
   London, 1932, p. 78.
31 Ed. A. Bell, Anglo-Norman Text Society, VII, 1947, vv. 42–3.
32 Ed. H. W. Robins, Lewisburg, 1925.

hand it would be foolish to read *sauver* as anything other than 'to know' (i.e. *saveir*) in the following:

> Pur ceo voudrey a dreit sauver K'est le seyn Abraam nomé
>
> [*Lumere as lais*[33]]

This uncertainty about diphthongs is often easy to interpret correctly, and it may be taken for granted, perhaps, that the reader would have little trouble in seeing *loisible* and *laisser* behind *lisible* and *lasser* of the following two phrases:

> tant soulement en lisible & aisee manere[34]

> De ces treis freres en voil lasser   [*Geste de Burch*[35]]

It is not so easy, however, to interpret this next passage:

> Sachez ke sire R. de E. esteit en la servise le rey a Lampaderwaur par comaundement le nostre seygnur le rey, pur le acounte rendre e fere la deliveraunce du chastel ke vus ben savez e tut le conseil le seet, e nus le tesmoynouns bien. Pur quoy nus vus prioms ke vus li facez aver un breef de cervise le rey a viscunte de Herteford de un play ke est entre l'avaunt dit R. e N. le Fraunceys dunt ses gens le fierent asoyngner de servise le rey a meme le houre ke il fust en Wales.[36]

What is at issue here is not the simple *fierent* for *firent*, although the diphthongal spelling is significant: the real difficulty lies in understanding *assigner* behind the *asoyngner* of the text. The only satisfactory sense to be read into this passage is that Sir Roger, whilst already serving the king in Wales, has been detailed for service elsewhere and is in trouble for not being in two places at once. The linguistic difficulty comes from the fact that, firstly, as a result of Anglo-Norman confusion of prefixes, it is not uncommon to find the noun *assoin*, etc., for *essoin* 'excuse' (and similarly in the verb forms, *assoiner* for *essoiner*), and secondly, just as diphthongs may be reduced, single vowels may conversely be spelt as diphthongs. Only common sense, then, can tell us whether this *asoyngner* is to be taken as *essonier* or *assigner*: grammars and manuals are of no avail.

The case just mentioned did not mislead Tanquerey in his edition of

---

33 Pierre d'Abernun, *La Lumere as lais*, York Minster ms. 16.N.3., f. 201r.31.
34 *Statutes of the Realm*, Record Commission, London, 1810–25, II, p. 20 vii.
35 *Geste de Burch*, ed. A. Bell, in *The Chronicle of Hugh Candidus*, Oxford, 1949, v. 64.
36 *Recueil de lettres anglo-françaises*, ed. F. J. Tanquerey, Paris, 1916, p. 28.

the *Recueil*, but a simple spelling variant, without any reduction of diphthongs, has apparently been sufficient to lead the editor of the *Anglo-Norman Political Songs*[37] into error in the Trailbaston poem. The stanza in question runs as follows:

> Vus cy estes endité, je lou, venez a moy,
> Al vert bois de Belregard, la n'y a nul ploy
> Forque beste savage e jolyf umbroy;
> Car trop est doteuse la commune loy.

Translation, glossary and notes all give *ploy* in the above as 'annoyance', but in view of the wholly legal flavour of the poem and in particular its reference to those *endité* (v. 53) and *la commune loy* (v. 56) it would appear unnecessary to go outside the vocabulary of the law for a meaning here: 'plea', 'pleading' (Latin *placitum*) would fit the bill perfectly. Miss Aspin again goes outside the legal framework of her text a few stanzas later:

> Si je sache plus de ley qe ne sevent eux,
> Yl dirrount: 'Cesti conspyratour comence de estre faus'.
> E le heyre n'aprocheroy de x. lywes ou deus.
> De tous veysinages hony seient ceux.   [vv. 89–92]

In a note on *heyre* (p. 78) she writes, 'Probably = *aire* ← *atrium*, meaning "threshing floor, yard", and by extension "home". The homonym *aire* "nest of the hawk, eyrie" has associations which might have influenced such a development of meaning.' The hawks may be left in peace, however, in their eyries, and the venerable 'rules' of phonological development may be left in their manuals of historical French grammar: no violent stretching of meaning is necessary to make good sense out of v. 91. The *heyre* referred to here is none other than the word we still find in the expression 'Justices in Eyre', the meaning being that, since the writer is convinced that he will not get a fair trial, he will not go within ten miles of the courts. Confirmation of this interpretation is to be found in stanza 8 of the poem:

> Si ces mavois jurours ne se vueillent amender,
> Que je pus a mon pais chevalcher e aler, . . .   [vv. 29–30]

pais having in this context a double meaning—'country' and also the legal sense *aler a pais* 'to opt for trial by one's fellow countrymen'. Finally, before leaving this poem it must be pointed out that *deus* v. 91) does not mean 'two', as the editor's translation would have us believe, but 'twelve'—yet another case of phonological 'rules' proving to be a snare and a delusion.

All the examples quoted illustrate one fundamental point: the correct appreciation of context will help the medievalist more than any theoretical knowledge of phonology or morphology. It would be interesting, for example, to see how the traditional 'rules' of phonology would help in dealing with *haut* in the following legal sentence:

> Le brief est a la commune ley, et si est le plus haut brief qe seit[38]

The meaning here is 'old', not 'high'. It is surprising to find that on occasion an editor will ignore both common sense and evidence in order to maintain an incorrect translation backed by an 'authority' of one kind or another. Presumably following Godefroy (IV, p. 698), Dr Owen translates *lay* in the following passage of Bibbesworth as 'réserve dans une forêt':

> Alez dount saunz delai Ou espleiteromes tut dreit au lay   [vv. 517–17a]

The Middle English glosses contradict this, however, giving 'great pol' and 'lake' respectively, an interpretation supported by other texts:

> un ville de Sessoine, qe fu aloiné de totes ewes et de tuz lays, . . . fu tote enfoundré   [Trivet, p. 265]

> vivers, pescheries, lays et parcs.   [Britton II, p. 78]

In this particular case Tobler–Lommatzsch do not follow Dr Owen and interpret the word correctly as 'See', but when dealing with *luire* from the same Bibbesworth text they unaccountably give credence to the editor and so fall into error. Bibbesworth gives a long list of collective nouns applied to various animals and birds (e.g. herd of deer, flock of sheep, etc.) and amongst these figures the following couplet:

> Greile de gelins, turbe de cerceles,
> Luire de faucouns, luyre de puceles   [vv. 233–4]

Dr Owen sees *luire* here as the modern French *leurre*' snare, lure' and is followed in this interpretation by Tobler–Lommatzsch, who translate as 'Lockspeise, Lockvogel' (v, col. 611, under *loirre*). Neither attempts to deal with *luyre*, clearly an arbitrary spelling by Bibbesworth in an attempt to differentiate it from its homonym *luire* (see his *aumaire, aumeire, aumere* on p. 131, etc.). This *luyre de puceles* cannot be

---

38 *Year Books of Edward II*, xxv, ed. J. P. Collas, Selden Society, 1964, p. 102.

other than 'band, company of maidens' and nothing in the surrounding context points towards *luire de faucouns* being necessarily 'lure' rather than a collective. In fact the *Nominale seu Verbale*,[39] which has close ties with the *Traité*, definitely sees *lure* as a collective noun, putting it under the rubric *congregacio Avium* and running on *Un lure de faucouns* (l. 835). The Middle English gloss *A lure of faucouns* supports the Latin here.

Still in the domain of Bibbesworth's difficult vocabulary comes *orer*:

Freid eit dil yver l'orer   [v. 585]

and

En yver quant l'orere chaunge   [v. 587]

Dr Owen is apparently beguiled by the spelling here and translates *abord*, although in both quotations Bibbesworth must be referring to winter weather.[40]

Usually the exercising of common sense on the basis of context will bring a solution to this kind of spelling difficulty, even if the spelling is in itself very deceptive. For instance, although *jeu* and *geus* in isolation would normally call to mind 'game(s)', when placed in context in the *Vie de Sainte Audree*[41] they turn out to mean 'yoke' and 'eyes':

menur peine et meins de haan Out el jeu de religion   [vv. 6240–1]
Un jur prist un cotel ageu, En un des geus l'en a fereu   [vv. 4266–7]

Similarly, although *hunir* is frequently found in Anglo-Norman texts for the standard Continental *honnir*, in this quotation it can only be read as *unir*:

Coment l'alme put estre huni o le cors[42]

Again, when faced with *livres* clearly meaning 'lips', one does not try to read into the word a homonymic clash, but simply takes it as yet another example of the vagaries of Anglo-Norman spelling:

Car en ses livres culur cum de rose Aparuit . . .
[*Miracles of Saint Richard*, v. 58]

39 Ed. W. W. Skeat, *Trans. Phil. Soc.*, 1906, pp. 1*–50*.
40 See Schellenberg, *op. cit.*, p. 52.
41 Ed. O. Södergård, Uppsala, 1955.
42 *La Lumere as lais*, ms. B. M. Harley 4390, f. 11*v*a.

There do arise, however, cases where semantic proximity allied to orthographic uncertainty can cause real difficulty. The ideas of 'laxity' and 'weariness', for example, are sufficiently close for one to hesitate between them, since Anglo-Norman tends to use either *lachesce* or *lassesce* for both. When Hue de Rotelande writes in *Ipomedon*:

> La fiere regarde la beste,
> Que de sa lachesce s'areste[43]

the meaning 'weariness' as opposed to 'slackness' suggests itself at once, since the text runs just previously:

> Et ly serfs par esteit si las . . .
> [Ke] n'alast avant mye un pas   [vv. 617-18]

Yet in the *Vie de Saint Auban lassesce* would appear to mean not 'weariness' but 'laxity, slackening':

> Auban en la chartre ne fina Deu urer;
> Ço fu sanz lassesce jur e nuit sun mester   [vv. 673-4]

The fact that the recent edition of this text does not include this word in the glossary or see fit to mention it in the notes would seem to indicate that the editor was led astray by the spelling. A further complication arises when we find *largesce* being used with the meaning 'laxity, indolence':

> por la odivesce e largesce (Latin: desuetudo) de lor armes qui enfeblisoient[44]

Another case of perhaps greater hesitation is to be found in Beneit's *Vie de Saint Thomas*:

> N'i out moine en l'abeie Ke plus demenast seinte vie
> Ke il feseit. N'aveit cure de lecherie,
> De chose ke turnast a folie[45]

At first sight one might translate *lecherie* here in its usual sense of 'lechery', but the line immediately following points rather to the meaning 'foolishness', i.e. *legerie* in standard Old French. The extent to which editors and dictionary makers have been misled by this pair —and not only in Anglo-Norman—may be seen by a careful examination of the Tobler–Lommatzsch entries for *lecherie* (v, 291-3) and

43 Ed. E. Köbling and E. Koschwitz, Breslau, 1889, vv. 623-4.
44 Vegetius, *De re militari*, Fitzwilliam Museum, ms. Marley Add, I, f. 18*v*.
45 Ed. B. Schlyter, Lund, 1941, vv. 937-41.

legerie (v, 307–8). Under the first of these headings (col. 293) is a whole group of quotations for which the translation of *lecherie* by 'Scherz, Spass' is proposed. In all these cases, however, we are really dealing not with *lecherie* but with *legerie*, as will be seen from a consideration of just two of the quotations given. In the first example Tristan in disguise is playing a trick for the benefit of Yseut:

> il le fait par lecherie, . . . Que ele en ait en son cuer joie   [vv. 3693–6]

The second example is even clearer, being an apologia for serious education as distinct from light, frivolous reading:

> est bonne chose de mettre ses enffans juennes a l'escolle et les faire apprendre es livres de sapience . . ., non pas les faire apprendre es livres de lecheries et des fables du monde

In neither of these cases is there any question of 'lechery'.

Conversely, Tobler–Lommatzsch fail to give any indication under *legerie* that a number of their quotations use this word quite clearly in the sense of 'lechery':

> 'Dame, donés moi vostre amor . . .' La contesse respont irié:
> 'Laissiés ester legerie'.

> Çou est bien drois, et se li doi, Que jou soie sa douce amie
> Sans malvestié, sans legerie'.

The translations 'Leichtfertigkeit, Leichtsinn, Unbesonnenheit' given by Tobler–Lommatzsch are quite erroneous here, where the idea of lechery is unmistakably present. The implications of these errors are important: firstly, since there is abundant evidence that this kind of confusion of spelling was rife on the Continent as well as in Anglo-Norman, one must ask whether the limitations of phonology as an aid to the understanding of medieval texts are not just as glaringly obvious in Continental French as in Anglo-Norman; secondly, here is as clear an example as could be desired of a genuine homonymic clash which, to judge from all appearances, did not incommode in the least those who used medieval French. That it seriously incommodes twentieth century philologists to the extent of forcing them into errors of interpretation must not be taken as implying any similar difficulty for medieval Frenchmen on either side of the Channel.

Nor is this case just an isolated instance. Sound and sense tend to confuse the products of Latin *augurium*, *hora* and *iter*, but the result need worry no one who reads medieval texts in order to understand a civilisation, since it is quite clear what is happening and the sense is not in doubt. When Rauf de Lenham wrote in his calendar *eur* for the standard Continental *eire* (iter) he was not running the risk of this being interpreted etymologically as a development of *augurium*:

> le solail . . .
> En yvern puis sun eur reprent;
> Vers l'autre coste vet muntant[46]

Nor did the anonymous writer of another calendar worry about corrupting French to the extent of making *hur* (←*hora*) rhyme with *jur*:

> de seigner est dunc bon hur[47]

There is clearly a contamination here—arising probably in the mind before being expressed in linguistic terms—between the idea of a good, favourable moment (*hora*) and good fortune (*augurium*).

In Anglo-Norman perhaps more than in any other field of French studies one is so often brought face to face with oddities and irregularities that one is forced to ask whether any outline or even detailed survey of its phonology and morphology can be of much practical help to the reader. What is needed, primarily, is a determination to make good sense of a text, given its historical and literary background. Phonology and morphology may play their part, but only a minor part. An editor must aim not at performing linguistic exercises on his text but at getting inside the skin of the medieval man who composed it.

46 Glasgow, Hunterian Museum, ms. Q.9.13, v. 1067.
47 H. J. Chaytor, 'An Anglo-Norman calendar', *Mod. Lang. Rev.*, II (1906–07), pp. 211–22, v. 307.

Paul S. N. Russell-Gebbett

Mossèn Pere Pujol's *Documents en vulgar dels segles XI, XII & XIII* . . . (Barcelona, 1913): a partial retranscription and commentary

In 1913 Mossèn Pere Pujol published his *Documents en vulgar dels segles XI, XII & XIII procedents del bisbat de la Seu d'Urgell*, Biblioteca Filològica de l'Institut de la Llengua Catalana, 1, Barcelona, Palau de la Diputació. The twenty-eight documents came from the Cathedral archives of Seu d'Urgell, whose archivist Mossèn Pujol was, and were the first in Catalan to be published 'segons un mètode o criteri llingüístic, ço és, posant en cursiu tot ço que en el pergamí és abreviatura, tot ço que se supleix'. However, Pujol did not separate words, capitalise, punctuate or provide stress marks according to modern usage, and neither did he regularise the use of *u* and *v*, *i* and *j*, *c* and *ç*. Consequently the texts, while far from impossible to interpret, were not especially clear.

When I decided to incorporate some of the Pujol documents in my *Mediaeval Catalan Linguistic Texts*[1] I attempted, but without success, to see the originals; Mossèn Pujol was unable to locate them. Since at least some of them were of great linguistic interest and could not be omitted from any anthology of early Catalan, I was obliged to base my versions upon Pujol's transcriptions. The *MCLT* texts 8, 15(10), 15(11), 18(2), 27, 29, 33(1) and 33(2) were produced in this way, while 18(1) was arrived at with the help of the one facsimile Pujol provided in his edition.

On a visit to the Cathedral's archives in the summer of 1968, however, I was at last able to unearth, with the help of the new archivist, twenty-one of the originals, to transcribe them and to have them microfilmed for later reference. Some of these new transcriptions were sufficiently different from Pujol's earlier versions (and so perforce from some of the *MCLT* adaptations) to warrant their publication, and I offer in what follows new and, I hope, definitive versions of seven of the first fifteen of Pujol's texts. The system of transcription I use is

---

1 *Mediaeval Catalan Linguistic Texts*, ed. Paul Russell-Gebbett, Oxford, 1965.

described in detail in *MCLT* pp. 50–2, and only where I depart from those norms are details provided in the introductory notes to each of the texts.

I

Pujol 1, *MCLT* 8. The passages between { } were not reproduced by Pujol because those parts of the original are stained and faded; they are, however, legible. In this text only I have retained the original's 'stress marks', for the reason that they do seem (except in line 2 *alíí*) to reflect stress or rhythm.

[*Sentència donada per En Miró, Vescomte i altres jutges en el* Placito *que's teníen el Bisbe de La Seu i En Raimón Gonball sobre els límits de Guissona i Ribelles.—Anys 1036–1079.*][2]

{Hoc est judicium quod judicavit Miro vice comite et Raimun Guada ⟨l⟩ /[2] de Kallers, et alíí judices que ibi fuerunt, de ipso placito que est inter domno Guilel /[3] mo episcopo et Raimundo Gonball de ipso termino que est inter Gissona et Ribeles. /[4] Unde abent entenzó que monstre predicto episcopo ipso termine ad Raimun /[5] Gonball per quale que loco se volet, et dicat per ipsas aprisiones et per ipsas /[6] tenezones quod fecerunt ipsos episcopos antecessores suos que fuerunt ante Guilel /[7] mo episcopo, et per ipsos akaptes quod illi fecerunt per dret et domno Guilelmo, /[8] quod melior est suo directo de jam dicto episcopo per ipso termine de Gissona que /[9] non est de predicto Remon Gonbal per aprisió ne per tenezó quod fecissent sui an /[10] tecessores que fuerunt ante predicto Raimundo, neque per ipsos akaptes quod /[11] illis fecissent per dret, nec illis neque jam dicto Raimundo, per ipso termine /[12] de Ribeles.} Et monstre Remon ipso termine ke proclame per Ribeles, que est de /[13] Ción ad enlá, che agtan ámple lo mónstre de la kom lo té de zá /[14] ad riba de Sció. Et si·n fan batalla et suo omine de Remon Gonball y venz, /[15] ut predicto episcopo feneschat ad jam dicto Remon Gonball ipso termine, et emen /[16] det ipso malo quod ibi apreenderit ipso kavallario de Raimundo sic quo /[17] modo fuerit judicatum per directum. Et si ipso suo omine de domno episcopo /[18] y venz, similiter fenescat Remon Gonball ipso termine {jam dicto supra nomina /[19] to ad jam dicto Guilelmo episcopo, et emendet ipso male

2 The titles of the texts are those which Pujol gave them.

ad ipso bataller quo /[20] modo erit judicatum per recte.} Et si i venz ipso suo omine de domno episcopo, quod /[21] Remon Gonball li·o jakescha e li·o defenescha per escrito; et si ipso suo /[22] omine i venz de Remon Gonbal, similiter feneschat et jakescat ipso episcopo per /[23] escrito. E ke sía en so assemblament de ipso episcopo si·o fará el prime /[24] rs {ipso fromiment} aut o rechulirá de Remon Gonball, et in quale que /[25] remanserit {de illos jam supra nominatos} ipsa batalla similiter jakeschat et de /[26] fenescat per exvacuacio scripture. Et ipso die que metránt illorum ca /[27] valers in potestate de ipsos omines qui·n faciant ipsa batalla, dicat /[28] ipso episcopo si phará el primers ipso fromiment o·l rechulirá de Remon /[29] Gonball.

Commentary[3]

1. *Miro* (M.Cat. *Miró*) shows the typical evolution of the suffix -ŌNE; cf. 4 *entenzó*, 9 *aprisió* and *tenezó*, 14 *Sció*(but 13 *Ción*). Similarly 13 *té* ← TĔNET.
   Raimun ←- RA(G)ĬNMŬNDU; cf. for the evolution of the diphthong [aj] 9, etc., *Remon*. Other examples of an early development [aj] --> [e] are here 19 *bataller*, 26-7 *cavalers*, 23-4 *primers*. The result [e] in the suffix -ARĬU is found in the earliest texts, cf. *MCLT* 1.2, 1.13, 1.15. The loss of the final vowel, also documented in the earliest texts, is further exemplified in 7 *dret*, 13 *kom* and the examples quoted above. Late final *n*, here from -ND-, remains.
   2. *Kallers*, if it is from CALĬDARĬOS, could reflect a development -L'D- -> [ll] frequent in O.Cat. See Coromines, *Lleis*,[4] pp. 28-30.
   que is throughout the text the form taken by the subject relative (cf. lines 3, 6, 10, 12) except for 27 *qui*—if this is not to be taken as introducing a final clause. The oblique form vacillates between *quod* and *ke*. Introducing a final clause *ut* (15), *quod* (20), *que*, *che*, *ke* (4, 13, 23) all occur, and here as in the case of the oblique forms the underlying reality is clearly Romance *que*. It is possible that 27 *qui* may herald a final clause in view of the following subjunctive *faciant*, since a subject relative would be more likely at this period to be followed by a (future) indicative. For examples of final *qui* in Hispanic Medieval Latin see Bastardas,[5] p. 187 n.
   ipso, etc., is regularly the form taken by the 'article'. The use of *predicto*,

---

3 In the commentaries the first figure refers to line numbers in the text under discussion. Other numbers refer either to line numbers in that same text (e.g. 4 *entenzó*), or to line numbers in other texts transcribed here (e.g. 'see §3.1 *fillg*'), or to a document or document and line number occurring in some other work (e.g. *MCLT* 1.2).

4 Joan Coromines, 'Algunes lleis fonètiques catalanes no observades fins ara', *Estudis romànics*, III (1951–52), pp. 201–30.

5 Juan Bastardas Parera, *Particularidades sintácticas del latín medieval (cartularios españoles de los siglos VIII al XI*, Barcelona (C.S.I.C.), 1953.

jam dicto, jam dicto supranominato and that of *ipso* referring to a hypothetical 16 *malo* all point to the loss of anaphoric value. On the article from ĪPSE see especially Bastardas, pp. 67–70, and Coromines, *Revista de filología hispánica*, V (1943), pp. 14–18.

3. The vacillation between *termino* and, elsewhere in the text, *termine* reflects, like 16 *malo* and 19 *male*, the scribe's difficulty in latinising his own undoubted *termen* and *mal*.

Ribeles shows the normal early development -AS → *-es*, presumably [es], and the voicing of -P- (cf. 14 *riba*). The result from the geminate -LL- is at this period still [ll], the scribe making some sort of distinction between this and the result from -LĬ- (19 *bataller*). For another graphy representing [ȼ] see §3.1 *fillg* and note.

4. *ad* throughout retains its consonant, even in the purely Catalan context of lines 13–14. For further examples see *GMLC*,[6] fasc. I, s.v. *ad*, and *MCLT*, glossary.

6. *tenezones* more frequently occurs in the form *tenedones*, and Rodón[7] quotes many examples from the eleventh and twelfth centuries, none with -*z*-. For a similar *d/z* vacillation in spelling cf. also §3.5 *fortedes* with Rodón *forteza* (s.v. *forcia*). On the phonology see Coromines, *Studia*,[8] pp. 129–34, *Lleis*, pp. 225–6, and Alarcos, *Consideraciones*,[9] pp. 14–17; both scholars postulate a development [dz] → [ð].

suos. Cf. the more correct 9 *sui* and the confusion 7 *illi* ∼ 11 *illis*. In spite of 23–4 *primers* it is clear that the scribe's own language did not have a two-case system.

7. *akaptes* is a post-verbal formation on AC(C)AP(Ĭ)TARE, on which see *GMLC*, fasc. I, s.v. *acapitum*, and Rodón's *acapte*. Like 13 *ample* the form shows the typical Catalan vowel of support *e*.

dret exemplifies the normal evolution -CT- --→ [jt] → [t]; cf. §2.6 *diretam*.

8. *quod* appears to introduce a completive clause after 5 *dicat*, while *que*. relates to *melior* and is the heir of QUAM.

suo (also 14 *suo omine*), alternates with 17, 20, 21 *ipso suo*—cf. O.Cat. *so(n)*

6 Mariano Bassols de Climent *et al.*, *Glossarium Mediae Latinitatis Cataloniae: voces latinas y romances documentadas en fuentes catalanas del año 800 al 1100*, Barcelona, Universidad de Barcelona, Departamento de Filología Latina del C.S.I.C., 1960—. To date six fascicles have appeared, taking us by 1971 as far as *cyrographare*.

7 Eulalia Rodón Binué, *El lenguaje técnico del feudalismo en el siglo XI en Cataluña: contribución al estudio del latín medieval*, Barcelona (C.S.I.C.), 1957.

8 Joan Coromines, 'De gramàtica històrica catalana: a propòsit de dos llibres', *Studia philologica et litteraria in honorem L. Spitzer*, Bern, 1958, pp. 123–48.

9 E. Alarcos Llorach, 'Algunas consideraciones sobre la evolución del consonantismo catalán', *Miscelánea homenaje a André Martinet: estructuralismo e historia*, II, Universidad de La Laguna, 1958, pp. 5–40.

and *lo seu*; O.Cat. *so* appears in line 23, and other early examples occur in *MCLT* 16.10, 19.51.

12. *monstre* (3 pres. subj.) and *proclame* (3 pres. ind.) show the fusion at least in writing of results from -ET and -AT. The modern language distinguishes in a number of different ways, e.g. standard *mostri* with [i] but *proclama* with [ə]. *proclame*'s *pro-* shows the same abbreviation as *per* in this text. On *per* and *pro* in Peninsular Latin see Bastardas, pp. 91 ff.

13. *agtan* ← *AC-TAM; see *GMLC*, fasc. 1.

14. *y*. Cf. 16 *ibi*, 20 *i*.

16. *apreenderit*. Though O.Cat. shows no traces of a derivative of the Latin future perfect (unlike Spanish and Portuguese), its use as a future subjunctive in official Latin documents is widespread. It also occurs instead of the future *imperfect*, which had early been replaced in speech by analytical constructions and whose Latin forms were with rare exceptions forgotten. Note in this connection 17 *fuerit judicatum* and 20 *erit judicatum*, occurring in identical contexts and both equally foreign to the scribe's underlying *será judgad*. See also below, 23 *fará*, n.

17. *fuerit judicatum*, like 20 *erit j.*, illustrates the replacement of synthetic forms of the passive by analyses.

20. *quod* introduces a final clause, cf. 2 *que*, n.

23. *so*. Cf. 8 *suo*, n.

fará, like 24 *rechulirá* and 26 *metránt*, shows the acclimatisation of the Romance future. This occurs commonly in the feudal oaths (see Bastardas, pp. 147 ff., and *MCLT* 6, 7, 9, 12, 15).

23–4. *primers*. Remants of the nominative case are not uncommon in the feudal oaths, where they may be attributed to formulaic conservatism. See *MCLT*, pp. 40–41, and §3.2 *fedels*.

26. *que* 'when, on which' (cf. *MCLT* 10.25 *per illas horas que*, 12.12 *totes celes veds che*). The relative pronoun introducing a complement of circumstances referring to time became early standardised as *que* without a preposition.

illorum reflects the O.Cat. possessive adjective *lur(s)*, which vacillated in the adoption of the adjectival *-s* when more than one item was possessed; cf. as late as 1323 *las lur mides* (*MCLT* 48.58). The form was probably never entirely popular, occasionally seems in O.Cat to be used with singular possessors, and is now replaced in normal usage by derivatives of *sŭŭs*.

27. *qui*. See 2 *que*, n.

Toponymy. *Gissona*, mod. Guissona, Segarra; *Ribeles*, mod. Ribelles, La Noguera; *Ción, Sció*, mod. R. Sió. It has not proved possible to locate with certainty *Kallers*.

2

Pujol II, *MCLT* 15(10). The original document of 1107 was found too late for it to be microfilmed, or for a complete and independent new transcription to be made. A comparison of the original with Pujol's version showed that there were no discrepancies of linguistic importance, but that apart from failing to italicise some uncontroversial abbreviations Pujol had not transcribed four or five lines of the first part of the oath. Since these show some interesting features, I transcribe below the first part of the text, enclosing in { } the sections omitted by Pujol.

[*Fragment d'un jurament feudal.—Any 1107.*]

Juro ego Ermengod Joçbert {filius q*ui* fuit d*e* Guilla femina que d*e* ista ora in /² antea fidelis ero} ad te Gauceran Mir {filiu*m* q*ui* fuisti de Sicards femi*n*a, et a filio tuo /³ Gauceran qui fuit filio de Adalet femi*n*a, *z* a Remo*n* Gauceran q*ui* fuit fil⟨i⟩us d*e* Aza /⁴ let femi*n*a si Gau⟨c⟩eran obierit sine i*n*fante d*e* legitimo coniugio, v*e*l ad illu*m* cui Gau /⁵ ceran dubitaverit sua*m* onore*m*, sine fraudo et ullo malo ingenio *z* sine ulla de /⁶ cepcione *z* sine engan p*er* diretam fide*m*.} *z* deincebs no*n* te dezebré {prephatu*m* /⁷ Gauceran Mir *z* Gauceran filio tuo} d*e* ipsos kastellos de Josa *z* d*e* Orsera et /⁸ d*e* Sa*n*cti Romani et de Gosal, neq*ue* d*e* ipsas fortedas {q*ue* in eis modo s*unt* aut in antea /⁹ eri*n*t. No les te tollré . . .

Commentary

1. *Joçbert ←* GAUCIBERT.

fuit for *fui*. This is a common confusion in the oaths, attributable not so much to hypercorrection as to vacillation between personal and impersonal expression.

2. *Gauceran.* Cf. §3.1 *Golceran*, n.

a. Cf. *ad te* earlier, and §1.4 *ad*, n.

3. *Adalet, Azalet ←* ADALHAID; a copy of this oath dated 1117 bears the form *Adzaled* and §3.1 has *Adalez.* Cf. for the graphies -*d*-, -*z*- and -*dz*- notes on §1.6 *tenezones* and §3.4 *aveds.*

4. *cui* exists in O.Cat. alongside its analytical competitor *a(d) qui*; cf. for the former *MCLT* 10.5 (five other examples in the text concerned), 10.34 (with one other example of *cui* and one of *que* incorrectly used), 12.4, 15.9, 15.86, and for the latter *MCLT* 7.4 (one other example), 9.3 (one other example), 14.21 (*a chuit*), 16.10 (*a cui*), 20.4 (*a cui*).

5. *dubitaverit* is a case of false etymology for DOTAVERIT; see Rodón's convincing argumentation s.v. *dubitare.*

fraudo is more commonly, and properly, found in the form *fraude*. The reality at the time was probably [fraw] or [frawŏ].

ingenio. Rodón gives only the definition 'máquina de guerra', but here the meaning must be almost synonymous with that of 6 *engan* 'treachery'. The two terms often occur in identical contexts—cf. Rodón's example *Ego mal engin ne mal engan no farei ne portarei ad prephatum comitem* (990–1050).

8. *fortedas*. See §1.6 *tenezones*, n.

Toponymy. Josa, mod. Josa de Cadí, Alt Urgell; *Orsera*, mod. Ossera, Alt Urgell; *Gosal*, mod. Gósol, Berguedà. *Sancti Romani* (§3 *Sen Roma*) remains unlocated.

3

Pujol III, *MCLT* 15(11). Although there are only a few discrepancies between Pujol's version and the original, given the brevity of the text it seems worth while providing a complete new transcription here.

[*Jurament de fidelitat atorgat per En Mir Guitart a En Galcaeran—Any 1131.*]

Juro ego Mir Guitard fillg de Gebelina ⟨femina⟩ ad te Golceran fillg de Adalez femina, *z* ad te Stefania /² filia de Loucia femina, *z* ad te Golceran fillg de Stefania femina, quod de ista ora inant fedels vos seré /³ de vostros quars et de vostres vides et de vostres membres qui en vostros cors (*vos) se tenen, *z* de vos /⁴ tra honor che ara aveds ne anant (*per) ab lo meu consellg acaptareds – per nomen de castro de Orsera /⁵ *z* de castro de Josa *z* de Sen Roma, et de fortedes chi ara i son ne enant i serán. Ego Mir G⟨u?⟩itard acsi /⁶ suo (*for* us o) tenré e·us o atendré per Deum *z* hec sancta. /⁷ Hoc fuit factum anno ab incarnacione domini nostri Jhesu Xpi. Cº XXXº Iº post Mº Xº k. aprilis.

Commentary

1. *fillg* and 4 *consellg*. The graphy representing [ʎ] is not common in O.Cat.; it is more reminiscent of scribal habits in Aragon or Southern France.

Golceran ← GAUZHRAMN. More commonly this name occurs with *a* in the first syllable (cf. §2.2 and §5.2 *Gauceran*), which accounts for Pujol's transcribing it with this vowel. Surrounded by the velars [g] and [w], the medial vowel had a natural tendency to retract.

2. *inant*. Cf. 4 *anant* and 5 *enant*. The variation in the spelling of the initial vowel may argue for a pronunciation [ə]; the *i* would be archaising.

fedels. Cf. §1.23–4 *primers*, n.

3. *quars* and *cors*. The first form seems to be a hypercorrection reflecting an early tendency [wa] → [o]; see *MCLT*, p. 27.

qui (*chi* in 5) and 4 *che* show the usual O.Cat. distinction between the subject and object relatives, but cf. §1.2 *que* n. For a more detailed treatment see *MCLT*, pp. 45–7.

4. *aveds*, *acaptareds* show an intermediate stage between -ĒTIS and the [ew] arrived at, via [dz] and then [ð], towards the end of the thirteenth century. For a more detailed explanation of this and related developments see *MCLT*, pp. 32–4, and J. Gulsoy, 'Nuevos datos sobre el imperativo segunda persona plural en catalán', *Boletín de la Sociedad Castellonense de Cultura*, XLIII (1967), pp. 153–77.

lo meu. Cf. §1.8 *suo*, n.

nomen seems at this date to be marginally more likely than *nome*.

5. *fortedes.* Cf. §1.6 *tenezones*, n.

acsi. Cf. §1.13 *agtan*, n.

6. *tenré.* O.Cat. long resisted, and some dialects resist still, the epenthetic *d* of the modern standard language; cf. the medieval forms in *MCLT*, glossary, s.v. [TENIR], [VALER], [VENIR], [VOLER].

Toponymy. See §2 above.

4

Pujol IV, *MCLT* 18(1) The *MCLT* version of this twelfth century text was transcribed from the facsimile of the document provided in Pujol's edition. A close comparison of my version with the original yielded two corrections: line 42 *teng-lo*, line 60 *Belvezer*.

More mature reflection has resolved the enigma of my reconstruction (ll. 47–8) *met-se en covenenza ab zos cavalers e ab los homens de PESQUELS PER fer dez seu*, where I invented a phantom toponym which I was not unnaturally unable to locate. After the conjunction *e* the phrase should read *ab los homens de pes* ('men of substance') *qu'el sper fer dez seu* ('so that he may hope to do what he wants'), or *qu'el sper[e] fer . . .* ('because he hopes . . .').

The toponyms are located in *MCLT*, pp. 243–50.

5

Pujol V. The original was not found, but Pujol's version as it stands is in places so misleading that we attempt a reconstruction here.

[*Relació d'alguns fets contra varies iglesies.—Segle XII.*]
R. de Ribes tol ecclesia de Ribes he de Fostega he de Chers Albs he de
Pardines, he totes les altres dentre la sua terra. El he Hug de Nava
[demaná] d'albergar he de forces ha fer als clergers. /² Gauceran
d'Urg trencá l'eglesia d'Adaç. B. d'Alb he Sanç qui sí han feit (*ed.*
feir) castel de l'eglesia d'Alb. N'Arsen d'Urg he En (*ed.* in) R. de
Castelbo macip qui albergen los (o)clergers forcivament (*ed.* forcuia
ment). /³ R. de Palerols hu mas ha Vila Labent. Arsen de Fula tol IIII
modios ha Ro . . . Sed. La donna de Macanos tol los alods [a] ecclesia de
Estol. Bacalars de Vilag tolgren lo mul /⁴ ad cap de scole. Raholf
Tarbera he so fil he·l monge de Cuxa qui tol ecclesia de Tartera.
B. Araculisa qui sa (*ed.* fa) ecclesia ha in Monte Cerdano a força del
bisbe.

Commentary
1. *Fostega* (mod. Fustanyà, Vall de Ribes, Ripollès) reflects the evolution
-ANU → [a], as do *Nava* (mod. Nevà, ibid.) and *Fula* (mod. Fullà, Conflent,
Pyr. Or.); cf. also *Castelbo*, mod. Castellbò, Alt Urgell. The graphy *g* in
Fostega, presumably representing [ɲ], recalls later spellings *Fusteya* and *Fustiya*
in the late thirteenth century Capbreu of the Vall de Ribes (*MCLT* 38).

dentre (mod. *dintre*) ← DE ĬNTRO. On the evolution of the tonic vowel see
J. Gulsoy 'Cat. *dins* y el problema de ĭ → *i*', *Romance Philology*, xviii (1964),
pp. 36-41. This particular example seems to have escaped his notice.

la sua. Cf. 4 *sa* and §1.8 *suo*, n.

[*demaná*] would supply this phrase with the verb it seems to need. It is not
inconceivable that a scribe, having just written *de naua*, might think he had already written a following *demana*. A singular verb with a plural subject is
parallelled in 4 *tol*.

clergers (mod. *clergues* ← CLERĬCOS) either reflects in a hypercorrection the
evolution [rs] → [s], or is a form not documented in the Catalan dictionaries
(listed in *MCLT*, p. 240) although known in Old French.

2. *Gauceran.* See §3.1 *Golceran*, n.

feit shows the retention of a diphthong from a late [aj]; the stage [ej] lasts
well into the fourteenth century, although cases of monophthongisation are
found by the end of the eleventh.

macip, like 4 *cap*, shows the devoicing of an earlier final [b]. Scribal practice
vacillates in this respect, but devoicing seems to have been general by the end
of the thirteenth century.

los is direct object of *albergen*, the sense being 'to whom the clergy are forced
to give hospitality'.

4. *cap de scole.* The final *-e* may represent a pronunciation [ə] of absolute
final *-a*, or may be a reminiscence of CAPŬT SCHŎLAE. Judging by examples in
S M L L—S

the *GMLC* the latter is the more likely conjecture, and the compilers suggest that the occurrence in our text may in fact be a more common *capud scole* misread by Pujol.

Araculisa (mod. Rigolisa, Cerdanya) appears to show a prosthetic vowel before initial *r*, a feature especially common in the Pyrenean area.

Toponymy. In the Vall de Ribes, RIPOLLÈS, are *Ribes*, mod. Ribes de Freser; *Fostega*, mod. Fustanyà; *Chers Albs*, mod. Queralbs; *Pardines*, mod. id.; *Nava*, mod. Nevà. In CERDANYA, to the north and north-west of the Vall de Ribes, are *Urg*, mod. Urtx; *Adaç*, mod. Das; *Alb*, mod. Alp; *Vila Labent*, mod. Vilallobent; *Estol*, mod. Estoll; *Vilag*, mod. Víllec; *Tartera*, mod. id.; *Araculisa*, mod. Rigolisa, and *Monte Cerdano*, mod. Puigcerdà. In ALT URGELL, to the west and south-west of Cerdanya, are *Castelbo*, mod. Castellbò, and *Sed*, mod. La Seu d'Urgell. In CONFLENT, Pyr. Or., are *Fula*, mod. Fullà, and *Cuxa*, mod. Cuixà. It has not proved possible to locate *Macanos*, but it may be mod. *La Maçana* in the Vall de Ribes. *Palerols* is most likely to be the place figuring to the south of Rigolisa in map I of Ramon d'Abadal i de Vinyals, *Catalunya carolíngia*, II, segona part, Barcelona, Institut d'Estudis Catalans, 1952, p. 489.

6

Pujol VI, *MCLT* 18(2). The original was not found, and mature reflection does not suggest the need for further comment upon or modification of the *MCLT* version.

7

Pujol VII.
[*Remembrança de les queixes dels homes d'Aiguatèbia (Conflent).—Principis del XIIIè segle.*]
{Hec *est* rememoracio *de* querimoniis *de* honines (*sic*) de Aqua Tepida.}
B. Od /² veger del comite levá *de* Els Pugals XVIII vacas, e nafrá I homi*ne* /³ *per* mo⟨r⟩t, e·l preborde dexé·s de la bestia e pres lo bajuli, e ac-ne CV sol. /⁴ P(*er*)ere Guilem *de* Vilafra*n*ca *per* I mul e *per* I garnaxa que vené /⁵ a·n Nunu CCC sol. pen⟨i⟩orá (*e XL ovelas). *P*er la ost d'Oltrera hac /⁶ B. Ot XXX sol. Altra vegada B. Ot [a] Aquatepida cavalcá e levá la *p*reda /⁷ e hac ne CC sol. e XL oveles que bareigá. (*Laeia) La meinada del /⁸ comte albergá ad Aquatepida CXX besties, e agren d'Els Pug /⁹ als XXX sol. Mes G. *de* Aniort albergá XV besties, Guile*m de* Çaporta les /¹⁰ i amená. Ponç d'Ixa albergá als Pugals II vegades e ag-ne XV sol. /¹¹ e ⟨V⟩XX sol. *de* Aqua Tepida. Los omes e les besties menare*n* a Cogols /¹² obrar ab comduit, e·l me*tex* comte albergá ad Aqua Tep⟨i⟩da (*a la ost /¹³ *de* So ab) a

l'emparar *de* So ab sa meinada. Al venir los ho*mines de* Vilafra*n* /¹⁴ ca
albe[r]gare*n* als Pujals. P*er de* Beders p*er* m*a*name*n*t *de* G. d'Aniort
(*p*er* I /¹⁵ ho*mine*) hac *de* nos L sol. p*er* I ho*mine* nostre q*ui* crem*d* III
cortals nostres / ¹⁶ metex. Al venir ades *de* Belvis B. Ot ab los aragones
hac *de* nos /¹⁷ LX sol. e·ls ho*mines de* Vilafra*n*[ca] albergare*n* ab nos al
venir: del primer /¹⁸ boage MC sol., del segon DCC sol., *de* altre
boage DCC sol . . .

Commentary

1. *Od.* Cf. 6 *Ot*, 3 *ac* (and §5.2 *macip*, n.) for devoicing of the final consonant.

2. *comite*, like *homine*, is latinising; cf. 8 *comte*, 11 *omes*.

Els arises from a reinforcement of enclitic ·*ls* ← ĪLLOS, on which see *MCLT*,
p. 44.

Pugals and 14 *Pujals* ← PODĪALES show common vacillation in the graphy for
[dʒ] or [ʒ], mod. standard [ʒ]. Cf. also 7 *bareigá*, and Alarcos, *Consideraciones*,
pp. 21–4.

vacas shows an unusual -*as* ← -AS, cf. 5 *ovelas*. In view of e.g. 7 *oveles*, 8
besties, 10 *vegades* it might be suspected that the final vowel was pronounced
[ə], as it is now in the eastern dialects.

3. *dexé·s* would appear to derive from a *DESCĒDIT SE 'dismounted' (cf. 4
vené ← VENDĪDIT). This verb is not documented in the dictionaries.

7. *bareigá* 'put to flight' would, according to the *DCEC*,¹⁰ derive from a
base VĔRRĒRE.

16. *aragones*, a normal phonetic development of ARAGONENSES, lacks a plural
marker. The medieval language also knew plural marked forms in -*es*, which
lacked a masculine *v*. feminine distinguishing feature. The modern standard
language has a m. *aragonesos*, which also occurs in the later medieval period.

Toponymy. Aqua Tepida, mod. Aiguatèbia, Conflent, Pyr. Or.; *Vilafranca*, mod.
Vilafranca de Conflent; *Oltrera*, Vallespir, Pyr. Or., now in ruins; *Ixa*, possibly
mod. La Guingueta (earlier La Guingueta d'Hix), Cerdanya Francesa, Pyr.
Or.; *Cogols*, mod. Cogullosa, Conflent, Pyr. Or.; *Beders*, mod. Béziers,
Hérault; *Belvis*, mod. Bellvís, La Noguera. It has not proved possible to locate
the following: *Els Pujals* (obviously near Aiguatèbia, and quite possibly not an
inhabited nucleus), *Aniort*, *Çaporta* (quite likely not a toponym, but possibly
Porta in French Cerdanya), *So*.

8

Pujol VIII, *MCLT* 27 (with some omissions). The *MCLT* version,
based on Pujol's, was the best that could be arrived at without seeing
the original text. Now that this has come to light a complete and more
reliable edition can be made.

10 Joan Coromines, *Diccionario crítico etimológico de la lengua castellana*, Bern,
1954–57. See s. v. *barajar*.

[*Mals causats a l'Iglesia de Puigfalconer (Pallars).—Any 1242.*]

Hec est memoria qe fa A. Borel de les contençons qui son estades entre
el e R. de Monçor /[2] e G. de Za Costa e·ls altres, per qe el ag a
eissir dez Pui Falchoner. In primis G. de Za /[3] Costa avie V ainels
e V porcels, e jo pregé-li qe me·n dés delme; e el dix-mi qe lo·n
soferís tro /[4] a l'altr'an. E fi·o, e ag-ne VII puis, e dix li qe me·n dés
delme, e no me·n v⟨o⟩lg donar, {e teng los az al /[5] berg} de G. de
Monçor. A cel altr'an s[í] ag-ne altres VII, e dix li e pregé-li qe me·n
donás lo delme, e dix /[6] qe no me·n darie gens. Co[n] foren III ans
dix-li e manné-li qe·m fermás dret tres vegades o qua /[7] tre, per tal
qar é per natura de l'eclesia e o devie fer. Dix qe no me·n fermarie res,
qe no·m tenie per/[8] seinor. Qaeg-me greu e ag-le·n a dir mal, e el
e·n R. de Mo[n]çor dixeren-me·n e feren-me·n, feri /[9] ren mi e pressren
mi [e] trencharen mi mon alberg e robaren la glesia—traseren·e pa e
forment, /[10] reqer(*e)(r)in·i mi ab bastons [e] ab sogovians qe jo·n
(n')ag a eissir ab lo vestiment vestid, qe no n'o /[11] sava eissir d'altrament.
Aqel dia eleis fo B. de Berga a Fonç, e pres ab els e ab mi qe lo dia de
Sen Mar /[12] (r)ch qe fossem a riba de Nugera, e el qe posarie·o si nos o
voliem. E no·ns en pog[re]m avenir /[13] per tal quar no i avie qui
tengés la mia rao. Manná·m R. de Burget qe li fermás dret, e jo /[14] dix
qe no, no·i avia agisad, for qe·m donás dia e qe seria·n agisad de
fermar e de respon /[15] dre. Ere divenres dia, [e] el dix qe lo dimenge
le·n fos agisad a Tremp, si no qe fos vedad; /[16] e a mi pareg mi qe i fos
mal jugad, qe a tercer dia donar no·m parie dret, e a di /[17] menge
sobre tot fom (for som?) falid, seinor, d'ajuda e omens de consel.
Foread e irad pregé /[18] a·n G. de Peralava qe los omens m'avien tolt
l'aver si el mis la orde i tolie, qe·m leissás /[19] morir no·m ere bel ni bo,
qe el a qual gisa podie qe·m trasqés de aqel trebal. E el /[20] parlá ab els
qe si anar me·n volia solt e quiti de totes coses qe fer o pogés, e qe /[21]
jaquisa l'eclesia. E jo pris l'assolta d'els per l'artiache, for anc aqesta
mia bocca no par /[22] lá qe renunciás, mes per lo mal qe om li avie feit
qe dix qe Deus i trametés /[23] malediccio, si els dien qe jo la e desfeita ni
endeutada quan jo·m n'emparé. P. de Zafont /[24] devie a A. Agilar
XXXII sol. e pagé-le·n jo XV sol., qe·m devie lo capela d'Orchau VII
sol. /[25] de forment, VIIII d'ordi e u[n] quintal d'oli. E devie a Blachet
III sol. de for[ment] per l'acapte del vispe /[26] e pagé·n jo VI sol., e
lesá-le·n B. de Burget la meitad de les exides e·l mas de B. Moix qe re
/[27] nu[n]ciás les ecclesies. Per tort qe·l capela d'Orchau tenie a la
ecclesia dez Pui fom en pleid em /[28] poder de B. de Burget, e ag n'a

fer missio, qe convengem al maestre V sol., e per aquels qe /²⁹
venem mig quintal d'oli. B. de Berga (e)refiná l'oli per decem sol., e
ag-ne B. de Burget VIII /³⁰ sol. e dos sol. de forment per tere, mes qe
la avia areda⟨d⟩ de besties groses e menudes e po /³¹ rcs e galines e
vexels e draps e areus d'alberg. E a perdud l'eclesia dez Pui e la /³² de
Fonç CCC ssacrifi[ci]s e de pus, e mil almones e pus remanides a donar,
/³³ tot per colpa de R. de Monçor; preg jo a Deu qe el lo·n leis penedir.
/³⁴ Veedors e oidors P. de Za Font, G. Riba, G. de Monçor, G. Picher,
/³⁵ P. de Riu, R. Pico e d'altres moltz, qe la vila dez Pui Falchoner
fo /³⁶ robada e trenccada qe no romás p[er] comunimenz de baile ni
de veins, /³⁷ e qe los omens de Fonç se·n mangaren un porc qui valie
be VIII sol. /³⁸ Tot aiço, sie be sie mal, fo feit per R. de Monçor, e
qe jo A. clerge i faré /³⁹ veritad cela qe sancta ecclesia vule per dret.
Actum est hoc M. CC. /⁴⁰ XLII. /⁴¹ Tot accest don e aqest destrig
met jo A. clerge in memoria a R. d'Orchat /⁴² qe·l deman qan
porá sens fi, qe jo no·n faré de mos dies vivenz senes els, /⁴³ qe tot
e ve[n]gud per G. de Za Costa e per R. de Monçor a l'eclesia dez
Pui.

Commentary

1. *contençons* (my cedilla) and not *contençoz* is clear in the original.

qui is here the normal form of the subject relative, *qe* that of the object (cf.
§3.3 *qui*, n.); 12 *qe* is to be viewed as introducing a completive clause, and 18
qe los is 'whose'—Catalan having lacked a derivative of cuïus.

2. *Za*, *dez* and 4 *az* show traces of the article from ïpse; see §1.2 *ipso*, n.,
and *MCLT*, p. 44.

3. *avie*, like 6 *darie*, 7 *devie*, etc., show the normal development of -ē(b)at
contrasting with 14 *avia*, *seria*, 20 *volia* ←-ē(b)a(m). In the modern standard
language the first and third persons singular of the imperfect are homophonic,
although this is not true of a number of the dialects. Our scribe's final vowels
may well have been for the first person [ə], for the third [e].

ainels ← agnĕllos, 8 *seinor* exemplify the most common representation of
[ɲ]; cf. for other possibilities §5.1 *Fostega*, n.

mi in this text occurs both as atonic direct object (ll. 9, 10) and as tonic and
atonic indirect object (ll. 3, 9, 11, 16 *a mi pareg mi*); a similar system operates in a
feudal oath reproduced in *MCLT* 7. Atonic *mi* does not occur when the original nexus was mĭhī ĭnde (→ *me·n*), nor when mē or mĭhī were enclitic to a
verb form ending in a vowel (13 *manná·m*), to *qe* (6 *qe·m fermás dret*, 19 *qe·m
trasqés*), or to *no* (7 *no·m tenie*, 16 *no·m parie*). The occurrence of *mi* or *m(e)* is
thus dictated by the phonetic context, as it is in the modern standard language:
me atonic, *mi* tonic.

The distribution of forms from ĭllī is the normal one of O.Cat.: ĭllī ĭnde →

le·n (8 *ag-le·n a dir mal*), but ĬLLĪ standing alone before or after the verb develops
to *li* (3 *pregé-li*, 13 *qe li fermás dret*).

4. *fi·o* ← FĒCĪ HOC, via *fiu·o*.

5. *cel* is more likely than *MCLT*'s *acel*. The ĬLLE demonstratives of O.Cat.
fall into two basic sets: *cel*, etc. ← *ECCE ĬLLU and *aquel*, etc. ← *ACCŬ ĬLLU.
Both are represented here, apparently indiscriminately: 5 *cel* (adj.), 11, 18
aqel (adj.), 28 *aqels* (pron.), 39 *cela* (adj.?). There is a third type, less common,
aicel(a), which appears to reflect usage north of the Pyrenees.

donás. Cf. 3, 4 *dés*.

6. *Co[n]*. Pujol had *eo*, separated *e o* in *MCLT*, but the original clearly shows *co*.

7. *per natura*. Pujol had an undocumented *pernates*. The abbreviation above
the *t* of the original is used by the scribe to represent *er*, *re*, *r*, *en*, *n* and *m*, which
does not make interpretation any easier.

8. *Qaeg*. Pujol had *que aegme greu*, regularised in *MCLT* as *que aeg-me greu*,
since this was the only solution open to me. The original shows the *q* to be no
more than a simple *q*, and the reading to be therefore *qaeg* (caeg) ← *CADĒDIT.
The *-d* or *-t* of an earlier *caded* or *cadet* would appear to have been replaced
by *-g* or *-c* through analogy with such common forms as *ag* ← HABŬIT,
deg ← DEBŬIT, etc. The loss of -D- before the stress is normal in O.Cat., and
contrasts with Provençal forms with *-z-* or *-s-*.

11. *eleis*—not Pujol's *eless*. The modern standard language prefers *mateix*,
cf. §7.16 *metex*.

12. *pog[re]m*. The original has *pogm* only. Given the scribe's habits, the most
likely missing abbreviation would be *re*, giving a past conditional form *pogrem*,
but the general sense of the passage seems to argue for a preterite, *pogem*.

17. *foread* is puzzling. The stem suggests FŎRIS or FŎRA, and the meaning
could well be something like 'put out, angry'.

18. *qe los* 'whose'.

l'aver. Pujol *laun* (from the scribe's *lau* plus his multi-purpose abbreviation),
accepted as *la un* in *MCLT* for lack of anything better.

el mis. Pujol and *MCLT* a clearly unsatisfactory *elimi*.

19. *qual*, M.Cat. *qualsevol*. Cf. §1.5 *quale que loco se volet*, 1.24 *quale que*
'whoever'.

21. *jaquisa* (first pers. s. imperf. subj.). The modern standard language shows
homophony between the first and third persons, e.g. *que jo (ell) dormís*, but
dialectally a distinction may still exist. Cf. 3 *avie*, n., for the situation in the
imperfect indicative.

26. *lesá*. The spelling is uncharacteristic, cf. 2 *eissir*, 11 *eleis*, 18 *leissás*, or 31
vexels.

27. *pleid*. The *d* is a hypercorrection, implying that the scribe's consistent
17 *irad*, 26 *meitad*, 28 *ag* conceal devoiced consonants.

30. *tere*. A spelling *r* for the result from -RR- is not uncommon (cf. *l* from
-LL-), but *-e* from absolute final -A is unusual this early.

aredad. At this period *aredada* would have been more likely, and is possibly what the scribe intended in view of e.g. 23 *la e desfeita ni endeutada.* On the other hand 31 *perdud* does not agree with the following *ssacrificis.*

Toponymy. The place names are located in *MCLT.*

9

Pujol ix, *MCLT* 29 (part). The original of this text was not found, and in view of the straightforward nature of its language Pujol's transcription provides no difficulty.

10

Pujol x reproduces the first twelve lines. The following is a transcription of the entire text taken from the original—badly faded but still readable.

[*Queixes contra Na Maria de Corsà.—1248, Febrer, 15.*]

Jo En P. Valenti me clam a vos En F. Zacosta, batle /² del senior bisbe en Sanaugia, de Na Maria de Corza que té les /³ coses de·n B. de Corza, les quals coses son a mi obligades per /⁴ rao de fermanza que feren a·n P. Pintor de XXX meins una /⁵ maz. per En G. de Ratera, de les quals dites maz. me clam a vos /⁶ per rao de Na Brunissen filia del davant dit En P. Pintor de /⁷ funt, que·ns en sie feita justicia e compliment de dret sal /⁸ ves totes mes raons e mes exceptions de crexer e de mir /⁹ var e de mudar tro a la fi del pleid. Anno domini M.CC.XLVIII. /¹⁰ XV k. marcii. /¹¹

Jo En P. Valenti me clam a vos En F. de Zaq⟨o⟩sta, batle del senior /¹² bisbe en Sanaugia, de Na Maria de Corza { d'aqueles cases /¹³ en que está, que son a mi obligades am totes les altres /¹⁴ coses qui foren de·n Ber. de Corza defunt per LXXX maz. /¹⁵ que·m devie, e de X maz. meins VIII sol. que·m foren jutga /¹⁶ des, salves totes mes raons e mes exceptions de crexer /¹⁷ e de mirvar e de mudar dentro a la fi del pleid. Anno domini /¹⁸ M.CC.XLVIII. XV k. marcii. /¹⁹

Aquests clams foren dads a Na Maria de Corza lo se /²⁰ gon dia de mag anno domini M.CC.XLVIII, al[s] quals ela /²¹ demana acord, lo qual libel deu aver.}

Commentary

2. *que* here seems to function as a conjunction rather than as a relative. The

same may be true of the second *que* in line 13, but the second one in line 15 is clearly a subject relative.

9. *tro*. Cf. 17 *dentro*.

13. *am*, more commonly *ab* in O.Cat. On the various forms taken by this preposition in the old and the modern language see J. Gulsoy, 'The descendants of Old Catalan and Provençal *ab* "with" ', *Revue de linguistique romane,* XXIX (1965), pp. 38–59.

Toponymy. Sanaugia, mod. Sanaüja, Segarra; *Corza,* mod. Corçà, La Noguera; *Ratera,* mod. id., Segarra.

The remainder of the twenty-eight documents Pujol published are, with one exception, letters written to the bishops of Seu d'Urgell. The exception is a fairly long text, written on both sides of the same piece of parchment (so that now much of the writing on the verso has been rubbed away), concerning heretical practices in Gósol (Berguedà). The text is particularly unusual in that it reproduces in direct speech the words of a number of the people concerned. I re-edit it below.

15

Pujol xv.

[Informe per qüestió d'heretges.—Any 1250.]

Anno d*omi*ni M.CC.L. Dix M*ari*a Pocha a·n G. clerge e a·n P. d'Anorra /² ca*n* los dava la primicia q*ue* fembres eretges ca*n* pregave*n* Deu ma*n*s /³ cubertes s'ajenolave*n*, e N'Ermesen d*e* Terrers fa aq*ue*l semblan*t* /⁴ ca*n*-(n)é en eglea. Dix M*ari*a Poca a·n G. c*ler*ge ja dit lo dia de Sen Vale*n* /⁵ ti dava*n*t so*n* fil q*ue* R*amo*na Fogeta dix ca*n* En Soler ere malaute /⁶ q*ue* tramesesen a·n Foget q*ue* vingés. E ca*n* el venie ere prim /⁷ son pasad, e viu les portes del castel desencadenar a Na /⁸ Barcelona q*ui*·n metie IIII homes q*ui* li fo semblan*t* q*ue* fosen /⁹ eretges. E Na Barcelona pregá·l q*ue* no·*n* fos dexelada, q*ue* amigs /¹⁰ eren, e el respós q*ue* saber o volrie.

'Diria·us·o si no-me·*n* dexela /¹¹ vets.'

'No faré.'

'Ja, azo é En Bla*n*c, e·n Talafer, e·n Guiamet /¹² es q*ui* vene*n* veer mo pare.'

E girá·s En Foget e viu-los entrar /¹³ en casa de·n Ferer drap*er*, e viu q*ue* ere*n* IIII homes. E l'e*n*dema /¹⁴ al vespre morie·s En Josa, e dix

Maria Poca a sa fila e a·n Miro que /[15] anasen veer qui·l vetlave, e els viuren lux tancad e·l malaute /[16] abian (*for* ab la u) d'aquels qui–l'abrigave. E·ncara ⟨dix *. . . ix⟩ mes Maria Poca aquel dia elex davan /[17] t son fil—que si no tornás En Pelicer a l'Agual que-s[e]·n entrave ⟨sa muler⟩ en aquel /[18] orde. Azo elex dix sa fila N'Aglea en casa de·n G. clerge davant Na /[19] Ripola e sa neta. E·ncara diren mes—que pocs albergs avie en Go /[20] sal que no·i tingesen. E·ncara dix Maria Poca que la vespra de Sen Valenti que /[21] veé X homes, e en aquels ere En Lorenz e Guiem son frare e·l ferer /[22] e G. Josa e P. Ferer e Ferer draper e R. de Serres, e fo–li semblant que tras⟨qesen⟩ /[23] los eretges de casa de·n R. de Serres. Dix Maria Poca que ab la muler d[e] B. de /[24] Riu e ab d'altres pastave a la casa de R. de Serres, e dix R. de Seres /[25] a R. de Bardines:

'Ara vos, compare, qui·us ensenave carera e·us /[26] tornave de mal a be?'

'Creuriets·o?'

'Oc jo volenters, for N'Amigo co /[27] neg.'

'Ara doncs calad, que trobad o avets.'

E respós la muler de·n Riu /[28] Na Maria Poca:

'Avets·o oid?'

'Oc, oid.'

Dix ela:

'Ai, mal dia·ls vinga! Si·ls costa /[29] va tant diner com feu a mon pare que–n'ag lo bispe ja no o preicarien /[30] tant com fan.'

Dix una fila de Na Vilela a Na Maria Poca que li dirie que a /[31] vie vist si no la·n dexel[a]ve.

'No faré. Ja, e que as vist?'

'Los promes qui son a ca /[32] sa de·n R. de Seres.'

Fo En G. clerge a casa de·n Balager e mogren–li questio, e dix Ferer /[33] draper:

'Negu clerge qui si metex no pod salvar, com pod salvar som poble? /[34] Que dig que negu clerge no p[o]d donar penitencia dreta a nul hom ne a /[35] neguna fembra pus a si elex no pod prod tenir.'

E respós Na Barce /[36] lona:

'Aquests eretges que axi encauze hom, qui·us en mostrave? En fe, com /[37] vos en cabtenriets?'

E el respós:

'No·ls quir ne·ls vul, que no (*·m a alt d) oizí /[38] anc que eretges feesen vertuds.'

E respós Ferer draper:

Pec sots, que nul hom /[39] qui entre em paradis torn[e] fer vertuts de
za.'

E respós G. clerge:

'Doncs /[40] frare Ponz, com fa Deus vertuds per el qui tam fort
encauza eretgia si tan /[41] bona orde tenen?'

E responeren Ferer draper e·n Balager e Na Barcenona /[42] que, ja
vertuds de frare Ponz no·ls pogesen proo tenir, que no·i avien lur /[43] fe.
Dix B. Paratge a·n G. clerge que no·s cuidare si les vesti[d]ures d'el
se fre /[44] gasen a celes dels eretges que el los aportás a mort. Azo dix
lo dia de Senta /[45] Maria de marz em plaza general davant la porta
de l'eglea. E respós R. /[46] de Seres que si el lo conseguie que el los
aportás a dexelament ne a mort que el lo /[47] pezejarie tot. Dix Na
Maria Martina a·n G. clerge que pocs albergs avie en Gosal qe /[48] . . .
no·i tingesen, 'que sí fa ma sor e mo cuniad e·l ferer e sa muler.' Dix
N'Aglesa /[49] en casa de·n G. clerge davant Na Ramona Ripola que pus
sant ere aquel cors axdubela /[50] . . . es que els donaven a pus sabeu que
aquel que·ls clerges donaven. //[51]

[verso]

Dix N'Aglesa a·n G. clerge lo jous . . . de . . . Maria de marz . . . /[52]
la vida dels eretges, e amonestá·l que el qe·i ti[n]gés, e axi aurie l'am /[53]
or de tots los omes de Gosal e aurie puxes tots sos drets /[54] d'els, 'que
pocs homes son qui rics sien qui no·i tingen, qe sí fa . . . /[55] ri'elex lo
bisbe. E pregaria Deu . . . que encara fose(s)ts bisbe de nos /[56] altres,
can be sapiats, En G. clerge, que pocs son en esta vila q . . . /[57] tingen.
E no ajats paor, que encara·us amarán tuit si vos i vo /[58] lets tenir. Per
estra sapiats be qe can vos mogés les paraule /[59] s que·ls eretges q'eren
a casa de·n R. de Seres, e jo qui i fui ab els /[60] tres vegades, e fa ta[n]
gran merce que·ls fa be ne . . . . /[61] que els pregen Deu per hom,
que en la vostra penitencia no·us . . . /[62] deds que·i aja nostra fe,
sino que·ns i venim per cuberta. E vos, /[63] si per aventura i voliets
tenir, vejats vos ab En Ferer draper e ab En /[64] R. de Seres e ab Na
Barcelona, e aprivadad vos-en ab els q[ue] els vos /[65] mostren. E asi
dien mal o be.'

Dix Na Maria Poca e sa fila Na Guialma /[66] e Na Maria Martina
a·n G. clerge que·n Josa e·n Gramened e·n Terrero /[67] que eren morts
en lur poder. Dix N'Aglaesa a·n G. clerge la ves /[68] pra de(·n) Se[n]
Jacme que estaven los bons homes a la casa /[69] de·n G. Maria, e trasc
los hom d'aquela casa lo dia de S /[70] en Felit e mes los hom en cela
de·n R. de Serres. /[71] E vengren tres e foren V, e estegren·i VIII dies, /[72]
e depuis aquels tres tornaren-se·n a Josa. D /[73] ix mes N'Aglesa, que

d'aquels bo[n]s homes que·n a /⁷⁴ vie a Solsona e a Agremunt e a Lerida
e a Sana /⁷⁵ uja e a La Sed e en la muntania de Prades e de Siurana.
/⁷⁶ E·l venres depuis Senta Maria d'agost dax (*for* dix) N'Aglesa a·n /⁷⁷
G. clerge que eren los bons homes a casa de B. Torner /⁷⁸ ... Torner ...
en la cavalcada de Ripol, e·n /⁷⁹ G. clerge aná a les garbes a aquela casa
per aestma ... /⁸⁰ trobá la muler e Na Ramona de l'Agual e coneg ...
/⁸¹ ... que·i eren. E al vespre torná·i En G. clerge per escolt ... /⁸² ...
a si·i eren, e costá·s·i per tal manera que·ls ozí fer ... /⁸³ ... enies, e·ls
ozí parlar e peure e pixar ... /⁸⁴ ... Aquel dia elex dix N'Aglesa
que ab En Gros ... der ... ... /⁸⁵ ... ... estads dos tres dies per la
fila, que no ere ... /⁸⁶ ... ... .fessada e dos homes ... ... /⁸⁷ ...
/⁸⁸ ... ... e·n Losada ... ... /⁸⁹ ab aquels qui ja s'i
eren e de ... ... /⁹⁰ ... en la val de ... ... /⁹¹ ...
/⁹² ... //

Commentary

1. *dava*. The O.Cat. third sing. imperf. more commonly ends in *-e*; cf.
notes §1.12 *monstre*, §8.3 *avie*. This text vacillates, though *-e* clearly predominates and is regular after *i*.

6. *tramesesen*, like 8 *fosen*, 15 *anasen* and all other examples of the imperf.
subj. show [s] unusually represented by *s* rather than *ss*.

7. *pasad*. Cf. notes §5.2 *macip*, §7.1 *Od*, §8.27 *pleid*. The scribe here shows
regularly *-d* in past participial forms and in the imperatives 27 *calad*, 64 *aprivadad*, but the devoicing of final consonants is betrayed in 39 *vertuts*.

10. *volrie*—cf. §3.6 *tenré*, n., and here also the substantive 76 *venres* ←
VENĔRIS.

10–11. *diria ... dexelavets* illustrates the normal O.Cat. structure for present-
cum-future conditions whether or not capable of realisation. Other examples
occur in lines 28–9 *costava ... preicarien*, 30–31 *dirie ... dexelave*, 46–7 *conseguie ... pezejarie*, 63 *voliets*.

13. *Ferer*. Cf. §8.30 *tere*, n., and e.g. the *Seres* ∼ *Serres* vacillation in line 24
of this text.

14. *vespre* is m. here, cf. 20 *la vespra*.

15. *lux*, clear in the original, is unusual. The normal O.Cat. evolution would
have been LUCE → [luð] →[luw], and a form *lud* appears in a late thirteenth
century text from Roussillon (see *MCLT* 41.15).

16. *elex*. Cf. 33 *si metex* ∼ 35 *si elex*, and §8.11 *eleis*, n.

17. *no tornás* has pluperfect sense ('had not come back') and in 'classical'
O.Cat. would be balanced here by a past conditional form *entrare* ('would
have entered') stemming from the C.L. pluperfect indicative. For another
example of an unrealised condition see 43–4: 'B. Paratge said to En G. priest
that he (B. P.) would not have thought (*no·s cuidare*) that if his (friar Ponz's)

vestments had brushed (*se fregasen*) against those of the heretics that he (friar Ponz) would have brought them (*los aportás*) to their deaths.' The subjunctive *aportás* instead of an indicative *aportare* is conditioned by the main verb of opining. The conditional clause system of O.Cat. is identical with that of O.Prov., on which see A.-J. Henrichsen, *Les Phrases hypothétiques en ancien occitan. Etude syntaxique*, in Universitet i Bergen Årbok, Historisk-antikvarisk rekke Nr. 2, 1955.

20. *no·i tingesen* 'did not hold (i.e. belong) to that order'. In O.Cat. the normal verb of possessing is, of course, *aver*.

21. *veé*. Cf. the strong perfect forms 7 *viu* and 15 *viuren*.

en. Cf. §10.13 *am*, n. If *en* here is from *ab* (← APUD) 'with', and not from ĬN (here 'among'), it is certainly the earliest example in Catalan. Gulsoy does not mention it in his article.

Guiem argues for a result [ʎ] from -LL-, absorbed by the preceding front vowel.

27. *calad*. See §3.4 *aveds*, n., *op. cit.*

35. *prod* is a conservative spelling, the reality at this period being [prow]— cf. 42 *proo* and 7 *viu* ← VĪDIT, but 75 *Sed* ← SEDE. Similarly conservative is 70 *Felit* ← FELĬCE—cf. 29 *feu*. Some other O.Cat. spellings with -*t* or -*d* for [w] are noted in *MCLT*, p. 33.

37. *oizí*, and 82 *ozí*. The result *z* from -D- is more proper to Pr ovençalthan it is to Catalan; cf. *MCLT*, pp. 33–4, and contrast above, 29 *preicarien*. The graphy *z* presumably represents here [dz], but the scribe also uses it throughout the text (except in learned words) for [ts]: 11 *azo*, 21 *Lorenz*, 36 *encauze*, 39 *za*, etc.

40. *tan*. Equally justifiable would be *tam*, in view of 40 *tam fort*, 39 *em paradis*, 33 *som poble*; similarly perhaps 29 *mom pare*.

42. *pogesen* is unusual—one expects *podien*.

43. *cuidare* is past conditional; see 17 *no tornás*, n.

44. *celes de*. Cf. 70 *cela de* but 69 *aquela casa*. The text shows forms in *aqu-* everywhere except before *de*.

51. *jous*. Cf. 76 *venres*. The modern language has *dijous*, *divendres*, etc.

55–6. *nos altres*. More normally *nos* in the medieval literary language except when used adversatively.

57 *tuit* as subject is common in O.Cat. but really belongs more properly to Provençal; cf. oblique 53 *tots* and 40 *Deus* ∼ 2 *Deu*.

83. *peure* appears, especially in view of the immediately following *pixar* 'to piss', to be a phonetically regular but otherwise undocumented Catalan derivative of PEDĔRE 'to fart'. Pujol has *penre*, a misreading.

Toponymy. Anorra, mod. Andorra; *Terrers*, probably mod. Tarrés, Garrigues; *Foget*, possibly mod. Foguet, Montsià; *Josa*, mod. Josa de Cadí, Alt Urgell; *Gosal*, mod. Gósol, Berguedà; *Vilela*, mod. Vilella, Berguedà; *Balager*, mod.

Balaguer, La Noguera; *Gramened*, mod. Gramenet, Pallars Jussà; *Solsona*, mod. id., Solsonès; *Agremunt*, mod. Agramunt, Urgell; *Lerida*, mod. Lleida, Segrià; *Sanauja*, mod. Sanaüja, Segarra; *La Sed*, mod. La Seu d'Urgell, Alt Urgell; *Prades*, mod. id., Baix Camp de Tarragona; *Siurana*, mod. Siurana de Prades, Priorat; *Ripol*, mod. Ripoll, Ripollès. The following have not been located: *l'Agual, Serres, Bardines, Terrero*.

There remain to be re-transcribed and considered the letters, seventeen in number, to the bishops of Seu d'Urgell—five to Bishop Ponz (1230–1257) and twelve to Bishop Abril (1257–69). These, of which I have been able to see thirteen of the originals, will be the object of a later study.

David J. Shirt
Chrétien de Troyes and the cart

Of all the romances of Chrétien de Troyes, his *Chevalier de la Charrete*[1] is undoubtedly the most paradoxical and ambiguous. The simple yet often graphic account of Lancelot's mission in the mysterious 'Land of No Return' gets to the heart of a problem which clearly fascinated and perplexed Chrétien's *salon* public – namely, to what extent, if at all, can the seemingly contradictory claims of feudal and courtly morality be explained? In order to direct attention to this problem, Chrétien makes the whole *raison d'être* for Lancelot's visit to Gorre totally ambiguous; the rescue of Queen Guinevere and King Arthur's captive subjects from the clutches of the villainous Meleagant gives Chrétien a splendid opportunity to demonstrate how, in one and the same act, Lancelot may possibly be attempting to serve two masters: his feudal lord, Arthur, on the one hand, and on the other, the God of Love. There are, however, never any serious doubts where Lancelot's true allegiance lies during his quest, for he regularly asserts that his own particular interest in this mission is the rescue of the queen and her alone. When his journey to Gorre is still in its early stages he confesses that his only interest in his quest is the rescue of Guinevere:

> Meüz sui por si grant afeire
> con por la reïne Guenievre.
> Ne doi mie avoir cuer de lievre
> quant por li sui an ceste queste . . .   [ll. 1098–101]

He reaffirms this aim later on when in answer to a vavassor's comment:

> An cest païs, ce cuit je bien,
> estes venuz por la reïne . . .   [ll. 2132–3]

Lancelot replies:

> Onques n'i ving por autre chose.

1 References are to *Le Chevalier de la Charrete*, ed. M. Roques, Paris (C.F.M.A), 1958.

Ne sai ou ma dame est anclose,
mes a li rescorre tesoil . . .   [ll. 2137-9]

Just after his arrival in Gorre and before the first battle with Meleagant,
as a result of which the queen is freed, Lancelot again admits, this time
to King Bademagu, that had it not been for Guinevere's presence in
Gorre he would never have set foot in the place:

autres besoinz ça ne m'amainne.   [l. 3347]

As we might expect, Guinevere is also firmly convinced that she
alone had inspired her lover's mission in Gorre:

qu'il vint an cest païs por moi . . .   [l. 4169]

Trop me fust ma joie estrangiee,
s'uns chevaliers an mon servise
eüst mort receüe et prise.   [ll. 4420-2]

However, Chrétien is careful to stress that it is only the two participants in the love affair who think that the dangerous journey to Gorre
has been undertaken solely in the service of Cupid. Various other
characters whom Lancelot meets on his travels see things in a rather
different light. This new note is first struck during Lancelot's visit to
the cemetery when he raises the tombstone. An old monk who had
watched Lancelot perform this feat explains that, as a result, Lancelot's
mission in Gorre will be successful in two ways: not only will
Guinevere be rescued but also the other prisoners will be freed as well:

Il vet secorre la reïne,
et il la secorra sanz dote,
et avoec li l'autre gent tote.   [ll. 1972-4]

The notion that Lancelot has undertaken his mission for the sake of the
common good is subsequently reiterated at several points in the
narrative:

Ce dïent an cest païs tuit
que il les deliverra toz . . .   [ll. 2300-1]

    Seignor, ce est cil
qui nos gitera toz d'essil
et de la grant maleürté
ou nos avons lonc tans esté . . .   [ll. 2413-16]

Before the first battle with Meleagant the girl prisoners fast for three
days and pray that God will grant Lancelot victory so that all the
unfortunate captives may be released:

por ce que Dex force et vertu
donast contre son aversaire
au chevalier, qui devoit faire
la bataille por les cheitis.   [ll. 3528–31]

After the battle, first the queen (l. 3877), then the prisoners (l. 3899)
are released; once the battle has taken place Chrétien is at great pains
to emphasise that the rescue of the queen and the rescue of the captives
is one and the same thing:

Par tot est la novele dite
que tote est la reïne quite
et delivré tuit li prison . . .   ]ll. 4107–9]

When he is fished out of the water, Gawain is informed of the twofold success of Lancelot's mission by some of the liberated prisoners:

Lanceloz del Lac, font se il,
qui passa au Pont de l'Espee;
si l'a resqueusse et delivree,
et, avoec, nos autres trestoz . . .   [ll. 5144–47]

The same news is likewise later reported to King Arthur:

Assez fu qui li sot retraire
comant Lanceloz a ovré,
comant par lui sont recovré
la reïne et tuit si prison.   [ll. 5346–49]

The outside world, therefore, sees a motivation behind Lancelot's
adventures which is quite different from that shared by the lovers
themselves. To restore to Arthur's safe keeping his queen and his
exiled subjects is the greatest public act of loyalty and devotion a feudal
servant could perform for his lord; this same act also constitutes the
greatest personal service a lover could render his lady. The paradox in
this romance is that these two forms of service, perfectly honourable
in themselves, cancel each other out: it is impossible for Lancelot to
be the perfect lover without, at the same time, insinuating himself into
his overlord's marriage bed, and yet he cannot retrieve the queen and
not seduce her in the process. Carefully—we might almost say, schematic-
ally—Chrétien invests Lancelot's mission in Gorre with this double
edge. In this ambiguous situation we know, of course, where the
lovers' interests lie; we know equally well where the prisoners' and
Arthur's interests lie; the really intriguing and more interesting point
is: do we know where Chrétien's interests lie?

Chrétien's personal attitude to the events related in this romance has long been the subject of scholarly speculation and interest. The various hypotheses and interpretations which we are offered by the critics are confusing and contradictory, and demonstrate, above all else, that Chrétien did his job well; the paradox surrounding Lancelot's expedition to Gorre has produced a plethora of even more paradoxical critical commentary.[2]

There could be no better illustration of this point than the treatment afforded by the critics to the cart episode. It would seem almost to state the obvious to point out that since Chrétien entitles his 'livre' *Del Chevalier de la Charrete* (l. 24) and since the poem is again referred to at the end by its continuator Godefroi de Lagny simply by the word *La Charrete* (l. 7103), Chrétien may have intended the cart to play more than an incidental role in the action of his romance. Such a view, however, has been expressed only by a mere handful of critics, such as Mme Lot-Borodine,[3] Cohen,[4] and more recently Diverres[5] and Holmes.[6] Of these, perhaps Mme Lot-Borodine is the most explicit; she suggests, although not without some hesitation, since her remarks on this point are rather discreetly confined to three footnotes, that the title of the romance 'exprime clairement l'idée directrice de toute l'œuvre';[7] at another point this same critic comments that the cart 'peut vraiment être appelé le *leitmotiv* de notre roman'.[8] Unfortunately, neither Mme Lot-Borodine nor any other critic develops this idea any further.

A completely contrary view is taken by Micha and Southward. For Micha the cart is, if anything, of only marginal importance in the romance, almost an irrelevance.[9] Southward is more outspoken in her opinions; she considers Chrétien's title to be 'illogical' and the cart 'one of the most pointless . . . trimmings' of the romance.[10] Such a view

2 The various conflicting views are neatly and conveniently summarised by F. D. Kelly, '*Sens*' *and* '*Conjointure*' *in the* '*Chevalier de la Charrette*', The Hague and Paris, 1966, pp. 4–21.

3 M. Lot-Borodine, *La Femme et l'amour au XIIe siècle, d'après les poèmes de Chrétien de Troyes*, Paris 1909, p. 155, n. 1; p. 158, n. 1; p. 177, n. 1.

4 G. Cohen, *Chrétien de Troyes et son œuvre*, Paris, 1931, p. 277 and p. 282.

5 A. H. Diverres, 'Some thoughts on the *sens* of *Le Chevalier de la Charrette*', *Forum for Modern Language Studies*, VI (1970), p. 25.

6 U. T. Holmes, *Chrétien de Troyes*, New York, 1970, p. 98.

7 M. Lot-Borodine, *op. cit.*, p. 155, n. 1.   8 *Ibid.*, p. 158, n. 1.

9 A. Micha, 'Sur les sources de la *Charrette*', *Romania*, LXXI (1950), pp. 345–58, especially p. 345: 'le reste, y compris l'épisode de la Charrette, n'est qu'accessoire'.

10 E. Southward, 'The unity of Chrétien's *Lancelot*', *Mélanges . . . Mario Roques*,

is unjustified and somewhat nonsensical, for Lancelot without the cart is almost as inconceivable as Roland without the horn or Tristan without the 'lovendrinc'. Fortunately, such eccentric opinions are shared by but a few commentators and most critics are inclined to admit that the cart is somehow or other important in the action of the poem, although a glance at recent work by critics such as Kelly Sargent, Rychner, Condren, Diverres, Fowler and Bogdanow[11] show that there is no unanimity on this question. And yet, although many critics talk freely about the significance of the cart episode in the romance as a whole, no one, up to now, has produced a convincing explanation of the cart episode as such; there have, of course, been several attempts to explain the *origin* of the cart[12] but, it must be admitted, such explanations are largely irrelevant when they fail to show that precise *function* Chrétien intended the cart to have in this specific context. Those few critics who have tried to deal with the cart episode are either simply evasive[13] or they shift the blame for their shortcomings as critics on to what they consider to be Chrétien's lack of artistry.[14] A re-examination of the cart episode in this romance requires, it would seem, no further justification. Several problems call for consideration in the course of such an investigation: firstly, what does the cart episode mean in itself? secondly, what bearing does this episode have on the remainder of the romance? thirdly, is there anything in the cart episode which could give us any indication of Chrétien's personal attitude towards his subject-matter? finally, how

Paris, 1953, II, p. 289. M. Roques, introduction, p. xxvi, also states that the cart 'ne joue pas de rôle utile après les premières scènes'.

11 Kelly, *op. cit.*; B. N. Sargent, 'L' "autre" chez Chrétien de Troyes', *Cahiers de civilisation médiévale*, X (1967), pp. 199–205; E. I. Condren, 'The paradox of Chrétien's *Lancelot*, *Modern Language Notes*, LXXXV (1970), pp. 434–53; Diverres, *op. cit.*; D. C. Fowler, 'L'Amour dans le *Lancelot* de Chrétien', *Romania*, XCI (1970), pp. 378–91; F. Bogdanow, 'The love theme in Chrétien de Troyes' *Chevalier de la Charrette*', *Modern Language Review*, LXVII (1972), pp. 50–61.

12 These are summarised and discussed by C. Foulon, 'Les Deux Humiliations de Lancelot', *Bulletin bibliographique de la Société internationale arthurienne*, VIII (1957), pp. 81–6.

13 Cf. J. Rychner, 'Le Sujet et la signification du *Chevalier de la Charrette*', *Vox Romanica*, XXVII (1968), p. 75.

14 Cf. R. S. Loomis, *Arthurian Tradition and Chrétien de Troyes*, New York, 1949, p. 214, says that 'the elements have been so garbled and shuffled . . .' Roques, introduction, p. xi, comments that the cart episode is 'sans grande clarté'.

far does the treatment of this particular episode contribute to the paradoxical nature of the romance as a whole?

The cart episode falls into two parts; during the first, ll. 314–77, the cart is described and Lancelot gets in; the second part of the episode, ll. 378–444, deals with Lancelot's cart journey to a castle and his reception there, and ends with the sudden disappearance of the cart.

The first part of the episode opens with a description of Gawain's seeing an unknown, unnamed and altogether faceless knight in full armour (to whom he had previously given a horse but whom he had not recognised as Lancelot) walking behind a cart (ll. 314–20). After stressing the fact that Lancelot's identity is completely concealed, Chrétien then intervenes in the narrative to give an explanation of what the cart was and what it was used for (ll. 321–44). He begins by stating that it was used 'lores', by which he presumably means in King Arthur's day in the kingdom of Logres, in the same way as the pillory is used in his own time; he then goes on to explain that although the pillory has taken over this specific function of the cart, carts as such have not disappeared; on the contrary, they are a common sight in every town. Next Chrétien again informs us that the cart to which he is referring was used 'a cel tans' in the same way as he claims the pillory is used in his own time; he elaborates further on the functions of the *charrete*, saying that it was used to transport criminals such as murderers (l. 328), robbers (alluded to twice in l. 328 and l. 330), and those defeated in judicial combat (l. 329). Criminals of this ilk were put in the cart and drawn through the streets in it; they were also deprived of their feudal privileges, 'enors', and no longer had any judicial rights (ll. 337–8). According to Chrétien, the cart was 'cruex', an epithet which suggests that it might have caused extreme physical discomfort to its occupant;[15] the author also explains that the cart was sometimes considered a sign of bad luck; this is why it is customary for some people to cross themselves when they see it and adopt a 'there but for the grace of God go I' attitude. Chrétien gives us more details about the physical appearance of the cart; 'sor les limons' there is a character who is no newcomer to his romances,[16] an ugly dwarf

---

15 Chrétien uses this word in a similar way, l. 2709, l. 3295 and l. 4204.
16 Cf. *Erec.* ed. Roques, ll. 145–8:

> devant ax, sor un grant roncin,
> venoit uns nains tot le chemin
> et ot et sa main aportee
> une corgiee an son noee.

who like a 'charreton' wields a big stick. From this description most
commentators almost automatically assume that Chrétien thought of
his *charrete* as a horse-drawn conveyance; this point will be discussed
later but here it is enough to say that there is nowhere in this account
any mention of a horse in so many words. Lancelot asks the dwarf if
he has seen Guinevere, and the dwarf offers to help him find her on
condition that the knight gets on the cart. After some deliberation
Lancelot jumps into the cart (l. 375).

At the beginning of the second part of this episode Gawain finds
Lancelot sitting in the cart being driven along by the dwarf. He
refuses to get into the cart himself but instead follows it at a safe
distance. Eventually, late in the afternoon, the cart and its occupant
come to a castle, where the people jeer and insult Lancelot as he is
carted through the streets (ll. 404–9). Their behaviour is a little surprising, since it does not altogether fit in with what Chrétien has said
previously about the sight of the cart inspiring the beholder with
God-fearing respect. The townspeople immediately assume that
Lancelot is on the way to be executed and they ask what death he
is going to die:

> A quel martire
> sera cist chevaliers randuz?
> Iert il escorchiez, ou panduz,
> noiez, ou ars an feu d'espines?   [ll. 410–13]

They also wonder what crime he has committed, and it is interesting to
note that the three criminal offences which Chrétien has previously
listed in the first part of this episode are all mentioned again:

> Est il de larrecin provez?
> Est il murtriers, ou chanp cheüz?   [ll. 416–17]

The dwarf, however, is not prepared to satisfy their curiosity; he drives
on to take Lancelot into the keep of the castle, where they are met
by three maidens. Once again the dwarf is asked what crime Lancelot
has perpetrated to merit public exposure in the cart:

> Nains, qu'a cist chevaliers meffet
> que tu mainnes come contret?   [ll. 438–40]

Instead of answering their question the dwarf makes Lancelot get down
from the cart, whereupon he drives off, never to be seen again.

A dwarf armed with a 'corgiees' also appears in *Yvain*, ed. Roques, ll. 4097–103.
Cf. also Kelly, *op. cit.*, p. 110, n. 15.

To explain away this episode as an absurd and even ridiculous
excursion by Chrétien into the realms of fantasy, as some critics do,[17]
is surely greatly to underrate Chrétien's talents as a writer. It also seems
rather improbable that a writer like Chrétien, who is usually extremely careful and attentive when it comes to presenting contemporary habits and customs to his aristocratic public, should base the
whole of a romance around an episode in which he deliberately sets
out to hoodwink his audience by dressing up a pack of lies as authentic
legal 'history'. Elsewhere in this romance, and notably in the episode
describing Lancelot's judicial combat with Meleagant, Chrétien
demonstrates a very detailed and exact knowledge of current legal
practices. At one point he even parades his knowledge of legal jargon:

> Et Lanceloz dist: 'Sire rois,
> je sai de quauses, et de lois,
> et de plez, et de jugemanz . . .   [ll. 4943-5]

Consequently, Rychner is probably very near the truth when he
remarks concerning the cart, 'cette charrette leur [i.e. Chrétien's con-
temporaries] disait sans doute plus de choses qu'à nous'.[18] If, for the
moment, it can be accepted that Chrétien may have based the cart
episode on some contemporary practice, several features in it call for
comment and explanation. Chrétien states that a cart was no longer
in use in his day to punish the sort of malefactors who were dealt with
by the pillory. He then states, on two separate occasions, that the sort
of people who were normally put in the cart were those who were
guilty of a capital offence and were, in fact, on their way to be executed. Chrétien's cart appears, then, to have been an instrument of
punishment in itself—it is 'cruex' and a ride in it is a humiliating,
degrading experience—but it is also a means of conveying convicted
criminals to the gallows—its associations with death cause it to be
feared and considered as an evil omen. How far does our knowledge
of medieval French legal practices help to elucidate this apparently
contradictory and confusing episode?[19] In this connection we come

17 G. Paris, 'Le Conte de la Charrette', *Romania*, XII (1883), p. 513 claims that
   Chrétien's explanation of the episode is 'bizarre'; A. Pauphilet, *Le Legs du
   moyen âge*, Melun, 1950, p. 147, comments: 'Son explication . . . ne répond
   à rien et est, au fond, assez absurde'; Roques, introduction, p. xxvi says,
   'l'on est tenté de l'attribuer à la seule imagination de l'auteur à la recherche
   d'une circonstance fâcheuse pour son héros'.
18 Rychner, *op. cit.*, p. 75.
19 F. C. Riedel, *Crime and Punishment in the Old French Romances*, New York,

across an initial stumbling block, namely a lack of documentary legal evidence for twelfth century France. The earliest handbook on the law or 'custumal' which has survived, the *Très Ancien Coutumier de Normandie*, dates from the period 1194–1204,[20] but its appearance was soon followed by that of several others,[21] including Beaumanoir's invaluable *Coutumes de Beauvais* (1280–83).[22] It is, however, generally agreed that the custumals codified practices which had changed little over the years and that they can be used as a guide to twelfth century as well as thirteenth century custom.[23]

Custumals from this period generally make a clear-cut distinction between two types of criminal offence—the serious crimes, the *causae majores*, punishable by loss of life and coming within the jurisdiction of High Justice, and the minor offences or misdemeanours, the *causae minores*, generally dealt with by the processes of Low Justice and punishable by loss of limb, the brand, some form of public degradation, or a fine.[24] A charter of 1153 from Sceaux-en-Gâtinais lists the serious crimes, *majores malificii*, as 'homicidium, proditio, furtum, raptum mulierum'.[25] The *Très Ancien Coutumier de Normandie* states: 'De larrecin, de murtre, de traïson ... de roberie ne puet nule pes estre fete o ceus qui en sont convaincu; mes se il sont pris, il soient pandu'.[26] Later on in the thirteenth century Beaumanoir includes a similar list of hanging offences in his catalogue of *criemes*: 'Quiconques est pris en

---

1938, and P. Jonin, *Les Personnages féminins dans les romans français de Tristan*, Aix, 1958, pp. 59–138, both show that in their treatment of law and custom many romance writers adhere remarkably closely to contemporary practice.

20 E. J. Tardif, *Le Très Ancien Coutumier de Normandie*, Rouen, 1903.

21 Cf. E. Chénon, *Histoire générale du droit français public et privé*, Paris, 1926, pp. 553–7; F. Olivier-Martin, *Histoire du droit français des origines à la Révolution*, Paris, 1951, pp. 112–18.

22 Philippe de Beaumanoir, *Les Coutumes de Beauvoisis*, ed. A. Beugnot, Paris 1842.

23 Jonin, *op. cit.*, p. 61: 'Il faut enfin ajouter que bien souvent les faits rapportés par les coutumiers le sont très longtemps après la date à laquelle ils se sont produits.'

24 Cf. A. Gautier, *Précis de l'histoire du droit français*, Paris 1882, p. 151; C. L. von Bar, *A History of Continental Criminal Law*, trans. T. S. Bell, London, 1916, pp. 146–97; Olivier-Martin, *op. cit.*, p. 141.

25 Cited by A. Luchaire, *Histoire des institutions monarchiques de la France sous les premiers capétiens, 987–1180*, Paris, 1883, p. 221. In the *Leges Henrici* passed in England between 1108–18, the following major crimes are listed: 'Furtum vero et proditio et murdrum ...' (cited by W. Stubbs, *Select Charters*, 4th edn., Oxford, 1891, pp. 106–7).   26 *Op. cit.*, p. 28.

cas de crieme et atains du cas si comme de murdre ou de traïson, d'omicide ou de feme efforcier, il doit estres trainés et pendus ... Qui emble autrui coze, il doit estre pendus.'[27] Murder, robbery, treason and rape are the principal *causae majores* for which the death penalty could be invoked at this period, although there are others as well, notably arson.[28] If we now turn to the cart episode in Chrétien's poem, we find that two of the *causae majores*, robbery and murder, are mentioned on two separate occasions (ll. 328–32 and 416–17) as offences for which one could be put into the cart; there is, however, no mention in Roques's edition of the text of the crimes of rape or treason. The omission of rape might be explained on the grounds that a great deal of the action of the poem preceding the cart episode has already illustrated the crime of rape—the abduction of the Queen by Meleagant —and there is no need to labour this point further. It is the omission from Roques's text of the crime of treason which is interesting;[29] Foerster's edition of the poem,[30] which is based at this point on ms. T (B.N. f. fr. 12560) has a different reading from ms. C (B.N. f. fr. 794), the base ms. for Roques's edition. In Foerster ll. 330–4 read:

> Qui traïson ou murtre font,
> Et as ceus qui sont chanp chëu,
> Et as larrons qui ont ëu
> Autrui avoir par larrecin
> Ou tolu par force an chemin.

This compares with Roques, ll. 328–32:

> a ces qui murtre et larron sont,
> et a ces qui sont chanp cheü,
> et as larrons qui ont eü
> autrui avoir par larrecin
> ou tolu par force an chemin ...

The only difference between these two passages is that ms. T includes treason in the list of 'cartable' crimes whereas ms. C avoids mentioning the word and can only do so by rather clumsily repeating the same

27 Beaumanoir, I, pp. 411–13.
28 Cf. von Bar, *op. cit.*, pp. 188–9; Chénon, *op. cit.*, p. 656; F. Pollock and F. W. Maitland, *A History of English Law*, Cambridge, I, 1898; II, 1911, II, pp. 470 and 511.
29 Cf. Riedel, *op. cit.*, pp. 19–26, and Pollock and Maitland, *op. cit.*, II, pp. 462– 511, for a discussion on the meaning of treason.
30 Christian von Troyes, *Sämtliche erhaltene Werke*, IV, *Der Karrenritter und das Wilhelmsleben*, ed. W. Foerster, Halle, 1899.

word, *larron*, twice. Vinaver has already shown[31] that some thirty lines later on in this same passage Foerster's reading is preferable to that of Roques, and it may be that ms. T is to be preferred to ms. C at this point as well.[32] But why did the scribe of ms. C feel it necessary to adopt a reading which avoided all mention of treason? Did he, for example, feel that it was rather indelicate at this point in the romance to associate Lancelot with the one capital crime he was in fact about to commit—namely the seduction of his overlord's wife?[33] It is quite clear that Chrétien himself was all too aware that fornication with the wife of one's overlord constituted a treasonable offence. This point emerges in the scene in which Meleagant accuses the wounded Kay of having slept with Guinevere:

> Le roi Artus a Kex traï
> son seignor, qui tant le creoit
> que comandee li avoit
> la rien que plus ainme an cest monde.   [ll. 4854-7]

We are reminded here of the other famous occasion in Arthurian romance, described by Wace in his *Brut*, when Guinevere committed adultery with Arthur's nephew, Mordred; Mordred is severely castigated by Wace:

> Aprés ceste grant felenie
> Fist Mordrez altre vilenie,
> Car, contre crestïene loi,
> Prist a son lit fame le roi,
> Fame son oncle et son seignor
> Prist a guise de traïtor.[34]

31 E. Vinaver, 'Les Deux Pas de Lancelot', *Mélanges . . . Jean Fourquet*, Munich and Paris, 1969, pp. 355–61.

32 Foerster's reading is adopted by J. Frappier, *Le Chevalier de la Charrette*, Paris, 1962, a translation into modern French of Roques's edition of the romance, see p. 13. Cohen, *op. cit.*, p. 229, also bases his comments on Foerster's reading.

33 Cf. Britton, *Summa de legibus Angliae*, London, 1540, ch. 8, 'De Treson' p. 21: 'Et le jugement de graund treson est de estre treyne et de suffrir mort pur la felonie et meme le jugement doit encontre ceux coure: que par appels de felonie sont atteyntz que ilz eient le seal lour seigneur countrefait ou autrement fause ou del avoutrie des femmes lour seigniours ou del purgiser des filles lour seigniours. . . .' cf. also Riedel, *op. cit.*, p. 149; Pollock and Maitland, *op. cit.*, II, p. 504: 'treason gathered round it and embraced some offences which can be regarded as the vilest breaches of the vassal's troth, such as adultery with the lord's wife, violation of his daughter, forgery of his seal'.

34 Wace, *La Partie arthurienne du roman de Brut*, ed. I. D. O. Arnold and M. M. Pelan, Paris, 1962, ll. 4463–8.

In *Cligès*, the romance which preceded *Le Chevalier de la Charrete*,
Chrétien had already made his feelings on adultery known; the deception practised by Fénice on Alis, her 'husband' and uncle and overlord
of her lover, Cligès, is qualified as 'traïson'.[35] In the light of Chrétien's
plainly disapproving attitude towards adultery between a vassal and
the wife of his overlord, if the reading of ms. T is to be accepted in
this part of the cart episode, it would seem that once again, but this
time in a rather more oblique way, Chrétien is drawing the attention
of his audience to the criminal nature of adultery, and more particularly to the treason inherent in Lancelot's mission to Gorre. But which-
ever ms. reading we accept as being correct, it is clear that in the cart
episode Chrétien deliberately associates his hero with two and possibly
three *causae majores* which were usually punishable by death and for-
feiture of lands and possessions.[36] But here we come across a puzzling
discrepancy in Chrétien's account of his *charrete*. If, as we hope to have
shown, Chrétien had a gallows cart in mind when he composed this
part of his romance, why does he say that in his day the cart was no
longer in use, and that its previous functions had been assumed by the
pillory? The known facts support neither of Chrétien's contentions.
We have found no instances from this period of the Middle Ages
where the pillory was used in connection with the execution of a
capital sentence; we have also found that the gallows cart was regularly
used to convey criminals to their place of execution and very often it
served as a 'drop'.[37] A gallows cart even makes an appearance in
romance: in Jean Maillart's *Roman du Comte d'Anjou* the wicked aunt
who is convicted of treason at the court of the Count of Bourges is
conveyed to the stake in a cart:

> A la prison vont sanz actendre.
> Hors la traient par l'eschelete;
> Mise l'ont en unne charete,
> Au feu s'en vont droite la voie.[38]

35 *Cligès*, ed. A. Micha, Paris (C.F.M.A.), 1962, l. 6651. Cf. also H. Euler,
   Recht und Staat in den Romanen des Crestien von Troyes, Marburg, 1906,
   p. 85, and Riedel, *op. cit.*, p. 64.
36 Cf. Beaumanoir, I, p. 412: 'et si meffet tout le sien quanques il a vaillant, et
   vient le forfeture au segneur desoz qui il est trouvés'. Cf. also Pollock and
   Maitland, *op. cit.*, II, p. 466.
37 Cf. P. Lacroix, *Moeurs, usages et costumes au moyen âge*, Paris, 1873, p. 455;
   L. Radzinowicz, *A History of English Criminal Law*, London, 1948–68, I,
   pp. 171–203.
38 *Le Roman du Comte d'Anjou*, ed. M. Roques, Paris, C.F.M.A., 1931, ll. 7810–13.

In Chrétien's romance it is not solely in the cart episode itself that the cart is closely identified with imminent death. Later on in the work, when Lancelot has just glimpsed Guinevere's procession and has tried to throw himself from a tower, a girl who has observed this behaviour remarks:

> don n'iert seüe la novele
> par tot de la maleürté
> qu'il a en la charrete esté?
> Bien doit voloir qu'il fust ocis,
> que mialz valdroit il morz que vis . . .   [ll. 576–80]

The boastful knight prefers death at the hand of Lancelot to a ride in the cart:

> Mialz voldroie estre, je cuit, morz
> que fet eüsse cest meschief.   [ll. 2774–5]

Perhaps Bademagu has this aspect of Lancelot's cart journey in mind when he says to Guinevere:

> Certes vos avez trop mespris
> d'ome qui tant vos a servie
> qu'an ceste oirre a sovant sa vie
> por vos mise an mortel peril . . .   [ll. 3950–3]

If we now turn from the capital offences and the gallows cart to the *causae minores*, we find that these less serious crimes were punished in a variety of ways. One of these was the use of the pillory, *collistrigium* or 'stretch-neck'—an instrument of punishment which consisted of a wooden post and frame arranged in such a way that an offender was kept standing behind it, his head and hands protruding through holes, so that he could be exposed to public scorn and degradation.[39] The pillory was certainly in existence in Chrétien's day,[40] and among the offences which could be punished by exposure in this instrument of punishment were the giving of false measure,[41] blaspheming,[42]

---

39 Cf. Lacroix, *op. cit.*, p. 458; L. Jewitt, 'The pillory and whom they put in it', *Reliquary*, I (1861), pp. 209–24; W. A. Andrews, *Punishments in the Olden Time*, Hull, 1881, pp. 50ff; *id.*, *Old-time Punishments*, Hull, 1890, pp. 63–89.

40 Cf. Godefroy, *Dictionnaire*, X, p. 339b; von Wartburg, *Französisches etymologisches Wörterbuch*, VIII, p. 478a.

41 Jewitt, *op. cit.*, p. 210; Andrews, *Old-time Punishments*, p. 69; Pollock and Maitland, *op. cit.*, II, p. 518.

42 von Bar, *op. cit.*, pp. 184 and 190.

certain types of forgery and bearing false witness,[43] slander and scandalmongering,[44] lewd behaviour[45] and adultery.[46] As well as being used in France, the pillory was also in use in England during the Middle Ages: the right to possess a pillory is mentioned in a charter granted by Henry I in the first quarter of the twelfth century to the monks of Middleton, in Dorset,[47] but its ancestry can be traced much further back to the 'healfang' or 'halsfang', literally, 'catch-neck', mentioned in the Anglo-Saxon laws of Withred in the seventh century.[48] A closer examination of legal documents relating to England reveals a most interesting feature which is entirely absent from legal documents intended for Continental use. In many English documents from the period the use of the pillory is coupled with that of another instrument of punishment, the *tumb(e)rellum*, the 'tumbril' or 'tumbrel'; both pillory and tumbril seem to have been used in England to punish similar types of misdemeanour. The celebrated thirteenth century jurist Bracton, in his *De legibus et consuetudinibus Angliae* (1250-58), talks of 'poena corporalis, scilicet pilloralis vel twymboralis'[49] and recommends for *crimina minora* the following punishments: 'fustigationem . . . vel poenam pilloralem vel twymboralem . . .'[50] Another justice, Britton, in his *Summa de legibus Angliae* (c. 1290), which in spite of its Latin title is the first great treatise on the law of England written in French, refers to the 'juise de pillori ou de tumberel'.[51] The 'Statute of Pillory and Tumbril', or, to give it its Latin title, *Judicium pillorie vel tumbrelli*, is generally thought to have been enacted by Henry III in 1266;[52] subsequently this statute is

43 Jewitt, *op. cit.*, p. 210; von Bar, *op. cit.*, pp. 174 and 190; Beaumanoir, I, p. 424: 'Qui porte faus tesmoins et en est atains, il doit estre tenus en longe prison et puis estre mis en l'esquele devant le pille.'
44 Jewitt, *op. cit.*, p. 213; Andrews, *Punishments in the Olden Time*, p. 50.
45 Jewitt, *op. cit.*, pp. 210 and 213; Andrews, *Punishments in the Olden Time*, p. 50.
46 Andrews, *Old-time Punishments*, p. 69; Pollock and Maitland, *op. cit.*, II, p. 544. Generally, however, adultery, along with fornication, incest and bigamy, was considered as an ecclesiastical offence and tried by canon law. Cf. Pollock and Maitland, *op. cit.*, II, pp. 543-4; von Bar, *op. cit.*, p. 170; Riedel, *op. cit.*, p. 64; Jonin, *op. cit.*, pp. 67-71.
47 Cf. W. Dugdale, *Monasticon Anglicanum*, London, 1891, II, p. 351.
48 Jewitt, *op. cit.*, p. 210.
49 Bracton, *De legibus et consuetudinibus Angliae*, ed. G. E. Woodbine, Cambridge, Mass., 1968, II, p. 340.   50 *Ibid.*, pp. 290 and 299.
51 Britton, ch. 19, 'De Fraunchises', p. 35.
52 *Statutes of the Realm*, London, 1810-28, I, pp. 201-2; the date of the statute is uncertain but it is generally ascribed to 51 Hen. III. Cf. also Jewitt, *op. cit.*, p. 211.

often cited, as, for instance, in a charter from the reign of Edward I: 'In tertio transgressu habeant judicium de pillorio vel tumberello.'[53] The right to possess a tumbril, along with a pillory and gallows, is often mentioned as a beneficial franchise which could be claimed by the lord of the manor; a typical example is the following charter granted in 1293 to the lord of the manor of Barnard Castle in County Durham: 'Item Johannes rex Scotiae habet apud Castrum Bernardi infra praedictas libertates: mercatum, feriam, pillorium et tumberell, furcas . . .'[54]

The nature and function of the tumbril have been the object of investigation by several antiquarians.[55] It appears to have been a mobile ducking stool, fitted with two wheels and two long poles forming shafts to which a chair was attached in which the offender had to sit —generally he or she was fastened to the chair; the tumbril was then drawn, sometimes pushed, through the town so that its occupant could be exposed to the mockery and derision of the public. Sometimes, though not inevitably, a ride in this conveyance ended with a public ducking of the offender in the local duck-pond or river; in this case the person drawing or pushing the tumbril let go of the shafts and upended the chair. It is especially interesting to note that in some parts of England this contraption was occasionally called the 'scolding cart',[56] since it was considered to be a particularly effective way of punishing gossips and quarrelsome women. Like the pillory, the tumbril seems to have been in use early on in the Middle Ages in England. Domesday Book contains a reference to a *cathedra stercoralis* employed in Chester to punish fraudulent alewives, and this is thought by some authorities[57] to be an ancestor of the tumbril. A *tumberellum* was certainly available for use in Durham around the year 1200.[58]

In the light of this evidence, it cannot be denied that the close

53 Cited by Du Cange, VIII, p. 206 under *Tumbrellum*.
54 Cited by J. C. Hodgson, *A History of Northumberland*, London, 1902, VI, p. 18, n. 3; cf. also Jewitt, *op. cit.*, p. 210; W. Dickinson, *A Practical Exposition of the Law*, London, 1813, II, p. 385.
55 L. Jewitt, 'A few notes on ducking stools', *Reliquary*, I (1861), pp. 145–58; W. A. Andrews, *Punishments in the Olden Time*, pp. 3–26; W. A. Andrews, *Old-time Punishments*, pp. 1–37.
56 Jewitt, 'Ducking stools', p. 150; Andrews, *Punishments in the Olden Time*, p. 25.
57 Andrews, *Punishments in the Olden Time*, p. 2.
58 'Feodarium Prioratus Dunelmensis', ed. W. Greenwell, Surtees Society, I (1871), p. 252, in a document dated 1199: 'quod vidit tumberellum erectum in terra monachorum. . . .'; cf. also p. 282.

connection which existed between the pillory and tumbril in the
correction of those guilty of minor offences in England is curiously
similar to the claims made by Chrétien about the pillory and the
'charrete'. The tumbril was especially effective in punishing those with
glib and wicked tongues; it is this same idea which is echoed by
Chrétien in his romance when Lancelot attempts to force the 'chevalier
orgueilleux' to ride in the cart:

> Et cil dit: 'Il te covandroit
> sor une charrete monter;
> a neant porroies conter
> quan que tu dire me savroies,
> s'an la charrete ne montoies
> por ce que tant fole boche as
> que vilmant la me reprochas.'   [ll. 2758–64]

There are also other features about Chrétien's *charrete* which call the
tumbril to mind. Before he was wheeled around in the tumbril the
victim was normally strapped to it in a sitting position; similarly, on
two separate occasions in the cart episode (l. 380 and l. 385) Chrétien
tells us that Lancelot was sitting on the *charrete*, and this idea is again
repeated soon after the cart episode when Lancelot has acquitted himself of the exploit of the flaming lance:

> s'an vint li chevaliers pansis,
> cil qui sor la charrete ot sis . . .   [ll. 541–2]

Moreover, the use of the word 'contret' (l. 440) by the maiden at the
Castle of the Flaming Lance to describe Lancelot's condition in the
charrete, might have been prompted by the fact that he was physically
immobilised or incapacitated in some way, possibly by being strapped
to the vehicle.[59] Once he was installed in the tumbril the victim was
pulled or pushed around manually; it is not easy to tell how Chrétien's
charrete was moved. On the one hand, the remark made to the dwarf
by the inhabitants of the castle:

> Di, nains, di, tu qui le traïnes,   [l. 414]

could be interpreted as meaning the dwarf was pulling the cart himself,
yet, on the other hand, the description of the dwarf:

---

59 *Contret* is glossed by Foerster as 'wie einen lahmen Krüppel', by Frappier as
'perclus' and by Roques as 'impotent'.

> sor les limons,
> qui tenoit come charretons
> une longue verge an sa main. [ll. 347-9]

suggests the presence of a horse. This passage, however, presents us with several difficulties. Firstly, not all the mss. agree about the reading 'sor les limons'; ms T. has 'sor les banons', reproduced by Foerster, l. 349, and causing him some concern;[60] in his *Wörterbuch* Foerster tentatively glosses this word as *Wagenleitern*—'shafts';[61] von Wartburg, however, under *benna*[62] lists *begnon*, *benion* and *bagnon*, all used in the Walloon dialect with the meaning of 'tombereau' or 'planche que l'on place sur les charrettes pour retenir le fumier'; is the dwarf on the cart itself or on the shafts? One might think that Chrétien's use of the word *charreton* to describe the dwarf is sure proof that the dwarf is driving a horse-drawn vehicle; however, the same word is used in l. 884 to refer to Lancelot:

> lors li vient sus li charretons,

and earlier, in l. 684, Lancelot is also called *charretiers*. Nor is the fact that the dwarf wields 'une longue verge' very significant, since this implement is a necessary accessory of almost every dwarf, and generally used to whip anyone unlucky enough to cross the dwarf's path, like the maiden in *Erec*, l. 182, or the four unfortunate knights in *Yvain*, l. 4100 ff.

The vexed question of how the cart is moved is far more difficult to resolve than first appears; indeed, it could be said that Chrétien is positively vague and obscure on this issue, but, as we hope to show below, such obscurities are possibly created deliberately by the author.

One of the principal aims of punishment by the tumbril was to shame its occupant publicly; this is also one of the effects which Lancelot's ride in the *charrete* has. The shaming nature of the cart is alluded to once in the cart episode itself:

> que de la honte ne li chaut . . . [l. 376]

When he is in the cart Lancelot hears himself publicly degraded and vilified:

> s'ot molt li chevaliers de lui
> vilenies et despit dire. [ll. 408-9]

---

60 Cf. edn. p. 366.
61 W. Foerster, *Wörterbuch zu Kristian von Troyes' sämtlichen Werken*, 4th edn., edn. H. Breuer, Tübingen, 1966, p 41. 62 *F.E.W.*, I, pp. 325-6.

The maiden at the Castle of the Flaming Lance also refers to Lancelot's shame:

> Honiz est chevaliers an terre
> puis qu'il a esté an charrete . . .   [ll. 486-7]

The 'chevalier orgueilleux' taunts Lancelot with the dishonour of the cart:

> Ce ne sai ge se tu honte as
> de ce que tu i fus montez: [ll. 2596-7]

Even Guinevere refers to the 'honte' which Lancelot may have felt as a result of his cart ride:

> Comant? Don n'eüstes vos honte
> de la charrete . . .   [ll. 4484-5]

In view of such close similarities between the tumbril which was used in Chrétien's day only in England in the same way as the pillory, and the *charrete* which, according to our author, was no longer in use in France and whose functions had been taken over by the pillory, it seems reasonable to assume that Chrétien may have had the tumbril in mind, as well as the gallows cart, when he composed the cart episode. This hypothesis, however, poses two problems: firstly, how could Chrétien have known about the English tumbril? secondly, if he is in fact alluding to the tumbril in part of the cart episode, why did he feel such a reference was necessary and apposite?

It is not difficult to see how Chrétien could at least have heard the tumbril discussed, living as he did in the prosperous and internationally famous market town of Troyes and also frequenting the court of the Count and Countess of Champagne, where, given the fact that the Countess of Champagne's mother was the Queen of England, there was probably fairly constant contact with England and the English court.[63] If, however, Chrétien himself visited England, as some critics think very possible,[64] he may even have seen the tumbril in operation. What, then, are the consequences for our interpretation of the cart episode if we are correct in thinking that Chrétien knew about the tumbril? First of all, it seems likely that when he conceived the episode

---

63 Cf. J. Longnon in *Histoire des institutions françaises au moyen âge*, ed. F. Lot and R. Fawtier, Paris, 1957, pp. 123-36.

64 G. Paris, *Mélanges de littérature français du moyen âge*, Paris, 1912, I, pp. 259-60; Cohen, *op. cit.*, p. 89, P. Rickard, *Britain in Medieval French Literature, 1100-1500*, Cambridge, 1956, pp. 107-13; Holmes, *op. cit.*, pp. 24-5.

about the *charrete* Chrétien had in the back of his mind not one cart but two—both of them instruments of justice but not of the same sort of justice; both carts were used in Chrétien's time in England and he must have assumed that they were also used there in the days of King Arthur. Out of the two carts Chrétien forges a third, his *charrete*, which is the corrective for all types of criminal offence, both great and small. It seems to us that there is ample evidence in the text to support the identification of the *charrete* with both the gallows cart and the tumbril; apart from their respective use, the only major difference between the two carts was that one was horse-drawn and the other was moved manually. Chrétien noticed this difference too and this is probably the reason why he is so evasive on the subject.

By introducing the *charrete* in the crucial first stage of Lancelot's mission to Gorre, Chrétien is implying that when his hero gets into the cart it looks as though he has fallen foul of all forms of justice, high and low. This may well be, therefore, a somewhat veiled but none the less virulent comment by Chrétien on Lancelot's future adultery. On the other hand, since there was a fairly clear distinction in medieval law between capital and non-capital offences, to a contemporary audience the association of the same person at one and the same time with both types of crime would appear a complete paradox. This paradox, which is at the heart of the cart episode, is the key to our understanding of it. In our view, the underlying tone of the cart episode is that, just as the *charrete* represents a paradoxical fusion of two different instruments of punishment connected with two different types of justice, so Lancelot's mission to Gorre, in which he hopes to play the roles of loyal feudal vassal and courtly lover, constitutes a similar paradox. And just as the *charrete* can exist only in the world of romance fiction, the double standard of the morality of Lancelot's mission is essentially the stuff of the author's imagination, impossible to realise in practice.

In his treatment of the cart episode, therefore, Chrétien reveals his own uneasiness and scepticism about Lancelot's predicament, but he is careful not to be too overt in the denigration of his hero and his subject-matter—indeed, at this stage in the romance any open condemnation of Lancelot's behaviour and situation, both aesthetically and politically, would have been quite out of keeping with his brief from Marie de Champagne. It is only when Lancelot has actually committed adultery with the queen that Chrétien is able to be more explicit about his feelings concerning such conduct. In the scene in which Meleagant ironically accuses Kay of having had improper relations with Guinevere (ll. 4744–889) Chrétien uses words to describe the terrible nature of adultery, some of which he has never used before in the romance: adultery is 'mal' (l. 4751), an 'outrage' (l. 4845 and l. 4850), an act of treason (l. 4854), a 'leidure' and 'torz' (l. 4864), a 'desconvenue' (l. 4887) and 'honte' (l. 4888). In the cart episode Chrétien's disapproval has to be more masked.

During the remainder of the romance we are constantly reminded of the *charrete* and the cart episode to the point that the recurrent allusions become almost an obsession on Chrétien's part. During many of the adventures which lead up to Lancelot's arrival in the 'Land of No Return' (ll. 445–3110) the cart is referred to at regular intervals. If we examine these references in more detail, a definite pattern seems to emerge. In the adventures which occupy the next 500 lines of the romance immediately after the cart episode (ll. 445–927), the cart is mentioned specifically on nine separate occasions.[65] During the next two adventures (the visit to the castle of the 'Amorous Hostess' and the discovery of Guinevere's comb, ll. 928–1648) there is no mention of the cart, but it is referred to twice in the next episode, Lancelot's adventures at the 'Pré aux Jeux' (ll. 1649–828), near the beginning (ll. 1666–7), and near the end (l. 1818); two further adventures follow (the visit to the cemetery and the visit to the hospitable host, ll. 1829–2195) and in neither is the cart alluded to. However, in the course of the next adventure at the 'Passage des Pierres' (ll. 2196–254), the cart is mentioned twice (ll. 2212–13 and ll. 2217–18), just as it was in the earlier 'Pré aux Jeux' episode. There then follows a series of adventures occupying some 300 lines (ll. 2255–565) during which the cart is temporarily forgotten; but during the episode which precedes Lancelot's crossing of the sword bridge (ll. 2566–941) the cart is again mentioned on no fewer than five different occasions.[66] Once Lancelot is in Gorre a change takes place. The cart is only referred to again on three more occasions; on two of these Lancelot himself alludes to his previous exploit in his monologue (ll. 4348–9 and l. 4371), and the last time the cart is mentioned in the romance is by Guinevere, during the interview which precedes the couple's night of love (ll. 4484–5). The cart is never mentioned by any of the inhabitants of Gorre, not even by Lancelot's arch-enemy, Meleagant. There are several reasons why Chrétien may have adopted this sudden change in technique. Firstly,

65 Cf. l. 477, l. 487, l. 542, l. 578, l. 627, l. 684, l. 711, l. 867, l. 884.
66 Cf. l. 2595, l. 2612, l. 2717, l. 2736, l. 2789.

Lancelot's pseudonym, 'Le Chevalier de la Charrete', is, strictly speaking, redundant once he is named in lines 3660–1 during his first battle with Meleagant; secondly, Chrétien may have felt that once Lancelot has to focus all his knightly energies in a trial of physical strength with King Arthur's enemy, the treacherous Meleagant, in which Lancelot's chivalric prowess has to be displayed and the forces of right vindicated, any attempt to belittle his hero's achievements by further references to the cart would, at this point, be out of place and in bad taste. In this connection it is interesting to observe that in the adventures which take place after Lancelot has crossed the sword bridge and before the episode in which he is named (ll. 3129–661), Chrétien gives Lancelot a new, temporary pseudonym; instead of being called 'Le Chevalier de la Charrete' Lancelot now becomes 'le chevalier estrange' (l. 3514) and, at another point, he is alluded to as 'cil qui ert au pont passez' (l. 3623).

As well as referring to the cart directly, at regular intervals in the narrative up to the point at which the lovers commit adultery, Chrétien reminds us of the cart incident in other ways, notably by indirect allusions to this adventure, all of which occur in the episodes after the night of love and before Chrétien abandons his romance (ll. 4737–6103). In the adventures immediately following the night of love, the accusation of Kay and his defence by Lancelot (ll. 4738–5043), Chrétien has no need to make any reference to the cart episode to make his opinions concerning adultery felt, since the whole of these adventures is strongly flavoured with elements from the Tristan story.[67] The introduction of a dwarf who spirits Lancelot away in the next episode (ll. 5044–91) brings to mind the dwarf of the cart incident, although there is no reason to suppose, as some critics do, that the two dwarfs are one and the same.[68] It is, however, in the episode dealing with the marriage tournament at Noauz (ll. 5506–6103) that Chrétien is most clearly attempting to remind us of the cart adventure.[69] Just as Chrétien tells us in the cart episode that when the cart is seen 'fei croiz sor toi' (l. 343), in the Noauz adventures, as soon as the herald espies Lancelot, 'si s'an seigna' (l. 5549). In the Noauz adventures Lancelot receives a

67 Cf. Cohen, *op. cit.*, p. 260; Loomis, *op. cit.*, p. 251; S. Bayrav, *Symbolisme médiéval*, Paris, 1957, pp. 44–5; J. Frappier, *Chrétien de Troyes*, Paris, 1957, p. 140; M. Lazar, *Amour courtois et 'Fin' Amors' dans la littérature du XIIe siècle*, Paris, 1964, p. 241; Kelly, *op. cit.*, p. 136.
68 Cf. Cohen, *op. cit.*, p. 261; Kelly, *op. cit.*, pp. 136–7.
69 Cf. Foulon, *op. cit.*, p. 89: 'Un certain parallélisme subsiste entre les deux moments où Lancelot se voit humilié'; Kelly, *op. cit.*, p. 148: 'The tournament at Noauz corrects and complements the cart episode'.

new pseudonym: 'li chevaliers vermauz' (l. 5714); 'celui as armes
vermoilles' (l. 5862); 'cil . . . as armes de sinoples taintes' (ll. 5956–7);
'cil qui porte l'escu vermoil' (l. 6026). In the cart episode Lancelot hears
the mocking crowd taunt him with 'vilenies et despit' (l. 409); at
Noauz he is told:

> Ja n'a el monde rien tant vil,
> si despite, ne si faillie.   [ll. 5864–5]

There is one more occasion in this romance where it seems to us
that Chrétien might be reminding us of the cart episode; immediately
after he has made love to Guinevere and just before he is forced to
leave her chamber at daybreak, Lancelot's tormented state of mind is
described:

> Au lever fu il droiz martirs,
> tant li fu griés li departirs,
> car il i suefre grant martire.   [ll. 4689–91]

Would it be reading too much into the text to suggest that the mention
of 'martire' here is meant to remind us of the only other time in this
romance when Chrétien uses this word in the cart episode:

> A quel martire
> sera cist chevaliers randuz?[70]   [ll. 410–11]

Perhaps Lancelot's punishment as a result of his ride in the cart is that
he must suffer the torment of being an adulterer and never being able
to marry the woman he loves.

In the course of this study we hope to have shown that the title
Chevalier de la Charrete was not given to this romance by Chrétien
without good reason. The cart episode is the first adventure confronted
by Lancelot on his way to Gorre, and it is undoubtedly the most
crucial; after it, the cart is a dominant motif in the remainder of the
romance. Although the presentation of the episode is apparently confusing, it is in fact deliberately ambiguous. Chrétien's *charrete* is a
literary fusion of the 'tumbril' or 'scolding cart' and the cart used to
take prisoners to the gallows, both of which were in use as instruments
of punishment in England in Chrétien's day. By making his hero step
on to a vehicle which punishes all types of crimes, both great and
small, Chrétien can direct our attention to the dubious morality of

---

70 For other uses of 'martire' by Chrétien, cf. *Erec.* l. 4461, and *Yvain*, l. 604.

Lancelot's mission in Gorre and also highlight the paradoxical predicament of Lancelot the feudal vassal and Lancelot the courtly lover. That Chrétien was able to express his feelings in such a clever and subtle way right at the start of his poem is yet further proof of his supreme greatness as a romancer and *mystificateur*.

Jane H. M. Taylor
Reason and faith in the *Roman de Perceforest*

The *Roman de Perceforest*, which has to many critics seemed simply a confused and highly derivative tangle of neo-Arthurian adventures,[1] can, as Mlle Jeanne Lods has demonstrated in her remarkable study of the romance,[2] be shown to have on the contrary a certain massive coherency, a certain number of *idées directrices*. Of these last, one of the most interesting, and one of the more complex, is the author's treatment of the religious development of his fictional Britain.

To give only the broadest of outlines, this immense romance relates how Alexander the Great, driven off course by a storm at sea, arrives in Britain and founds a dynasty whose last and greatest representative is King Arthur. The *chronique*, as the author calls it, covers some two hundred years of British 'history', added to Geoffrey of Monmouth's *Historia Regum Britanniae* after the obscure king Pir, and preceding the coming of the Grail to Britain, which is virtually the last event of the romance.[3] It covers several generations of British monarchs and heroes, but concentrates perhaps particularly on two: Betis (later and more generally known as Perceforest) and his brother Gadifer, made by Alexander kings respectively of England and Scotland, and responsible, to a large extent, for the civilising of Britain. Perceforest and Gadifer are, of course, pagans at the beginning of the romance, believing in the Greek pantheon; but they will survive until the coming of the Grail, and be converted to Christianity. Between the two extremes of paganism and Christianity, however, the author introduces a far more original conception, which is the concern of this study: a cult whose beliefs prefigure the Christian.

1 See, for example, Paulin Paris, *Les Manuscrits français de la Bibliothèque du Roi*, Paris, 1836-48, I, p. 143; U.T.Holmes, *A History of Old French Literature*, New York, 1962, pp. 327-8.

2 *Le Roman de Perceforest: origines, composition, caractères, valeur et influence*, Geneva and Lille, 1951 (Société de publications romanes et françaises, XXXII).

3 The author indeed copies a part of the *Queste del Saint Graal* virtually verbatim; see J. Lods, *op. cit.*, pp. 41-3.

The *Roman de Perceforest* can be seen as the history of a civilisation.
The barbarous, sorcerer-ridden, unruly, pagan Britain which Alexander
finds at the opening of the romance has by its end, and even before
the coming of the Grail, adopted the chivalrous and courtly codes,
and many of its inhabitants have also become converted to a monotheistic, quasi-Christian religion. The details of the beliefs of this creed
have been listed by Mlle Lods, but so far no one has attempted to set
this imaginary religion in the context of thirteenth or fourteenth
century thought, scholastic or popular.[4]

Our first introduction, and Perceforest's, to this new religion comes
fairly early in Book I of the romance. Perceforest, riding alone through
a forest in search of malefactors, makes his way with some difficulty
to a remote temple. He is at first afraid to enter; between him and
the altar there is what appears to be a pit full of spears, and more
spears hang from the ceiling. At last, however, he realises that this is,
at least in part, only an optical illusion, goes into the temple, and after
suffering various vicissitudes to which I shall return later, sees the
servant and builder of the temple, the old hermit Dardanon. Dardanon
sings a hymn or rhymed prayer which convinces Perceforest of the
necessity of monotheism and which sets out the 'dogma' of the creed
in a conveniently summarised form.[5]

The basic tenets are simple. The adherents of the new religion
believe in one God:

> Philozophie aproeuve des enfance
> Qu'il n'est qu'un Dieu qui sur tous ait puissance,   [14–15]

variously called the *Dieu Souverain* or the *Dieu dessus Nature*. This God
is a God of love, and the creator of the world:

> Dieu tout-puissant de figure incongnute
> Qui as formé toute chose congnute . . .   [1–2]

Himself uncreated and eternal,

> En toy n'est fin ne fut commencemens . . .   [28]

He is all-powerful:

> Dieu tout-puissant, Dieu sur tous mouvemens . . .   [27]

---

4 *Op. cit.*, pp. 246 ff. Mlle Lods' main concern is, of course, less with the sources
  than with the structure of the romance.

5 It is printed in full as No. 3 in *Pièces lyriques du Roman de Perceforest*, ed. J.
  Lods, Geneva and Lille, 1953 (Société de publications romanes et françaises,
  xxxvi), pp. 25–7. Line references are given to this edition.

and unsubstantial:

> Tu es partout, ne t'estoet remouvoir . . .   [58]

The followers of this religion have moreover some knowledge of the Trinity:

> Encore n'est pas en vie
> Dieu, le tien corps, qu'on voit en trois partir.   [39-40]

and of the Incarnation:

> Tu te puez bien a noz membres sartir
> Sans le tien corps de nul lés dessartir,
> Car tu poeulx tout sans autruy decepvoir.
> Affule toy pour noz coeurs enhardir . . .   [43-46]

In adopting the new religion they realise the fact of a one God, dismiss the many gods of antiquity as powerless mockeries and abjure the practice of idolatry:

> Gens humaine, ne soyez si laniere
> Que ydole d'or ou pourtraicte en paniere
> Soit de par nous desormais aouree;
> Mars, Jupiter n'ont puoir ne maniere,
> Venus aussi n'est, fors filz, en cariere . . .   [66-70]

The new single God is beyond the compass and comprehension of the human mind:

> Ta grant clarté nous feroit couardir,
> Ta deïté ne puet nul percevoir . . .   [47-8]

but His followers live in the hope that He will come down to earth and reveal himself to the faithful, as Dardanon says later in conversation with Perceforest:

> Mais le meilleur est encores a venir: c'est que Dieu visitera encore son peuple, si comme je tieng, d'une visitacion esmerveillable et proffitable. Or luy prie je qu'il se voeuille haster, car c'est mon desir, et est ma priere, toute ma vie.
> [I, 181v; P. I, 66r6]

6 References to the prose text of the romance are given from the following mss.: Books I, II, III, V from ms. B.N., f.f., 345-8; Book IV from B.N., f.f., 108; Book VI from Bibl. de l'Arsenal, Paris, ms. 3493-4. Since the romance is unpublished, references for more important points will also be given (preceded by the letter P.) to the earliest printed edition: *La Treselegante Delicieuse Melliflue et tresplaisante hystoire du tresnoble Victorieux et excellentissime roy Perceforest Roy de la grand Bretaigne, etc.*, Paris, 1528.

All this is quite clearly Christian; indeed, there is nothing in the 'dogma' *per se* of the author's imagined religion which betrays any theological originality. That this is so obvious, but two points clinch the matter. Mlle Lods[7] has said that the author's definition of God as a God of love is foreign to Jewish and pagan thought, M. Pierre Sage that the dogma of the creation *ex nihilo* which the author puts forward is foreign both to Jewish and to ancient philosophy.[8] The tenets of the author's imagined religion are in fact those of Christianity itself.

What is original, however—indeed, unorthodox—is the invention in the pre-Christian era of a sect whose beliefs are indisputably Christian. The hermit's rhymed prayer, after all, is being sung some two hundred or so years before the birth of Christ. And yet not only do these pre-Christians, who are not even Jewish, accept a monotheistic creed, they also understand and accept the doctrines both of the Incarnation and of the Trinity. It is in this context that Pierre Sage has talked of 'une religion naturelle, avouable à la raison'.[9]

Francis Bacon defined natural theology as 'that spark of knowledge of God which may be had by the light of nature and the consideration of created things'.[10] In so far, however, as we may speak of a 'natural religion' in the *Perceforest*, it must be taken one step further to include a knowledge not only of God but also of Christian dogma, prior to the Revelation. As I shall show, belief in this paradoxical state of affairs is not unusual in the Middle Ages; but before we go any further it is essential to establish with precision the role that pure reason plays in propagating the new religion in the romance.

Information on this point comes mainly from the author's accounts of the 'conversions' of three main characters of the romance. The hermit Dardanon is the source of the new religion in Britain. The initial impulse towards a reconsideration of the polytheistic universe which he had until then accepted unconditionally is given by something which resembles a miracle. Dardanon had originally come to

7 *Op. cit.*, p. 253.
8 Pierre Sage, 'Sur la religion de *Perceforest*', *Bibliothèque d'Humanisme et de Renaissance*, XIII (1951), p. 394.
9 *Op. cit.*, p. 393.
10 'Diffinitur autem [Theologia Naturalis] ut sit talis scientia, seu potius scientiae scintilla, qualis de Deo haberi potest per lumen naturae et contemplationem rerum creatarum.' (*De dignitate et augmentis scientiarum libri IX*, Paris, 1624 Lib. III, cap. ii, p. 156. Quoted by C. C. J. Webb, *Studies in the History of Natural Theology*, Oxford, 1915, p. 2, who points out that the phrase *natural religion* is not used before Raymond of Sebonde.)

Britain with Cassandra, who was able to escape the destruction of
Troy because of her gift of prophecy (this also appears to be an invention of the author). Cassandra, besides being a sorceress, naturally
worships the Greek pantheon, and because of this, according to
Dardanon:

> le Souverain Dieu en prinst telle vengence que Dieu avoit commandé
> qu'elle ardist du feu celestial   [I, 179*v*; P. I, 65*r*]

Dardanon looks for reasons for this terrible punishment:

> et vey qu'elle avoit creu en plusieurs dieux, que je tenoie a bien fait adont,
> mais la science des philozophes me fist recongnoistre qu'il n'est que
> ung createur, et la manoit vraye boneureté.   [I, 179*v*; P. I, 65*r*]

Finally, he repents and builds his temple:

> Sy me pensay que bon me seroit a repentir de ma mauvaise creance et
> laissier tous pechiez dont je pouoie courroucier mon createur qui est Souve-
> rain Dieu. Sy me pensay que je esliroie ung lieu secret ou je porroie servir le
> Dieu Souverain. Sy m'embaty sur ceste montaigne qui estoit inhabitable,
> et y fiz faire ce temple que vous veés ou nom du Dieu tout-puissant.
>   [I, 179*v*; P. I, 65*r*]

Perceforest, too, receives a warning that his belief in the Greek
pantheon is wrong and sinful. When he reaches Dardanon's temple he
naturally prays to the heathen gods, the only ones he knows; as a
result, he is struck by spears falling as if by magic from the ceiling of
the temple, and temporarily blinded:[11]

> Lors [Perceforest] se traist en ung anglet par derriere l'autel et prinst a prier
> a Marcus son dieu et a Dame Venus sa deesse et a plusieurs autres qu'il avoit
> acoustumé de prier. Mais sy tost qu'il les eut nommez, il ne veyt entour luy
> neant plus que s'il eust eu les yeulx crevez, et sy fut feru sur son heaume, ne
> sceut de quoy, ung sy grant cop qu'il ne sceut ou il fut l'espace de demye
> lieue de terre.   [I, 176*r*; P. I, 64*r*]

He is unable, however, to understand why he has been thus punished,
until he hears the hermit's rhymed prayer, whereupon he realises that
he has sinned in praying to some of the many gods of antiquity:

> Dont pensa en son coeur comme cellui qui parler ne pouoit que jamais ne
> aoureroit plusieurs dieux, car bien luy estoit advis que pour ce luy estoit
> advenue sa meschance.   [I, 177*v*; P. I, 64*v*]

11 This looks like a deliberate reminiscence of the account of the conversion of
St Paul (Acts 9.1–22).

These two 'conversions' have in common, then, the fact that they start from a supernatural or divine warning that previous polytheistic beliefs are wrong and sinful. This, however, is only a preliminary; the formulation of belief in a one God comes to Dardanon only after study of the 'science des philozophes', while his acceptance of the doctrines of the Trinity and of the Incarnation appears to arise from the use of reason. This knowledge, the fruit of reason and study, is then passed on to Perceforest, who is apparently incapable even after the warning of understanding alone the truths of religion.

From this point of view the most interesting of these 'conversions' is that of the Reine Fée, Perceforest's sister-in-law. She is the wisest of the three, having been taught magic, astronomy and philosophy by Aristotle in her childhood. We cannot speak, in her case, of there being any supernatural occurrence to move her to quasi-Christian belief; but it is significant that, with all her knowledge and wisdom, all her study of the philosophers, she has not been able to come to a true knowledge of the one God:

> Haa, Dieu Souverain, je vous recongnois comme Dieu tout-puissant. Je vous requiers mercy de ce que j'ay aouré autre dieu que vous, et qui n'ont pouoir synon ce que presté leur avés. Moult ay plus mesfait que une simple personne qui ne scet rien synon par la doctrine de pere et de mere. Car moy qui tout ay leut les sentences des philozophez, qui aucunement donne a congnoistre ce qu'on doit aourer, par dessus tous les deusse avoir recongneu. Mais petitement ay interpretee la verité quant j'ay laissié le createur et aouré les creatures.   [IV, 149v; P, IV, 73v]

Just as for Perceforest the hermit's prayer is the source of the new belief, so the Reine Fée must come to Dardanon's temple and hear his prayer before being convinced of the truths of religion. Henceforward she will accept the one God:

> Je suis l'une des creatures de cellui que vous conseilliés tant a croire et aourer dessus tous dieux. Et moy pecheresse ay esté contre lui jusques a present, mais vostre dittier qui a resjouy et a ouvert ma cognoissance et destruit les tenebres de mes sentences le me fait recongnoistre a Souverain et Dieu tout-puissant.   [IV, 149v; P. IV, 73v]

Dardanon will transmit to her his own conclusions, the result of years of study and reflection. Her intellect is insufficient alone to find the one God, but on the other hand hers is no miraculous conversion, of the type which medieval hagiography, for instance, gives us in abundance; her acceptance of the new religion is again a reasoned one rather than a supernatural illumination. We are dealing, then, with a religion for the understanding and acceptance of which both reason and faith are required. Reason alone and totally unaided is not enough. In the author's imagination, pagan beliefs must first be eradicated by a supernatural or divine warning. But given this warning, Dardanon is capable of the reflection and reasoning which enable him to find the one God, and he in turn is able to pass on his conclusions to Perceforest or the Reine Fée. But this cannot be done piecemeal; evidently, each of the protagonists must come himself to the temple and hear for himself the hermit's prayer. The part that reason plays is, then, large; and if we cannot talk of a wholly natural religion, it is still a religion of a Christian type which pagans are able to understand and accept without a genuinely divine illumination, without the Revelation, and principally by the use of reason.

These questions—those of reason and faith, of whether certain pagans were able through reason to apprehend certain of the truths of the Christian religion—were topics which in the Middle Ages engaged wide interest on many levels, as this study will show. As Mlle Lods says in concluding her chapter on the author's religious ideas:

> Ce romancier rencontre les grands problèmes de la philosophie de son temps, les rapports de la foi et de la raison, le problème du libre arbitre; il ne les pose pas dans les termes scolastiques [. . .] mais il les pense à sa manière et sa pensée, parfois hardie, n'est pas sans intérêt.[12]

But how far is the author really reflecting the thought of his time, and how far might he have been aware of contemporary or near-contemporary thought and controversy on the subject? How bold, in fact, are his ideas? It will not be possible to point to any precise sources for his account; it seems unlikely, indeed, that any such precise source exists, as I hope to demonstrate. But in order to assess the author's originality and inventiveness in this interesting field we need to know precisely how widespread such thinking was, whether it was confined to the scholastic circles of the theologians and philosophers, and whether a writer of romance in relatively remote Hainaut[13] was likely

---

12 *Op. cit.*, p. 258.
13 For discussion of the author's country of origin see J. Lods, *op. cit.*, pp. 275 ff., and L.-F. Flûtre, 'Etudes sur le *Roman de Perceforêt*', *Romania*, LXXI (1950), pp. 377–8.

to be aware of it. To do this we shall need to examine the precise way in which such questions are treated on the philosophical level, on the level of the educated but not philosophically inclined layman or cleric, and finally on the level of popular legend and of fiction. Given this information, we shall be able more clearly to judge how far the author's conception is in itself original, and how far too he is original in his elaboration of it.

Philosophically speaking, there is, of course, nothing very new in the belief that certain pre-Christian philosophers had some conception, more or less precise, more or less close to Christian belief, of a one God, the ruler of all things. Pierre Sage traces this back to Arnobius in the third century A.D.[14] But such a belief is much more widespread in philosophical circles than this might suggest, and among the most orthodox and impeccably respectable of Christian philosophers and patristic writers. Biblical authority gave support to such a viewpoint; St Paul in saying that

> Invisibilia enim ipsius a creatura mundi per ea quae facta sunt intellecta conspiciuntur; sempiterna quoque ejus virtus et divinitas   [Rom. 1.20]

and that the infidel therefore has no excuse for his unbelief, had laid a foundation for philosophical speculation on the subject.[15] St Paul does not here maintain, however, that any particular pagan or infidel has in actual fact used the evidence of the physical world to deduce the existence of a one God, and we must distinguish between those thinkers who maintain merely that the existence of one God is susceptible of proof, and those who maintain that certain pagans were able to prove or at least apprehend, rationally and intellectually, without the Revelation, the existence of one God. The first type, for instance, includes Duns Scotus, who denies that any of the attributes of God is susceptible of proof, but accepts that his existence may be proved.[16] Even this, it should be said, is disputed by the more extreme Nominalists, by a William of Ockham for instance, who says that even the existence of God cannot be proved in the rational sense.[17] The next stage is to suggest that certain pagans were believers in a monotheistic religion; this was the belief, for instance, of St Augustine, who finds such

---

14 *Op. cit.*, p. 394.
15 See E. Gilson, *L'Esprit de la philosophie médiévale*, I, Paris, 1932, pp. 27–8.
16 *Tractatus de primo principio*, ed. and trans. A. B. Wolter, Chicago, 1966, p. 147.
17 See E. Gilson, *Reason and Revelation in the Middle Ages*, New York and London, 1946, pp. 86–7.

knowledge foreshadowed in the *Platonici*,[18] and of such philosophers as Scotus Erigena and William of Avergne, who share what Gilson calls: 'a general confidence in the translucency of a universe in which the least of all beings was a living token of the presence of God'.[19] Aquinas himself accepts that natural reasoning is capable of proving the existence and unity of God.[20]

What is far more unorthodox, philosophically and theologically, is the author's assertion that his pre-Christian converts knew of the doctrine of the Trinity. Here a majority of medieval theologians and philosophers is quite clear: reason alone is insufficient to allow us to apprehend the doctrine of the Trinity. St Thomas Aquinas says:

> Impossibile est per rationem naturalem ad cognitionem Trinitatis divinarum Personarum pervenire.[21]

John the Scot Erigena, who had admitted the capability of reason to demonstrate the existence of one God, is equally categorical:

> Non enim est unitas neque trinitas, talis qualis ab humano quamvis purissimo cogitari, aut angelico intellectu etsi serenissimo, considerari potest.[22]

This is the orthodox view; but not all medieval philosophers accept or uphold it. And here the same distinction as before must be made. Certain thinkers believe that reason alone, without the Revelation, can understand and apprehend the Trinity. Ramon Llull, for instance, in the early fourteenth century, wrote a treatise, *Liber de demonstratione per aequiparantium*,[23] designed to give logical and incontrovertible arguments to be used in converting the heathen, and of which two chapters prove:

—Quod sint Tres Divinae personae, et non plures, nec pauciores.
—Quod Divinae Personae sint Pater, Filius et Sanctus Spiritus.

And St Anselm, in the *De Divinitatis essentia monologium*, undertakes to prove the Trinity by dialectical argument.[24]

None of these thinkers, however, takes the argument a stage further to maintain that pagans, Greek and Roman or otherwise, had been able through reason alone to apprehend the Trinity. This is, however, the

18 *Confessions*, VII, cap. ix (Migne, P. L. XXXII, cols. 740–2).
19 *History of Christian Philosophy in the Middle Ages*, London, 1955, pp. 352–3.
20 Webb, *op. cit.*, p. 235.
21 *Summa Theologiae*, I, q. XXXII, art. I, 1964–71, VI, pp. 101 ff.
22 *De divisione naturae libri quinque*, Oxford, 1681, p. 8.
23 *Opera*, Mainz, 1721–29, IV.   24 Migne, P. L., CLVIII, col. 220.

contention of Abelard, who finds frequent heathen witness to the
doctrine of the Trinity—in Plato, for instance; in Virgil, in Seneca and
Hermes Trismegistus[25]—and maintains that:

> prius hanc [i.e. given at the Revelation] divinae trinitatis distinctionem, non
> a Christo inceptam, sed ad ipso apertius ac diligentius traditam esse osten-
> damus, quam quidem divina inspiratio et per prophetas Judaeis et per
> philosophos gentibus dignata est revelare, ut utrumque populum ad cultum
> unius dei ipsa summi boni perfectio agnita invitaret.[26]

Indeed, it is not only the sometimes unorthodox Abelard who maintains this; St Augustine himself, in the *Confessions*, finds the doctrine
of the Trinity foreshadowed in the *Platonici*.[27]

In the same way, for medieval thinkers, the Incarnation will be
understood and prophesied not only by Old Testament prophets but
also by certain pagans. Virgil's famous fourth eclogue is, of course, a
case in point.[28] According to the English friar Ridevall, Plato, because of his virginity, was given a revelation of Christ Himself;[29]
St Augustine finds that the Sibyl prophesied the coming of Christ.[30]

All this is, however, probably on too rarefied a level for the author
of the *Perceforest*. It seems unlikely, after all, that he would be an avid
reader of scholastic controversy, and there is no evidence of his having
had any direct acquaintance with the theologians. Not that we can
dismiss entirely the possibility of his knowing something of such
matters. If he was a cleric—and this is a question which is still uncertain[31]—he might well at some point have had contact with questions
of this sort, while even as a layman he could have heard quoted in
some sermon the views of Augustine and Abelard, Duns Scotus and
William of Ockham; the sermon literature of the time quotes abun-
dantly and often verbatim.

Such questions are in any case frequently raised in sermons, fre-

---

25 Webb, *op. cit.*, pp. 222 ff.
26 *Tractatus de unitate et trinitate divina*, ed. R. Stolzle, Freiburg-im-Breisgau,
   1891, p. 4.   27 *Loc. cit.*, cols. 740–2.
28 See D. Comparetti, *Vergil in the Middle Ages*, tr. E. F. M. Benecke, New York,
   1908, pp. 96 ff.
29 See B. Smalley, *English Friars and Antiquity in the Fourteenth Century*, Oxford,
   1960, p. 119.
30 *De civitate Dei*, XVIII, 23 (Migne, P. L. XLI, col. 579).
31 Mlle Lods thinks he was a layman; *op. cit.*, pp. 278 ff.; Flûtre, however, takes
   the opposite viewpoint; see 'Etudes sur le *Roman de Perceforêt*', *Romania*, LXXI
   (1950), p. 377.

quently treated in *Summa* or encyclopedias and collections of *exempla* intended for sermon writers—in other words, on a level probably more accessible to the unlearned writer we must assume him to have been. Gerson, for instance, returns frequently to debate the question in his sermons. In the sermon *Rex in sempiternum vive* he says:

> Dit S. Jerome en la glose sur cette histoire, que Dieu veut reveler ses secrets a un païen pour la cure qu'il avoit du bien commun.[32]

In another sermon, the *Videmus*,[33] he maintains that reason alone can demonstrate the existence, the unity and the attributes of God, but in order to prove the doctrine of the Trinity requires the help of faith. Ridevall, in a lecture on the Apocalypse, tells us that Hermes Trismegistus found from reason alone the doctrine of the Trinity.[34] G. R. Owst quotes from a sermon in English which tells us:

> Many philosophres and hethen men couthe knowe God thorgh his creatures, as it were thorgh a myrour. But right savour of him had thei none. Thei seyh thorgh understondynge and resoun his fairnes, his goodnes, his myght, and his wisdom, thorgh sight of the creatures that he had made so faire, so good, so wel ordeyned bi skile to oure bihove.[35]

The sermon writers also make themselves the purveyors of the sort of legendary material which might have suggested his idea to the author of the romance. In a sermon attributed to Peter of Blois, the *De Trinitate*, Plato is found reading the *libri Moysi*:

> gloriatus est se maxime ex hoc loco invenisse unum quod operabatur et alterum per quod illud operabatur; tertium autem se invenire non posse non diffitetur.[36]

And in a sermon for Lent by Michel Menot we are even told that Plato was excommunicate.[37]

Such legends proliferate particularly, and in particularly developed form, in the encyclopedias of the period, which often serve as source books for sermons, as well as having considerable popularity in their

32 See Jean Gerson, *Opera omnia*, ed. Ellies du Pin, Antwerp, 1706, iv, col. 662.
33 See Jean Gerson, *Six Sermons français inédits*, ed. L. Mourin, Paris, 1946 (Etudes de théologie et d'histoire de la spiritualité, viii), pp. 151–72.
34 See B. Smalley, *op. cit.*, p. 120. The text is to be found in appendix i, pp. 313 ff.
35 *Literature and Pulpit in Medieval England*, Cambridge, 1933, p. 184.
36 See J.-B. Hauréau, *Notices et extraits de quelques manuscrits latins de la Bibliothèque Nationale*, Paris, 1890, i, p. 371.
37 Michel Menot, *Sermons choisis*, ed. J. Nève, Paris, 1924 (Bibliothèque du XVe siècle, xxix), pp. 479–80.

own right. One of the main claims to fame, for instance, of the pre-Christian 'philosopher' Sidrach, in the *Livre de Sidrach*, consists in his having demonstrated incontrovertibly to the pagan King Boccus the doctrine of the Trinity:

> Sidrac demanda maintenant i vaissel de terre, et le fist amplir d'yawe, et iii fus et le fist asseoir sus les iii fus et regarda dedens celle yawe ou non de Dieu et vit l'ombre de la Sainte Trinité. Et cria a haute voiz: 'Regarde, roys Boccus, en l'yawe, si i verras le Dieu de tout le monde.' Ly rois vint par grant ire et regarda dedens l'yawe et vit l'ombre de la Trinité, Pere et Fil et Saint Esprit, en sieges ou ciel, l'un samblant a l'autre, et les angles chantans devant et loans Dieu le Pere et le Fil et le Saint Esperit et touz trois ensamble.[38]

Similarly, in Gautier de Metz's *Image du Monde* we are told:

> Puis vint li sages Platons,
> Li souverainz des philosophes,
> Et ses clers k'ot non Aristotes [. . .]
> prouva il droite Trinité:
> Son pooir, son sens et son bien,
> Ces trois clamment li crestien
> Pere et Fil et Saint Esperit.
> Li Peres la puissance dit,
> Et li Filz dit la sapience;
> Sainz Esperiz la bienvoillance.[39]

The author of the Perceforest is thus dealing here with questions which had a very wide circulation in the thinking circles of his day, whether philosophical or more mundane. But how far had such questions percolated into a context of fiction, in other words to a more popular level? No other purely fictional work in French, so far as I am aware, depicts the details of a pre-Christian monotheistic religion, but several mention such matters in passing. The prose *Tristan*, for instance, briefly describes a pagan *philosophe* living at Norhout in Cornwall who, having heard of St Augustine, builds a temple to the unknown God:

> Li philosophes, quant il oï que Sainz Agustins fu venus en Loenois, e que ciaus de cele terre avoit torné a la loi crestiene, il se merveilla que ce pooit estre, car de celui Dieu n'avoit il onques oï parler. Quant il sot qu'il ne pooit mais vivre, il fist el temple un autiex loing des autres, e escrist letres en un leu; e disoient ses letres: 'CIL EST L'AUTEL DOU DIEU DES MERVEILLES.'

38 *Le Livre de Sidrach*, ms. B.N., f.f., 1161, f. 18r.
39 Gautier de Metz, *L'Image du monde*, ms. B.N., f.f., 1548, f. 38v.

The *philosophe*, whose name is Augur, is martyred for this faith, but not before God has performed a miracle for him: he is made to drink poison, but is able to do so without coming to any harm.[40] To look at non-French literature for a moment, the question of whether such learned men as Aristotle or Trajan can be saved is discussed in the *Vision of Piers Plowman*.[41] Even in a work as wholly secular as the *Livre des faits du maréchal de Boucicaut* we find said, in passing:

> A propos des payens, lesquels sans loy escripte eurent par raison naturelle congnoissance de Dieu et des choses divines.[42]

In having pre-Christian pagans, then, believing in a one God, understanding the Trinity and expecting the Incarnation, the author of the *Perceforest* is not propounding anything which in its essence is original, whether in philosophical terms or in terms of legend and fiction. He is transferring into his romance ideas which were prevalent in his own time, and which he could have derived from a variety of sources, from sermons, from encyclopedias, or indeed from even a fairly limited knowledge of scholastic controversy. It is even possible that he could have taken the bare idea from, say, the *Roman de Tristan* and used this as the basis of his portrayal. We cannot, in fact, speak of the conception itself, the 'dogma', as being in any way original, nor of originality in his attributing them to pre-Christian pagans. But as we have already seen and as I shall show more fully now, the author has clothed the bare bones of his conception in a considerable mass of detail, and this in itself is highly original, since, as I have said, no other work of fiction in French makes so extensive a use of this type of pre-Christian religion. Beyond this basic originality, moreover, we may distinguish two other respects in which the author's inventiveness and imagination are at work: in the detail of his account, and in the emphasis which he places on the particular role which this new religion plays in his fictional Britain.

The groups of medieval writers whom we have discussed treat the problem of reason and faith from differing points of view and use this information to fulfil different purposes. Broadly speaking, scholastic philosophers are concerned with two aspects of the problem, the

---

40 *Le Roman de Tristan*, ed. R. L. Curtis, Munich, 1963, pp. 106–7.
41 See Langland, *The Vision of William concerning Piers the Plowman*, ed. W. Skeat, London, 1873 (Early English Text Society), III, xv, pp. 192 ff.
42 Ed. Michaud and Poujoulat, Paris, 1836 (Nouvelle collection pour servir à l'histoire de France, 1re série, II), p. 319.

epistemological and the theological (that is, the distinguishing of those of the pre-Christian era who may be saved, and the theological justification for this). The writers of the sermons tend to use the pagans principally as *exempla* and for polemical purposes, and are saying in effect, 'Even the pagans were able to know God—and very often, without the example of Christ, were able to live better lives than so-called Christians.' The writers of encyclopedias mention such matters apparently as *faits divers*, of general interest or as demonstrating the peculiar sagacity of the ancient philosophers.

None of the writers goes beyond asserting that certain pre-Christian philosophers had some knowledge of God. There is in general no sustained account given, except that, from time to time, we are told that some one of the pagans raised an altar to the unknown God, a detail presumably suggested by the account of the altar of the Unknown God found by St Paul in Athens.[43] There is to my knowledge no other account which so fully describes not only a belief but a cult.

What we are given in the *Perceforest* is on the contrary a fully imagined cult. Mlle Lods[44] has detailed some of its characteristics, and this is not the place for a full description and analysis of it. Briefly, however, it is a cult with two temples, the architecture and furnishings of which, interestingly, betray some considerable effort of imagination on the part of the author, especially in being apparently deliberately independent of contemporary church building. This independence is demonstrated in particular by his condemnation of the luxury of the churches of his own time, which contrasts unfavourably with the austerity of the two temples of the *Dieu Souverain*:

> Et n'y avoit nul fenestraige, fors autant qu'il en faloit pour donner competamment clarté, afin que l'en peust veoir pour aler par le temple, et aussi que l'ymage du Dieu fust veue et congneue [. . .] combien qu'il me samble que ceulx qui ont regné depuis la passion de N.S.J.C. ont esté trop deceus selon les fais anciens que les sages experimenterent dilligentement en leur longs eages, quant ilz ont souffert que vanité et orgueil a effondré et troué les murs des temples que les anciens fonderent [. . .] pour avoir veue champestre, qui empesche devotion et simplesse, mais a present, l'en les a tant ouvers et esclarcis que vanité est venue a son intencion. Car elle de sa nature veult estre veue et regardee et veir et regarder.
>
> [III, 316r; P. III, 120v[45]]

---

43 Acts 17.23.   44 *Op. cit.*, pp. 256 ff.
45 Quoted by Mlle Lods, *op. cit.*, pp. 256–7. I hope to discuss this passage, interesting as illustrating the thought of the author, in greater detail elsewhere.

The temples of the imaginary religion are furnished only with an altar and with symbols which are to represent the *Dieu Souverain*: a lamp in Dardanon's temple, a richly made reliquary containing fragments of all four elements in the temple which Perceforest later builds in honour of the one God. The temples are both brightly lit, but with 'carbuncles' known for their power to shine in the dark. There appears to be no other church furnishing, a considerable contrast with normal fourteenth century architectural and artistic habits.

This is also—and here again we detect an original conception—a religion without priests or clerics. True, Dardanon appears at first sight to fulfil this role, but this is illusory, since he does not preach or officiate at any services and administers no sacraments. It is perhaps significant that he performs none of the several marriage ceremonies which take place during the course of the romance, and that these—in default, one supposes, of any priest in the new religion—continue to take place in the temples of the old heathen gods, the ceremonies being directed by the priests of the pagan cult. Because of the lack of priests this is principally an interior cult, highly meditative. The prayers which the author gives as those of the heroes are meditations on the nature of God, as in the rhymed prayer we have already mentioned or in the long prayer printed in full by Mlle Lods,[46] or else simple affirmations of faith.

All this obviously owes much to the author's own Christian experience, or to his own observations. What the author has made is, however, a very interesting synthesis. The independence of the new religion both from paganism (as the Middle Ages understood it, and as it is portrayed in the *Perceforest*[47]) and from Christianity is underlined. Many of the details of the new sect, in particular its 'dogma', are Christian, but the cult itself is equally clearly and deliberately not Christian. At the same time the heroes of the romance, even when they adopt the new cult, remain pagans, and the author is skilful enough not to turn them into Christians *avant la lettre*; not, for instance, to invent some sort of baptismal ceremony, but to allow them quite simply to have some comprehension, some intimations, of the dogma of Christianity, and to live in the hope of the coming of Christ. This is a synthesis which suggests on the part of the author a certain sophistication, and a considerable originality.

The author is original also in the role in the romance which he gives the cult of the *Dieu Souverain*; it becomes an important and

46 *Op. cit.*, pp. 252–3.
47 See Mlle Lods, *op. cit.*, pp. 247 ff.

central theme. Let me make it quite clear that in discussing the romance one must be careful not to overstress its coherency or to give the impression that every theme stands out clearly. In actual fact, only too often we lose sight of such themes under a mass of adventures, tournaments, jousts and quests. But Mlle Lods has demonstrated that the author appears to see as the central thread of his romance the slow evolution of Britain from barbarism to the civilisation represented ultimately by the Britain of King Arthur. This process rests on the propagation of two main ideals, the chivalrous and the religious (the courtly ideal can, I feel, legitimately be included under the chivalrous).

There is no doubt that to the author the more important of the ideals is the chivalrous. What is emphasised again and again throughout the first book, for instance, of the romance is the chivalrous degeneration of the native British knights, a physical and moral weakness which in the case of one particular group, the *lignage Darnant*, descends to actual crime and to rebellion. This must be cured by a rapid programme of chivalrous reform on the part of the new kings and of the Greek heroes. This is the constant theme, the author's main preoccupation, which makes of the romance something approaching a 'manuel de chevalerie'.[48]

In terms of space and time devoted to it, the religious and spiritual ideal occupies a much less important place. The sixth book, which represents the spiritual culmination of the romance, is the only one in which the attention of the reader is directed preponderantly to the religious development of Britain, and it must be admitted that the sixth book is also by far the least successful in structure and style. Moreover, the spiritual ideal is to some extent dependent on the chivalrous ideal. When Perceforest, in the first book, is able, as we have shown, to enter the temple of the *Dieu Souverain*, the first to do so in some four hundred years, and thus becomes worthy to be the first to accept Dardanon's new religion, this is primarily because of his prowess and because he has successfully begun the task of subduing the rebellious elements in his kingdom and restoring the chivalry of Britain. As Dardanon tells him:

> Sachiez que j'ay vescu au siecle quatre cens ans ou plus, sy ay bien demouré en ceste forest trois cens, dont j'ay bien demouré ceans les neuf vings ans qu'il n'entra chevalier estrange ceans. [. . .] Puis que je vins ceans ilz ont esté

---

48 The phrase is that of Mlle Lods; see her analysis of the author's treatment of chivalry, *op. cit.*, pp. 201 ff.

a l'uys de ce temple cincq cens chevaliers qui oncques n'oserent entrer ens. Dont je tieng, ou je suis deceu, que le malice des forestz d'Angleterre sera abatu temprement. [I, 180r–v; P. 1, 66v]

A similar scale of values is evident in a later episode. Certain of the heroes of Britain, Perceforest among them, will be transported to the Ile de Vie, where they will survive until the coming of the Grail and of Christianity to Britain; these too, with the exception of Dardanon himself and the Reine Fée, are chosen for their prowess, and include the greatest heroes of Britain.

Nevertheless, the religious ideal is a central theme and a recurring one. It could be seen as providing the culmination of the romance. In the author's imagination, it seems that the sixth book provides not only the spiritual culmination of the romance but also the high point overall of the history of pre-Arthurian Britain, the goal to which the previous five books are tending. A large portion of this book is devoted to spiritual matters. Several threads combine, not always very happily, and one senses that the author hoped to build events up to a triumphant crescendo. The adventures of Gallafur, Perceforest's grandson, which occupy the early part of the book, have both a chivalrous and a spiritual significance. Carrying the 'escu a l'estrange signe' (a red cross on a white ground) he has as his mission to rid the forests of Britain of evil spirits, by conjuring them, in a phrase which he uses without understanding it, in the name of the 'filz de la Vierge'. His son, Gallafur II, gives himself to meditation and after being cured of leprosy by the mere sight of the Grail is converted to Christianity by Alain le Gros. Finally, in a grand climax, Gallafur II is transported to the Ile de Vie, where he finds Perceforest, Dardanon, the Reine Fée and others, and tells them of the 'bonne nouvelle', the birth and passion of Christ. They are converted to Christianity, and die on returning to the soil of Britain. This climax of the sixth book represents the final stages of the chivalrous and spiritual progress which has been described in the romance as a whole. Britain is purged of evil and of evil spirits, and the great survivors of the earlier, Alexandrian age have accepted Christianity and been baptised. The country is thus ready, spiritually and otherwise, for the advent of Arthur's world.[49]

Moreover, although the weight attached to the more spiritual and religious themes is greater in the sixth than in any other book of the

49 For a summary of the events of Book VI see J. Lods, *op. cit.*, pp. 32–4, and Flûtre, 'Etudes', *Romania*, XCI (1970), pp. 198–226.

romance, their importance in the climax of the 'chronique' is not unexpected or unprepared. Throughout the romance—at intervals, true, and often somewhat overwhelmed by a mass of detail—the spiritual and the religious, the cult of the *Dieu Souverain*, have intervened at crucial moments in the history of Britain. Only a few examples can be given here, but they will show how important an element is represented by the spiritual themes, as a force for good and for civilisation, as opposed to the forces of evil and anarchy.

In the second book of the romance Perceforest, on hearing of the death of Alexander, falls into a profound melancholy, a shameful lethargy from which nothing can arouse him. The king being, as the writer says 'ydeote et rassotté (II, 84*v*; P. II, 46*r*), the forces of evil begin to reappear; the rebellious *lignage Darnant*, painfully suppressed in the first book of the romance, emerges from the forests, and in alliance with certain other dissident elements rebels against the king; as the author says:

> Des lors en avant cesserent joustes et tournoiz et toutes gentillesses. Et les mauvais commencerent a apparoir petit a petit qui devant ne s'osoient monstrer, et les justices emprindrent a estre lasches et recreans. Car l'en dist pieç'a: "Quant le chief est malade, tous les membres se deulent." Et par ceste occasion emprindrent dedens brief temps les mauvais a regner et a faire les maulx en appert, et quant les justices en parloient, ilz les couroient sus et les fourmenoient. Et quant les bons veirent batre ceulx qui garder les devoient, ilz s'espardirent et s'en fuyoient par les boscaiges. Ainsi par deffaulte de souverain ala le royaume a perdicion.   [II, 85*v*; P. II, 46*r*]

Perceforest's 'merencolie' is incurable, until finally he is persuaded to visit the temple of the *Dieu Souverain*. Here he is cured, and finds the energy and the will to undertake the repression of the *lignage Darnant* and of the other rebellious elements in his kingdom.[50] The cult of the *Dieu Souverain* is thus a potent force against anarchy and rebellion.

The cult is also naturally associated with the greatest moments in the

50 Is this episode a reminiscence of a similar one in the *Perlesvaus* (ed. Nitze and Jenkins, Chicago, 1932, Branch I)? The relations between the two romances need clarifying; I hope to do this at a later date. If this incident is derivative, this does not invalidate the argument; the author has transferred the incident into the pre-Christian world and still chosen to make it central to his romance. Moreover, the balance of the episode is interestingly changed. In the *Perlesvaus* Arthur's lethargy is condemned by the author only because it has led to a decline in chivalry, to a falling off of numbers at Arthur's court because of his lack of 'largesse'. There is no suggestion of widespread discontent, or of political and social decay.

history of Britain. In the author's scheme of things the high points of pre-Arthurian Britain, as indeed of Arthur's kingdom later, are represented by the great feasts given either by Perceforest or by his brother and their descendants, and many of these are associated directly with the cult of the *Dieu Souverain*. The great feast at the beginning of Book IV of the romance (IV, 1–29*v*; P. IV, 1–13*v*), for instance, which is the last triumphant manifestation before the downfall of Perceforest's kingdom to the Romans under Julius Cæsar, is given in honour of the *Dieu Souverain*. And although the great feast held to celebrate the founding of the Order of the Franc Palais (II, 327*r* ff.; P. II, 241 ff.) is not directly under the patronage of the *Dieu Souverain*, the author, by introducing in imitation of Arthurian romance a 'siege perilleux' and a knight who is rash enough to sit at it, is able to give a long sermon from Perceforest exhorting the new knights, in the name of the *Dieu Souverain*, to chivalry, courtesy and humility (II, 341*v* ff.).[51]

The cult of the *Dieu Souverain* is also regularly associated, but less actively, with the critical moments in the history of Britain. It is, for instance, at the temple of the *Dieu Souverain* that we learn the extreme danger menacing Britain from Julius Caesar, and that the premonitory dreams of the Reine Fée and Dardanon, who have foreseen the disaster in the stars, are explained.[52] And after the disaster it is the believers in the cult of the *Dieu Souverain* who, mortally wounded, are carried to the Ile de Vie to await the coming of Christ.

The cult of the *Dieu Souverain* is thus vitally important in the author's imagination and central to the *Roman de Perceforest*. Its role is essentially a civilising, one might almost say a secular, one; this is not a near-mystic, allegorical work like the *Queste del Saint Graal*. The author is concerned not with the spiritual growth of the individual, but with describing, on a larger if more impressionistic scale, the development of civilisation in Britain, and showing how the Britain of Alexander the Great and Perceforest foreshadows the kingdom of Arthur. In this the spiritual development of Britain plays a part, and the *Dieu Souverain*, that one God whom the author's pagans are able to apprehend, and the idea for whose cult is derived from the philosophical or theological commonplaces of the time, is a potent force against barbarity and unchivalrousness.

51 Quoted in part by Flûtre, 'Etudes', *Romania*, LXXXIX (1968), pp. 499–500.
52 IV, 148*r* ff.; P. IV, 72*v* ff.; for a full summary from the printed edition see Flûtre, 'Etudes', *Romania*, XC, (1969), pp. 342–4.

We are dealing, then, with a religion and a cult which is not in its conception original. We have no evidence of any direct sources, but the prevalence of this *motif* in legend, sermon literature or indeed in philosophical treatises shows that the author need have had no precise source. His originality lies not in the conception itself but in the details with which he surrounds it and in the use that he makes of it. The cult of this new God, whose adherents eagerly await over the centuries the coming of Christ and his Incarnation, is thus an element which takes its place in the grand design of an author of whom Mlle Lods says:

> L'audace et le mérite de l'écrivain est d'avoir eu l'idée de montrer dans un roman comment, au cours des siècles, la civilisation, la morale et la religion se transforment.[53]

53 *Op. cit.*, p. 273.

Lewis Thorpe
Merlin's sardonic laughter

After having disguised himself as 'a man called Britaelis' so that he might play a minor part in the scurrilous episode of the seduction by Utherpendragon of Ygerna, Duchess of Cornwall, Merlin disappeared from the narrative of the *Historia Regum Britanniae*.[1] He was to be mentioned only once more, in retrospect, towards the end of the story, when the Angelic Voice announced that the time had not yet come for the rejuvenation of Britain which Merlin had prophesied to Vortigern.[2] It follows that, while he was certainly lurking nearby in the castle at Tintagel at the moment when Ygerna was being dishonoured, Merlin never set eyes on Arthur, who, in the course of nature, was born nine months later. Even more curious is the fact that Geoffrey of Monmouth should have allowed himself to forget the circumstance. When in A.D. 689 or thereabouts the Angelic Voice spoke to Cadwallader in a peal of thunder, it told him that 'God did not wish the Britons to rule in Britain any more, until the moment which Merlin had prophesied to Arthur'.[3] In the *Vita Merlini*,[4] Geoffrey's

---

1 Geoffrey of Monmouth, *The History of the Kings of Britain*, Penguin Classics, Harmondsworth, 1973, my translation, VIII.20, p. 207.

2 *Ibid.*, XII.17, p. 282.

3 *Loc. cit.* In both ms. Camb. Univ. Libr. 1706 and ms. Trin. Coll. Camb. 1125 the actual words are 'quod Merlinus Arturo prophetaverat', where 'Arturo' is presumably a slip for 'Vortegirno' and where the reference is to VII.3, p. 175. The adaptor of ms. Jesus Coll. Oxf. LXI was more careful: 'yny ddelai yr amsser a ddroganoedd merddin emrys gair bron gwrtheyrn', f. 134*v* (information supplied by Professor Idris L. Foster). The Brut Dingestow, Llanstephan ms. 1 and Peniarth ms. 23 all have 'Arthur'; ms. B.M. Cotton Cleopatra B. v has 'gortheyrn gwrthenev', and it is this that ms. Jesus Coll. Oxf. LXI seems to be following; Peniarth ms. 44 lacks the section (information supplied by Dr Brynley R. Roberts).

4 1529 Latin decasyllabic lines. There is only one complete manuscript, B.M. Cotton Vespasian E. IV, ff. 112b–138b, late thirteenth century. The most modern editions are J. J. Parry, *The Vita Merlini*, Urbana, 1925; and Edmond Faral, *La Légende arthurienne, études et documents, Première partie, Les plus anciens*

second work, written *c.* 1150—some fourteen years after the *Historia*, at a moment when the College of St George had already been made over to Oseney Abbey but before Geoffrey's election as Bishop of St Asaph—the position was more or less reversed. Merlin was then an old man, the Man of the Woods, Merlinus Silvester, but Arthur was presumably long since dead, or, at least, he had been 'carried off to the Isle of Avalon, so that his wounds might be attended to'.[5] In effect, Arthur was never mentioned in the *Vita*.

A feature of Merlin's behaviour in the *Vita* was his disconcerting habit of suddenly giving vent to bursts of sardonic laughter. He laughed first at the apparently happy marriage of Ganieda,[6] his own sister, who was the wife of King Rodarchus;[7] he laughed a second time at a doorman who was begging for alms; he laughed thirdly at a man who was buying not only a pair of new shoes but some patches with which to repair them should they ever begin to wear out.

The seemingly innocent and affectionate love-play of Rodarchus and his queen makes an endearing picture, a husband who embraces and kisses his wife in public when she comes to him, and then, without a thought of the reason for its being there, plucks a leaf from her unbraided hair and absent-mindedly drops it on the ground.

> Interea visura ducem regina per aulam
> Ibat et, ut decuit, rex applaudebat eunti,
> Perque manum suscepit eam, jussitque sedere,
> Et dabat amplexus, et ad oscula labra premebat;
> Convertensque suos in eam per talia vultus,
> Vidit in illius folium pendere capillis.
> Ergo suos digitos admovit, et abstrahit illud,
> Et projecit humi, laetusque jocatur amanti.   [254–61]

Ganieda's brother was not so pleased with what had happened. Much against his will he had just been dragged back to civilisation from his self-imposed exile in the Caledonian Forest, where for some time he had been living contentedly on a mixed diet of grubbed-up roots, woodland plants, acorns and the wild fruit which hung thick from the

---

textes, III, *Documents*, Paris, 1929, pp. 307–52. A new critical edition, with an introduction and an English translation, is to be published by Basil Clarke, Cardiff, 1973.

5 *H.R.B.*, my translation, XI.2, p. 261.
6 *V.M.*, 215: Ergo fratre suo gaudet regina recepto, ...
7 *V.M.*, 32: Rex ... Cumbrorum Rodarcus, ...

forest branches. The great warmth of the welcome which he had been
given by his sister and her husband had made Merlin even more vexed;
or perhaps what was rankling in his mind was the fact that they had
thought it necessary to keep him chained up like a dog, to prevent him
from running back to the woods again. He was determined to teach
them both to leave him alone. He stared fixedly at the leaf, at the care-
free, amorous king, and at his sister, the queen, whose loosened hair
rippled down over her lovely shoulders: and he laughed for the first
time.

> Flexit ad hoc oculos vates, risumque resolvit, . . .[8]

The king's courtiers were astonished. Rodarchus himself was idly
curious. He tried to bribe his brother-in-law to explain his sardonic
laughter; but only one concession could possibly induce Merlin to
break his silence, that of his freedom and of permission to return to the
woodland glades. In the end Rodarchus offered even this, and it was
accepted, to his own immediate discomfiture. Queen Ganieda had
been down in the woods, this being a compulsive habit in her family.
Her purpose had not been to gather blackberries or to pluck the rosy
crab-apples which hung from the bough. She had gone there to meet
her lover. She knew a secluded spot deep in the bushes. There she lay
on her back and soon the worst, or the best, had inevitably happened.
In the excitement her hair had come down, and without her noticing it
a leaf had caught in her tresses.

> 'Dum traheres folium modo, quod regina capillis
> Nescia gestabat, fieresque fidelior illi
> Quam fuit illa tibi, quando virgulta subivit,
> Quo suus occurrit secumque coivit adulter;
> Dumque supina foret, sparsis in crinibus haesit
> Forte jacens folium, quod nescius eripuisti.'   [288–93]

Ganieda naturally swore that she was innocent, maintaining that her
brother's unkind insinuations were nothing more than the ravings of
a mind unhinged. To prove her case she brought before him a young
servant in three different disguises, the third time dressed as a girl.
For this one boy Merlin prophesied three different deaths: that he
would die by falling off a rock, that he would meet his death in a
tree and that he, or she, would drown in a river. Ganieda then revealed
her subterfuge, and her husband was persuaded that if Merlin could

8 *V.M.*, 262.

err in this he could have been wrong about the leaf. Later the boy toppled down from a rock, tore his foot off in a tree as he fell and landed in a river, where what was left of him sank to the bottom.

Merlin was given his freedom and he promptly made off again for the woods. Not long after, he fell into a river in his turn and was brought home more dead than alive by the king's servants, who tied him up and handed him over to his sister. Again he languished and refused to eat or drink. To divert him from his melancholy Rodarchus had him taken to the market place. There Merlin laughed a second and a third time, at the doorman who was begging for alms and at the man who was buying shoes.

> Inspicit ante fores famulum sub paupere cultu,
> Qui servabat eas, poscentem praetereuntes
> Ore tremente viros ad vestes munus emendas;
> Mox stetit et risit vates miratus egentem.
> Illinc progressus nova calciamenta tenentem
> Spectabat juvenem commercantemque tacones;
> Tunc iterum risit . . .   [491–7]

Once again Rodarchus promised Merlin his freedom if he would say why he had laughed. The doorman who was begging so piteously for money to help him buy new clothes was ridiculous because, without knowing it, he was standing on a cache of buried treasure.

> 'Janitor ante fores tenui sub veste sedebat
> Et velut esset inops rogitabat praetereuntes,
> Ut largirentur sibi quo vestes emerentur:
> Ipsemet interea subter se denariorum
> Occultos cumulos occultus dives habebat.
> Illud ergo risi: tu terram verte sub ipso,
> Nummos invenies servatos tempore longo.'   [508–14]

The man who was buying shoes from a stall in the market place and providing himself with extra patches against the day when he would wear holes in them was ridiculous because, in effect, he would never live even to put the shoes on. That very same day he was drowned in the sea, and even as Merlin spoke his body was already floating shorewards.

> 'Illud item risi, quoniam nec calciamentis
> Nec superadditis miser ille taconibus uti
> Postmodo compos erit, quia jam submersus in undis
> Fluctuat ad ripas. Tu, vade videre: videbis.'   [519–22]

It is clear that the tale of the leaf in Ganieda's loosened hair is, of the
three, the one which Geoffrey savoured most, and artistically it is
extremely rewarding. In its warm lasciviousness and its laconic
brevity it has great charm: the young Queen who comes to greet her
husband, her face still flushed from exercise in the fresh air, her hair
dishevelled and her beauty disarrayed, her limbs now tired yet her
whole body fortified by contact with our Mother Earth, who, like
her wanton daughters, knows too well the quickening of seedtime
and the hot agony of harvest. There is nothing like it in the *Historia
Regum Britanniae*. Where did Geoffrey find this story of the telltale
leaf? Had he a source for the two more prosaic happenings in the
market place? What gave him the idea of the framework of Merlin's
three bursts of sardonic laughter? One can only proceed by listing
analogues.

1 In *The Testament of Solomon*,[9] an anonymous Christian Greek text
allegedly of the third century, there is a not dissimilar tale of sardonic
laughter by the devil Ornias, in an incident which is supposed to have
occurred when Solomon was building the Temple:

> 110. And behold, in those days one of the workmen, of ripe old age,
> threw himself down before me, and said: 'King Solomon, pity me,
> because I am old.' So I bade him stand up, and said: 'Tell me, old man,
> all you will.' And he answered: 'I beseech you, King, I have an only-born
> son, and he insults me and beats me openly, and plucks out the hair of my
> head, and threatens me with a painful death. Therefore I beseech you,
> avenge me.'
>
> 111. And I Solomon, on hearing this, felt compunction as I looked at
> his old age; and I bade the child be brought to me. And when he was
> brought I questioned him whether it were true. And the youth said: 'I
> was not so filled with madness as to strike my father with my hand. Be
> kind to me, O King. For I have not dared to commit such impiety, poor
> wretch that I am.' But I Solomon, on hearing this from the youth, ex-
> horted the old man to reflect on the matter, and accept his son's apology.
> However, he would not, but said he would rather let him die. And as the
> old man would not yield, I was about to pronounce sentence on the youth,
> when I saw Ornias the demon laughing. I was very angry at the demon's
> laughing in my presence; and I ordered my men to remove the other

9 The most recent edition of the Greek text is by C. C. McCown, *The Testament of Solomon*, Leipzig, 1922, vol. IX in the series *Untersuchungen zum Neuen
Testament*. Of the dating McCown writes: '. . . the conditions of language
and subject matter are best met by supposing the *Testament* to have been written in the third century' (pp. 107–8).

parties, and bring forward Ornias before my tribunal. And when he was brought before me, I said to him: 'Accursed one, why didst thou look at me and laugh?' And the demon answered: 'Prithee, King, it was not because of thee I laughed, but because of this ill-starred old man and the wretched youth, his son. For after three days his son will die untimely; and lo, the old man desires to foully make away with him.'

112. But I Solomon, having heard this, said to the demon: 'Is that true that thou speakest?' And he answered: 'It is true, O King.' And I, on hearing that, bade them remove the demon, and that they should again bring before me the old man with his son. I bade them make friends with one another again, and I supplied them with food. And then I told the old man after three days to bring his son again to me here; 'and', said I, 'I will attend to him.' And they saluted me, and went their way . . .

115. And I Solomon, having heard this, ordered the demon to be guarded for five days. And after five days I recalled the old man, and was about to question him. But he came to me in grief and with black face. And I said to him: 'Tell me, old man, where is thy son? And what means this garb?' And he answered: 'Lo, I am become childless, and sit by my son's grave in despair. For it is already two days that he is dead.' But I Solomon, on hearing that, and knowing that the demon Ornias had told me the truth, glorified the God of Israel.[10]

2 In his anthology of Jewish *haggadah*, *The Legends of the Jews*,[11] Louis Ginzberg tells a much more detailed story of sardonic laughter by the devil Asmodeus:[12]

> While Solomon was occupied with the Temple, he had great difficulty in devising ways of fitting the stone from the quarry into the building, for the Torah explicitly prohibits the use of iron tools in erecting an altar. The scholars told him that Moses had used the shamir, the stone that splits rocks, to engrave the names of the tribes on the precious   5 stones of the ephod worn by the high priest. Solomon's demons could give him no information as to where the shamir could be found. They surmised, however, that Asmodeus, king of demons, was in possession of the secret, and they told Solomon the name of the mountain on which Asmodeus dwelt, and described also his manner of life. On this   10 mountain there was a well from which Asmodeus obtained his drinking

---

10 This English translation is by F. C. Conybeare, 'The Testament of Solomon', *Jewish Quarterly Review*, XI (1899), pp. 1–45, of which see pp. 39–40.

11 Louis Ginzberg, *The Legends of the Jews*, written in German but translated into English by Henrietta Szold, Philadelphia, 1946–47, of which see IV, pp. 165–169.

12 Asmodeus plays a part in *The Testament of Solomon*, F. C. Conybeare's translation, pp. 20–1, but he has no occasion to laugh.

water. He closed it up daily with a large rock, and sealed it before going
to heaven, whither he went every day, to take part in the discussions
in the heavenly academy. Thence he would descend again to earth in
order to be present, though invisible, at the debates in the earthly houses 15
of learning. Then, after investigating the seal on the well to ascertain
if it had been tampered with, he drank of the water.

Solomon sent his chief man, Benaiah the son of Jehoiada, to capture
Asmodeus. For this purpose he provided him with a chain, the ring on
which the Name of God was engraved, a bundle of wool, and a skin of 20
wine. Benaiah drew the water from the well through a hole bored
from below, and, after having stopped up the hole with the wool, he
filled the well with wine from above. When Asmodeus descended
from heaven, to his astonishment he found wine instead of water in the
well, although everything seemed untouched. At first he would not 25
drink of it, and cited the Bible verses that inveigh against wine, to
inspire himself with moral courage. At length Asmodeus succumbed
to his consuming thirst, and drank till his senses were overpowered,
and he fell into a deep sleep. Benaiah, watching him from a tree, then
came, and drew the chain about Asmodeus's neck. The demon, on 30
awakening, tried to free himself, but Benaiah called to him: 'The
name of thy Lord is upon thee'. Though Asmodeus now permitted himself to be led off unresistingly, he acted most peculiarly on the way
to Solomon. He brushed against a palm-tree and uprooted it; he
knocked against a house and overturned it; and when, at the request of 35
a poor woman, he was turned aside from her hut, he broke a bone. He
asked with grim humor: 'Is it not written, "A soft tongue breaketh
the bone"?' A blind man going astray he set in the right path, and to a
drunkard he did a similar kindness. He wept when a wedding party
passed them, and laughed at a man who asked his shoemaker to make 40
him shoes to last for seven years, and at a magician who was publicly
showing his skill.

Having finally arrived at the end of the journey, Asmodeus, after
several days of waiting, was led before Solomon, who questioned him
about his strange conduct on the journey. Asmodeus answered that he 45
judged persons and things according to their real character, and not
according to their appearance in the eyes of human beings. He cried
when he saw the wedding company, because he knew the bridegroom
had not a month to live, and he laughed at him who wanted shoes to
last seven years, because the man would not own them for seven days, 50
also at the magician who pretended to disclose secrets, because he did
not know that a buried treasure lay under his very feet; the blind man
whom he set in the right path was one of the 'perfect pious', and he
wanted to be kind to him; on the other hand, the drunkard to whom

he did a similar kindness was known in heaven as a very wicked man, 55
but he happened to have done a good deed once, and he was rewarded
accordingly.[13]

Now, it is dangerous to argue from analogues. With few if any dates
to rely on, one puts them in the wrong order and mistakes cause for
effect. One underrates the inventive faculty of two different authors
who, without influencing each other, both think spontaneously of the
same story. Where there is a real link one sees it as immediate contact,
whereas there are often innumerable stages in between. When a
narrative theme is going the rounds it may often inspire a dozen tale-
tellers, each in a different way, without there being direct or conscious
imitation. One is so hypnotised by possible source relationships that
one fails to enjoy or even notice the literary talent of the writer who
comes towards the end of the chain. Here there can surely be no
doubt. The story of the sardonic laughter of the demon Ornias exists
in a third century text, and there were probably a few more stages in
the development which preceded it. The *haggadah* of *Solomon and
Asmodeus* is not dated, but it is extraordinarily similar in flavour and
subject-matter to *The Testament of Solomon*, although again there were
probably earlier versions. In an article in *The Jewish Encyclopedia*[14]
Louis Ginzberg contents himself with saying that it goes back to very
early rabbinical literature, adding that Asmodeus/Ashmedai derives
possibly—although he himself doubts this—from the arch-demon
Æshma in the Zend Avesta and in Pahlavi texts, in some postulated
form such as Æshma-dæva. What is certain is that the story of the
demon Asmodeus provides the outer framework of the capture of the
demon—not all that relevant to the *Vita Merlini*, but its importance
will be seen later—the inner framework of the bursts of sardonic
laughter during the bringing in of the captive, and even two of the
three individuals laughed at, the man who stood without knowing it
above a forgotten cache of treasure and the man who bought shoes.
Maybe nine hundred years divide *Solomon and Asmodeus* from the
incident in the *Vita Merlini*. How shall we link them? These are the
old folk stories of laymen and of clerics, the 'iucundi narratiunculi
salsaque dicta' told down the long years by a thousand raconteurs,
both amateur and professional, collected in anthologies of exempla,

13 *The Legends of the Jews*, IV, pp. 166–8.
14 See *The Jewish Encyclopedia*, II, 1902, pp. 217–20, s.v. 'Asmodeus, or Ashmedai
[Aᶜhmadai]'.

sometimes set, as here, in embryonic *romans à tiroir*. These bursts of sardonic laughter came to Geoffrey of Monmouth by the same obscure and devious routes which the stories in *Les Sept Sages de Rome* and in *Marques de Rome* followed in their journey from the Middle East and beyond to Western Europe.[15] *The Seven Sages of Rome* is thought to go back to a lost Indian version of the fifth century B.C. and to trace its later descent, including possible offshoots, through Arabic, Syriac, Greek, Persian, Hebrew, Old Spanish and Latin, to appear eventually in France about 1150, the very moment which we are considering. Æshma/Ashmedai/Asmodeus/Ornias/Merlin travelled the same long dusty trackway, laughing sardonically as he went, and he was occasionally given a lift in the same primitive ox cart by the same kind fellow wayfarer.[16]

There remains still the leaf in Ganieda's hair. The forgotten treasure and the pair of shoes are tawdry enough as anecdotes. At some time some one, maybe even Geoffrey himself, thought of adding a more titillating theme. One can laugh at most things if one has no conscience but a good digestion: at other people's poverty, at death, the macabre joker in all our slender, well thumbed packs, at man's carnal lusts and appetites, for we are all like brute beasts that have no understanding. Stories of wantonness abound in *The Thousand and One Nights*, *Les Sept Sages de Rome*, *Marques de Rome*, the *fabliaux*, the *Gesta Romanorum*, the *Decameron*, the *Canterbury Tales*, the *Confessio Amantis*. The dates of these collections, as we have them, matter little, for the stories had been told and re-told down the centuries. In the two which precede the *Vita Merlini* in date—*The Thousand and One Nights* and *Les Sept Sages de Rome*—there is nothing closely resembling the tale of the leaf; Cathon's story called *Avis* in *Les Sept Sages de Rome* is of the same type, as are many of the stories in *Marques de Rome*, but they all differ in detail. We can give the greater credit to Geoffrey.

It is perhaps less dangerous and more rewarding to look forwards rather than backwards over one's shoulder. The theme of Merlin's

---

15 For a consideration of this fascinating problem see Lewis Thorpe, *Le Roman de Laurin, fils de Marques le Sénéchal*, 1950, pp. 89–117.

16 To move beyond the life span of Geoffrey of Monmouth, but not outside the confines of this article, can anyone doubt that Bauduins Butors was aware of the Asmodeus legends, if not of *The Testament of Solomon* itself? See Lewis Thorpe, 'The four rough drafts of Bauduins Butors', *Nottingham Mediaeval Studies*, XII (1968), pp. 3–20; XIII (1969), pp. 49–64; XIV (1970), pp. 41–63.

laughter was used a second time in that section of the Arthurian prose
Vulgate which is called the *Estoire Merlin*.[17]

The emperor Julius Caesar had a dream in which he saw a coroneted
sow being served in turn by twelve wolf cubs. He was greatly puzzled
by what he had dreamed. Merlin appeared before Caesar in the guise of
a five-tined stag and told him that only the Wild Man of the Woods
could explain its significance. Later the stag appeared a second time,
to Grisandoles, the Seneschal of Rome, and described to him how he
could capture the Wild Man. Deep in the forest he must prepare a
meal of highly seasoned pork, fresh bread, milk and honey. The
Wild Man would then appear, gorge himself on the food, and assuage
his thirst with the milk and honey. As a result he would fall asleep
by the fire, and it would be a simple matter for Grisandoles and his
companions to capture him. The Seneschal did exactly as he was told,
and soon the Wild Man of the Woods found himself encircled with
chains and bound with ropes to a horse's saddle.

On the way back to Rome as a captive the Wild Man laughed four
times. First he looked at Grisandoles, his captor, and burst into a
paroxysm of mirth.

> Lors se metent al chemin et li homs salvages se regarde et vit Grisandoles,
> si commencha moult durement a rire.[18]

As they rode by the gates of an abbey they saw a crowd of poor folk
waiting for alms, and the Wild Man laughed a second time.

> Einsi chevalchent ensamble parlant de maintes choses et ont tant alé k'il
> passerent .j. jour devant une abeie, si virent devant la porte grant plenté
> de povre gent ki atendoient l'aumousne. Et quans li homs salvages les vit,
> si commencha a rire.[19]

They entered a wayside chapel to hear mass and there the Wild Man
gave a threefold burst of laughter as he watched a squire slap his
knight's face on three different occasions during the service.[20] Eventually they entered Rome. Julius Caesar's leaders assembled and the
Wild Man was ordered to interpret the emperor's dream before the
court. He asked that the empress and her twelve attendant maidens

---

17 *The Vulgate Version of the Arthurian Romances*, II, *L'Estoire de Merlin*, ed. H. O.
   Sommer, Washington, D.C., 1908, pp. 281–92.
18 *E.M.*, 284, 38–9. I have regularised Sommer's transcription in accordance
   with modern conventions.
19 *E.M.*, 285, 7–10.
20 *E.M.*, 285, 15 to 286, 8.

might also be present. As they came in, the Wild Man laughed for the last time.

Quant l'empereis et ses .xij. puceles furent venues, si leverent li baron sus contre li. Et si tost comme li salvages homs les vit, si torna la teste en travers et commencha a rire ausi comme par despit. Et quant il ot .j. poi ris, si regarda l'empereis et l'empereor tout a estal et Grisandoles et les .xij. puceles, et puis se tourne vers les barons, si commenche a rire moult durement aussi comme en escarnisant.[21]

After some debate, Merlin agreed to interpret the emperor's dream on condition that he should be given his freedom. First he repeated the details of the dream, and then he explained its meaning.

'Sire,' fait li homs salvages, 'li grant truie que vous veistes senefie vostre feme, l'empereis ki la esta, et la soie qu'ele ot si longe senefie la robe qu'ele a vestue, et li cercles d'or ke ele avoit el chief senefie la grant corone dont le fesistes coroner—et se vostre plaisirs i estoit je m'en tairoie a tant sans plus dire.' 'Chertes,' dist li empereres, 'dire le vous esteut, se vous volés aquiter vostre creant.' 'Sire,' fait li homs salvages, 'et je le vous dirai. Les .xij. loveaus ke vous veistes issir de vostre cambre senefient les .xij. puceles ki sont avoec vostre feme. Et sachiés de fi que che ne sont mie femes, ains sont homme comme autre. Et faites les desvestir, si savrés se ce est voirs ou non. Et sachiés ke toutes les fois que vous alés fors de la vile se fait servir en ses cambres.'[22]

That the twelve attendant maidens were really men in disguise was easily proved. The guilt of the libidinous empress seemed clear enough, and all thirteen offenders were condemned to be burnt to death.

The reason why Merlin laughed when he was captured by Grisandoles was because the doughty Seneschal was really a woman in disguise.

'. . . la premiere fois que jou ris ce fu por çou ke feme m'avoit pris par sa poisance et par son engin, che que nus homs ne pooit faire de tout vostre pooir. Et bien saciés que Grisandoles est la plus bele feme et la plus boine de tout vostre terre, et s'est pucele. Et por ce fis je le ris.'[23]

He laughed at the poor men begging outside the abbey because there was a vast treasure hidden in the ground directly beneath where they were standing.

'Et aprés le ris que je fis devant l'abeie jou le fis por chou k'il i a le plus grant tresor del monde devant la porte en terre. Et por chou fis je le ris que

21 E.M., 287, 20–6.   22 E.M., 288, 14–26.   23 E.M., 289, 13–17.

li tresors estoit desous les piés a chaus qui atendoient l'aumousne, et plus
avoient de richoise desous leur piés que toute l'abeie ne valoit ne quanques
il i apent, et por ce fis je le ris por le tresor qui devers els estoit et prendre
ne le savoient.'[24]

It was not the three blows given by the squire during mass to the
knight, his master, which Merlin found so amusing, but rather the
symbolism which he detected behind these blows. Again they were all
standing on a treasure hidden in the earth. Merlin laughed to think of
the ill effect this treasure would one day have upon the character and
the behaviour of the man who eventually discovered it; in a more
general way he laughed when he considered how pathetic was the way
in which rich and miserly men doted upon their wealth, and how
sinister the hatred which the poor bore them; at the third blow he
laughed when he thought of the lack of honesty and conscience shown
by lawyers in their pleading and their refusal to offer loving kindness
to their fellow human beings, for 'a mal voisin il a mal matin'.[25]

When all the explanations were over and the empress had been
burnt at the stake with her team of lovers, the emperor Julius Caesar
married his Seneschal, who was really Avenable, the beautiful daughter
of the exiled Duke Mathem de Soane.[26]

In the Grisandoles/Avenable episode there is no mention of the man
buying shoes. The reason is not far to seek. The compiler of the
Estoire Merlin had used the story already, with yet another not dissimilar tale, at an earlier point in his narrative, when the fatherless boy
Merlin was brought in to blend the cement of Vortigern's tower with
his blood. As he was being conducted to Vortigern, Merlin twice gave
vent to enigmatic and sardonic laughter. Soon after passing through
a market place he saw a man who had bought shoes and patches with
which to mend them.

Et Merlins chevauche avoec les messages tant qu'il passerent parmi une
ville ou il avoit marchiet. Et quant il orent la ville passee, si troverent .j.
vilain qui avoit achaté un moult fors solers, et portoit le quir por ces solers
afaitier quant il seroient depechiet, car il voloit aler en pelerinage. Et
Merlins vint pres del vilain, si commencha a rire. Et cil qui le menoient li
demanderent por quoi il avoit ris, et il lor dist: 'Por cel vilain que vous veés
chi. Ore li demandés qu'il veut faire de cel quir que il enporte, et il dira
qu'il en vaudra ses solers afaitier. Si le suivés, car je vous di vraiement que
il sera mors anchois qu'il viegne a sa maison.'[27]

24 E.M., 289, 17–22.   25 E.M., 290, 8–29.
26 E.M., 291, 4–15.   27 E.M., 28, 32 to 29, 1, etc.

Not long after this they passed a cemetery, where, in the midst of general lamentation, a priest was burying a woman's son.

Un jour avint qu'il passoient par mi une ville, si avint que on portoit .j. enfant por enterrer, si avoit entor le cors moult grant duel d'ommes et de femes. Et quant Merlins vit cel deul et les provoires et les clers qui chantoient et portoient le cors por enterrer moult vistement, si arresta Merlins et commencha a rire. Et cil qui le menoient li demandent por quoi il rioit, et il dist: 'D'une grant mervelle que je voi'. Si lor dist: 'Veés vous cel preudome la qui fait tel duel et cel provoire qui si chante?' Et il dient: 'Oïl, bien.' Et Merlins dist: 'Li provoires deust faire le duel que li preudoms fait, que je voel bien que vous saciés que cis enfes fu ses fiex por qui chiex a qui il n'apartient de riens fait tel duel, et cil qui fiex il est chante, si qu'il m'est avis que c'est grant mervelle.'[28]

Merlin's sardonic laughter was used for the third time in the denouement of *Le roman de Silence*, by Heldris de Cornuälle.[29] At the suggestion of Queen Eufeme, his consort, Ebains, king of Britain, sent the knight Silence to find Merlin, who had not been seen since he helped King Fortigierne to build his tower many years before. This was tantamount to perpetual banishment, for when he disappeared Merlin had prophesied that only a woman could find him. Silence searched the woods and the desert places for six months or more. Then one day he met the White-haired Man, who told him how to set a trap for Merlin by preparing a meal of salted roast meat, milk, honey and wine, and leaving it by a water hole in the forest. Merlin came to the spring, ate the vast meal, fell asleep and was duly captured by Silence. As he was being led back to Ebains' court, Merlin laughed three times. They entered the town and a crowd came out to gape at them. In the crowd Merlin observed a peasant with a new pair of shoes.

> Voit Merlins venir un vilain:
> Uns nués sollers porte en sa main
> Bien ramendés de cuir de tacre.
> Merlins le voit de deseur l'acre,
> Si en commenche fort a rire
> Mais ne volt onques un mot dire
> Por quele oquoison il a ris.   [6191–7]

28 *E.M.*, 29, 22–32, etc.
29 *Le Roman de Silence, a thirteenth-century Arthurian verse romance by Heldris de Cornuälle*, ed. Lewis Thorpe, 1972, ll. 5779–6683.

They passed the gateway of an abbey, and there a leper was shaking his
rattle and begging for alms.

> Dont vien devant une abeÿe
> Et voit un mezel tarteler
> Et por Deu l'almosne apieler.
> Dont rit Merlins, por poi ne derve, . . .   [6202-5]

Next they passed a cemetery, where a priest was conducting a burial
service in the presence of a single mourner, who was crying his eyes out.

> Ilueques ot un cimentire,
> Joste l'eglize, a un descors.
> Voit Merlins enfoïr un cors,
> Entre .ii. pieres ensierer.
> Uns priestres cante a l'entierer
> Et uns prodom i crie et pleure.
> Et Merlins en rist en esleure.   [6210-16]

When they reached the king's court they were given a cold reception,
for both Ebains and his queen had been convinced that they would
never see Silence again, in that his quest for Merlin was condemned to
failure from the start. Merlin was thrown into prison for three days
and given no food; then he was brought back to court and threatened
with immediate death unless he could explain satisfactorily his three
bursts of laughter. His reply was to laugh a fourth time, at King
Ebains, at the queen and the nun who accompanied her everywhere,
at the knight Silence and at himself. In the end, to save his life, he
agreed to explain his odd behaviour, with the entire court listening.
He had laughed at the villein who had just bought some new shoes
and had had strengthening patches put on them because the man
would die before he reached home and never have occasion to wear
his shoes.

> 'Quant ens en la cité entrai,
> Un fol vilain i encontrai
> Si com il venoit del marchié.
> Uns nués sollers ot encargié:
> Sis ot fais ramender tols nués
> Mais onques ne li orent wés.
> De rire oi jo bone oquoison,
> Car ains qu'il venist en maison
> Morut li vilains, c'est la voire.'   [6315-23]

Merlin's second burst of laughter had been at a leper shaking his rattle

outside an abbey gateway and begging for alms. Not without significance, the leper became a group of 'povres gens' in the explanation.

'... Jo ris, mais ne fu pas mervelle,
Des povres gens qu'illuec estoient
Et por Deu l'almosne apieloient.
Il demandoient la le mains
Et li plus ert devant lor mains.
Desor lor piés ot un tresor
Moult mervellols d'argent et d'or,
A .ii. piés et demi sos terre.'   [6330–7]

Merlin next explained his unfeeling laughter when he and Silence
passed the cemetery. It was a young boy who was being buried,
although we had not previously been told so.

'Uns priestres cantoit por le mort,
Et uns prodom i ploroit fort.
Li prodom en deüst liés estre
Car li enfes estoit le priestre,
Ki en deüst par droit plorer
Et li prodom Deu aörer
De cui feme li enfes fu.'   [6359–65]

For dramatic effect and because it brings the story to an end, Merlin's
explanation of why on entering the court he laughed at King Ebains,
at the queen and her attendant nun, at the knight Silence and at himself
is left until last.

'Cil doi, Silence et la none,
Sont li doi qui gabés nos ont,
Et nos li doi qui gabé sunt.
Rois, cele none tient Eufeme.
Escarnist vos ses dras de feme.
Rois, or vos ai jo bien garni.
Silences ra moi escarni
En wallés dras, c'est vertés fine,
Si est desos les dras meschine.
La vesteüre, elle est de malle.
La nonain, qui n'a soig de halle,
Bize, ni vent, ki point et giele,
A vesteüre de femiele ...   [6528–40]

Sire, jo ris de cest affaire.'   [6552]

Queen Eufeme and her lover were drawn apart by horses. King
Ebains made the knight Silence his wife.

The *haggadah* of *Solomon and Asmodeus* goes back to the early centuries
of our era and perhaps beyond. The *Vita Merlini* is dated *c.* 1150.
Both the *Estoire Merlin* and *Le roman de Silence* were written in the
second half of the thirteenth century. They all use the theme of sardonic laughter by a demon soothsayer. How closely they resemble
each other in their narrative sequences and to what similar use they
put the topos the accompanying table shows.

		Solomon and Asmodeus	Vita Merlini	Estoire Merlin	Silence
A	Setting	1–10	212–14	282, 19–42	5779–872
B	Soothsayer in first guise			283, 1–284, 6	5873–977
C	Capture of soothsayer in second guise	10–32		284, 7–38	5978–6136
Ia	Reaction of soothsayer to captor			284, 38–285, 3	6137–60
IIa	Tears at wedding party	39–40			
IIIa	Laughter at beggar(s)	41–2	491–4	285, 7–14	6202–9
IVa	Laughter at shoes	40–41	495–7	[28, 32–6]	6191–201
Va	Laughter at knight			285, 17–286, 16	
VIa	Laughter at burial service			[29, 22–6]	6210–20
D	Arrival at court	43–7	215–53, 481–9	286, 17–31	6161–227
VIIa	Laughter at queen/empress		254–61	287, 20–6	6228–64
VIIb	Explanation of VIIa		285–93	288, 14–32	6471–552
E	Fate of queen/empress		342–6	288, 32–42	6651–63
Ib	Explanation of Ia			289, 13–17	6534–7
IIb	Explanation of IIa	47–9			
IIIb	Explanation of IIIa	51–2	508–14	289, 17–22	6329–37
IVb	Explanation of IVa	49–50	515–22	[28, 36–29, 11]	6314–23
Vb	Explanation of Va			290, 8–29	
VIb	Explanation of VIa			[29, 26–43]	6359–70
F	Outcome			291, 4–15	6664–83

From the lists one can make certain tentative deductions. It is best to
work backwards. In this section *Le roman de Silence* is a direct adapta-

tion from the *Estoire Merlin*. Heldris de Cornuälle has more space at
his disposal, since for him this is the dramatic denouement of a single-
theme verse romance told in 6,706 octosyllables; he omits the threefold laughter at the squire and the knight as being too complicated in
its symbolic explanation; in a curious way, remembering the *Estoire
Merlin*, when he explains the plight of his single leper, he changes
him to a group of 'povres gens', just as, in the description of the villein
and his shoes, he adds a meaningless line,

Un roi i ot qu'ot a non Ris,   [6198]

which can come only from a confusion in his reading of his source;
he has the taste to give Queen Eufeme one lover only, disguised as a
nun. Between the *Estoire Merlin* and the *Vita Merlini* there may well be,
and in fact there must be, a great number of hidden stages. The compiler of the *Estoire Merlin* develops enormously the theme of sardonic
laughter by his demon soothsayer, but he spoils it by using it twice;
he gives to his empress twelve transvestite lovers, which is to move
from libido to luxuria; he alone uses the difficult theme of the knight
who is hit three times by his squire during mass; he alone explains
the villein's preoccupation with his footwear by adding convincingly
that 'il voloit aler en pelerinage'. Between the *Vita Merlini* and *Solomon
and Asmodeus*, with *The Testament of Solomon* at its side, lie long centuries of tale telling. Geoffrey of Monmouth brings Merlin in from the
wilderness twice, just as the *Estoire Merlin* divides the sardonic laughter
into two sections, and this is perhaps a blemish; of the four authors,
or five, he is the first to introduce a theme of wantonness, which is a
welcome variation after such mundane matters as beggars and shoes;
alone among the erring women, Geoffrey's queen defends herself, and
one thinks of *Les Sept Sages de Rome*; of all the stories told, that of the
leaf in Ganieda's hair is the one perfect gem. In the capture of the
demon by a substitution of wine for water *Solomon and Asmodeus*
leads unmistakably on to the *Estoire Merlin* and *Le roman de Silence*,
but by-passes strangely the *Vita Merlini*. The theme of the beggars and
that of the shoes are unbreakable links in a long chain which joins
together all four stories.

Eugène Vinaver
Remarques sur quelques vers de Béroul

Autour du *Tristan* de Béroul les travaux d'exégèse se multiplient
et si pour rendre hommage à la mémoire d'un ami j'ai choisi, au
risque de ne rien trouver de neuf, d'examiner quelques problèmes que
nous pose l'unique manuscrit conservé de ce texte, c'est que l'œuvre de
Béroul a toujours été pour nous deux un lieu de rencontre privilégié
où se confirmait à chaque épreuve l'harmonieuse convergence de nos
vues. Les réflexions réunies dans les pages qui suivent n'ont pour
objet que d'en renouveler l'émouvant souvenir.

Dans le domaine de la critique des vieux textes, nous étions, lui et
moi, «non-interventionistes»: aucune correction ne nous paraissait val-
able qui ne s'appuyât en premier lieu sur la découverte des conditions
dans lesquelles l'erreur à corriger a pu se produire. D'après ce principe,
que Frederick Whitehead lui-même a admirablement illustré dans son
édition de la *Chanson de Roland*, seules sont corrigibles les erreurs dont
nous pouvons reconstituer le mécanisme et l'origine; et inversement,
toute trace d'une telle erreur peut appeler l'intervention du critique:
il suffit pour la justifier que le texte accuse une irrégularité quelqconque
et que l'on voie comment cette irrégularité a pu résulter d'un accident
de copie.

Un vers contaminé?

Aux vers 711-14 du *Tristan* de Béroul, nous lisons:

> Pus dist: «Bien tost a ceste place
> Espandroit flor por nostre trace
> Veer, se l'un a l'autre iroit.
> Qui iroit or que fous feroit.»

C'est Tristan qui parle ainsi en voyant le nain Frocin s'affairer
autour du lit d'Iseut. Ce texte suppose que *nostre trace* est le complément

direct du verbe *veer* et *se l'un a l'autre iroit* une proposition condition-
nelle qui veut dire«si l'un de nous allait rejoindre l'autre.» Or, comme
le fait remarquer dans un commentaire tout récent M. T. B. W.
Reid,[1] une telle construction appelle en principe un imparfait, soit du
subjonctif, soit de l'indicatif: on s'attendrait à *se l'un a l'autre aloit* ou
alast au lieu de *iroit*. M. Reid estime néanmoins que parce que *iroit* se
trouve ici confirmé par la rime riche *iroit:feroit*, il faut laisser le vers
713 tel qu'il est et ajouter une virgule après *nostre trace*: «... espandroit
flor por nostre trace, veer» etc. Or il me semble que la richesse même
de la rime *iroit:feroit* pourrait être considérée comme un motif de
suspicion contre elle: d'abord parce que Béroul, on le sait, ne sacrifie
jamais l'usage syntaxique normal aux raffinements prosodiques; et
puis, et surtout, parce que dans le cas qui nous occupe une rime
normale comme *aloit:feroit* a très bien pu devenir rime riche à la
faveur d'une distraction de copiste. Tout copiste est susceptible de se
laisser égarer par le contexte immédiat du vers qu'il transcrit. Au
moment où il copiait le vers 713, le scribe de notre manuscrit ne
pouvait ne pas voir, au vers 714, la terminaison *roit* dans *iroit* et *feroit*;
et sans y penser, victime d'une aberration visuelle dont on sait combien elle est difficile à éviter, il remplaça *aloit* par *iroit*. La rime riche
qui résulta de cette erreur détonne un peu dans un contexte où dominent
les rimes en *oit* sans consonne d'appui: *devoit/soloit, estoit/doloit*, etc.
Mais ce qui la juge surtout c'est qu'elle nous oblige à prêter à Béroul une
syntaxe dans laquelle il eût eu de la peine à se reconnaître. La virgule
qui suit *veer* dans toutes les éditions du texte, celles de Muret, de
Ewert et de «L. M. Defourques»,[2] n'arrange rien; celle que M. Reid
nous propose d'ajouter après *nostre trace* donne une construction
singulièrement estropiée, où le verbe *veer* n'est plus relié à *espandre*

---

1 T. B. W. Reid, The 'Tristran' of Beroul: a Textual Commentary, Oxford,
1972.
2 Beroul, The Romance of Tristran, ed. A. Ewert, Oxford, 1939. Le premier
volume de cette édition, publié en 1939 et réimprimé plusieurs fois depuis
cette date, contient l'introduction, le texte et le glossaire; le deuxième, con-
tenant un commentaire détaillé, n'est sorti qu'en 1970, quelques semaines
après la mort de l'auteur. La première édition publiée par Ernest Muret parut
dans la collection de la Société des anciens textes français en 1903. Elle fut
réimprimée trois fois (en 1913, 1922 et 1928) dans la collection des Classiques
français du moyen âge. Une nouvelle édition «revue par L. M. Defourques»
vit le jour en 1947 dans le même collection. Sous ce masque transparent se
cachaient deux grands romanistes, Lucien Foulet et Mario Roques, qui estimai-
ent sans doute cette «révision» trop superficielle pour mériter leurs signatures.

par la préposition *por*. En substituant *aloit* à *iroit* on rétablit la construction normale en s'appuyant sur la plus vraisemblable des hypothèses, celle d'une contamination.

Le saut de la chapelle

L'évasion des amants se situe, chez Béroul, à la limite du merveilleux et du réel. Voici comment Béroul décrit le fameux «saut de la chapelle» (je supprime toute ponctuation sauf l'apostrophe):

Triés l'autel vint a la fenestre   943
A soi l'en traist a sa main destre
Par l'overture s'en saut hors
Mex veut sallir que ja ses cors
Soit ars voiant tel aunee
Seignors une grant pierre lee   948
Out u mileu de cel rochier
Tristran i saut mot de legier
Li vent le fiert entre les dras
Quil defent qu'il ne chie a tas   952
Encor claiment Corneualan
Cele pierre le saut Tristran
La chapele ert plaine de pueple
Tristran saut sus l'araine ert moble   956
Toz a genoz sot en ligliglise
Cil l'atendent defors l'iglise
Mais por noient Tristran s'en vet
Bele merci Dex li a fait.   960

Jusqu'au vers 956, le texte ne présente aucune difficulté: «Tristan court au vitrail derrière l'autel, tire la fenêtre vers lui de la main droite et saute à travers l'ouverture; il aime mieux sauter que de se laisser brûler vif en présence d'une telle assemblée. Seigneurs, il y avait, au milieu de ce rocher, une large pierre. Tristan y saute légèrement. Le vent qui se prend en ses vêtements, l'empêche de tomber comme une masse. Les Cornouaillais appellent encore cette pierre le *Saut Tristan*. La chapelle était pleine de gens. Tristan fait un saut en l'air. Le sable est mou.» Admirable ellipse que ce dernier vers, qui supprime tout ce que le poète n'avait pas besoin de dire: que Tristan, ayant sauté d'abord sur une pierre plate, en contrebas de la chapelle et juste au-dessus du rivage, s'est jeté de là sur le sable, assez mou pour lui éviter les suites fâcheuses que pourrait avoir une telle chute. Au vers 957, *ligliglise*

est une corruption évidente de *liglise*. Mais que veut dire *liglise*?
L'iglise ou *la glise*? Pour éviter de prêter à Béroul une rime du même
au même Muret avait choisi *la glise* (glaise) et remplacé *sot* par *chiet*. Et à
la suite de cette correction on a vu, dans toutes les éditions du texte sauf
celle de Ewert, Tristan s'enfoncer jusqu'aux genoux dans la glaise[3] et
en ressortir indemne pour fuir *granz sauz* le long du rivage. Certes,
Béroul ne manque pas de dire que la miséricorde divine y était pour
quelque chose, mais les miracles, chez Béroul, ne sont jamais contraires
à la vraisemblance, le détail précis, concret y est toujours scrupuleuse-
ment respecté. Ainsi lorsque Tristan saute sur la *pierre lee*, c'est le vent
qui l'empêche d'y tomber trop lourdement. Or, est-il concevable qu'un
homme, sautant d'une grande hauteur, rentre jusqu'aux genoux dans
une couche de glaise sans se casser les deux jambes? Le vers précédent
dit bien que Tristan est tombé sur une plage de sable. Que vient donc
faire ici cette chute dans la glaise, catastrophique si elle avait jamais pu
avoir lieu, contradictoire dans son contexte, et textuellement indéfen-
dable, puisqu'il n'y a aucune raison pour que sous la plume d'un copiste
chiet devienne *sot*? Et pourquoi ne pas lire tout simplement *Toz a genoz
sont en l'iglise* («tous, dans la chapelle, se sont mis à genoux») en laissant
iglise rimer avec *iglise*, puisque nous connaissons au moins neuf autres
cas où Béroul rime du même au même?[4] Ainsi transcrit, ce vers
pourrait s'entendre comme une suite naturelle du vers 955 (*La chapele
ert plaine de pueple*), ces deux touches superposées donnant au tableau
un relief que la correction introduite par Muret risquait d'effacer.

Cette interprétation, adoptée par Ewert, n'a pas rencontré les suf-
frages de «L. M. Defourques» ni ceux de M. Reid. Celui-ci propose
d'intervertir les vers 955 et 956 pour obtenir ce qu'il appelle «a much
less disjointed narrative». Il ne semble pas se rendre compte que la
vraie réussite stylistique de Béroul tout au long de ce récit réside précisé-
ment dans sa structure entrelacée. La description détaillée des deux
étapes du «saut Tristan» alterne avec celle des deux groupes de témoins:
les spectateurs agenouillés à l'intérieur de la chapelle et les gardes qui
attendent que Tristan en ressorte. La transposition que propose M.

3 A moins qu'il ne faille comprendre que Tristan tombe tout droit (*toz* au sens
   de «en plein») sur les deux genoux, ce qui serait encore plus absurde.
4 Grant : grant (193-4), vot : vot (1301-2), paine : paine (1783-4), demorer :
   demorer (2121-2), cheval : cheval (2571-2), reter : reter (3057-8), loiauté :
   loiauté (3421-2), esperon : esperon (3677-8), harberges : herberges (4079-80).
   Sur l'emploi des rimes «homonymes» en vieux français voir l'article de P.
   Rickard dans *Neuphilologische Mitteilungen*, LXVI (1965), pp. 335-401.

Reid ne ferait que nuire à l'effet de simultanéité que produit le texte conservé. Pour ce qui est du vers 957 que Muret avait remanié afin de faire rimer *iglise* avec *glise*, M. Reid y voit une anomalie grammaticale plutôt que prosodique. La forme *toz*, dit-il, ne saurait être un pluriel parce que partout ailleurs le scribe a respecté la forme *tuit* ('since else-where the scribe has regularly copied *tuit* correctly as the masc. nom. pl. form').[5] M. Reid a-t-il tenu compte des vers 3395-6:

Devant le roi vint a l'estage
Ou s[e]oient tuit li barnage,

où *tuit* remplace visiblement *toz*? A-t-il surtout pris en considération ce fait que la correction proposée par Muret suppose qu'un scribe a changé le *chiet* du texte primitif en *sont*, non par distraction, mais sciemment, qu'il a pris l'initiative de passer du singulier *chiet* au pluriel *sont*, et que par conséquent pour ce scribe comme pour beaucoup d'écrivains et de copistes du XIIe et du XIIIe siècle *toz* était une forme légitime du pluriel, interchangeable avec *tuit*? Adopter la leçon *chiet*, comme le veut M. Reid, c'est affirmer le contraire de ce qu'il soutient lui-même, c'est reconnaître—et Muret ne l'a jamais nié—que *toz* dans notre texte peut signifier soit *tout* soit *tous*, selon ce qu'exige la phrase. Inutile donc de pousser l'invraisemblance jusqu'à faire rentrer Tristan *toz a genoz* dans une couche de glaise. La Providence, chez Béroul, emprunte pour agir des voies moins excentriques.

Indiscrétion ou calomnie?

Il n'est pas toujours interdit d'intervertir les vers d'un couplet pour retrouver la bonne leçon. Dans l'édition Ewert, on lit, aux vers 1341-6:

Au roi dient priveement:
«Roi, nos savon ton celement».
Li rois s'en rist et dist: «Ce mal,

5 *Ouvr. cité*, p. 38. Au vers 956 (*Tristran saut sus, l'araine ert moble*), M. Reid propose de corriger *sus* en *jus* parce que, dit-il, le scribe confond souvent les prépositions et les adverbes qui correspondent à *on*, *over* et *under*. Or, dans le cas qui nous occupe, il s'agit justement d'un saut en hauteur: quittant le rocher, Tristan saute en l'air et retombe sur le sable. *Sus* est le seul adverbe qui puisse traduire ce mouvement. Ewert (*ouvr. cité*, II, p. 138) décrit ainsi le

Que j'ai orelles de cheval,
M'est avenu par cest devin;
Certes, ja ert fait de lui fin.»

Muret avait interverti les vers 1342 et 1344, remplacé *s'en rist* par
s'iraist, j'ai orelles par *as orelles* et imprimé le tout comme suit:

Au roi dient priveement:
«Roi, nos savon ton celement,
Que as orelles de cheval.»
Li rois s'iraist et dist: «Ce mal
M'est avenu par cest devin;
Certes, ja ert fait de lui fin.»

Il ne semble pas s'être aperçu que les vers 1343 et 1344 une fois inter-
vertis, il n'avait plus besoin de les corriger. Il suffisait de les reponctuer
ainsi:

«Roi, nos savon ton celement.»
«Que j'ai orelles de cheval?»
Li rois s'en rist et dist: «Ce mal
M'est avenu par cest devin, *etc.*

Dès lors, le rire du roi s'inscrit tout naturellement dans un échange
de répliques entre lui et ses barons. Ceux-ci lui disent: «Nous connaissons ton secret». «Lequel? leur répond-il en riant. Vous a-t-on dit que
j'ai des oreilles de cheval? C'est la faute de ce devin.» Au lieu d'être
une affirmation, «que j'ai orelles de cheval» devient une interrogation
à laquelle répond le rire de Marc, rire ambigu comme *ce mal* qui,
dans sa bouche, pourrait bien signifier «cette calomnie», le bruit mali-
cieux que fait courir le nain Frocin. Béroul se garde bien d'en dire
davantage; et rien ne nous empêche de croire que l'histoire des oreilles
de cheval a été inventée de toutes pièces par le nain.[6] Toute précision
risquerait d'alourdir inutilement cette jolie scène de comédie.

Une correction qui abolit le poème

De toutes les corrections proposées par Muret celle qui fournit le
meilleur exemple des méfaits de l'interventionisme se situe dans un des

---

«saut de la chapelle»: 'Tristran first leapt from the chapel to a flat stone half-way
down the cliff, the impact being broken by his cloak billowing out, parachute-
like, under the wind, and from this stone he leapt to the soft sand of the sea-
shore.'

6 Le nom de Marc s'y prêtait, puisque *marc* en gallois, comme *march* en breton,
veut dire «cheval».

plus beaux passages du texte; la description de la vie des amants pendant
leur exil dans la forêt de Morois:

> Chascun d'eus soffre paine elgal,
> Qar l'un por l'autre ne sent mal. [1649-50]

Muret corrige:

> Qar l'un por l'autre *resent* mal.

J'ai essayé de montrer ailleurs[7] que cette correction, qui fausse la
signification d'un des thèmes centraux du poème, repose sur un con-
tresens: *soffrir paine elgal* ne veut pas dire ici «éprouver la même dou-
leur», mais «subir, sans en souffrir, les mêmes privations». Le vers
suivant, avec la négation *ne* devant *sent mal*, prolonge et précise la
même pensée, et supprimer cette négation, c'est dire le contraire de
ce qu'a voulu dire le poète. Chose curieuse, Ewert a retenu ici la
leçon du manuscrit, tout en laissant subsister la ponctuation introduite
par Muret. Le vers 1650 apparaît chez lui comme chez Muret suivi de
deux points pré-explicatifs:

> Qar l'un por l'autre ne sent mal:
> Grant poor a Yseut la gente
> Tristran por lié ne se repente, *etc.*

Quelle relation de cause à effet peut-il y avoir entre *ne sent mal* et le
fait qu'Iseut craint les regrets de Tristan? Aucune, selon Muret, et c'est
pourquoi dans son édition *ne sent* devient *resent*. Sans adopter cette
correction Ewert ponctue le texte comme s'il l'avait adoptée. D'où le
curieux *non sequitur* de la traduction qu'il en donne:[8]

> The sufferings of the lovers are shared equally, for neither of them feels
> their pangs because of the other, the fear of Iseut being that Tristran should
> repine because of her.

Si les amants ne souffrent pas (*neither of them feels*, etc.) à quoi introduire
ici, par le truchement de la ponctuation, un lien causal entre cette
affirmation et celle qui suit (*the fear of Iseut being*, etc.)? La version de
Muret avait au moins l'avantage d'être logique avec elle-même. Les
deux points pré-explicatifs y exprimaient le raisonnement que le

---

7 D'abord dans un article des Mélanges Ewert (*Studies in Medieval French,*
Oxford, 1961, pp. 90-5), ensuite dans une étude publiée dans les *Cahiers de
civilisation médiévales* (janvier–mars 1968) et tout récemment dans *A la
Recherche d'une poétique médiévale*, Paris, 1970, pp. 88-92.

8 *Ouvr. cité*, II, p. 173.

critique croyait devoir prêter au poète, raisonnement qui appelait la substitution de *resent* à *ne sent*. Que le poème obéisse à une logique plus subtile, c'est ce que ni Muret, ni Ewert, ni «L. M. Defourques»[9] ne semblent avoir compris. Béroul nous dit, en effet:

> Ils subissent tous les deux les mêmes épreuves, de sorte que ni l'un ni l'autre ne sent sa misère. La noble Iseut craint que Tristan ne se reproche l'état où elle se trouve, *etc.*

La deuxième phrase est ici en rupture totale avec la première, comme le monde auquel les amants viennent d'échapper avec le philtre d'amour qui les a rendus insensibles à la *paine* qu'ils subissent l'un et l'autre dans la forêt de Morois. Le *qar* du vers 1650 ne saurait être, dans ce contexte, qu'un *qar* consécutif («de sorte que», «à telles ensignes que»), comme dans ce passage où Béroul décrit l'accueil que les gens de Cornouailles avaient réservé à Iseut:

> D'Iseut grant joie demenoient,
> De lui servir molt se penoient,
> Quar, ce saciez, ainz n'i ot rue
> Ne fust de paile portendue   [2965-8]

Si pourtant M. Reid estime qu'au vers 1650, il faut ou bien rétablir la correction proposée par Muret, ou bien remplacer le *qar* par un *mais*, c'est que pour lui *soffrir paine elgal* veut toujours dire «endurer les mêmes tourments».[10] A cet égard son commentaire ne marque aucun progrès sur celui de Ewert. Mais ce qu'il a très bien vu, c'est qu'après le vers 1650 *non corrigé* il faudrait mettre un point au lieu de deux points. «The following lines, dit-il, are no longer explanatory, but contradictory.» On ne saurait mieux dire pour toucher au nerf le

---

9 L'édition Defourques reproduit ici sans le commenter le texte de Ewert.
10 *Ouvr. cité*, p. 62. On ne manquera pas d'être surpris de voir M. Reid affirmer que le sens consécutif de *qar* n'est attesté «ni à l'époque ni dans la région de Béroul», et qu'il faut par conséquent remplacer *qar* par *mais*. Ce sens est attesté, nous venons de le voir, par Béroul lui-même, au vers 2964; et même s'il ne l'était pas, il s'agit là d'une acception si généralement répandue en vieux français (*quar*, après tout, est un doublet de *que*) qu'on n'aurait guère besoin d'en chercher des exemples «dans la région et à l'époque de Béroul». L'«époque» de Béroul n'a d'ailleurs jamais été strictement définie; tout ce qu'on sait, c'est que son œuvre date, selon toute probabilité, du dernier tiers du XIIe siècle; et l'on connaît la fragilité des analyses linguistiques qui cherchent à la localiser aver trop de prècision. La langue de Beroul est le français littéraire de son temps. Elle autorisait certainement l'emploi de *que* et de *quar* au sens de «de sorte que», «si bien que».

plus sensible de l'œuvre, par où s'expliquent toutes les complexités de sa structure morale. La refus de la souffrance n'exclut pas, chez les amants, l'évocation d'un autre ordre de choses qu'ils craignent lorsqu'ils y songent, sans que leur crainte change quoi que ce soit à ce refus, présent prestigieux de la magie du philtre.

Que faut-il restaurer?

«Ne restaurer à aucun prix.» Ce conseil de l'archéologue Didron, dont Bédier s'est si souvent prévalu dans ses travaux, n'en avons-nous pas parfois abusé? Et ne devrions-nous pas, chaque fois qu'il nous revient à l'esprit, nous demander quelle est la chose que nous restaurons: est-ce un état antérieur de la tradition manuscrite, générateur de son état actuel et donc plus proche de l'original, ou cet original même, dans la mesure où nous nous croyons capables de le retrouver? Dans le premier cas, on fait l'histoire du texte en sens inverse, en partant des leçons conservées et en s'arrêtant là où s'arrêtent les données fournies par elles; dans le second cas, on réinvente l'original, on le récrit de confiance, en partant de l'idée que l'on se fait de l'auteur et de son œuvre, et c'est là surtout que la règle de Didron peut rendre de réels services: elle condamne d'avance les corrections qui ne sont pas historiquement défendables.

Aux vers 1653-5 on se trouve, semble-t-il, en présence d'un texte irrémédiablement corrompu:

> Et a Tristran repoise fort
> Que Yseut a por lui descort
> Quil repente de la folie.

Muret avait d'abord remplacé, au vers 1655, *Quil* par *Qu'el*, puirétabli la leçon du manuscrit en la faisant précéder de points de suspension pour indiquer une lacune entre le vers 1654 et le vers 1655. M. Reid, moins avare de remèdes grammaticaux, en propose trois à la fois. Et voici comment il propose de récrire ces trois vers:[11]

> Et a Tristran *poise si* fort
> Que Yseut a por lui descort
> Qu'il *se repent* de la folie.

Ces corrections supposent qu'au premier vers le scribe a laissé tomber

11 *Ibid.*, pp. 63-4. Ces corrections ont d'abord été proposées par M. Reid dans un article de mes Mélanges (*Medieval Miscellany*, Manchester 1966, p. 282).

un *si*, ce qui évidemment n'a rien d'impossible; mais on se demande pourquoi le scribe l'aurait fait, sachant que ce *si* était métriquement indispensable. M. Reid pense qu'un *si* aurait été caduc après *se*, autrement dit que le *se* de *poise* devant *si* aurait entraîné un saut du même au même. Or un saut du même au même dans le groupe *poise si* aurait fait disparaître la deuxième syllabe de *poise*, laissant le *si* intact, ce qui donnerait *poisi* et non *poise* et ne ferait qu'éloigner le texte de la leçon du manuscrit. Ces corrections supposent également qu'au vers 1655 un copiste a substitué *repente* à *se repent*. Encore une fois, il n'y a là rien d'impossible, mais a-t-on le droit de postuler une erreur non motivée mécaniquement dans une phrase où elle aurait eu pour seul effet de rendre celle-ci inintelligible? Qui plus est, ces trois vers ainsi « corrigés» seraient plus difficiles que jamais à situer dans leur context immédiat. Au moment où le philtre n'a encore rien perdu de sa puissance, où malgré tout ce qu'exige d'eux la vie *aspre et dure* dans la forêt de Morois les amants n'en ressentent ni l'âpreté ni la dureté, pourquoi Tristan se repentirait-il de la «folie» qui l'y avait amené? Craindre, comme le fait Iseut, que Tristan ne déplore son *descort* avec le roi Marc, ce n'est pas s'en repentir, ni prévoir le repentir de Tristan, et c'est aller bien au-delà du texte que de faire dire à Béroul que Tristan *se repent de la folie*, lui qui vient de dire à l'ermite Ogrin que jamais il ne s'en repentira, ni ne cessera d'aimer Iseut *a merville*.[12] Tout porte à croire que Muret avait raison: une lacune difficile à combler a rendu indéchiffrable le vers 1655.

Qu'est-ce à dire sinon que l'ambition du critique ne devrait pas aller au-delà de la correction des accidents identifiables de lecture ou de copie? Limiter ainsi notre champ d'action, ce n'est pas renoncer aux joies de la découverte: c'est les rendre moins éphémères. Dans la scène où Marc trouve les amants endormis dans leur refuge au fond de la forêt, on lit cette phrase:

> Li rois en haut le cop leva,
> Iré le fait, si se tresva.   [1991-2]

---

12 Cf. Béroul, vers 1401-8:

> Sire, j'am Yseut a merville,
> Si que n'en dor ne ne somelle;
> De tot an est li consel pris:
> Mex aim o li estre mendis
> Et vivre d'erbes et de glan
> Q'avoir le reigne au roi Otran, *etc.*

Le texte de Béroul, comme nous le dit très justement M. Reid, donnait sans aucun doute:

Iré le fait, si tresua.[13]

Le jour où quelqu'un a lu *tresva* au lieu de *tresua*, il a fallu, pour rétablir à la fois la mesure du vers et l'usage normal du verbe *tresaler*, y ajouter le pronom réfléchi, et c'est ainsi qu'au lieu de corriger l'erreur initiale on en commit une autre: deux erreurs successives, l'une et l'autre identifiables et partant corrigibles. L'histoire de leur découverte résume symboliquement la longue épopée de l'exégèse béroulienne. En 1921, à Oxford, très jeune étudiant, j'assistais à une des leçons de Mildred Pope sur Béroul. Arrivée au vers 1992, la distinguée élève de Gaston Paris avoua ne rien y comprendre: aucun des sens attestés de *tresaler* ne lui semblait convenir au contexte. Non sans quelque appréhension, je hasardai une suggestion: *tresua* au lieu de *tresva*. Sans hésiter, Mildred Pope s'en déclara satisfaite. Elle proposa seulement, pour rétablir le compte des syllabes, de lire *sis* au lieu de *si se*, et envoya aussitôt cette double correction à Muret. Celui-ci n'en tint aucun compte dans les rééditions du texte parues en 1922 et en 1928, pas plus que Ewert à qui j'en fis part au cours de nos nombreux entretiens sur Béroul. Par contre, Whitehead l'accueillit avec enthousiasme et en parla plusieurs fois dans ses cours. Beaucoup plus tard, et indépendamment de nous, M. Brian Blakey, qui était son élève et le mien, proposa cette même correction dans un article de *French Studies*,[14] et de nouveau Ewert la rejeta d'emblée, croyant que le présent de *tresaler* convenait mieux à la phrase que la passé simple de *tressüer*.[15] Et il faut savoir gré à M. Reid, non seulement d'avoir remis la question sur le tapis, mais d'avoir ajouté aux suggestions antérieures un détail capital. C'est lui qui a proposé tout récemment de lire *si tresua* sans pronom réfléchi. L'emploi réfléchi de ce verbe n'est attesté nulle part ailleurs (au vers 4431 on lit: *d'ire tresua*), alors que n'importe quel scribe face au vers

13 Sur ce vers voir entre autres A. Henry, *Études de syntaxe expressive*, p. 64, n. 2. M Henry préfère lire *ire* sans accent aigu au lieu de *iré*, la forme normale du participe passé étant, selon lui, *irié*. Argument sans grande valeur, puisque le scribe confond souvent *e* avec *ie*. Cf. Ewert, *ouvr. cité*, II, p. 187.
14 'On the text of Béroul's *Tristan*', *French Studies*, XXI (1967), pp. 99–103.
15 *Ouvr. cité*, p. 187. Cette objection, comme l'a montré M. Reid (*ouvr. cité*, p. 74), ne tient pas compte du fait qu'après le *leva* du vers précédent on s'attend à un passé simple plutôt qu'à un présent. Le présent de *Iré le fait* en fait une parenthèse qui se situe hors du récit proprement dit.

hypométrique *Iré le fait si tresva* aurait automatiquement ajouté *se* devant *tresva, se tresaler* étant en vieux français de fort bonne langue. Argument décisif, dont on ne manquera pas d'apprécier l'élégance, et qui couronne en les complétant les efforts conjugués de trois générations de chercheurs.

Rosemary E. Wallbank
Emperor Otto and Heinrich von Kempten

The nonchalance of medieval authors with regard to naming their
works, though surprising to modern readers, has not on the whole
been a source of confusion and controversy among scholars. The
sound advice given by Kirchner,[1] 'bei der Katalogaufnahme (den)
Titel stets so zu wählen, dass er der in der Literaturgeschichte üblichen
Form entspricht', has generally been followed, and where major works
are concerned critics have sensibly remained faithful to traditional titles
(often chosen by an early editor) even where they appear inept or
positively misleading (as in the case of the *Nibelungenlied* or *Diu Crône*).
There is, however, one area where dual titles have tended to proliferate,
namely in the *Märe*, or short verse tale. The exhaustive list of *Mären*
in Fischer's *Systematische Forschungsbibliographie zur Märendichtung*[2]
shows how frequent are alternative titles for works of this *genre*; just
occasionally a poem has achieved the doubtful distinction of collecting
three or even four titles on its progress through successive editions of
Verserzählungen. Fischer has demonstrated the extent of this problem;
and in this small field, as in the major areas of his subject, has offered
a solution which ought properly to provide a reliable foundation for
future investigation, and so fulfil the hope he expressed before his
untimely death while mountaineering in 1968. The *Gesamtverzeichnis
der Mären*[3] is as complete an inventory as his unique knowledge of the
material could supply, and it is devoutly to be wished, in the interests
of clarity, that the titles he uses here will now be adopted in the literature. In most cases they are anyhow unproblematic and familiar. There
are some new ones, admittedly: in the most extreme cases Fischer
took it upon himself, as he says,

> sprachlich und sachlich schiefe alte Titel durch prägnantere neue (und
> wirklich neuhochdeutsche) zu ersetzen, die den Inhalt des bezeichneten
> Gedichts möglichst unverwechselbar nach dem dargestellten äusseren oder

1 J. Kirchner, *Germanistische Handschriftenpraxis*, Munich, 1950, pp. 84-5.
2 Hanns Fischer, *Studien zur deutschen Märendichtung*, Tübingen, 1968, pp. 296-
382. See especially the *Titelkonkordanz* pp. 379 ff.   3 *Op. cit.*, pp. 65-71.

inneren Vorgang, den handelnden Personen oder einem markanten Requisit charakterisieren'.[4]

In many cases, of course, it was not necessary to invent a new title to replace an infelicitous one, or to modify one that was neither Middle High nor Modern German (like *Frauenzucht*) to conform to the modern standard (as *Frauenerziehung*); but to choose between two existing titles, both hallowed by tradition and both having some claim according to Fischer's own standards. Such a case is Konrad von Würzburg's *Heinrich von Kempten* or *Otte mit dem Barte*, where Fischer decides in favour of *Heinrich von Kempten*, without—quite naturally, in the framework of his book—spelling out his reasons for doing so. This particular example may be worth a closer look, partly because opinions are still divided, partly because the issue is the acceptance of an apt and generally approved title for one of the most important representatives of its *genre*, and above all, because it raises fundamental questions concerning the interpretation of the poem itself.

Heinrich von Kempten (*Otto mit dem Barte, Kaiser Otto*), the latest of Konrad's four *Mären*, composed sometime between 1260 and 1275, is the story of a knight who calls down on his head the fury of the emperor Otto for killing the court chamberlain, an act of unpremeditated vengeance on that official, who had belaboured Heinrich's charge, the Duke of Swabia's young son, for helping himself, as children will, from the imperial table. Heinrich is promptly condemned to death and saves himself by grabbing the emperor by the throat and extorting a free pardon as the price of Otto's life. Ten years later, having reluctantly followed the emperor on an Italian campaign and being understandably anxious to keep out of his way, he nonetheless leaps naked from his bath to save his sovereign's life, when he sees him treacherously attacked while parleying alone and unarmed with the burghers of the besieged city. The story ends with joyful reconciliation and a generous reward for Heinrich's courage.

The poem was first published by Karl August Hahn in 1838 under the title *Otte mit dem Barte*, following the Heidelberg manuscript cpg. 395, which has the superscription *Keiser Otto mit dē barte*.[5] Lambel[6] and

4 *Op. cit.*, p. 64.

5 *Otte mit dem barte von Cuonrat von Würzeburc*, ed. K. A. Hahn, Quedlinburg and Leipzig, 1838 (Bibliothek der gesammten deutschen National-Literatur, XIII, 3).

6 Hanns Lambel, *Erzählungen und Schwänke*, Leipzig, 1872 (Deutsche Classiker des Mittelalters, XII), p. 244.

Piper[7] followed his lead. In the (itself misleadingly named) *Gesammtabenteuer* of 1850 von der Hagen departs from previous editorial practice and calls the poem *Heinrich von Kempten und des Kaisers Bart*.[8] In the first (and still standard) critical edition Edward Schröder declares categorically that the only proper name for the poem is that of its hero, and accordingly heads his text *Heinrich von Kempten*.[9] This might be thought to have settled the matter, but there is still not complete agreement among literary historians. A few examples may suffice: Hermann Schneider deliberately reverts to *Kaiser Otto* ('er scheint mir die Hauptfigur')[10] and Gustav Ehrismann to *Otte mit dem Bart* (in brackets, *Heinrich von Kempten*).[11] From more recent references[12] Schröder appeared to be winning the battle, if only for lack of organised resistance. But in 1950 Lutz Röhrich for the first time argued the case more fully and came to the conclusion that the poem should most fittingly receive its title from its central theme, not from its characters, but that if this were considered too drastic an innovation the only proper alternative must be *Kaiser Otto und Henrich von Kempten*.[13] The suggestion is not regarded in the two major works of the 1960s dealing with the *genre*.[14] Heinz Rölleke,[15] basing his recent

7 Paul Piper, *Höfische Epik*, III (Deutsche National-Litteratur, IV), n.d., p. 183 ff. Similarly K. Goedeke, *Grundriss zur Geschichte der deutschen Dichtung*, I, Dresden, 1854, p. 217: *Kaiser Otte*.

8 F. H. von der Hagen, *Gesammtabenteuer. Hundert altdeutsche Erzählungen*, Stuttgart and Tübingen, 1850, repr. 1961, I, p. 59.

9 Edward Schröder, *Kleinere Dichtungen Konrads von Würzburg*, Berlin, 1924, 2nd edn., 1930, frequently repr., I, p. xii, p. 41 ff.

10 Hermann Schneider, *Heldendichtung, Geistlichendichtung, Ritterdichtung*, Heidelberg, 2nd edn., 1943, I, p. 565.

11 Gustav Ehrismann, *Geschichte der deutschen Literatur bis zum Ausgang des Mittelalters*, II, 2, *Schlussband*, Munich, 1935, p. 42.

12 E.g. Wolfgang Stammler, *Verfasserlexikon des deutschen Mittelalters*, Berlin and Leipzig, 1933–55; K. H. Halbach, 'Epik des Mittelalters' in Stammler, *Deutsche Philologie im Aufriss*, II, Berlin, 2nd edn., 1960, p. 642 ('*Heinrich von Kempten alias Otte mit dem Barte*'); Helmut de Boor and Richard Newald, *Geschichte der deutschsen Literatur von den Anfängen bis zur Gegenwart*. III. *Die deutsche Literatur im späten Mittelalter*, Munich, 1962, p. 42; *Reallexikon der deutschen Literaturgeschichte*, 2nd edn., II, Berlin, 1963, p. 704.

13 Lutz Röhrich, '*Kaiser Otto oder Heinrich von Kempten*? Eine Studie zu Konrad von Würzburg', *Germ.-rom. Monatsschrift*, XXXII (1950), pp. 151–4.

14 Fischer, *op. cit.*, and Arend Mihm, *Überlieferung und Verbreitung der Märendichtung im Spätmittelalter*, Heidelberg, 1967.

15 *Konrad von Würzburg. Heinrich von Kempten, Der Welt Lohn, Das Herzmaere, nach der Ausgabe von Edward Schröder, übersetzt, mit Anmerkungen und einem Nachwort versehen von Heinz Rölleke*, Stuttgart, 1968.

edition on Schröder's text, also explicitly accepts Schröder's verdict as
to the title—'Kein Zweifel, dass Edward Schröder in seiner Edition
aus dem Jahre 1924 mit vollem Recht die Dichtung wieder Heinrich von Kempten genannt hat . . .'—but without taking issue with
Röhrich, though his comment on p. 156 echoes one of Röhrich's
arguments.[16]

Röhrich's reasons for objecting to the then (1950) fairly well
established title were twofold: first the manuscript evidence and
second the burden of the tale. On the first point he asserts that of the
ten known mss., nine have a superscript mentioning Emperor Otto.
Despite a long-standing preoccupation with the mss. of Konrad's
Mären, I have been able to find no more than seven of Heinrich von
Kempten,[17] namely those listed by Fischer (*op. cit.*, p. 334) in his
Systematische Forschungsbibliographie, which he strove to make as
complete as possible. Mihm appears to know of no others either.[18] Of
these seven mss. one is a fragment containing only the last few lines
of the poem, so the question of a heading does not arise. In the remaining mss. the superscriptions are as follows:

Heidelberg, cpg. 341 (H): *Ditz buchel ist keyser Otte genant   Got der helf
vns in sin lant*
Kalocsa (K) (now lost): *Ditz ist von keiser otten ein mer Nv helf vns got von
aller swer*
Heidelberg, cpg. 395: *Kaiser Otto mit dē barte*
Vienna, Österreichische Nationalbibliothek, 2885 (w): *Von Kaiser Otten*
Innsbruck, Tiroler Landesmuseum Ferdinandeum, FB 32001 (i): *Von
chaiser Otten*
Vienna, Österreichische Nationalbibliothek, 10 100ᵃ (w⁶): *Die Rede haizt
Chaiser Ott vnd hat geticht maister Chunrad von Wirczpurckh.*[19]

16 *Loc. cit.*, p. 152.
17 See my forthcoming edition of *Heinrich von Kempten* based on cpg. 341.
18 Is it possible that Röhrich has been misled by a phrase of Schröder's? Namely
op. cit., *Einleitung xi*, where, speaking of *Heinrich von Kempten*, he says, 'Weil
in der 1. Zeile der Kaiser Otto genannt wird, setzen die Schreiber, welche *in
neun von zehn Fällen* [my italics] den Titel, resp. die Inhaltsangabe aus den
ersten Versen ihrer Vorlage entnehmen, kurzweg darüber: "keiser Otte":
diese Überschrift bieten resp. setzen voraus alle Handschriften. . . .' This
'nine out of ten cases' refers, of course, not to actual mss. of *Heinrich von
Kempten* but merely to the common practice of copyists in such matters.
Schröder himself describes only the seven mss. mentioned above.
19 This title does appear in the ms. (own copy), though Schröder does not
mention it.

Of these six mss., K is copied from H[20] and i from w, so that not too much can be made of the consensus of opinion they appear to reveal. More interesting in this connection are Mihm's observations on the titles of H. He argues[21] that verse superscriptions of the type found in cpg. 341 (H), using formulae such as *Ditz bvchel ist . . . genant* or *heizet* are characteristic of the blocks of *Mären* which he distinguishes in the ms. (as opposed to those sections presumed to be derived from *Sammelhss.*) and suggests that these couplets enshrine 'echte Buchtitel . . . , die in den Vorlagen des Sammlers zugleich Dichtungs- und Editionseinheiten bezeichnet haben'. Unfortunately it is impossible to say, for all Mihm's perspicacity, how many stages separate the model of H from such individual editions, nor whether the use of a particular title formula denotes anything more than the preference of one scribe. Certainly the copyist of K shows scant respect for the superscriptions he found in H and prefers a variant with *von* as quoted above.[22] Nor is the use of the word *buchel* or *buch* very reliable evidence for 'eine kleinere, selbständige Editionseinheit', for its Middle High German meaning is much wider than this, as Mihm readily admits. There is no doubt that Mihm has caused a light to shine in the darkness with his pioneering and scholarly work on the late medieval *Märenhandschriften*; but as regards the naming of medieval poems in general one cannot in the end help coming back to Schröder's judgement that in nine out of ten cases it depended on the whim of the copyist, who simply lifted a likely-looking name from the first few lines, regardless of its suitability.

The mss. being thus unhelpful, let us turn to Röhrich's other (and main) arguments for rejecting *Heinrich von Kempten* as the best title for Konrad's poem. He agrees that, although the emperor Otto appears at the beginning of both episodes, the more important character in each is Heinrich: '. . . alles, was von Kaiser Otto und seiner Umgebung allein berichtet wird, gibt offenbar nur den historischen Hintergrund, . . . scheint . . . lediglich Voraussetzung für das Auftreten des Haupt-handelnden Heinrich von Kempten zu sein.[23] . . . Kaiser Otto ist dagegen meist nur Objekt.' All of which seems to vindicate Schröder's choice. What Röhrich requires, however, to clinch the matter is 'ein

---

20 For the most part, and certainly the sections that concern us here. Cf. Mihm *op. cit.*, pp. 51–7.   21 *Op. cit.*, pp. 58–60.

22 Similarly in *Der Welt Lohn: Ditz ist von der werlde lon vnd stet niht vmb ein bon* K *Ditz buchel heizet der werlt lon vn stet mir fvr ein bon* H.

23 Rölleke, *loc. cit.*, p. 156, has almost exactly the same wording, but without referring to Röhrich or his views.

einheitliches Charakterbild' and this, he maintains, emerges for neither protagonist. It is true—as he himself points out—that throughout the poem Konrad uses only positive epithets for Heinrich and negative ones for the emperor: Otto is 'ein übel man', whose 'herze in argem muote bran'; he is 'übel unde rôt', etc.[24] Even in the second part of the poem, with the emperor grateful and reconciled, the poet goes no further than 'maere' and 'hôchgeborn', epithets relating only to his rank and reputation. Heinrich, on the other hand, is and remains from start to finish 'ein helt', 'der unverzagte ritter', 'der werde ritter', 'der ûzerwelte man', possessed of 'edel muot' and 'rîlichiu manheit', etc., etc.[24] But the emperor does also, according to Röhrich, have 'liebenswerte Züge': he does thank his rescuer and reward him suitably—the least he could do, one might think, and in any case essential in terms of the plot.

More controversial is Röhrich's interpretation of Heinrich's character and motivation, which he feels is not presented positively:

> Was Heinrich von Kempten als Minuszeichen anhaftet, ist vor allem sein zorniges Aufbrausen . . . Auch die Entschlossenheit des Ritters bei seinem Auftreten gegen den Kaiser im 1. Teil geht etwas zu weit und entspricht nicht ganz der Wohlerzogenheit, Höflichkeit und Gesittung, die Konrad von Würzburg uns sonst so beredt von Heinrich zu schildern weiss.

All of which brings him to the conclusion that there is more to this little piece than an exciting and well constructed tale idealising the qualities of courage and resolution. The action is only foreground: 'Im Hintergrund steht ein sittliches Ziel. Es geht dem Dichter um den blinden Jähzorn, um die aufbrausende, unbeherrschte Rachsucht, die er bekämpfen will'. He proceeds to argue that the first half of the poem demonstrates through five examples (the seneschal's excessive punishment of the boy, Heinrich's angry reprisal, the emperor's fury, his refusal to pardon the killer, and Heinrich's desperate attack on his sovereign) the results of uncontrolled violence arising from trivial causes. The second half brings reconciliation and a resolution of the conflict. Heinrich redeems his honour by saving the emperor's life. The trouble with this interpretation is that the author has never uttered a word of criticism of Heinrich's actions nor given the slightest hint that his honour is in need of repair. On the contrary, as we have seen, none but laudatory epithets are attached to him throughout. And what does Konrad say of him in the crucial moment of his *lèse majesté*?

24 Further examples in Röhrich, *loc. cit.*, p. 152.

> Der werde ritter Heinrich
> verstuont wol bî dem eide sich
> den der übel keiser tete,
> daz er benamen an der stete
> daz leben müeste hân verlorn.
> des wart im alsô rehte zorn
> daz er sich gerne wolte wern
> und daz leben sîn genern. . . .   [vv. 245–52]

Heinrich is even here 'der werde ritter' as opposed to 'der übel keiser'. His action is represented as self-defence, and a justification is put into his own mouth:

> Dâ von sprach er: 'nu merke ich wol
> daz ich benamen sterben sol;
> nû ist zît daz ich mich wer[25]
> und daz leben mîn gener
> al die wîle daz ich kan.'   [vv. 257–62]

In the first part of the poem, as in the second, it is difficult to find any evidence for the view that the whole thing is a protest against violence. Konrad is not an obscure poet. On the contrary, if a reproach is to be made against him, it is rather of being too repetitiously explicit than of making his points obliquely or by implication. It is natural, therefore, that Röhrich should turn to the *Schlussbemerkung*, the valedictory moral, in which, as he says, 'der Kerngedanke des ganzen Gedichts steckt', for confirmation of his interpretation:

> Dar umbe ein ieslich ritter sol
> gerne sîn des muotes quec,
> werf alle zageheit enwec
> und üebe sînes lîbes kraft.
> wan manheit unde ritterschaft
> diu zwei diu tiurent sêre:
> si bringent lob und êre
> noch einem iegelîchen man
> der si wol gehalten kan
> unde in beiden mag geleben.   [744–53]

But here we come up against Röhrich's understanding of the word *ritterschaft*. Is he justified in reading it as 'ritterliche Selbstbeherrschung'?

25 Cpg. 341 reads here: *Des han ich reht daz ich mich wer*, even more emphatically vindicating Heinrich's right to defend his life.

This is certainly not its primary meaning in Middle High German. Lexer gives 'ritterlicher Brauch und Beruf, ritterliches Leben und Tun; Kampf; Turnieren'.[26] That self-discipline was an essential element in the chivalrous ideal is not in dispute, and Middle High German is not without the means to express this (*zuht, mâze*). But the word *ritterschaft*, thus unmodified, is much more commonly associated with the *military* aspect of that ideal, and its use here in conjunction with *manheit* looks like a modest example of the *Doppelformel*, which was one of the distinguishing features of Konrad's style, the two nouns being more or less synonymous, rather than a confrontation of conflicting values. More especially as the whole passage is concerned with the rewards attendant on 'manheit vrevel unde starc' (v. 740) and the exhortation that every knight shall be bold and shall cast off all timidity (vv. 755–6). 'Manheit unde ritterschaft' appear in these surroundings to express the closely related values of 'valour and knightly prowess' rather than the contrasted qualities of 'valour and self-control', and the 'Zwiespältigkeit' and 'doppelte pädagogische Zielsetzung' which are the vital factors in Röhrich's interpretation become illusory. Equally imaginary, in consequence, is the notion that Konrad is here preaching a more general moral, 'von stadtbürgerlichem Geiste bestimmt', rather than the specifically military–chivalrous one on which to the naive reader the poem appears to be based. If we did not know from other sources of Konrad's rank and position in life, we could certainly not deduce them from this poem. It will not do to project a bourgeois ethic which we feel Konrad *ought* to have been propagating into a work which is informed by quite another spirit.

It is true that in *Der Welt Lohn* 'die äusseren Schicksale des Ritters Wirnt von Grafenberg den Dichter im Grunde herzlich wenig interessieren'.[27] It would be surprising if it were otherwise, for that poem is wholly concerned with a spiritual experience, the hero's conversion from the service of Lady World to the service of God. Quite the reverse in *Heinrich von Kempten*.[28] 'Die äusseren Schicksale des Ritters' are here the very substance of the poem. Everything is action, half exciting, half comic. Neither Otto nor Heinrich is given to self-examination. Each acts spontaneously, governed only by his temperament and the feudal ethic to which both subscribe. The peculiar merit

26 *Mittelhochdeutsches Handwörterbuch*, II, Leipzig, 1876, p. 466.
27 Röhrich, *loc. cit.*, p. 154.
28 *Contra* Röhrich, *loc. cit.*, p. 154: '. . . so geht es auch in unserem Gedicht um eine innere Haltung'.

of the poem rests partly on the liveliness and humour of Konrad's presentation—with wholehearted admiration for his hero, but with an ironical appreciation of the twists of fortune, which now banish him from court, now return him to favour; even more perhaps on the aesthetically satisfying equilibrium between the two parts.[29] So far from contrasting the violence of the opening with the reconciliation at the end of the affair, the whole point he is making is that the *very same* quality, namely impetuous courage, which got him into trouble in the first part, restores his fortunes in the second. The mainspring of his action is exactly the same in both episodes: fearlessness and resolution; no less when he leaps from his bath to save the emperor's life than when he drags him from his throne to save his own. The identity of motivation in both episodes is underlined by the fact that Konrad uses exactly the same epithet for Heinrich just before each of his intrepid acts: 'der ûzerwelte man' (v. 262) and 'ein ûzerwelter degen' (v. 576). And more discreetly, but no less effectively, by the fact that Otto unhesitatingly recognises in his rescuer that same quality of daring (*getürstekeit*) which had led him to pluck the imperial beard:

> der keiser wîte erkennet
> sprach dâ wider sâ zehant:
> 'und ist er komen in diz lant,
> daz weiz ich gerne sunder wân,
> wer haete ouch anders diz getân
> daz er nacket hiute streit?
> wand er ouch die getürstekeit
> truog in sîme herzen hôch
> daz er bî dem barte zôch
> einen keiser über tisch.   [vv. 663–73]

Then the emperor had suffered from Heinrich's impetuosity, *now* he is benefiting from it. Neither has changed: only the circumstances.

Heinrich von Kempten—and we must now accept with Schröder that this is the only proper name for the poem—is one of Konrad's most attractive pieces—in fact, one of the best of the Middle High German short verse tales. Its excellence stems from the lively yet restrained presentation, the combination of earnestness (in the commendation of the chivalrous ideal) and humour (in the somewhat absurd circum-

29 On Konrad's achievement in creating this unity and on the whole question of his sources, see my forthcoming edition of *Heinrich von Kempten*.

stances of its application); and above all in its structural unity, the nicely considered balance of the two parts, with their identity of motivation and diversity of outcome. This is all the poet's intention, his 'eigentliche Absicht'.[30] There is no need to look further.

30 Röhrich, *loc. cit.*, p. 154.

Z. P. Zaddy

Le Chevalier de la Charrete and the *De amore* of Andreas Capellanus

One of the most important points raised by Gaston Paris in his study of the *Conte de la charrette*[1] is the similarity between the views on love and lovers expressed in Chrétien's romance and those contained in the first two sections of that twelfth century handbook for intending lovers, the *De amore* of Andreas Capellanus.[2] According to Paris, the thirty-one rules of love which a British knight is described as bringing back from Arthur's court in Book II, chapter vii, of Andreas' treatise provide 'la théorie dont le poème de Chrétien nous montre la pratique', a claim that he illustrates by quoting some of the more important rules:

> . . . il ne sera pas inutile, pour montrer combien l'esprit de ce chapitre s'accorde avec celui que nous avons constaté dans notre roman, d'en citer ici quelques-unes:
>
> 1. Causa conjugii ab amore non est excusatio recta. [Marriage is no real excuse for not loving.]
> 12. Verus amans alterius nisi sue coamantis ex affectu non cupit amplexus. [A true lover does not desire to embrace in love anyone except his beloved.]

1 Paris, 'Etudes sur les romans de la Table Ronde. Lancelot du Lac. II. Le Conte de la Charrette', *Romania*, XII (1883), pp. 459–534.
2 *Andreae Capellani regii Francorum De amore libri tres*, recensuit E. Trojel (Munich, 1972). For convenience, quotations from this work in the rest of this article will be taken from J. J. Parry's translation: Andreas Capellanus, *The Art of Courtly Love*, New York, 1959. The precise date of the *De amore* is unknown. According to Trojel, the *terminus a quo* is 1174, the date of a letter ascribed to Marie de Champagne in the seventh dialogue (p. ii), and the *terminus ad quem* 1238, the date of a treatise by Albertanus of Brescia mentioning the work and quoting from it (p. vi). The reference to Hungarian affairs on p. 62 of Trojel's edition (Parry, p. 57), which Trojel sees as a reference to the marriage of 1186 between Béla III and the daughter of King Louis of France (p. ix) has led J. F. Benton to claim that 'the most comprehensive dating of the *De amore* . . . places it between 1186 and 1196' ('The court of Champagne as a literary center', *Speculum*, XXXVI (1961), pp. 562–3).

13. Amor raro consuevit durare vulgatus. [When made public love rarely endures.]

14. Facilis perceptio contemptibilem reddit amorem, difficilis eum carum facit haberi. [The easy attainment of love makes it of little value; difficulty of attainment makes it prized.]

15. Omnis consuevit amans in coamantis aspectu pallescere. [Every lover regularly turns pale in the presence of his beloved.]

16. In repentina coamantis visione cor tremescit amantis. [When a lover suddenly catches sight of his beloved his heart palpitates.]

18. Probitas sola quemque dignum facit amore. [Good character alone makes any man worthy of love.]

20. Amorosus semper est timorosus. [A man in love is always apprehensive].

23. Minus dormit et edit quem amoris cogitatio vexat. [He whom the thought of love vexes eats and sleeps very little.]

24. Omnis amantis actus in coamantis cogitatione finitur. [Every act of a lover ends in the thought of his beloved.]

25. Verus amans nichil beatum credit nisi quod cogitat coamanti placere. [A true lover considers nothing good except what he thinks will please his beloved.]

28. Modica presumptio cogit amantem de coamante suspicari sinistra. [A slight presumption causes a lover to suspect his beloved.]

30. Verus amans assidua sine intermissione coamantis imagine detinetur. [A true lover is constantly and without intermission possessed by the thought of his beloved.][3]

For the most part Paris' views on the parallelism between the *De amore* and the *Charrete* seem to have been accepted. He is followed, for example, by T. P. Cross and W. A. Nitze in their study of the *Charrete* ('The fact is that Andreas' concept of love and that of Chrétien just about coincide').[4] J. Frappier finds that certain precepts in the *Charrete* are closer to the '*Regulae* contenues dans le *De amore*' than to the views expressed in Chrétien's other works.[5] Although M. Lazar does not directly relate the *Charrete* and the *De amore*, he sees both as expressions

3 'Etudes', pp. 531–2. Paris also pointed out that the similarity between the two works goes beyond similarities of erotic doctrine and extends to the Arthurian matter contained in the account of the discovery of the Rules of Love. This, he maintains, was drawn from Chrétien ('Etudes', p. 532). He did not, however, point out the similarity in the conceits used by Andreas and those employed by Chrétien in *Cligés*, *Yvain* and the *Charrete*.

4 Cross and Nitze, *Lancelot and Guenevere: a study on the Origins of Courtly Love* Chicago, 1930, p. 68.

5 Frappier, *Chrétien de Troyes*, Paris, 1968, pp. 141–2.

of *fin'amors*, the one being 'dans le genre romanesque du XIIe siècle, l'illustration la plus complète et la plus absolue de l'idéologie amoureuse des troubadours'[6] and the other assembling 'les divers thèmes' des troubadours', integrating them into a system and giving them 'un aspect plus doctrinal'.[7] Similarly, F. D. Kelly draws certain parallels between the two works in his discussion of the 'sens' of the *Charrete*, although he does not specifically relate them to one another.[8] Recently, however, Paris' views have come under attack. J. Rychner, for example, has accused him of reading Andreas' ideas into Chrétien's romance:

> Gaston Paris, croyant (à tort ou à raison) que le livre d'André le Chapelain témoignait des goûts de la comtesse pour la *fin'amors*, pensant d'autre part que Marie avait donné le *san* du roman à Chrétien de Troyes, projetait tout naturellement les idées du *De amore* sur le *Lancelot*.[9]

For R. Dragonetti the differences between Andreas and poets like Chrétien are such as to lead him to declare that the *De amore* 'n'est en aucune manière ... la transcription théorique du *Conte de la Charrette*', for all there seems to be an 'air de famille' between them.[10] At the other extreme, we find D. W. Robertson affirming that Andreas' preface, his closing statements and the general discussion of love in the first five chapters of his treatise show that he 'was not concerned with what has been called "courtly love" at all'.[11] In the opinion of this critic the *De amore* is nothing other than a condemnation of lust (*fornicatio*), as is fitting in a cleric:

> When the opening chapters of the *De amore* are examined in the light of theological, philosophical, and literary conventions prevailing in the twelfth century, two conclusions emerge. First, it is evident that Andreas employs the literary device of irony and, second, that, if we take this irony into

6 Lazar, *Amour courtois et 'fin' amors' dans la littérature du XIIe siècle*, Paris, 1964. p. 235. See pp. 235–43 for a discussion of the *Charrete* as the 'version romanesque de la *fin'amors*'.

7 Lazar, *Amour courtois*, p. 268. See pp. 268–77 for a discussion of Andreas' work.

8 Kelly, *'Sens' and 'Conjointure' in the 'Chevalier de la Charrette'*, The Hague, 1966, pp. 36–85.

9. Rychner, 'Le prologue du *Chevalier de la charrette*', in *Mélanges offerts à Rita Lejeune, professeur à l'Université de Liège*, II, Gembloux, 1969, p. 1124.

10 Dragonetti, 'Trois motifs de la lyrique courtoise confrontés avec les *Arts d'aimer*', *Romanica Gandensia*, VII (1959), pp. 6–7.

11 Robertson, 'The subject of the *De amore* of Andreas Capellanus', *Modern Philology*, L (1953), p. 145

account, there is no doctrinal inconsistency in the *De amore* as a whole. . . . The subject of the *De amore* is *fornicatio* used with its full connotations as the opposite of *caritas*, and Andreas does nothing except condemn it. His lesson is exactly what we should expect from a chaplain in a great feudal court . . . .

[p. 161]

Faced with this divergence of opinions, I find myself siding with Gaston Paris. Having recently examined both texts for an analysis of the structure of the *Charrete*,[12] I feel that the weight of the evidence is as much in Paris' favour in this matter as it is against him in the matter of the composition of Chrétien's romance. It seems to me, therefore, that there is a definite need for the comparison between the *Charrete* and the *De amore* to be pursued in far greater detail than has hitherto been attempted, and I hope that such a study may form a fitting tribute to the late Frederick Whitehead.

★

On comparing the *Charrete* and the *De amore*, one finds in the first place that Chrétien and Andreas give a very similar picture of love and its effects.

(*a*) Both authors, for example, present the lover as a man constantly preoccupied with thoughts of the beloved. In the *Charrete* we find Lancelot totally absorbed in thoughts of Guenevere as he makes his way towards Gorre:

> . . . cil de la charrete panse
> con cil qui force ne deffanse
> n'a vers Amors qui le justise;
> et ses pansers est de tel guise
> que lui meïsmes en oblie,
> ne set s'il est, ou s'il n'est mie,
> ne ne li manbre de son non,
> ne set s'il est armez ou non,
> ne set ou va, ne set don vient;
> de rien nule ne li sovient
> fors d'une seule, et por celi
> a mis les autres en obli;
> a cele seule panse tant
> qu'il n'ot, ne voit, ne rien n'antant.   [*Charrete*, ed. Roques, vv. 711–24]

12 Zaddy, 'The structure of the *Charrete*', in *Chrétien Studies: Problems of Form and Meaning in 'Erec', 'Yvain', 'Cligés' and 'The Charrete'*, Glasgow, 1973.

Indeed, so complete is his abstraction that he fails to hear himself challenged by a knight guarding a ford (vv. 730–66) and is only brought back to outer realities when he is toppled from his horse into the water:

> Quant cil sant l'eve, si tressaut;
> toz estormiz an estant saut,
> ausi come cil qui s'esvoille,
> s'ot, et si voit, et se mervoille
> qui puet estre qui l'a feru. [vv. 767–71]

At a later stage in the journey Chrétien again shows him given up to reverie and ignoring the damsel who insists on accompanying him:

> Cele l'aresne et il n'a cure
> de quan que ele l'aparole,
> einçois refuse sa parole;
> pansers li plest, parlers le grieve [vv. 1332–5]

In the *De amore* rule 30 of the thirty-one rules of love brought back from Arthur's court by a British knight states that 'a true lover is constantly and without intermission possessed by the thought of his beloved' (P., p. 186). What these thoughts are is specified at the end of Book I, chapter i ('What love is'):

> ... when a man sees some woman fit for love and shaped according to his taste, he begins at once to lust after her in his heart; then the more he thinks about her the more he burns with love, until he comes to a fuller meditation. Presently he begins to think about the fashioning of the woman, and to differentiate her limbs, to think about what she does, and to pry into the secrets of her body, and he desires to put each part of it to the fullest use.
> [P., p.29]

(*b*) That love renders a man indifferent to the attractions of other women is a point that Chrétien and Andreas both deal with. In the *Charrete* it is illustrated by Lancelot's dealings with the Seductive Damsel whose bed he is forced to share very much against his will on the journey to Bade (vv. 931–64, 1195–212). Having described how Lancelot tries to avoid all contact with his hostess (vv. 1213–22), Chrétien explains that if his hero rejects an opportunity that most men would welcome, it is because his desires and interests are totally directed elsewhere:

> Bel sanblant feire ne li puet.
> Por coi? Car del cuer ne li muet,
> qu'aillors a mis del tot s'antante,

mes ne pleist mie n'atalante
quan qu'est bel et gent a chascun.
Li chevaliers n'a cuer que un
et cil n'est mie ancor a lui,
einz est comandes a autrui
si qu'il nel puet aillors prester.   [vv. 1223-31]

We are then told that Lancelot's behaviour is directly due to his being
dominated by Love and that, for his part, Chrétien feels he should be
congratulated, not censured, for obeying Love's commands and
rejecting what she forbids:

Tot le fet en un leu ester
Amors, qui toz les cuers justise.
Toz? Nel fet, forz cez qu'ele prise,
Et cil s'an redoit plus prisier
cui ele daigne justisier.
Amors le cuer celui prisoit
si que sor toz le justisoit
et li donoit si grant orguel
que de rien blasmer ne le vuel
s'il lait ce qu'Amors li desfant
et la ou ele vialt antant.   [vv. 1232-42]

Chrétien's lesson is then driven home still further when these self-
same sentiments are attributed to the rejected damsel herself. For,
seeing Lancelot's total lack of interest, she withdraws from his bed
(vv. 1243-60) and returns to her chamber, filled with admiration for
him (vv. 1261-78).

In his turn, Andreas states in his chapter on the effects of love that:

There is another thing about love that we should not praise in a few words:
it adorns a man, so to speak, with the virtue of chastity, because he who
shines with the light of one love can hardly think of embracing another
woman, even a beautiful one. For when he thinks deeply of his beloved
the sight of any other woman seems to his mind rough and rude.

[P., pp. 31-2]

Andreas' words here could be taken for a comment on Lancelot's
behaviour towards the Seductive Damsel—and an excuse for his
neglect of her when she insists on accompanying him through Logres
(vv. 1332-5), which some critics have censured severely.[13]

(c) The fact that lovers seem indifferent to the price they have to pay

13 Lancelot's treatment of the Seductive Damsel is censured by A. H. Diverres
   in his article 'Some thoughts on the *Sens* of *Le Chevalier de la Charrette*', *Forum
   for Modern Language Studies*, VI (1970), pp. 27-8.

for loving is again one to which Andreas and Chrétien both call attention. In the words of Andreas:

> ... in the sight of a lover nothing can be compared to the act of love, and a true lover would rather be deprived of all his money and of everything that the human mind can imagine as indispensable to life rather than be without love, either hoped for or attained. For what under heaven can a man possess or own for which he would undergo so many perils as we continually see lovers submit to of their own free will? [P., p. 30]

To this Lancelot's conduct in the *Charrete* fully testifies. The hardships he bears and the injuries he receives for Guenevere are as nothing in his eyes, as we see from his reaction to the wounds he received in wrenching the bars out of her window:

> Et lors a primes se mervoille
> de ses doiz qu'il trueve plaiez;
> mes de rien n'an est esmaiez
> por ce qu'il set tot de seür
> que au traire les fers del mur
> de la fenestre se bleça;
> por ce pas ne s'an correça,
> car il se volsist mialz del cors
> andeus les braz avoir traiz fors
> que il ne fust oltre passez;
> mes s'il se fust aillors quassez
> et si laidemant anpiriez,
> molt an fust dolanz et iriez.   [vv. 4724-36]

(*d*) The effect that the sight of the beloved can have upon a lover is noted in both the *De amore* and the *Charrete*. According to Andreas, the fifteenth rule of love states that 'every lover regularly turns pale in the presence of his beloved', whilst the sixteenth runs: 'when a lover suddenly catches sight of his beloved his heart palpitates' (P., p. 185). In the *Charrete* Lancelot's reactions are rather more extreme. The news that a comb contains some of Guenevere's golden hairs almost makes him faint:

> Quant cil l'ot, n'a tant de vertu
> que tot nel coveigne ploier:
> par force l'estut apoier
> devant a l'arçon de la sele.
> . . .
> qu'il avoit au cuer tel dolor
> que la parole et la color
> ot une grant piece perdue.   [vv. 1424-37]

On a later occasion, the knowledge that he is fighting in Guenevere's presence makes him lose his head completely. He totally forgets the matter he has in hand, and thinks only of keeping his adoring gaze turned towards her until recalled to his senses:

> Qant Lanceloz s'oï nomer,
> ne mist gaires a lui torner:
> trestorne soi et voit a mont
> la chose de trestot le mont
> que plus desirroit a veoir,
> as loges de la tor seoir.
> Ne, puis l'ore qu'il s'aparçut
> ne se torna ne ne se mut
> de vers li ses ialz ne sa chiere,
> einz se desfandoit per derriere;
> et Meleaganz l'enchauçoit
> totes voies plus qu'il pooit.   [vv. 3669–80]

When one comes to consider what Andreas and Chrétien expect of lovers, one finds that they are in close agreement. The characteristics exhibited ¡by Lancelot on the journey to Bade—and elsewhere in the *Charrete*—tally with those listed in the third dialogue of the *De amore* as needful in a man 'who asks for the love of an honorable woman' and who, accordingly, 'ought to be of great fame and of all courtliness' (P., p. 58):

(a) Lancelot's dealings with the Seductive Damsel, for instance, meet Andreas' requirement that a lover 'should never cheat anyone with a false promise' (P., p. 60). In spite of the repugnance he feels, he forces himself to get into her bed because he had given her his word to do so:

> Un lit ot fet en mi la sale,
>
> . . .
>
> et la dameisele s'i couche,
> mes n'oste mie sa chemise.
> Et cil a molt grant poinne mise
> au deschaucier et desnüer:
> d'angoisse le covint süer;
> totevoies par mi l'angoisse
> covanz le vaint et si le froisse.
> Donc est ce force? Autant le vaut;
> par force covient que il s'aut
> couchier avoec la dameisele;. .
> covanz l'en semont et apele.   [vv. 1195–212]

(*b*) The fact that Lancelot stops at a wayside chapel to pray and then speaks with becoming courtesy ('molt dolcemant') to the monk he meets there indicates that he treats God and his ministers with due respect:

> . . . truevent en un leu molt bel
> un mostier et, lez le chancel,
> un cemetire de murs clos.
> Ne fist que vilains ne que fos
> li chevaliers qui el mostier
> entra a pié por Deu proier.
> . . .
> Quant il ot feite sa proiere
> et il s'an revenoit arriere,
> si li vient uns moinnes molt vialz
> a l'encontre, devant ses ialz.
> Quant il l'encontre, se li prie
> molt dolcemant que il li die
> que par dedanz ces murs avoit.   [vv. 1837–51]

The *De amore* likewise stresses that a lover 'should not utter harmful or shameful or mocking words against God's clergy . . . but should always and everywhere render them due honor. . . . He ought to go to church frequently and there listen gladly to those who are constantly celebrating the divine service' (P., p. 61).

(*c*) Lancelot's handling of the exiles who clamour for the honour of entertaining him after the fighting in Gorre shows that he is, as Andreas advises, 'so far as [is] possible, a composer of differences' (P., pp. 59–60). He succeeds in satisfying them all by promising to take the word for the deed:

> . . . herbergier le vialt chascuns
> ausi li juenes con li vialz,
> et dit chascuns: 'Vos seroiz mialz
> el mien ostel que an l'autrui.'
> Ce dit chascuns androit de lui;
> et li uns a l'autre le tost,
> si con chascuns avoir le vost,
> et par po qu'il ne s'an conbatent.
> Et il lor dit qu'il se debatent
> de grant oiseuse et de folie:
> . . .
> 'Ne dites mie ancore bien.
> fet li chevaliers, a mon los,

li plus sages de vos est fos
de ce don ge vos oi tancier.

. . .

Se vos m'avïez tuit en ordre
li uns aprés l'autre a devise
fet tant d'anor et de servise
com an porroit feire a un home,
par toz le sainz qu'an prie a Rome,
ja plus boen gré ne l'en savroie,
quant la bonté prise en avroie,
que je faz de la volanté.
Se Dex me doint joie et santé,
la volantez autant me haite
con se chascuns m'avoit ja faite
molt grant enor et grant bonté;
si soit an leu de fet conté.'
Ensi les vaint toz et apeise.   [vv. 2448–89]

(d) If the De amore insists that 'nothing is considered more praiseworthy in a lover than to be known to be generous' (P., p. 152),
Lancelot proves to be eminently endowed with that virtue. As
Chrétien is at pains to stress, he insists on exchanging the horse presented to him by his host with the mount ridden by his young companion:

Mes une chose vos cont gié
por ce que rien ne vos trespas,
que li chevaliers ne volt pas
monter sor le cheval presté
qu'an li ot a l'uis presanté;
einz i fist, ce vos voel conter,
un des deus chevaliers monter
qui venu erent avoec lui.
Et il sor le cheval celui
monte, qu'ainsi li plot et sist.   [vv. 2988–97]

Again, we find from the two single combats which he fights on the
way to Bade that he is magnanimous to the defeated and generous to
the suppliant. On both occasions he is willing to spare his opponents
when they sue for mercy (vv. 898–910, 2852–60). On both occasions,
too, he grants the request of the young woman who approaches him
after the fight—the one to beg for the liberty of her lover (vv. 912–24),
the other to ask for the head of her enemy (vv. 2796–933). In the second
case Lancelot finds himself caught between the conflicting claims of

compassion (*pitiez*) and liberality (*largece*): a moral dilemma that Chrétien describes at length (vv. 2831–65), and which Lancelot resolves with the wisdom of a Solomon. For he allows the man a second chance to defend himself and then presents the girl with his head when he defeats him again (vv. 2866–927).

(*e*) The injunction that a lover 'ought to be courageous in battle and hardy against his enemies, wise, cautious and clever' (P., p. 60) is gloriously true of Lancelot. His crossing of the sword bridge—his culminating act of courage—is seen by Bademaguz as 'le plus grant hardemant / qui onques fust mes nes pansez' (vv. 3192–3). The three victories over Meleagant show him to be the greatest warrior in the world and confirm the opinion expressed at the time of his exploit in the wayside chapel that 'onques voir d'ome ne de fame / ne nasquié, n'en sele ne sist / chevaliers qui cestui vausist' (vv. 1978–80). There is, then, every reason why Lancelot should, as the world's greatest knight, be accepted as a lover by the world's greatest lady, Guenevere. Her choice certainly receives—informal—ratification at the tournament of Pomelegoi, where Lancelot emerges as the man all women would choose as a husband or lover.[14] By the end of the tournament the damsels who have come expressly to choose themselves husbands can think only of Lancelot, and, despairing of their chances with him, are ready to forswear marriage for the time being:

> Et les dameiseles disoient
> qui a mervoilles l'esgardoient,
> que cil les tolt a marïer,
> car tant ne s'osoient fïer
> en lor biautez n'an lor richeces,
> n'an lor pooirs, n'an lor hauteces,
> que por biauté ne por avoir
> deignast nule d'eles avoir
> cil chevaliers, que trop est prouz.
> Et neporquant se font tex vouz
> les plusors d'eles, qu'eles dïent
> que s'an cestui ne se marïent

14 The queen's choice of Lancelot as a lover, therefore, is in accord with the fourth commandment ascribed to the God of Love in the fifth dialogue: 'Thou shalt not choose for thy love anyone whom a natural sense of shame forbids thee to marry' (P. p. 81) and, *mutatis mutandis*, the eleventh of the rulings given in Book II, chapter viii: 'It is not proper to love any woman whom one would be ashamed to seek to marry' (P., p. 185).

ne seront ouan mariees,
n'a mari n'a seignor donees.
. . .
Et lor volentez est comune
si qu'avoir le voldroit chascune;
et l'une est de l'autre jalouse
si con s'ele fust ja s'espouse,
por ce que si adroit le voient,
qu'eles ne pansent ne ne croient
que nus d'armes, tant lor pleisoit,
poïst ce feire qu'il feisoit.   [vv. 5993–6022]

When one comes to the question of how a love affair should be conducted, the *Charrete* and the *De amore* prove to be in agreement over
the way a courtship should be pursued. Both make it clear that a man
can expect to be admitted to a lady's favour only after he has been
thoroughly sounded, and then, only by degrees. Both again make it
clear that it lies with the woman to decide whether or not a relationship shall be established. The theoretical exposition of these doctrines
is provided by the *De amore*:

The point that a man must expect to find himself on probation is
expressly made in Dialogue 8. There a too urgent suitor finds himself
rebuked in the following terms:

> Your urging seems to me too insistent, because you are trying to obtain the
> gift of love in such a hurry. For even if your good qualities made you
> most worthy of every honor, you ought not ask to have love granted you
> so suddenly. No woman of character ought to be so quick to assent to her
> lover's desire, for the quick and hasty granting of love arouses contempt
> in the lover and makes the love he has long desired seem cheap. . . . There-
> fore a woman ought first to find out the man's character by many tests and
> have clear evidence of his good faith.   [P., p. 132]

As for the various stages by which a man should be admitted to a
lady's favours, these are detailed in Dialogue 3:

> From ancient times four distinct stages have been established in love: the
> first consists in the giving of hope, the second in the granting of a kiss,
> the third in the enjoyment of an embrace, and the fourth culminates in the
> yielding of the whole person. . . . if a woman wants to select a lover in the
> fourth stage, all at once without waiting to think it over, then it is profitable
> for her to select the man who has done many good deeds instead of [the]
> one who hasn't done any. . . . But it is not seemly for wise women to give

themselves so hastily to anyone, passing over the preliminary stages and jumping at once to the fourth. Women usually proceed in this order: first a woman should make use of the granting of hope, and then if she sees that her lover, after receiving this, improves in conduct, she need not fear to go on to the second stage. And so step by step she may come to the fourth stage, if she finds that he is in every respect worthy of it.   [P., pp. 42-3]

The speaker ends his description of the four stages of love by observing that:

. . . until the third stage is passed a woman may withdraw without blame; but if love has been established in the fourth stage, after that she ought not to go back except for the very best of reasons, not only because she has ratified her love, which is done by the fourth step, but also because of the great thing that the yielding of her person is to a woman. For what greater thing can a woman give than to yield herself to the mastery of someone else?
[P., p. 43]

Lastly the point that it is up to the woman to decide whether or not a relationship is to be established is made in Dialogue 2:

Although (Love) sees that all men are by the natural desire of their passions drawn to anybody of the opposite sex, he considers it shameful for him to pitch his tent at once over against the other person, so that she whose love is sought must immediately be driven to love. If he did this, any rough, shaggy person who spent his time in farming or in begging his bread publicly in the streets might impel a queen to love him. But lest such an impropriety or absurdity happen, *Love regularly leaves it to the choice of each woman either to love or not, as she may wish, the person who asks for her love.*
[P., p. 47; my italics]

A practical illustration of the courtly views on the correct way to pursue a courtship is to be found in the *Charrete*, where the conduct of Lancelot and Guenevere complies with the three conditions specified in the *De amore*.

First, we find that Lancelot patiently provides long and ample proof of his good faith and worth before he becomes the queen's lover. From the way Guenevere is able to supply the name of the champion who has come forward to challenge Meleagant (vv. 3634-61), it is plain that she has been fully aware of Lancelot's devotion for some time. At the same time, her reaction to the news of his supposed death makes it equally clear that this devotion has never been repaid. For in her remorse for her heartless rejection of him after his victory over

Meleagant (vv. 4157–223), we find Guenevere regretting that she has
never once requited his love:

> 'Ha! lasse! Con fusse garie
> et com me fust granz reconforz
> se une foiz, ainz, qu'il fust morz,
> l'eüsse antre mes braz tenu.'   [vv. 4224–7]

Next, it is indeed the woman who decides that a relationship shall be
established in the case of Lancelot and Guenevere. For they do not
become lovers until she has come to reciprocate his desire. This
happens only when her remorse leads her—as we have just seen—to
wish that she had granted him his heart's desire at least once before he
died. At this point the queen suddenly becomes aware of the full
implications of her wish and accepts them freely:

> 'Comant? Certes, tot nu a nu,
> por ce que plus an fusse a eise.'   [vv. 4228–9]

Thereafter her attitude to Lancelot is completely changed. Her satisfied
and half-amused acceptance of his devotion gives way to an answering
desire, and a relationship will be able to develop between them when
and as circumstances permit.

Lastly, the relationship between Lancelot and Guenevere progresses
along the lines indicated in the *De amore* once they are reunited on
Lancelot's return to Bade. At their first meeting Lancelot is given
ample grounds for hope. He receives a smiling welcome, is invited to
sit by the queen—a privilege that a lady may grant to a man of lower
degree as a special favour, according to Andreas (P., p. 62)—and is
engaged in very agreeable conversation:

> Lors ne lessa mie cheoir
> la reïne ses ialz vers terre;
> einz l'ala lieemant requerre,
> si l'enora de son pooir,
> et sel fist lez li aseoir.
> Puis parlerent a lor pleisir
> de quan que lor vint a pleisir,
> ne matiere ne lor failloit,
> qu'Amors assez lor an bailloit.   [vv. 4460–8]

With this encouragement Lancelot feels able to enquire the cause of
the queen's earlier displeasure, whereupon the lovers are reconciled
(vv. 4469–500). This emboldens Lancelot to ask for a more private

interview (vv. 4501–5): a request that is granted, though only the promise of a kiss and an embrace are held out to him:

> . . . 'Venez parler a moi
> a cele fenestre anquenuit,
> . . .
> Ceanz antrer, ne herbergier
> ne porroiz mie vostre cors;
> je serai anz, et vos defors
> que ceanz ne porroiz venir.
> Ne je ne porrai avenir
> a vos, fors de boche ou de main.'   [vv. 4508–17]

At the rendezvous the lovers pass rapidly through the second and third stages of love, exchanging, as best they may, kisses and embraces through the bars of Guenevere's window (vv. 4583–93). Then, when they find that the bars need be no impediment to their mutual desire (vv. 4594–649), they proceed to the fourth stage of love:

> Et la reïne li estant
> ses bras ancontre, si l'anbrace,
> estroit pres de son piz le lace,
> si l'a lez li an son lit tret,
> et le plus bel sanblant li fet
> que ele onques feire li puet
> que d'Amors et del cuer li muet.   [vv. 4654–60]

If it is felt that the relationship between Lancelot and Guenevere proceeds with rather more haste than Andreas would countenance, it should be remembered that he also says that 'a wise and discreet woman is usually moderate about delaying the grant of her lover's request' (P., p. 133) and advises that 'if she finds him persistent during [his] long-continued probation, she ought not delay much longer the fulfillment of her promises' (P., p. 120).

Andreas and Chrétien are likewise in agreement over the need for lovers to be discreet in conducting their affairs. In discussing the behaviour that is to be expected of a lover Andreas states that 'great prudence is necessary in the management of a love affair and diligence in all one does' (P., p. 60). The need for secrecy is stressed again in his discussion of the way love may be retained once it has been acquired in Book II, chapter i:

> The man who wants to keep his love affair for a long time untroubled should above all things be careful not to let it be known to any outsider, but

should keep it hidden from everybody; because when a number of people begin to get wind of such an affair, it ceases to develop naturally and even loses what progress it has already made.   [P., p. 151]

At a later stage in the discussion he specifies the conduct to be avoided if an affair is to be kept secret:

And every man ought to be sparing of praise of his beloved when he is among other men; he should not talk about her often or at great length, and he should not spend a great deal of time in places where she is. When he is with other men, if he meets her in a group of women, he should not try to communicate with her by signs, but should treat her almost like a stranger, lest some person spying on their love might have opportunity to spread malicious gossip. Lovers should not even nod to each other unless they are sure that nobody is watching them.   [P. pp. 151–2]

In the *Charrete* Lancelot and Guenevere conduct themselves with exemplary—and very necessary—discretion. Guenevere is careful to hide her grief at the news of Lancelot's supposed death:

. . . tant duremant s'an esmaie
qu'a po la parole n'an pert;
mes por les genz dit en appert:
'Molt me poise, voir, de sa mort;
et s'il m'an poise, n'ai pas tort;
qu'il vint an cest païs por moi,
por ce pesance avoir an doi.'
Puis dit a li meïsme an bas,
por ce que l'en ne l'oïst pas,
que de boivre ne de mangier
ne la covient ja mes proier
se ce est voirs que cil morz soit,
por la cui vie ele vivoit.
Tantost se lieve molt dolante
de la table, si se demante,
si que nus ne l'ot ne escoute.   [vv. 4164–79]

In the same way she is discreet in arranging the rendezvous with Lancelot, indicating the window by a mere glance (vv. 4506–7). She prudently arranges to avoid being seen near the window whilst Lancelot is wrenching out the bars (vv. 4618–26). At the tournament she shrewdly hits on the one sure way of discovering whether or not the unknown champion is Lancelot (vv. 5634–45), for, as she is fully aware (vv. 5872–5), only one man is likely to expose himself to public humiliation at her behest a second—or even a first—time. Finally, Guenevere shows a restraint which is held up for praise on Lancelot's arrival at court for the final duel with Meleagant. Her wild desire to greet him is held in check until such time as a more suitable occasion presents itself (vv. 6820–53). In his turn Lancelot shows a similar discretion when this is demanded of him. On the night of his rendez-vous with the queen he carefully covers his movements, adopting tactics which Chrétien suggests were familiar enough to some of his public:

> Quant il vit le jor enublé,
> si se fet las et traveillié,
> et dit que molt avoit veillié,
> s'avoit mestier de reposer.
> Bien poez antendre et gloser,
> voz qui avez fet autretel,
> que por la gent de son ostel
> se fet las et se fet couchier;
> mes n'ot mie son lit tant chier
> que por rien il n'i reposast,
> n'il ne poïst ne il n'osast,
> ne il ne volsist pas avoir
> le hardemant ne le pooir.
> Molt tost et soëf s'an leva,
> ne ce mie ne li greva
> qu'il ne luisoit lune n'estoile,
> ne an la meison n'avoit chandoile,
> ne lanpe, ne lanterne ardant.
> Ensi s'an ala regardant
> c'onques nus garde ne s'an prist,
> einz cuidoient qu'il se dormist
> an son lit trestote la nuit.   [vv. 4546–67]

Where the attitude to be adopted towards love is concerned, a comparison between the *Charrete* and the *De amore* shows Chrétien and Andreas to be in complete agreement.

To begin with, both works glorify sexual love as inspiring all that is highest and best in man. For its part, the *De amore* proclaims that love 'is the fountain head and source of all good things' (P., p. 68) and maintains that 'no one does a good or courteous deed in the world unless it is derived from the fount of love' (P., p. 40). These two statements are the basic tenets of the ethic expounded in the first two books of the treatise and figure repeatedly in the dialogues where various lovers plead their particular cases. In the sixth dialogue, for example, a nobleman tries to impress a commoner with the following arguments:

> Now I shall prove to you that you cannot properly deprive me of your love. Loving is either a good thing or a bad thing. It is not safe to say that it is a bad thing, because *all men are clearly agreed and the rule of Love shows us that neither woman nor man in this world can be considered happy or well-bred, nor can he do anything good, unless love inspires him.* Wherefore you must needs conclude that loving is a good thing and a desirable one. *Therefore if a person of either sex desires to be considered good or praiseworthy in the world, he or she is bound to love.*   [P., p. 88; my italics]

Or again, in the eighth dialogue, a lady tactfully prefaces her rejection of a suitor with the following observation:

> *Now I say that there is nothing in this life more praiseworthy than to love wisely, and no man can do to the full those things that make a man worthy of praise unless he does them under the compulsion of love.* Therefore you do rightly if you seek for yourself a suitable love through whom your determination to do well may always be increased.   [P., p. 114; my italics]

The *De amore* also provides a clue as to the basis of this view of love as a major, if not the major, influence for good in man's life. From the discussion of the effects of love (Book I, chapter iv), it would seem to be founded on the beneficial changes love can be seen to produce in the habits and characters of lovers:

> Now it is the effect of love that a true lover cannot be degraded with any avarice. Love causes a rough and uncouth man to be distinguished for his handsomeness; it can endow a man even of the humblest birth with nobility of character; it blesses the proud with humility; and the man in love becomes accustomed to performing many services gracefully for everyone. *O what a wonderful thing is love, which makes a man shine with so many virtues and teaches everyone, no matter who he is,* so many good traits of character!   [P., p. 31]

The *Charrete* provides a practical illustration of the view that love represents and inspires all that is highest and best in men. It is, after all, the ruling passion of a hero who not only proves to be the greatest knight in the world, but is also a paragon of all the virtues, social and moral. Furthermore, Chrétien is at pains to stress that it is love which inspires the hero's greatest acts of heroism and valour. It is the thought of Guenevere that urges Lancelot to rescue the Seductive Damsel from her assailant and his six formidable henchmen:

Li chevaliers a l'uis s'areste
et dit: 'Dex, que porrai ge feire?
Meüz sui por si grant afeire
con por la reïne Guenievre.
Ne doi mie avoir cuer de lievre
quant por li sui an ceste queste:
se Malvestiez son cuer me preste
et je son comandemant faz,
n'ateindrai pas ce que je chaz;
honiz sui se je ci remaing.
Molt me vient or a grant desdaing,
quant j'ai parlé del remenoir;

. . .

or en ai honte, or en si duel
tel que je morroie mon vuel,
quant je ai tant demoré ci.'   [vv. 1096–111]

Again it is love that makes Lancelot cross the sword bridge—which for
Bademaguz is 'le plus grant hardemant qui onques fust'—regardless of
the cost to himself, and even glorying in it:

Mains et genolz et piez se blece,
mes tot le rasoage et sainne
Amors qui le conduist et mainne,
si li estoit a sofrir dolz.   [vv. 3112–5]

And finally, it is love that enables him, when on the point of defeat
(v. 3622–33), to rally and to prevail against Meleagant:

. . . force et hardemanz li croist,
qu'Amors li fet molt grant aïe.   [vv. 3720–1]

. . .

Ensi Lanceloz molt sovant
le menoit arriers et avant
par tot la ou boen li estoit,
et totevoies s'arestoit,
devant la reïne sa dame
qui li a mis el cors la flame,
por qu'il la va si regardant;
et cele flame si ardant
vers Meleagant le feisoit,
que par tot la ou il pleisoit
le pooit mener et chacier.   [vv. 3720–1, 3745–55]

It has been alleged that love is shown in the *Charrete* as a destructive
force, undermining the social order, demeaning and diminishing

Lancelot. For some, his riding in the cart is a contravention of all the laws of chivalry:

> Ainsi l'amour, ou plutôt Guenièvre, en commandant à Lancelot de monter dans la charrette, a volontairement et sciemment confondu les valeurs que la chevalerie s'acharne à distinguer. Tout se passe donc comme si la reine prenait à cœur d'humilier la chevalerie en bafouant les conventions établies par elle.[15]

For others, the display of cowardice at Pomelegoi is a shaming instance of knighthood being forced to yield to love:

> Décidément l'amour a vaincu la chevalerie, la femme a triomphé de l'exploit, la féminité l'emporte sur la virilité. Et c'est un homme qui écrit l'ordre du jour de cette victoire.[16]

In fact, however, there are no grounds in either case for claiming that love has overborne chivalry, duty or honour. Rather it is self-interest that has been so vanquished.[17] On both occasions it is Lancelot, and Lancelot alone, who is exposed to public mockery—not the order of knighthood. In neither case is any real disgrace or dishonour involved, since his humiliation is undeserved. In both instances Lancelot sees his humiliation as serving the interests of the queen, and in both he accepts the sacrifice demanded of him as willingly as he puts his life and safety at risk on her behalf on other occasions. Here, as when he hazards life and limb for Guenevere, his attitude is that of the Christian martyr, willing and ready to accept death or dishonour—in the eyes of men—for 'the Lord's sake'. The whole position is put clearly enough by Lancelot himself when he comes to speculate on the cause of the displeasure the queen showed when he was led into her presence after his victory over Meleagant. The only explanation that he can think of is that he was paraded in a cart like a common malefactor. But this, he argues, could not be taken by any true lover as a disgrace. Since it was done for love's sake, it should, on the contrary, be recognised as an honourable and gracious act of service. For love—and here Lancelot is as much a maximist as Andreas himself—ennobles every deed undertaken in the service of the beloved:

15 P. Jonin, 'Le vasselage de Lancelot dans le *Conte de la Charrette*', *Le Moyen Age*, LVIII (1952), p. 291.

16 G. Cohen, *Un Grand Romancier d'amour et d'aventure au XIIe siècle, Chrétien de Troyes et son œuvre*, Paris, 1931, p. 265.

17 For a full discussion of the significance of the cart episode in the *Charrete* see Zaddy, *Chrétien Studies*, pp. 132–6, 190–2.

'Dex, cist forfez, quex estre pot?
Bien cuit que espoir ele sot
que je montai sor la charrete.
Ne sai quel blasme ele me mete
se cestui non. Cist m'a traï.
S'ele por cestui m'a haï,
Dex, cist forfez, por coi me nut?
Onques Amors bien ne conut
qui ce me torna a reproche;
qu'an ne porroit dire de boche
riens qui de par Amors venist
qui a reproche apartenist:
einz est amors et corteisie
quan qu'an puet feire por s'amie.
Por m' "amie" nel fis je pas.
Ne sai comant je die las!
Ne sai se die "amie" ou non,
ne li os metre cest sornon.
Mes tant cuit je d'amor savoir,
que *ne me deüst mie avoir*
por ce plus vil s'ele m'amast,
mes ami verai me clamast.
quant por li me sanbloit enors
a feire quan que vialt Amors,
nes sor la charrete monter.
Ce deüst ele amor conter;
et c'est la provance veraie;
Amors ensi les suens essaie,
ensi conuist ele les suens.
Mes ma dame ne fu pas buens
cist servises; bien le provai
au sanblant que an li trovai.
Et tote voie ses amis
fist ce don maint li ont amis
por li honte et reproche et blasme;
s'ai fet ce geu don an me blasme
et de ma dolçor m'anertume,
par foi, car tex est la costume
a cez qui d'amor rien ne sevent
et qui enor en honte levent:
mes qui enor an honte moille
ne la leve pas, einz la soille.
Or sont cil d'Amors non sachant
qui ensi les vont despisant,

et molt an sus d'Amors se botent
qui son comandemant ne dotent.
Car, sanz faille, molt en amande
qui fet ce qu'Amors li comande,
et tot est pardonable chose;
s'est failliz qui feire ne l'ose.'   [vv. 4347–96; my italics]

So far from its being true, then, that love acts as a destructive and anti-
social force in the *Charrete*, one may safely claim that, with the one
exception which will be dealt with presently, its commands never run
counter to Lancelot's feudal or chivalric obligations in Chrétien's
romance. Love never gives him occasion there to experience the remorse and the disgust which afflict Beroul's Tristan once the effects of
the potion wear off. Nor does Lancelot ever know, as Bernier does
in *Raoul de Cambrai*, the agony of being torn between conflicting
loyalties.

The glorification of sexual love which is found in the *Charrete* and
in the first two books of the *De amore* was, of course, entirely contrary
to the teachings of the Church. In the eyes of that institution such love
was a source of evil and corruption and, even within wedlock,[18] a sin
to be avoided. The point is clearly made in the third section of Andreas'
treatise, which is a counterblast to all lovers and loving:

> Now for many reasons any wise man is bound to avoid all the deeds of love
> and to oppose its mandates. The first of these reasons is one which it is not
> right for anyone to oppose, for no man, so long as he devotes himself to the
> service of love, can please God by any other works, even if they are good
> ones.   [P. p. 187]

> But still another argument seems very much opposed to love. Many evils
> come from love, but I do not see that anything that is good for men comes
> from it: the delight of the flesh which we embrace with such great eagerness
> is not in the nature of a good, but rather, as men agree, it is a damnable sin
> which even in married persons is scarcely to be classed among the venial
> faults which are not sins, according to the word of the prophet, who said,
> 'For behold I was conceived in iniquities and in sins did my mother con-
> ceive me'.
> . . .

> Besides this we know beyond a doubt that God Himself is the fountain-
> head and origin of chastity and modesty, and from Scripture we know that

18 This we gather from the *De amore* (P., p. 103): '. . . the too ardent lover, as
we are taught by the apostolic law, is considered an adulterer with his own
wife'. Parry's footnote to this statement (No. 47) concludes by saying that 'it
seems to have been a commonplace of medieval theology . . .'.

the Devil is really the author of love and lechery. And so, because of their sources, we are bound forever to observe modesty and chastity and to shun lechery completely, because we agree that that which the Devil has given rise to cannot be at all wholesome for men or give them anything that we can praise. [P., pp. 193-5]

What we see in the *Charrete* and in the first two sections of the *De amore*, then, is a deliberate rejection of the Church's rulings on sex. This rejection is explicit in Andreas' eighth dialogue, where the teachings of the Church are presented as an ideal to be pursued by a few rare souls prepared to eschew the world entirely, whilst an alternative ethic, more in line with human instincts, is advocated in their place for the average woman and man:

> Your statement that God is offended by love cannot keep you from it; it seems to be generally agreed that to serve God is a very great and extraordinarily good thing, but those who desire to serve Him perfectly ought to devote themselves wholly to His service, and according to the opinion of Paul they should engage in no worldly business. Therefore if you choose to serve God alone, you must give up all worldly things and contemplate only the mysteries of the Heavenly Country, for God has not wished that anybody should keep his right foot on earth and his left foot in heaven, since no one can properly devote himself to the service of two masters. Now since it is clear that you have one foot on earth from the fact that you receive with a joyful countenance those who come to you and that you exchange courteous words with them and persuade them to do the works of love, I believe you would do better to enjoy love thoroughly than to lie to God under cloak of some pretense. I believe, however, that God cannot be seriously offended by love, for what is done under compulsion of nature can be made clean by an easy expiation. Besides it does not seem at all proper to class as a sin the thing from which the highest good in this life takes its origin and without which no man in the world could be considered worthy of praise. [P., pp. 110-1]

The second point to emerge from a comparison of the views on love expressed in the *Charrete* and the *De amore* is that Chrétien and Andreas both see fulfilment as the aim of love. In the words of Andreas:

> Every attempt of a lover tends towards the enjoyment of the embraces of her whom he loves; he thinks about it continually, for he hopes that with her he may fulfill all the mandates of love. . . . Therefore in the sight of a lover nothing can be compared to the act of love. [P., p. 30]

It is true that in the eighth dialogue Andreas advocates the practice of pure love, which stops short of consummation, rather than that of mixed love, which culminates in the 'final act of Venus'. But this is on grounds of expediency (because 'no injury comes from it'), and not because he sees it as intrinsically superior. Mixed love, he hastens to add, is also 'real love, and . . . is praiseworthy, and . . . is the source of all good things, although from it grave dangers threaten' (P., pp. 122–3).

In the *Charrete* the joy the lovers experience together is described as the finest and most exquisite it is given to man to know:

> . . . il lor avint sanz mantir
> une joie et une mervoille
> tel c'onques ancor sa paroille
> ne fu oïe ne seüe;
> mes toz jorz iert par moi teüe,
> qu'an conte ne doit estre dite.
> Des joies fu la plus eslite
> et la plus delitable cele
> que li contes nos test et cele.   [vv. 4676–84]

Lastly, the *Charrete* and the *De amore* coincide in extolling extra-marital love. The example of Lancelot and Guenevere shows that in the *Charrete* the rights of the heart—where its affections are worthily bestowed—take precedence over the laws of Church and State which prohibit adultery. The charge that Kay has committed adultery with the queen is rebutted by them both as a betrayal unthinkable in her or in a loyal servant of Arthur's:

> '*Je cuit que Kex li seneschax*
> *et si cortois et si leax*
> *que il n'an fet mie a mescroire;*
> *et je ne regiet mie an foire*
> *mon cors, ne n'an faz livreison.*
> *Certes, Kex n'est mie tex hom*
> *qu'il me requeïst tel outrage,*
> *ne je n'en oi onques corage*
> *del faire, ne ja ne l'avrai.*'
> 'Sire, molt buen gré vos savrai,
> fet Meleaganz a son pere,
> se Kex son outrage conpere,
> si que la reïne i ait honte.
> . . .
> Le roi Artus a Kex traï
> son seignor, qui tant le creoit
> que comandee li avoit

la rien que plus ainme an cest monde.'
'Sire, or sofrez que je responde,
fet Kex, et si m'escondirai.
Ja Dex, quant de cest siegle irai,
ne me face pardon a l'ame,
se onques jui avoec ma dame.
Certes, mialz voldroie estre morz
que tex leidure ne tiex torz
fust par moi quis vers mon seignor.' [vv. 4839–65]

In spite of these protestations, however, neither Guenevere nor
Lancelot have the slightest compunction about betraying Arthur
themselves, although the one is shown as a dutiful and gracious consort of a loving husband[19] and the other as a loyal knight and a God-
fearing man in all other respects. All that holds the queen back is lack
of desire in the first place, and then, once this has been awakened, lack
of opportunity. And all that Lancelot waits upon is his lady's pleasure
and then opportunity.

In the *De amore* it is a matter of principle that love is necessarily
adulterous. The ruling is first given in the letter ascribed to the Countess
of Champagne in the seventh dialogue:

We declare and we hold as firmly established that love cannot exert its
powers between two people who are married to each other. For lovers give
each other everything freely, under no compulsion of necessity, but married
people are in duty bound to give in to each other's desires and deny themselves to each other in nothing. . . . And we say the same thing for still
another reason, which is that a precept of love tells us that no woman, even
if she is married, can be crowned with the reward of the King of Love
unless she is seen to be enlisted in the service of Love himself outside the
bonds of wedlock. But another rule of Love teaches that no one can be in
love with two men. Rightly, therefore, Love cannot acknowledge any rights
of his between husband and wife. . . .
Therefore let this our verdict, pronounced with great moderation and
supported by the opinion of a great many ladies, be to you firm and indu-
bitable truth. [P., pp. 106–7]

The countess's decision is quoted by the suitor who finds himself
rebuked in the eighth dialogue for rejecting a 'most beautiful wife [to]
seek for love away from home' (p. 116). A similar ruling is given by
Lady Ermengarde of Narbonne in the eighth love case on p. 171, and

19 Arthur's feeling for the queen can be judged from the description of his joy
   at her return in vv. 5355–8.

the first of the thirty-one rules of love brought back from Arthur's court runs: 'Marriage is no real excuse for not loving' (P., p. 184).

The glorification of adultery that we find in the *De amore* and the *Charrete* is yet another attempt to assert the rights of the heart in a society where marriages were arranged with an eye to dynastic and strategic necessities rather than to private inclinations. In Chrétien's other romances the remedy proposed is the union of love and marriage. In the *Charrete* the solution is to make a virtue of necessity and to exclude marriage from love in a world where all too often love must have been excluded from marriage.

The last point to emerge from a comparison of the *Charrete* and the *De amore* is that both advocate treating women with respect. Both show that they are to be served and honoured because they are, to quote the words of 'Andreas the Lover', 'the cause and origin of everything good' and because 'men cannot amount to anything or taste of the fountain of goodness unless they do this under the persuasion of ladies' (P., p. 108). But over the degree of respect to be shown them the views expressed in the two works vary very considerably.

In the *Charrete* one gathers from the example of Lancelot that women are to be revered as superior beings—as representing, quite literally, all that is highest and best in this life. In his eyes Guenevere is clearly a divinity—albeit an alternative one—to be revered with a quasi-religious devotion.[20] On coming into her presence or leaving it he genuflects as before the deity:

> . . . puis vint au lit la reïne,
> si l'aore et se li ancline,
> car an nul core saint ne croit tant.   [vv. 4651-3]

> Au departir a soploié
> a la chanbre, et fet tot autel
> con s'il fust devant un autel.   [vv. 4716-18]

Her hairs are venerated by him as holy relics, more efficacious against disease than the help of God's saints:

> Ne cuidoit mie que reoncles
> ne autres max ja més le praigne;

20 The fact that it is worship that Lancelot offers Guenevere is one which is fully recognized by M. Lazar in *Amour courtois et 'fin'amors'*, pp. 237-8; and—with abhorrence—by Jonin in 'Le vasselage', pp. 294-6.

dïamargareton desdaigne
et pleüriche et tirïasque,
neïs saint Martin et saint Jasque;
car an ces chevox tant se fie
qu'il n'a mestier de lor aïe. [vv. 1472–8]

In Guenevere's service Lancelot shows a martyr's willingness to hazard
life and limb (as he does most spectacularly in braving the perils of the
sword bridge, vv. 3008–109), and, like a martyr, he glories in the pains
he suffers in her cause:

Mains et genolz et piez se blece,
mes tot le rasoage et sainne
Amors qui le conduist et mainne,
si li estoit a sofrir dolz. [vv. 3112–15]

For Guenevere he is prepared to forfeit his standing in the world and
to endure public humiliation, which is what he consents to in agreeing
to be driven in a cart to get news of her whereabouts:

Qui a forfet estoit repris
s'estoit sor la charrete mis
et menez par totes les rues;
s'avoit totes enors perdues,
ne puis n'estoit a cort oïz,
ne enorez ne conjoïz. [vv. 333–8]

And from this sacrifice we see that Lancelot is capable of total self-
abnegation. For it is the ultimate sacrifice to be demanded of a knight
if we can judge from the example of Lancelot's opponent who finds
death preferable to such degradation:

'. . . por Deu, vos quier et demant
merci, fors que tant seulemant
qu'an charrete monter ne doive.
Nus plez n'est que je n'an recoive
fors cestui, tant soit grief ne forz.
Mialz voldroie estre, je cuit, morz
que fet eüsse cest meschief.' [vv. 2769–75]

In the circumstances it is not surprising to find that for Lancelot
Guenevere's every command is a law to be obeyed immediately
(vv. 3798–804), even though it may cost him his life (as in the two
duels with Meleagant, where Lancelot stops fighting in obedience to
the queen, although his opponent continues to belabour him with

blows, vv. 3805–17, 5019–25); or even if it means exposing himself to
public ridicule (as it does at the tournament, where he is ordered to
play the coward, vv. 5654–99, 5856–7). Nor, again, is it surprising that
he accepts her will without murmuring, even when his services
deserve a better reward than the show of cold displeasure he meets
with after his victory over Meleagant:

> Ez vos Lancelot trespansé,
> se li respont molt belemant
> a meniere de fin amant;
> 'Dame, certes, ce poise moi,
> ne je n'os demander por coi.'   [vv. 3960–4]

Turning to the *De amore*, one finds that what is demanded there is
that women be treated with the respect due to equals—and it is
significant that the term used to denote the female partner in a love
relationship is *coamans*. The two points that Andreas particularly strives
to impress upon his friend Walter are: the need for a man to consider
his partner's interests and the need to respect her wishes—provided
always that she is a woman of rank, for with a peasant or a serving
wench he can expect to make free.[21]

(*a*) It is made very plain that there can be no question of forcing
one's desires on a lady:

> . . . what sort of love can it be that is undertaken against the desire of the
> heart? Only that which is first desired by the heart and the will should have
> the rewards of love.   [P. p. 89]

The granting of love should be seen as lying entirely in the gift of
the lady:

> . . . it is left to the decision of every woman, when asked for her love, to
> refuse it if she will, and no one has a right to be injured thereby. . .
>   [P., p. 87]

It is therefore to be looked upon as a favour:

> . . . what greater favor can be shown to any man in the world than for him
> to have the love of the women he desires?   [P., p. 160]

---

21 See Andreas' remarks on the love of peasants (P., pp. 149–50). The following
statement there is particularly enlightening: 'And if you should, by some
chance, fall in love with some of their women, be careful to puff them up with
lots of praise and then, when you find a convenient place, do not hesitate to
take what you seek and embrace them by force.'

(*b*) It is also stressed that a man must broach the subject of his desires with due decorum:

> . . . all lovers must realize that after the salutation they should not immediately begin talking about love, for it is only with their concubines that men begin in that way.   [P., p. 36]

> . . . the wise and well-taught lover, when conversing for the first time with a lady whom he has not previously known, should not ask in specific words for the gifts of love, but he should try hard to give a hint to the lady he loves, and should show himself pleasant and courteous in all that he says; then he should be careful to act in such a way that his deeds praise him truly to his love, even when he is absent. Then as the third step he may with more assurance come to the request for love.   [P., p. 97]

In particular, a suitor is warned to be courteous and modest in approaching great ladies:

> If a man of the higher nobility should seek the love of a woman of the same class, he should first above all things follow the rule to use soft and gentle words, and he should take care not to say anything that would seem to deserve a reproof. For a noblewoman or a woman of the higher nobility is found to be very ready and bold in censuring the deeds or the words of a man of the higher nobility, and she is very glad if she has a good opportunity to say something to ridicule him.   [P., p. 107]

Andreas even gives advice on when it is proper for a lover to seat himself by a lady:

> . . . it is the usual rule that when a man is considered to be of a more privileged rank than the woman, he may, if he wishes, sit down beside her without asking permission. If they are of the same rank, he may ask permission to sit beside her, and if she grants it he may sit down by her side, but not unless she does. But where the man is of lower rank than the woman, he must not ask permission to sit beside her, but he may ask to sit in a lower place. If, however, she gives him permission to sit beside her, he may without fear oblige her.   [P., p. 62]

(*c*) Great emphasis is laid in the *De Amore* on the right a woman has to safeguard her interests by putting a suitor on probation until his character and intentions have been thoroughly scrutinised:

> . . . when a woman is asked for her love, before she grants it she should make every effort to find out the character and the good faith of the man who is asking, so that there will be nothing she does not know about him; because

after she has heedlessly gone into the affair it is too late to seek the advice
of a wise man or to torment herself with a tardy repentance.   [P., p. 161]

There is not in the world a lady or damsel . . . who cannot easily recognize
the faith and truth of a man who asks for her love if she sets about investigating his love. . . . a woman ought not to assent immediately to the desire of
a suitor, but should first make him a great many cautious promises and should
with proper moderation postpone giving him the good things she has
promised him; then, to test the purity of his faith, she should sometimes say
that she has completely changed her mind. . . . No lover is so cautious and so
clever that if the fruition of his love is long postponed, . . . , he will not
either be made a worthy man thereby or openly reveal his falseness.
                                                                     [P., p. 120]

To judge from the example of the suitors in the various dialogues, a
lover is clearly expected to submit to such investigations and to await
their outcome patiently:

. . . since it is not easy for all a man's good deeds to become known to
everybody, it may be that mine are unknown to you, and so perhaps in view
of the state of your knowledge this time for consideration for which you
ask would be reasonable.   [P., p. 83]

I give you all the thanks of which I am capable that you have so prudently
promised that after much labor I may have your love, and I hope that neither
I nor anyone else may enjoy the love of a woman as worthy as you are
until I have acquired it with much labor. It is not likely that so prudent a
woman as you would give her love hastily to anyone, nor would she permit
the efforts of any worthy man in her behalf to go unrewarded.   [P., p. 44]

(*d*) Andreas makes it equally plain that, besides concern for his partner's well-being, a lover should show respect for her wishes and
a willingness to please her in every possible way. The advice he gives
in discussing the way love may be retained once it has been acquired
tallies in this with Chrétien's observation that a lover is ever obedient
(vv. 3798–801) and with his comment that Lancelot's courteous acceptance of Guenevere's rejection of him after his duel with Meleagant is
that of a true lover (vv. 3960–2):[22]

22 The passages in question are:

       Molt est qui aimme obeïsanz,
       et molt fet tost et volentiers
       la ou il est amis antiers,
       ce qu'a s'amie doie plaire   [vv. 3798–801]
   and

Furthermore a lover ought to appear to his beloved wise in every respect and restrained in his conduct, and he should do nothing disagreeable that might annoy her. Moreover every man is bound, in time of need, to come to the aid of his beloved, both by sympathizing with her in all her troubles and by acceding to all her reasonable desires. Even if he knows sometimes that what she wants is not so reasonable, he should be prepared to agree to it after he has asked her to reconsider. And if inadvertently he should do something improper that offends her, let him straightway confess with downcast face that he has done wrong, and let him give the excuse that he lost his temper or make some other suitable explanation that will fit the case. [P. p. 151]

These same points appear among the rules brought back from Arthur's court to the lovers of Britain:

Rule xxv. A true lover considers nothing good except what he thinks will please his beloved.
Rule xxvi. Love can deny nothing to love. [P., p. 185]

In particular Andreas stresses the need to respect the woman's wishes in sexual matters. The failure to do so, he tells us, is one of the ways in which 'love may be decreased':

Love decreases, too, if the woman finds that her lover is foolish and indiscreet, or if he seems to go beyond reasonable bounds in his demands for love, or if she sees that he has no regard for her modesty and will not forgive her bashfulness. For a faithful lover ought to prefer love's greatest pains to making demands which deprive his beloved of her modesty or taking pleasure in making fun of her blushes; he is not called a lover, but a betrayer, who would consider only his own passions and who would be unmindful of the good of his beloved. [P., p. 155]

Not surprisingly, two of the rules of love devised by the God of Love himself are concerned with this point:

Rule viii. In giving and receiving love's solaces let modesty be ever present.
Rule xii. In practicing the solaces of love thou shalt not exceed the desires of thy lover. [P., pp. 81–2]

(e) Finally, Andreas makes it plain that all ladies are to be treated

---

Ez vos Lancelot trespansé
se li respont molt belemant
a meniere de fin amant. [vv. 3960–2]

with courtesy and consideration by lovers, and not merely those who
are the object of their affections:

> A lover should always offer his services and obedience freely to every lady.
> [P., p. 152]

> [A man] should not be a lover of several women at the same time, but for
> the sake of one he should be a devoted servant of all.   [P., p. 60]

The seventh rule of the God of Love indeed runs: 'Being obedient in
all things to the commands of ladies, thou shalt ever strive to ally
thyself to the service of Love.'

If Andreas insists that women are entitled to the respect and consideration of their lovers, he makes it very plain that this is as equal
partners, not as superior beings. The need for reciprocity in love is
stressed throughout the *De amore*, and as much emphasis is placed
there on a woman's obligations as upon her rights.

(*a*) A woman is clearly expected to give merit and service their due
reward:

> . . . it is clear that every man should strive with all his might to be of service
> to ladies so that he may shine by their grace. But the ladies are greatly
> obligated to be attentive to keeping the hearts of good men set upon doing
> good deeds and to honour every man according to his deserts. For whatever
> good things living men may say or do, they generally credit them all to the
> praise of women, and by serving these they so act that they may pride
> themselves on the rewards they receive from them, and without these
> rewards no man can be of use in this life or be considered worthy of any
> praise.   [P., p. 108]

> A woman ought to inquire diligently whether the man who asks for her
> love is worthy of it, and if she finds that he is perfectly worthy, she ought
> by no means to refuse him her love unless she is obligated to love someone
> else.   [P., p. 51]

> We believe we must firmly hold that when a woman has granted any man
> the hope of her love or has given him any of the other preliminary gifts,
> and she finds him not unworthy of this love, it is very wrong for her to try
> to deprive him of the love he has so long hoped for. It is not proper for any
> honest woman to put off without good cause the fulfillment of any of her
> promises; if she is fully determined not to listen to a suitor, she must not
> grant him hope or any of the other preliminary gifts of love, because it is
> considered very deceitful for her not to do what she has promised him. It is
> thought very shameful in a woman not to be careful to keep her promises;
> that is usually looked upon like the deceit of harlots, who in all their deeds
> and words are full of falsehood and all of whose thoughts are full of guile.
> [P., p. 166]

(*b*) Although the right of a woman to safeguard her interests is fully conceded, she is not expected to prolong the probation of a suitor longer than is reasonable or necessary:

> . . . if she finds him persistent during this long-continued probation, she ought not delay much longer the fulfillment of her promises, lest he feel that his labor gets him very little profit.   [P., p. 120]

> A wise and discreet woman is usually moderate about delaying the grant of her lover's request.   [P., p. 133]

(*c*) In a love relationship the obligation to study and consider the well-being and the desires of the beloved are as binding on the woman as on the man. This we see when the question of changing from the practice of pure to that of mixed love is discussed. The woman is advised to give way to her partner's desires on the score that 'love can deny nothing to love':

> Although all men ought to choose a pure love rather than a mixed or common one, still one of the lovers may not oppose the desire of the other unless at the beginning of the attachment they made an agreement that they would never engage in mixed love except by the free will and the full consent of both parties. But even if the lovers have made an agreement that neither may ask for anything more unless both are agreed to it, still it is not right for the woman to refuse to give in to her lover's desire on this point if she sees that he persists in it. For all lovers are bound, when practicing love's solaces, to be mutually obedient to each other's desires.   [P. p. 167]

Indeed, the obligations are more stringent for women than for men in some respects, as we see from the discussion on infidelity in lovers:

> The old opinion, held by some, is that when the woman is at fault the same rule should be followed as in the case of the man just mentioned. But this rule, although old, should not be respected on that account, since it would lead us into great error. God forbid that we should ever declare that a woman who is not ashamed to wanton with two men should go unpunished. Although in the case of men such a thing is tolerated because it is so common and because the sex has a privilege by which all things in this world which are by their nature immodest are more readily allowed to men, in the case of a woman they are, because of the decency of the modest sex, considered so disgraceful that after a woman has indulged the passions of several men everybody looks upon her as an unclean strumpet unfit to associate with other ladies.   [P., p. 162]

That the *De amore* should advocate treating women as equal partners in love where the *Charrete* would have them revered as superior beings is not difficult to understand. For the one work was written at the behest of a man and the other at that of a woman. It is hardly likely that a man would take kindly to the idea of female domination —how unlikely, indeed, can be judged from the reactions of Chrétien's modern critics![23] Even to suggest that they should be treated as equals, though not quite as equal as men, must have seemed revolutionary enough at the time, if the behaviour of the amorous count in *Erec* or of Erec himself are anything to go by.[24] For a woman, on the other hand, the idea of being reverenced as a near-divinity must have been gratifyingly flattering.[25] At all events, such a role must have been more acceptable than the one assigned her in the third book of the *De amore* by Andreas, the churchman, who denounces womankind as compounded of all the vices and as an evil to be avoided at all costs:

> Not only is every woman by nature a miser, but she is also envious and a slanderer of other women, greedy, a slave to her belly, inconstant, fickle in her speech, disobedient and impatient of restraint, spotted with the sin of pride and desirous of vainglory, a liar, a drunkard, a babbler, no keeper of secrets, too much given to wantonness, prone to every evil, and never loving any man in her heart.   [P., p. 201]

> Therefore Solomon, that wisest of men, who knew all the evils and misdeeds of womankind, made a general statement concerning their crimes and wickednesses when he said, 'There is no good woman.' Why therefore, Walter, are you striving so eagerly to love that which is bad?   [P., p. 209]

*

Now that the comparison between the *Charrete* and the *De amore* is complete, it can be seen that Paris was right in claiming that the one provides the theory behind the practice described in the other, whereas

23 Adverse reactions to the domination of Lancelot by Guenevere are to be found in: Jonin: 'Ce n'est plus un homme, encore moins un guerrier, mais un jouet' ('Le vasselage', pp. 292–3); Rychner (who sees it as yet another reason for looking for an alternative to the traditional—realist—view of the *Charrete*): 'Il devient proprement absurde qu'une pareille loque libère les prisonniers de Gorre' ('Le prologue', p. 1132); and Cohen, whose reaction to the queen's domination of her lover has already been seen on p. 382 of this study. Even Frappier sees a basic immorality in the subject of the *Charrete* which stems, he claims, 'moins du fait même de l'adultère que de l'esclavage mystique de l'amant' (*Chrétien*, p. 124).

24 For a discussion of the development of Erec's attitude towards his wife see Zaddy, *Chrétien Studies*, pp. 19–23.

25 A point fully appreciated by Frappier: 'Il [Lancelot] sert à exalter la féminité idéale ou réelle des précieuses de la cour de Champagne' (*Chrétien*, p. 138).

the charge which Rychner brought against him was unjustified. For the examination of the two texts has shown that they coincide in the views on love and loving advanced in them. Both glorify a love that is extra-marital and frankly sensual. Both insist on respect for women, though they differ over the degree of respect to be shown in a way to be expected when the one work was written for a woman and the other for a man. They agree over the proper conduct of a love affair and the qualities to be required of those who would practise the art of loving. They coincide in their descriptions of the effects of love.

At the same time this comparison of the two texts confirms Paris' view that they illustrate ideas on love current among the great ladies of Chrétien's day ('Etudes', p. 534), but lends no support to those who share Robertson's desire to dissociate Andreas, Chrétien and his patroness, Marie de Champagne, from such frivolous preoccupations.[26] For a detailed examination of the *Charrete* and the *De amore* leaves one with the very distinct impression that certain sections of twelfth century society, and in particular the circles for whom Chrétien wrote, were greatly intrigued by the possibilities of finding an alternative to the sexual code imposed by Church and State. This impression, moreover, is strongly reinforced by the fact that both Chrétien and Andreas testify to the interest taken in love at certain courts. In *Cligés*, for example, Chrétien addresses his public as a body of experts on all matters concerning love:

> Vos qui d'Amors vos feites sage,
> et les costumes et l'usage
> de sa cort maintenez a foi,
> n'onques ne faussastes sa loi,
> que qu'il vos an doie cheoir,
> dites se l'en puet nes veoir
> rien qui por Amor abelisse
> que l'en n'an tressaille ou palisse.   [*Cligés*, ed., Micha, vv. 3819–29]

26 The desire to find a more edifying theme in the *Charrete* than the glorification of 'courtly'—in the sense of adulterous—love is expressed by Robertson in his article 'Some medieval literary terminology with special reference to Chrétien de Troyes', *Studies in Philology*, XLVIII (1951), p. 691: 'An interpretation which showed the "courtly love" in the *Roman* to be merely a feature of the *cortex* would constitute an act of kindness to Chrétien and to his Lady, . . . As the matter now stands, amongst most critics, the poet is made out to be a heretic of a very peculiar kind, guilty of writing an empty fable which is indeed "porcorum cibus", and his Lady is accused of foisting upon him his rather silly heresy.'

whilst in *Yvain* we find him bewailing that love has proved a passing fashion among his patrons, who are no longer prepared to follow Love's commands (vv. 8–28), or even to allow a poet to dwell on erotic conceits:

> De ceste plaie vos deïsse,
> Tant que hui mes fin ne preïsse,
> se li escouters vos pleüst;
> mes tost deïst tel i eüst,
> que je vos parlasse d'oiseuse,
> car la janz n'est mes amoreuse,
> ne n'aimment mes si come il suelent.   [*Yvain*, ed. Reid, vv. 5389–95]

As for Andreas, he attributes many of the doctrines which appear in the first two sections of his treatise to the teachings of the same Countess of Champagne who commissioned Chrétien's romance (according to its prologue). Besides ascribing to her the letter in Dialogue 7 which deals with the incompatibility of love and marriage, Andreas quotes her as his authority for one of his observations on the love of harlots ('We know, from some of her remarks, that the Countess of Champagne knew this'—P., p. 166) and attributes to her one third of the rulings in the love cases described in Book II, chapter viii, of the *De amore*. The rest he imputes to Eleanor of Aquitaine, Ermengarde of Narbonne or the Countess of Flanders.

Those who still share Robertson's unwillingness to think of that 'rather silly heresy', courtly love, as the subject of the *Charrete* or the *De amore* might do well, perhaps, to consider two last points:

(*a*) The consistency which Robertson claims that his interpretation gives to the *De amore* is not necessarily a virtue. It is surely no particular weakness in the treatise if Andreas' closing statements are taken at their face value, so that we see him as setting out the arts of polite gallantry in his first two books, in compliance with Walter's wishes, and then, in the third book, providing a counterblast to all lovers and loving designed to persuade his friend to follow a wiser course:

> In the first part [of the treatise] we tried to assent to your simple and youthful request . . . so we set down completely, one point after another, the art of love, as you so eagerly asked us to do, and now that it is all arranged in the proper order, we hand it over to you. If you wish to practice the system, you will obtain, as a careful reading of this little book will show you, all the delights of the flesh in fullest measure; but the grace of God, the companionship of the good, and the friendship of praiseworthy men you will with

good reason be deprived of, and you will do great harm to your good name, and it will be difficult for you to obtain the honors of this world.

In the latter part of the book we were more concerned with what might be useful to you, and of our own accord we added something about the rejection of love, although you had no reason to ask for it, and we treated the matter fully; perhaps we can do you good against your will. If you will study carefully this little treatise of ours and understand it completely and practice what it teaches, you will see clearly that no man ought to misspend his days in the pleasures of love. . . .

Therefore, Walter, accept this health-giving teaching we offer you, and pass by all the vanities of the world, so that when the Bridegroom cometh to celebrate the greater nuptials, and the cry ariseth in the night, you may be prepared to go forth to meet Him with your lamps filled and to go in with Him to the divine marriage. . . . [P., p. 211]

(*b*) The fact that no evidence has been found of adulterous practices at the court of Marie de Champagne cannot be taken, as J. F. Benton takes it, for proof positive that she did not commission Chrétien to extol courtly love in the *Charrete*.[27] There are no grounds for assuming, as he does, that had Chrétien received such a commision this would necessarily mean that his romance was intended to be the manifesto of an active subversionist group. Nor would it necessarily mean that Marie practised the doctrines she set Chrétien to preach. There is, in fact, no reason at all why the religion of love should have been anything other than a purely literary and intellectual pastime in twelfth century courtly circles—much as the geography of love was to be in the *salons* of the seventeenth century.

27 See Benton's article 'The court of Champagne as a literary center', pp. 562–3, 586–90, where he stoutly combats the idea that 'courtly love', in the sense of adulterous love, was encouraged by Marie de Champagne 'as either a social or a literary phenomenon'. His case rests on (*a*) the unjustified assumption that had writers at Marie's court extolled adulterous love this would necessarily imply that she practised what they preached (p. 590); and (*b*) the claim that no criticism of courtly ideas was forthcoming from writers at her court who did not hold with her views (p. 588). This objection is likewise unfounded. It overlooks the criticism of certain aspects of the courtly doctrine found in the *Charrete* and the *De amore* made by Chrétien himself, namely the criticism of adultery as the courtly solution to loveless marriage made in *Cligés* (see my *Chrétien Studies*, pp. 165–6, 171) and of female domination in *Erec* (see *Chrétien Studies*, pp. 44–8).

Subscribers

P. F. Ainsworth, Esq., Littleborough
Dr W. R. J. Barron, Manchester
Professor Jeanette M. A. Beer, New York
G. C. Birkett, Esq., Southsea
Miss Madeleine Blaess, Sheffield
Dr David Blamires, Manchester
Professor Marco Boni, Bologna
G. N. Bromiley, Esq., Belfast
Dr Leslie C. Brook, Birmingham
Dr G. S. Burgess, Liverpool
Professor André Crépin, Amiens
Michael Crowe, Esq., Chester le Street
Malcolm Currie, Esq., Sale
D. E. Curtis, Esq., Hull
Dr Jasmine Dawkins, Bingley
Professor Ruth J. Dean, Philadelphia, Pa.
Dr Jacques de Caluwé, Liège
Professor Maurice Delbouille, Chênée
Dr Jean Deroy, Heemstede
Professor A. D. Deyermond, London
Miss E. M. R. Ditmas, Oxford
A. H. and A. D. Diverres, Aberdeen
Professor Jean Frappier, Paris
Wilson L. Frescoln, Esq., Wallingford, Pa.
J. C. Gillis, Esq., London
Dr Ida L. Gordon, Broughton in Furness
Mr and Mrs A. C. Grand, Manchester
Professor D. H. Green, Cambridge
Mrs Elizabeth Greenhalgh, Oadby
Dr Peter R. Grillo, Toronto
Miss P. B. Grout, Swansea
Dr and Mrs. G. E. Gwynne, Manchester
Dr W. M. Hackett, Birmingham
Professor N. Hampson, Newcastle upon Tyne
Professor A. T. Hatto, London
Dr R. F. Hobson, West Wickham

Miss C. Hogetoorn, Utrecht
Professor Lillian Herlands Hornstein, New York
Tony Hunt, Esq., St Andrews
M. Bernard Jean, Manchester
Dr Omer Jodogne, Namur
Professor R. C. Knight, Swansea
Professor Roy F. Leslie. Ottery St. Marys
Dr J. Linskill, Liverpool
David Lister, Esq., Grimsby
Dr Eleanor R. Long, Santa Clara, Cal.
Dr F. Lyons, London
Professor Geoffrey MacCormack, Aberdeen
Professor James Mahoney, Queensland
Mrs Georgette Marks, Manchester
Dr J. H. Marshall, Durham
Mrs Linda Marshall, Bracknell
Professor G. R. Mellor, Salford
Professor Philippe Menard, Toulouse
Professor Ian Michael, Southampton
Dr M. Mills, Aberystwyth
James Milroy, Esq., Belfast
Dr M. R. Morgan, Cambridge
Dr L. R. Muir, Leeds
Professor Guy Muraille, Grez-Doiceau
Professor D. D. R. Owen, St Andrews
Mrs Hanneke Paardekooper van Buuren, Eindhoven
Professor C. E. Pickford, Hull
Albert Gordon Redpath, Esq., New York
Professor J. W. Rees, Harlech
M. Claude Régnier, Vincennes
Professor T. B. W. Reid, Oxford
Dr Barbara Reynolds, Nottingham
Professor William Roach, Philadelphia, Pa.
Professor Ruth E. Roberts, Fredonia, N. Y.
Miss Gillian Rogers, Newcastle upon Tyne
Professor J. S. Roskell, Manchester
F. W. Saunders, Esq., Manchester
Professor Harvey L. Sharrer, Santa Barbara, Cal.
Dr David J. Shirt, Newcastle upon Tyne
M. S. Sidorski, Esq., Manchester
Dr Sarah V. Spilsbury, Aberdeen
Professor F. E. Sutcliffe, Manchester
Dr and Mrs M. J. Swanton, Exeter
Dr Jane H. M. Taylor, Manchester

Professor Lewis Thorpe, Nottingham
Professor Madeleine Tyssens, Liège
Dr Kenneth Urwin, London
Professor Francis Lee Utley, Columbus, O.
Dr Wolfgang G. van Emden, Lancaster
Professor Alberto Varvaro, Naples
Professor Eugène Vinaver, Evanston, Ill.
Professor Ronald N. Walpole, Berkeley, Cal.
W. Loraine Wilson, Esq., Southampton
Professor Brian Woledge, Wendover
Thomas L. Wright, Esq., Auburn, Ala.
Professor John A. Yunck, Ann Arbor, Mich.

Libraries

Centro de Estudos Filológicos, Lisbon
Keble College library, Oxford
Millersville State College library
New University of Ulster library
Queen Mary College library, London
Queen's University of Belfast library
Royal Holloway College library
St Anne's College library, Oxford
St Peter's College library, Oxford
University College library, Aberystwyth
University College library, Cardiff
University of Aberdeen library
University of Berne, Institut des langues et littératures romanes
University of Birmingham library
University of Bristol library
University of Dundee library
University of Exeter library
University of Hull, Brynmor Jones Library
University of Kent library
University of Manchester, John Rylands University Library
University of Minnesota library
University of Münster, Romanisches Seminar
University of Reading library
University of St Andrews library
University of Sheffield library
University of Southampton library
University of Vienna, Germanistisches Institut
University of Warwick library
Westfield College library, London